# Linux®

## ALL-IN-ONE

7th Edition

## by Richard Blum

## Linux® All-in-One For Dummies®, 7th Edition

Published by: **John Wiley & Sons, Inc.**, 111 River Street, Hoboken, NJ 07030-5774, www.wiley.com

Copyright © 2023 by John Wiley & Sons, Inc., Hoboken, New Jersey

Published simultaneously in Canada

For general information on our other products and services, please contact our Customer Care Department within the U.S. at 877-762-2974, outside the U.S. at 317-572-3993, or fax 317-572-4002. For technical support, please visit https://hub.wiley.com/community/support/dummies.

Wiley publishes in a variety of print and electronic formats and by print-on-demand. Some material included with standard print versions of this book may not be included in e-books or in print-on-demand. If this book refers to media such as a CD or DVD that is not included in the version you purchased, you may download this material at http://booksupport.wiley.com. For more information about Wiley products, visit www.wiley.com.

Library of Congress Control Number: 2022945629

ISBN 978-1-119-90192-1 (pbk); ISBN 978-1-119-90194-5 (ebk); ISBN 978-1-119-90193-8 (ebk)

SKY10036326_100322

# Contents at a Glance

# Table of Contents

# Introduction

Linux is truly amazing when you consider how it originated and how it continues to evolve. From its modest beginning as the hobby of one person — Linus Torvalds of Finland — Linux has grown into a full-fledged operating system with features that rival those of any commercial Unix operating system. To top it off, Linux — with all its source code — is available free to anyone. All you have to do is download it from a website or get it on a USB flash drive, CD, or DVD for a nominal fee from one of many Linux CD vendors.

Linux certainly is an exception to the rule that "you get what you pay for." Even though Linux is free, it's no slouch when it comes to performance, features, and reliability. The robustness of Linux has to do with the way it is developed and updated. Developers around the world collaborate to add features. Incremental versions are continually downloaded by users and tested in a variety of system configurations. Linux revisions go through much more rigorous beta testing than any commercial software does.

If you're beginning to use Linux, what you need is a practical guide that not only gets you going with Linux installation and setup but also shows you how to use Linux for a specific task. You may also want to try out different Linux distributions before settling on one.

## About This Book

*Linux All-in-One For Dummies* gives you eight quick-reference guides in a single book. Taken together, these eight minibooks provide detailed information on installing, configuring, and using Linux, as well as pointers for passing the vendor-neutral certification exams available from CompTIA and the Linux Professional Institute (LPI) to authenticate your skills.

What you'll like most about this book is that you don't have to sequentially read the whole thing chapter by chapter — or even read through each section in a chapter. You can pretty much turn to the topic you want and quickly get the answer to your pressing questions about Linux, whether they're about using the LibreOffice.org word processor, setting up the Apache web server, or a wide range of topics.

Topics that correspond to the certification objectives are important after you've become comfortable enough with the operating system to consider taking the certification exams. As I discuss the material, Tips draw your attention to the key concepts and topics tested in the CompTIA Linux+ or LPI LPIC-1 exams. Note, though, that not all Tips indicate material that's on the exams; I also share other types of information in Tips.

If you are a novice to Linux, ignore the certification objective information as you read. Only after you become comfortable with the operating system and are considering authenticating your skills by taking the CompTIA or LPI exams should you revisit the book and look for this information.

Each minibook zeros in on a specific task area — such as using the Internet or running Internet servers — and then provides hands-on instructions on how to perform a series of related tasks. You can jump right to a section and read about a specific task. You don't have to read anything but the few paragraphs or the list of steps that relate to your question. Use the Table of Contents or the Index to locate the pages relevant to your question.

You can safely ignore text next to the Technical Stuff icons, as well as text in sidebars. However, if you're the kind of person who likes to know some of the hidden details of how Linux works, then, by all means, dig into the Technical Stuff icons and the sidebars.

Within this book, you may note that some web addresses break across two lines of text. If you're reading this book in print and want to visit one of these web pages, simply key in the web address exactly as it's noted in the text, pretending as though the line break doesn't exist. If you're reading this as an e-book, you've got it easy — just click the web address to be taken directly to the web page.

# Foolish Assumptions

I assume that you're familiar with a PC — you know how to turn it on and off and you've dabbled with Windows. (Considering that most new PCs come preloaded with Windows, this assumption is safe, right?) And I assume that you know how to use some Windows applications, such as Microsoft Office.

When installing Linux on your PC, you may want to retain your Windows installations. I assume that you don't mind shrinking the Windows partition to make room for Linux. For this procedure, you can invest in a good disk-partitioning tool or use one of the partitioning tools included with most Linux distributions.

I also assume that you're willing to accept the risk that when you try to install Linux, some things may not quite work. Problems can happen if you have some uncommon types of hardware. If you're afraid of ruining your system, try finding a slightly older, spare PC that you can sacrifice and then install Linux on that PC. Alternatively, you can install a virtual server software package such as Oracle's VirtualBox and install Linux as a virtual machine inside your Windows desktop.

*Linux All-in-One Desk Reference For Dummies* has eight minibooks, each of which focuses on a small set of related topics. If you're looking for information on a specific topic, check the minibook names on the thumb tabs or consult the Table of Contents.

# Icons Used in This Book

Following the time-honored tradition of the *All-in-One For Dummies* series, I use icons to help you quickly pinpoint useful information. The icons include the following:

**REMEMBER**

The Remember icon marks a general, interesting fact — something that you want to know and remember as you work with Linux. You might even find interesting trivia worth bringing up at an evening dinner party.

**TIP**

When you see the Tip icon, you're about to read about something you can do to make your job easier. Long after you've finished with the first reading of this book, you can skim the book, looking for only the tips.

**WARNING**

I use the Warning icon to highlight potential pitfalls. With this icon, I'm telling you: "Watch out! Whatever is being discussed could hurt your system." They say that those who are forewarned are forearmed, so I hope these entities will save you some frustration.

**TECHNICAL STUFF**

The Technical Stuff icon marks technical information that could be of interest to an advanced user (or those aspiring to be advanced users).

# Beyond the Book

In addition to the book you have in your hands, you can access some helpful extra content online. Check out the free Cheat Sheet by going to www.dummies.com and entering **Linux All-in-One For Dummies** in the Search box. You'll find common Linux commands and where to go for more help with Linux.

Occasionally, we have updates to our technology books. If this book does have any technical updates, they'll be posted at www.dummies.com.

# Where to Go from Here

It's time to get started on your Linux adventure. Turn to any chapter and let the fun begin. Use the Table of Contents and the Index to figure out where you want to go. Before you know it, you'll become an expert at Linux!

I hope you enjoy consulting this book as much as I enjoyed writing it!

# 1

# Getting Started with Linux

# Contents at a Glance

# Chapter **1**

# Introducing Linux

The Linux operating system has become one of the most widely used operating systems, popular among researchers, application developers, and hobbyists alike. These days, the Linux operating system can be found in an amazing range of computer environments, from mobile phones to satellites.

This chapter examines just what the Linux operating system is and why there are so many different Linux distributions available to choose from. With this information, you can select the right Linux distribution for your environment.

## What Is Linux?

If you've never worked with Linux before, you may be confused as to why there are so many different versions of it available. You've most likely come across terms such as *distribution*, *LiveDVD*, and *GNU* when looking at Linux packages, and you may have been confused. This section takes some of the mystery out of the Linux system for you.

Although people usually refer to the Linux operating system as just "Linux," in reality there are quite a few parts that make up a complete Linux system. The four main parts of a Linux system are

- » The Linux kernel
- » The GNU utilities
- » The user interface
- » Application software

Each of these four parts has a specific job in the Linux system. Although each of the parts by itself isn't very useful, put together, they create what people refer to as "Linux." Figure 1-1 shows the basic diagram of how these parts fit together to create the overall Linux system.

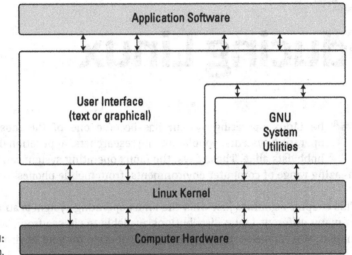

FIGURE 1-1:
The Linux system.

The following sections describe these four parts in detail and give you an overview of how they work together to create a complete Linux system.

## The Linux kernel

The core of the Linux system is the *kernel*. The kernel controls all the hardware and software on the computer system, allocating hardware when necessary and executing software when required.

If you've been following the Linux world at all, no doubt you've heard the name Linus Torvalds. Linus is the person responsible for creating the first Linux kernel software while he was a student at the University of Helsinki. He intended it to be a copy of the Unix system, at the time a popular operating system used at many universities.

After developing the Linux kernel, Linus released it to the Internet community and solicited suggestions for improving it. This simple process started a revolution in the world of computer operating systems. Soon Linus was receiving suggestions from students as well as professional programmers from around the world.

Allowing anyone to change programming code in the kernel would result in complete chaos. To simplify things, Linus acted as a central point for all improvement suggestions. It was ultimately Linus's decision whether to incorporate suggested code in the kernel. This same concept is still in place with the Linux kernel code, except that instead of just Linus controlling the kernel code, a team of developers has taken on the task.

The kernel is primarily responsible for four main functions:

>> System memory management

>> Software program management

>> Hardware management

>> File system management

The following sections explore the first three functions in more detail. File system management in Linux can be somewhat complicated; Book 2, Chapter 5 dives into that topic.

## System memory management

One of the primary functions of the operating system kernel is memory management. Memory management is the ability to control how programs and utilities run within the memory restrictions of the system. Not only does the kernel manage the physical memory available on the system, but it can also create and manage *virtual memory* (memory that doesn't actually exist but is created on the hard drive and treated as real memory).

It does this by using space on the hard disk called the *swap space*. The kernel swaps the contents of virtual memory locations back and forth from the swap space to the actual physical memory. This allows the system to think there is more memory available than what physically exists, as shown in Figure 1-2.

The memory locations are grouped into blocks called *pages*. The kernel locates each page of memory either in the physical memory or the swap space. The kernel then maintains a table of the memory pages that indicates which pages are in physical memory and which pages are swapped out to disk.

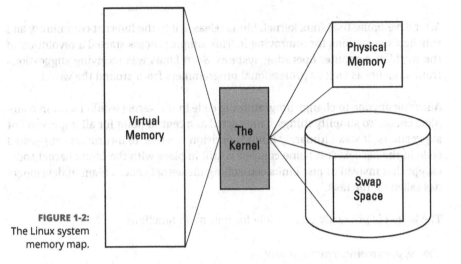

**FIGURE 1-2:**
The Linux system
memory map.

The kernel keeps track of which memory pages are in use and automatically copies memory pages that have not been accessed for a period of time to the swap space area (called *swapping out*) — even if other memory is available. When a program wants to access a memory page that has been swapped out, the kernel must make room for it in physical memory by swapping out a different memory page and swapping in the required page from the swap space. Obviously, this process takes time and can slow down a running process. The process of swapping out memory pages for running applications continues for as long as the Linux system is running.

## Software program management

With the Linux operating system, a running program is called a *process*. A process can run in the foreground, displaying output on a display, or it can run in the background, doing work behind the scenes. The kernel controls how the Linux system manages all the processes running on the system.

The kernel creates the first process, called the *init process*, to start all other processes on the system. When the kernel starts, it loads the init process into virtual memory. As the kernel starts each additional process, it gives it a unique area in virtual memory to store the data and code that the process uses.

A few different types of init process implementations are available in Linux, but these days, the two most popular are

>> **SysVinit:** The SysVinit initialization method was the original method used by Linux and was based on the Unix System V initialization method. Though it is not used by many Linux distributions these days, you still may find it around in older Linux distributions.

» **systemd:** The systemd initialization method was created in 2010 and has become the most popular initialization and process management system used by Linux distributions.

The SysVinit initialization method primarily utilizes scripts to start and stop applications as needed, while the systemd initialization method uses configuration files. Book 4, Chapter 2 explores how each of these initialization methods works and how you can configure them to customize which applications your Linux system starts automatically.

## Hardware management

Still another of the kernel's responsibilities is hardware management. Any device that the Linux system must communicate with needs driver code inserted inside the kernel code. The driver code in the kernel allows the kernel to pass data back and forth to the device, acting as a middleman between applications and the hardware. There are two methods used for inserting device driver code in the Linux kernel:

» Drivers compiled in the kernel

» Driver modules added to the kernel during runtime

Originally, the only way to insert device driver code was to recompile the kernel and restart the system. Each time you added a new device to the system, you had to recompile the kernel code and restart. This process became even more inefficient as Linux kernels supported more hardware and as removable storage devices (such as USB sticks) became more popular. Fortunately, Linux developers devised a better method to insert driver code into the running kernel.

Programmers developed the concept of *kernel modules* to allow the insertion of device driver code into a running kernel without having to recompile the kernel. Also, a kernel module could be removed from the kernel when the system had finished using the device. This greatly simplified and expanded using hardware with Linux.

Book 4, Chapter 2 also dives into driver modules and how to use them in your Linux system.

## GNU utilities

Besides having a kernel to control memory, software, and hardware devices, a computer operating system needs utilities to perform standard functions, such as handling files and programs. Although Linus created the Linux system kernel, he had no system utilities to run on it. Fortunately for him, at the same time he was working, a group of people were working together on the Internet trying to develop a standard set of computer system utilities that mimicked the popular Unix operating system.

The GNU Project (GNU stands for GNU's Not Unix — a recursive acronym) developed a complete set of Unix utilities but had no kernel system to run them on. These utilities were developed under a software philosophy called open-source software (OSS).

The concept of OSS allows programmers to develop software and then release it to the world with no licensing fees attached. Anyone can use the software, modify it, or incorporate it into their own system without having to pay a license fee. Uniting Linus's Linux kernel with the GNU operating system utilities created a complete, functional, free operating system.

Although the bundling of the Linux kernel and GNU utilities is often just called Linux, you'll see some Linux purists on the Internet refer to it as the GNU/Linux system to give credit to the GNU Project for its contributions to the cause.

The GNU Project was mainly designed for Unix system administrators to have a Unixlike environment available. This focus resulted in the project porting many common Unix system commandline utilities. The core bundle of utilities supplied for Linux systems is called the coreutils package.

The GNU coreutils package consists of three parts:

>> Utilities for handling files

>> Utilities for manipulating text

>> Utilities for managing processes

Each of these three main groups of utilities contains several utility programs that are invaluable to the Linux system administrator and programmer.

## Linux user interfaces

Having a world-class operating system that can manage your computer hardware and software is great, but you need some way to communicate with it. With the popularity of Microsoft Windows, desktop computer users expect some type of graphical display to interact with their system. This spurred more development in the OSS community, and the Linux graphical desktops emerged.

Linux is famous for being able to do things in more than one way, and no place is this more relevant than in graphical desktops. There are a plethora of graphical desktops you can choose from in Linux. The following sections describe a few of the more popular ones.

## The X Window system

There are two basic elements that control your video environment: the video card in your workstation and your monitor. To display fancy graphics on your computer, the Linux software needs to know how to talk to both of them.

The X Window software is a lowlevel program that works directly with the video card and monitor in the workstation and controls how Linux applications can present fancy windows and graphics on your computer.

Linux isn't the only operating system that uses X Window; there are versions written for many different operating systems. In the Linux world, there are a few different software packages that can implement it, but there are two that are most commonly used:

>> **X.org:** Based on the original Unix X Window System version 11 (often called X11), it's the older of the two packages.

>> **Wayland:** More Linux distributions are migrating to the Wayland software, a newer X Window package that is touted to be more secure and easier to maintain.

When you first install a Linux distribution, it attempts to detect your video card and monitor and then creates an X Window configuration file that contains the required information. During installation, you may notice a time when the installation program scans your monitor for supported video modes. Sometimes this causes your monitor to go blank for a few seconds. Because there are lots of different types of video cards and monitors out there, this process can take a little while to complete.

The core X Window software produces a graphical display environment but nothing else. Although this is fine for running individual applications, it isn't too useful for day-to-day computer use. There is no desktop environment allowing users to manipulate files or launch programs. To do that, you need a desktop environment on top of the X Window system software.

## The KDE Plasma desktop

The K Desktop Environment (KDE) was first released in 1996 as an open-source project to produce a graphical desktop similar to the Microsoft Windows environment. The KDE desktop incorporates all the features you're probably familiar with if you're a Windows user. Figure 1-3 shows the current version, called KDE Plasma, running in the openSUSE Linux distribution.

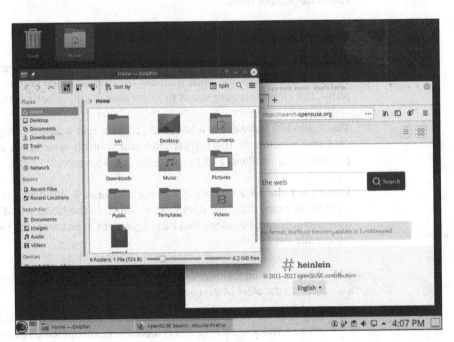

**FIGURE 1-3:**
The KDE Plasma
desktop in
openSUSE.

The KDE project also maintains lots of common desktop applications that run in KDE Plasma. Book 2, Chapter 2 explores all the features of the KDE Plasma desktop environment.

## The GNOME desktop

The GNU Network Object Model Environment (GNOME) is another popular Linux desktop environment. First released in 1999, GNOME has become the default desktop environment for many Linux distributions (the most popular being Red Hat Enterprise Linux).

The GNOME desktop underwent a radical change with version 3, released in 2011. It departed from the standard look and feel of most desktops that use standard menu bars and task bars, and instead made the interface more menu-driven so it would be user-friendly across multiple platforms, such as tablets and mobile phones. This change led to controversy, spawning many new desktops that kept the GNOME 2 look. Figure 1-4 shows the standard GNOME 3 desktop used in the Ubuntu Linux distribution.

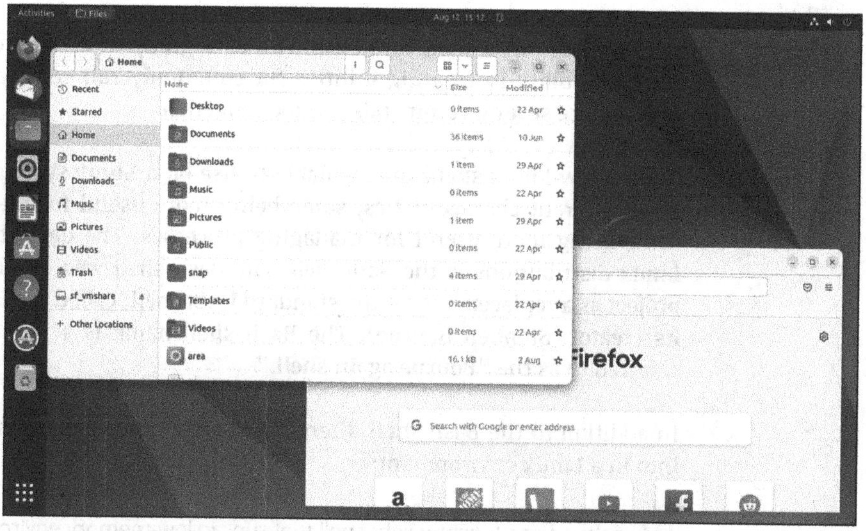

**FIGURE 1-4:**
A GNOME 3
desktop on an
Ubuntu Linux
system.

Not to be outdone by KDE, the GNOME developers have also produced a host of graphical applications that integrate with the GNOME desktop. Book 2, Chapter 1 shows the GNOME desktop environment and the many applications it contains.

## The command-line interface

While having a fancy graphical desktop interface is nice, there are drawbacks. The extra processing power required to interact with the graphics card takes away crucial CPU time that can be used for other programs. Nowhere is this more important than in a server environment.

Because of that, many Linux servers don't load a graphical desktop, and instead rely on a text-based interface called the *command-line interface* (CLI). The CLI provides a way for users to start programs, manage files on the file system, and manage processes running on the Linux system using simple text commands. The CLI is produced by a program called a *shell*. The shell allows you to enter text commands; then it interprets the commands and executes them in the kernel.

The shell contains a set of internal commands that you use to control things such as copying files, moving files, renaming files, displaying the programs currently running on the system, and stopping programs running on the system. Besides the internal commands, the shell also allows you to enter the name of a program at the command prompt. The shell passes the program name off to the kernel to start it.

You can also group shell commands into files to execute as a program. Those files are called *shell scripts*. Any command that you can execute from the command line can be placed in a shell script and run as a group of commands. This provides great flexibility in creating utilities for commonly run commands or processes that require several commands grouped together.

Quite a few Linux shells are available to use on a Linux system. Different shells have different characteristics, some being more useful for creating scripts and some being more useful for managing processes. The default shell used in all Linux distributions is the *Bash shell*. The Bash shell was developed by the GNU project as a replacement for the standard Unix shell, called the Bourne shell (after its creator, Stephen Bourne). The Bash shell name is a play on this wording, referred to as the "Bourne again shell."

In addition to the Bash shell, there are several other popular shells you can run into in a Linux environment:

>> **ash:** A simple, lightweight shell that runs in low-memory environments but has full compatibility with the Bash shell

>> **korn:** A programming shell compatible with the Bourne shell but supporting advanced programming features like associative arrays and floating-point arithmetic

>> **tcsh:** A shell that incorporates elements from the C programming language into shell scripts

>> **zsh:** An advanced shell that incorporates features from bash, korn, and tcsh, providing advanced programming features, shared history files, and themed prompts

**TIP**

Most Linux distributions include more than one shell, although usually they pick one of them to be the default. If your Linux distribution includes multiple shells, feel free to experiment with different shells and see which one fits your needs.

## Linux Distributions: Why So Many?

You may be wondering how you're going to get all the components of Linux put together to make a Linux system. Fortunately, there are people who have already done that for you.

A complete Linux system package is called a *distribution*. Lots of different Linux distributions are available to meet just about any computing requirement you could have. Most distributions are customized for a specific user group, such as business users, multimedia enthusiasts, software developers, or typical home users. Each customized distribution includes the software packages required to support specialized functions, such as audio and videoediting software for multimedia enthusiasts, or compilers and integrated development environments (IDEs) for software developers.

The different Linux distributions are often divided into two general categories:

>> Core Linux distributions

>> Specialized distributions

The following sections describe these different types of Linux distributions and show some examples of Linux distributions in each category.

# Core Linux distributions

A *core Linux distribution* contains a kernel, one or more graphical desktop environments, and just about every Linux application that is available, precompiled for the provided kernel. It provides one-stop shopping for a complete Linux installation. Here are some of the more popular core Linux distributions:

>> **Debian:** Popular with Linux experts and commercial Linux products

>> **Gentoo:** A distribution designed for advanced Linux users, containing only Linux source code

>> **openSUSE:** Different distributions for business and home use

>> **Red Hat Enterprise:** A commercial business distribution used mainly for Internet servers

>> **Slackware:** One of the original Linux distribution sets, popular with Linux geeks

In the early days of Linux, a distribution was released as a set of floppy disks. You had to download groups of files and then copy them onto disks. It would usually take 50 or more disks to make an entire distribution! Needless to say, this experience was painful. Nowadays, Linux distributions are released as an ISO image file, which is a complete disk image on a DVD as a single file. You use a software application to burn the ISO image file onto a DVD or create a bootable USB stick. Then you just boot your workstation from the DVD or USB stick to install Linux. This makes installing Linux much easier.

Having the entire Linux world at your fingertips is pretty amazing, but beginners often run into problems when they install one of the core Linux distributions. To cover just about any situation in which someone may want to use Linux, a single distribution has to include lots of application software. This includes everything from high-end Internet database servers to common games.

Most distributions ask a series of questions during the installation process to determine which applications to load by default, which hardware is connected to the PC, and how to configure the hardware. Beginners often find these questions confusing. As a result, they often either load way too many programs on their computer or don't load enough and later discover that their computer won't do what they want it to.

Fortunately for beginners, there's a much simpler way to install Linux.

## Specialized Linux distributions

A subgroup of Linux distributions is aimed specifically at beginning Linux users. These distributions are typically based on one of the core distributions but contain only a subset of applications that would make sense for a specific area of use.

Besides providing specialized software (such as only office products for business users), customized Linux distributions also try to help beginning Linux users by automatically detecting and configuring common hardware devices. This makes installing Linux a much more enjoyable process.

Here are some of the specialized Linux distributions available and what they specialize in:

>> **Fedora:** A free distribution based on the Red Hat Enterprise distribution, used as a testing ground for Red Hat Enterprise Linux

>> **Mint:** A free distribution based on the Debian distribution, intended for home entertainment use

>> **MX Linux:** A free distribution based on the Debian distribution, intended for home hobbyist use

>> **Puppy Linux:** A free small distribution based on Debian that runs well on older PCs

>> **Ubuntu:** A free distribution based on the Debian distribution, commonly used for school and home use

This is just a small sampling of specialized Linux distributions. There are literally hundreds of specialized Linux distributions and more are popping up all the time on the Internet. No matter what your specialty, you'll probably find a Linux distribution made for you.

Many of the specialized Linux distributions are based on the Debian Linux distribution. They use the same installation files as Debian but package only a small fraction of a full-blown Debian system.

**TIP**

If you're interested in exploring different Linux distributions, a great place to start is DistroWatch.com (`https://distrowatch.com`). They post updates as different Linux distributions release new versions, as well as review many of the popular distributions.

Most Linux distributions also have a LiveDVD version available. The LiveDVD version is a self-contained ISO image file that you can burn onto a DVD or USB stick to boot up a running Linux system directly, without having to install it on your hard drive. Depending on the distribution, the LiveDVD contains either a small subset of applications or, in the case of specialized distributions, the entire system. The benefit of the LiveDVD is that you can test it with your system hardware before going through the trouble of installing the system.

# Chapter **2**

# Installing Linux

There are three major approaches for installing Linux. If you have a spare computer that's only going to run Linux and nothing else, you're in luck! You can skip the "Installing Ubuntu" section and start your installation. If you do run into any problems, you can find troubleshooting information in Book 1, Chapter 4 as well.

Of course, many people don't have the luxury of having more than one computer to use for Linux. To install Linux permanently on an existing PC, you'll need to have a hard disk area set up for it. There are three common solutions to this problem:

» Completely replace an existing operating system on the hard drive.

» Install Linux on a second hard drive.

» Partition an existing hard drive to include Linux.

The first solution is the easiest way to install Linux on a PC. Most Linux installations even include an automatic process that guides you through converting a PC entirely to Linux. However, this is an all-or-nothing approach — you'll be replacing your existing operating system entirely with Linux! If you're okay with replacing your existing Windows or macOS operating system, you too can jump to the "Installing Ubuntu" section of this chapter.

**WARNING**

If you do replace your existing operating system, be aware that when you're done, you won't have your original data files anymore! If you want to keep any files from your Windows PC, you'll need to back them up yourself to a media that you can read from Linux.

The other two methods require a dual-boot scenario, which makes things much more complicated. In a dual-boot scenario, both Linux and Microsoft Windows reside on hard drives on the same computer. When you boot the computer, a menu appears, asking you which operating system you want to use. This allows you to keep your original Windows applications and files, plus use Linux — all on the same computer!

If you're using a desktop PC, you may be able to add a second, fresh hard drive to install Linux on. This is by far the easiest solution for a dual-boot system and should be used if at all possible. Unfortunately, most laptops don't have the space to add a second hard drive, so you'll have to resort to partitioning the existing hard drive, as I explain in the next section.

If you do add a second hard drive, just make a note of which drive is which as far as the computer sees them: You want to make sure that you leave your Microsoft Windows installation untouched. All you need to know is which drive (Windows or Linux) is first and second as far as the computer is concerned. For this scenario, you'll first want to read the "Partitioning an existing drive" section of this chapter. When you're sure that you know which drive is which, proceed to the "Installing Ubuntu" section.

**WARNING**

It's extremely important that you know which hard drive has your original Windows installation on it. When it comes time to load Linux you don't want to accidentally install it over the original Windows drive! This is another reason it's important to back up any important files before starting this process. Accidents can (and often do) happen!

Those who can't spare an entire hard drive for Linux and already have Microsoft Windows installed will have to resize their current Windows installation to make room for the Linux partition. If this is your situation, you'll most likely need to work through this entire chapter.

**TIP**

A few Linux distributions (such as Ubuntu) have the ability to shrink existing Windows partitions and add a Linux partition automatically as part of the installation process. Hopefully this feature will become more common among other distributions. Check with your particular Linux distribution installation documentation first before forging ahead.

If you don't want to dual-boot using your hard drive, you have three other options. (I know I said that there were three approaches in total and adding three more here brings us up to six, but give me a moment to explain.)

» You can use a virtual server software package, such as VMware or Oracle's VirtualBox (see Book 1, Chapter 3) to install a "virtual" Linux machine that lives in a window inside your existing Windows installation. You keep your Windows disk as is, without any modifications. You just install Linux within the virtual area created by the VMware or VirtualBox software.

» You can do the opposite — install only Linux on the computer and then use KVM, VMware, or VirtualBox to install a virtual Windows machine that lives in a window within your Linux installation. If you do this, remember to back up your original Windows files before installing Linux; then restore them in the new Windows area.

» If the thought of changing anything on your computer gives you hives, you can wi just use a LiveDVD distribution (see Book 1, Chapter 1) to boot your computer into Linux without installing anything. By running Linux from the DVD drive or USB stick, Linux will be slower (perhaps even painfully slow on older PCs), but it will work — and it'll give you an idea of just what Linux is all about.

Give some thought to which of the options detailed here you prefer and then read on.

# Dual-Booting with Linux and Microsoft Windows

If you're planning to run Linux and Microsoft Windows on the same machine, odds are you already have Windows installed and you've been using it for some time. Because I hate to hear screams of anguish from new Linux users, take a moment to assess what you have and what you need to do.

**TIP**

On the off chance that you actually don't have Windows installed yet and still want that dual-boot capability, you should install Windows *before* you install Linux. Otherwise, during installation, Windows will overwrite the part of your hard drive that Linux uses to store its boot menu. (This factor can create a mess later when you want to boot back into Linux!) Then, after you have Windows installed, come back here.

Most people want to dual-boot because they've got one machine and it's already running a Windows installation that they really don't want to redo. The following sections walk you through the processes required to get your computer ready for a dual-boot environment.

## Installing a second hard drive

Next to replacing the existing operating system, the second easiest way to get Linux onto a PC is to install a second hard drive. Many desktop PCs support multiple hard drives either by chaining two hard drives together on the same disk cable or by providing multiple cables to handle hard drives.

You'll have to crack open the PC case and take a look inside to see what you're up against. The standard disk controller cards in most PCs allow up to two devices per controller, and many PCs have more than one controller installed on the motherboard. If you see two cables with the long multi-pin connectors in them, you're in luck. If you see only one cable with an empty connector on it, you should be okay, too.

Usually, you can determine your disk controller configuration by looking at the BIOS setup screen for your PC. Besides the hard drive, controllers also support connecting CD/DVD drives, so you'll need to be careful when evaluating your disk controller situation.

TIP

If your motherboard contains only one disk controller and uses it for the hard drive and the DVD device, you won't be able to add a second hard drive on that controller. Usually, you can find plug-in disk controller cards to add a second controller to the PC. You'll need to do just that if you want to add another hard drive.

After you get the second hard drive installed, you're ready to get going with Linux. As I mention earlier, it helps to know which hard drive is the Windows one and which one will be used for Linux. If you don't know, you can use one of the disk management tools discussed in the following section.

## Partitioning an existing drive

If you only have a single hard drive available in your PC, you'll need to create separate areas (called *partitions*) on the hard drive for Windows and Linux. This section walks you through the process of how to do that, but first, let's examine just how partitions work.

Three types of partitions are available: primary, extended, and logical. A hard drive can have three primary partitions and one extended partition. Inside that extended partition, you can have up to 12 logical partitions. Think of an extended partition as a cardboard box that contains the logical partitions. Logical partitions hold data; extended partitions just hold logical partitions.

Before you try partitioning your hard drive, you'll need to evaluate just how much space you'll need for the Linux installation. I can't predict what software you want to install, so I recommend having at least 15GB of space available for Linux. More is always better because it gives you more room for downloads and even more programs.

**TIP**

Make a note of the partition you dedicate to Windows and the one you dedicate to Linux. Jot down which hard drive each partition is on (the first, second, third, and so on) and the partition number each is on the disk (again, first, second, and so on). You'll need this information when installing Linux.

If you aren't starting from scratch for a dual-boot, you likely need to make changes to your current installation. Proceed to the next section to find out how.

## Partitioning using Windows tools

If you already have Windows installed on the entire hard drive, you'll need to shrink that partition down so that there's room for Linux. The first step is to check your existing hard drive for how much free space is available to dedicate to Linux. The easiest way to do that is to open the File Explorer tool in Windows, and then click the This PC icon in the navigation window on the left. You'll see the hard drive(s) installed on your PC and how much space is used on each.

When you've determined how much disk space is available, you'll want to create a new partition on the drive. The Windows utility you'll want to use is the Windows Disk Management tool, as shown in Figure 2-1.

**WARNING**

As shown in Figure 2-1, many modern PCs create one or more hidden partitions that aren't assigned drive letters in Windows. These partitions don't appear in File Explorer but are used by the PC to contain recovery data to reinstall Windows in an emergency. Don't mess with those partitions!

Right-click the partition that contains the C: drive, and select Shrink Volume from the pop-up menu. Enter the amount of space you want to assign to the Linux partition, and then click the Shrink button.

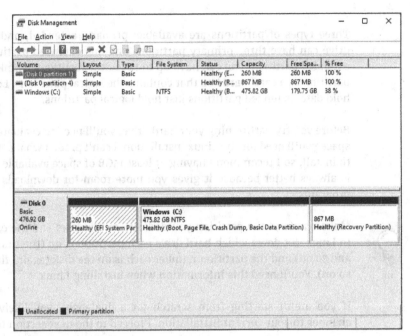

FIGURE 2-1:
The Windows
Disk Management
tool.

## Partitioning using Linux tools

If you're in a situation where you don't currently have Windows installed on the hard drive but you'd like to partition the drive first, you can use Linux tools to do the work for you. There are plenty of Linux LiveDVD distributions that include disk management tools by default, but by far the most popular is the KNOPPIX Linux distribution.

The KNOPPIX Linux distribution was the first to create a live Linux version, even back before there were DVDs and it was called a LiveCD! What keeps KNOPPIX at the top of the list of popular Linux distributions are the utilities it includes by default. It touts itself as a rescue disk — a way to boot your PC if things go horribly wrong with the existing operating system and be able to troubleshoot and possibly fix issues.

After you boot your KNOPPIX, click the Start menu icon in the toolbar, select System Tools, and then select GParted. This opens the GParted partition editor tool, as shown in Figure 2-2.

The GParted tool provides a graphical display showing the disk drives and partitions, making it a breeze to change things.

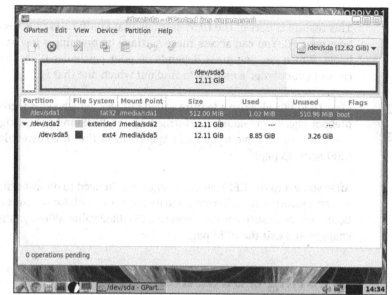

**FIGURE 2-2:**
The Linux
GParted partition
editor tool main
window.

# Finally, Finally, Before You Get Started

Before you can install Linux, you'll need to make sure that you and your PC are ready to boot a Linux distribution. There are two things you'll need to check before you move on to the next chapter and install Linux:

≫ Make sure that your PC can boot an alternative operating system.

≫ Create a bootable media for your Linux distribution.

The following two sections discuss both of these requirements in detail.

## Disabling the secure boot feature

Thanks to all the various attacks against PCs these days, most modern PCs include extra security to prevent booting using an "unauthorized operating system." Unfortunately, by default, the only authorized operating system for most PCs is Microsoft Windows (go figure). You'll need to disable this feature to boot most Linux distributions.

Systems that use the Unified Extensible Firmware Interface (UEFI) boot method are locked down so that the boot record can't be changed to either boot from Linux or do a dual boot between Linux and Windows. You'll need to disable this feature so that you can install Linux on your PC.

This feature is part of the UEFI settings that you'll need to access when you first boot your PC. You can access these settings by pressing a key as the system first boots. Which key you press depends on your particular PC brand; you'll need to consult your owner's manual to find out which one that is.

**TIP**

Most UEFI PCs also use a feature called *fast boot*, which skips through many of the preboot checks previously performed by the BIOS and jumps right into booting Windows. You'll have to be extra speedy in hitting the correct key to get to the UEFI settings page!

After you get to the UEFI settings pages, you'll need to do some hunting. Different systems incorporate different security features. Look for settings related to Secure Boot, and make sure you set them to a Disabled value. When you're done, save the changes and exit the UEFI page.

## Creating a boot disk

A bootable DVD or USB stick is the last thing you need before proceeding to install Linux. Remember that Linux distributions come as ISO image files. For most situations, you'll need to burn the ISO file onto a DVD or use a utility to create a bootable USB stick. This section walks through those processes.

### Creating a bootable DVD

If you currently have a Windows PC available, you can use the built-in features of Windows 10 to burn the Linux ISO image to a DVD. Just follow these steps:

1. **Open File Explorer and navigate to the location of the downloaded ISO image file.**

2. **Right-click the image file and select Show More Options, and select Burn Disc Image.**

   This starts the Windows Disc Image Burner, as shown in Figure 2-3.

3. **Insert a blank DVD into the DVD tray, and then click Burn to initiate the process.**

4. **When the burn process completes, remove the DVD and label it with the operating system and version.**

Although it may seem funny to include labeling the DVD as the final step, after you start experimenting with Linux, you'll be surprised how many different DVDs you'll start to accumulate. I can't tell you how many unlabeled DVDs I have lying around my office with various Linux distributions on them.

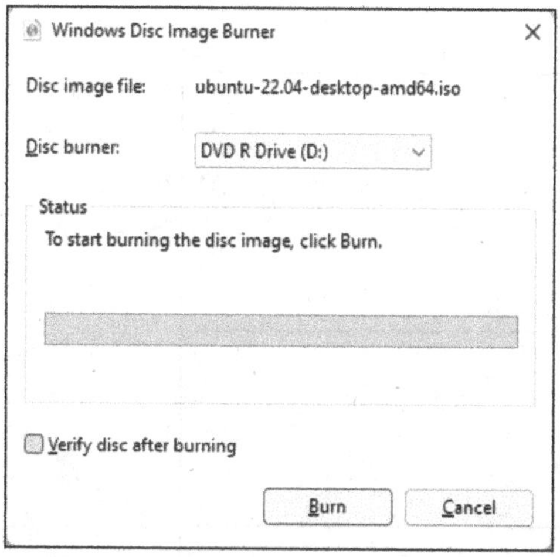

**FIGURE 2-3:**
The Windows
Disc Image
Burner.

## Creating a bootable USB stick

A trend in modern desktop and laptop PCs these days is to forgo the DVD drive. With the ease of downloading software from the Internet, a DVD drive just takes up space that can be used for other things (or in the case of laptops, just allows them to be smaller). If your PC doesn't have a DVD drive, don't fret — there's another way to boot Linux.

Modern PCs include the option to boot from a USB stick. However, there's somewhat of a trick in creating a USB stick that the PC can boot from. You can't just burn the ISO image file to the USB stick the way you do with a DVD — there has to be some extra work done so that the PC can recognize the USB stick as a bootable device.

Fortunately, many Linux distributions now include utilities for creating bootable USB sticks with their distribution. Check with your Linux distribution's documentation to see if they support such a utility.

If your particular Linux distribution doesn't have its own utility for creating a bootable USB stick, you can use a third-party one. One of the more popular tools for this is Rufus (https://rufus.ie). After you download Rufus, just insert a blank USB stick into a USB port on your PC, fill out the necessary information in the Rufus window (see Figure 2-4), and click Start to begin creating the bootable USB stick.

Now you should be able to boot your PC from the bootable USB stick. Most PCs require you to select the option to boot from a USB device at startup. You may need to interrupt the normal boot process to see that selection menu.

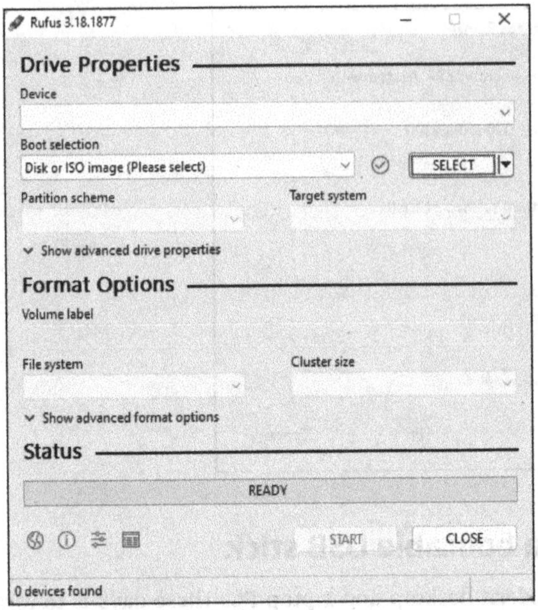

Rufus 3.18.1877

**Drive Properties**

Device

Boot selection

Disk or ISO image (Please select)    SELECT

Partition scheme                          Target system

˅ Show advanced drive properties

**Format Options**

Volume label

File system                               Cluster size

˅ Show advanced format options

**Status**

READY

START    CLOSE

0 devices found

**FIGURE 2-4:** The Rufus program for creating a bootable USB stick.

If you've made it this far, you should be all ready to start installing Linux! Go ahead and proceed to the "Installing Ubuntu" section.

# Installing Ubuntu

As an example of installing Linux, I'll use the Ubuntu 22.04 LTS distribution. *LTS* stands for long-term support, which means Ubuntu will continue to publish updates and security patches for five years after the release date (indicated by the year and month in the version name, 22.04). Ubuntu has a reputation for being a great distribution for first-time Linux users; it makes many of the installation decisions for you. Most Linux distributions have a great installation wizard tool that guides you through the installation. Ubuntu does just that — guiding you through all the steps required to set up the system and then installing the entire Ubuntu system without prompting you for too much information.

After you boot your computer using the Ubuntu LiveDVD image, you can start the installation process from two locations:

>> Directly from the boot menu without starting Ubuntu

>> From the Install desktop icon after you start the Ubuntu Live system

Both locations start the same installation process, which guides you through several steps of options.

**WARNING**

To begin the installation from the DVD or USB stick, you may first need to change your system to *boot* (start) from a DVD or USB stick — many systems today are configured to do this already, so you may not need to make any changes. You'll need to look at your BIOS or UEFI settings to determine if your system can boot from the DVD drive or USB stick.

After you have a LiveDVD or USB stick in your hand, you can start the installation process. Just follow these steps:

1. **Place the Ubuntu LiveDVD in the DVD tray of your PC (or plug the USB stick into a USB port), and restart your PC.**

   This should boot your PC from the Ubuntu LiveDVD, and you'll see the main Ubuntu LiveDVD menu, as shown in Figure 2-5.

2. **From the menu, select your language and then choose either to install Ubuntu directly or to first try out Ubuntu by running it from the LiveDVD.**

   The great feature about the LiveDVD is that you can test drive Ubuntu without having to mess with your hard drive. This will give you an idea of what works and what doesn't. After you've completed your test drive, if you decide to install Ubuntu, just click the Install icon on the desktop.

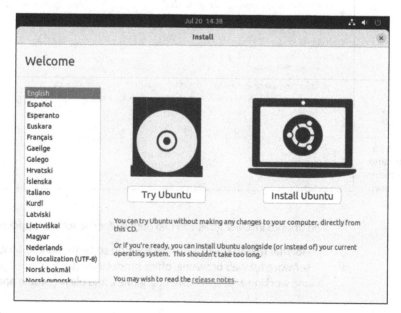

**FIGURE 2-5:**
The Ubuntu
LiveDVD Install
menu.

3. **Select the language to use for the installation, and click Continue.**

   If you install Ubuntu from the desktop installation icon, it asks you again for the default language. If you install Ubuntu directly from the LiveDVD boot menu, it skips this step, because you've selected the language at the boot menu.

4. **Select a keyboard, and then click Continue.**

   Next up in the installation process is identifying the keyboard you'll use with the Ubuntu system. This option may sound simple, but it can get complicated if you have a keyboard that includes special keys. Ubuntu recognizes hundreds of different keyboard types and lists them all in the keyboard layout window.

5. **Select what software you'd like installed by default in your Ubuntu desktop, and then click Continue.**

   The Ubuntu installer gives you some choices as to what software to install, as shown in Figure 2-6.

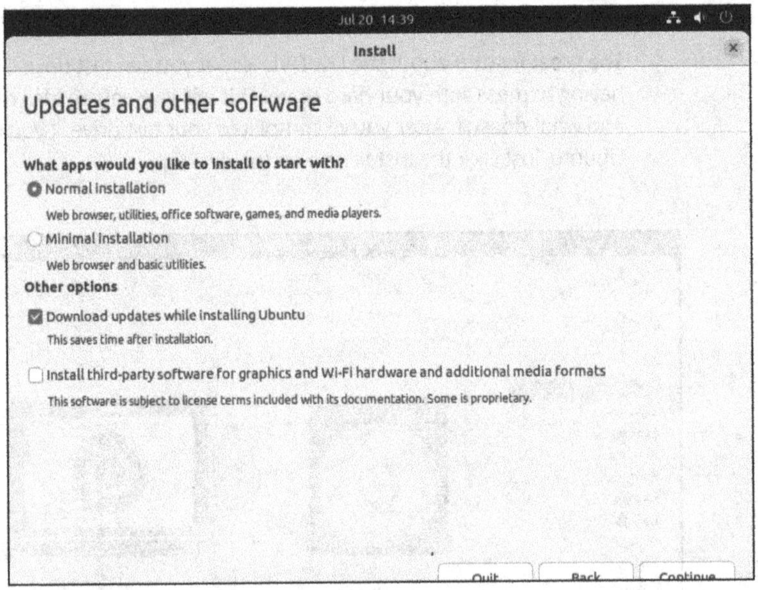

FIGURE 2-6:
The Updates and
Other Software
window.

The Ubuntu installer gives you two options for the software packages to install:

- **Normal Installation:** A normal desktop software bundle, including software for web browsing, office productivity (such as word processing and working with spreadsheets), games, and playing audio and video)

- **Minimal Installation:** A minimal desktop software bundle, which includes only software for web browsing and standard desktop utilities to control your desktop environment

For most Ubuntu desktop installations, you'll want to install the normal software package bundle. If you're using an older workstation with a small hard drive, you may have to go with the minimal desktop installation and then manually install any other software packages you need.

If your PC is connected to a network, the installer gives you the option to install any available updates from the Ubuntu software repository now if you prefer. Selecting this option will increase the installation time, but it will also ensure that your Ubuntu desktop software is up-to-date with the latest security patches and bug fixes when you first log in.

The last option is to install third-party software. This topic is a bit controversial in the Linux world. Some hardware companies use proprietary drivers so Linux can interact with their hardware. These drivers aren't open source, so many Linux purists prefer not to use them. Certain audio and video formats are proprietary as well, and as you may suspect, they also cause consternation among Linux purists. I'll leave the decision as to whether to select this option up to you, but just beware that if you choose to *not* install this bundle, your Linux desktop may not work with some of your hardware devices or be able to play some of the more popular audio and video formats.

6. **Select how to install Ubuntu on your hard drive, and then click Install Now.**

This step in the installation process is quite possibly the most important and also the most complicated. Here's where you need to tell the Ubuntu installer exactly where to place the Ubuntu operating system on your system. One bad move here can really ruin your day.

The options that you are given in this window during the installation depend on your hard-drive configuration and whether you have any existing software on your hard drive. If you went through the steps in the "Dual-Booting with Linux and Microsoft Windows" section, earlier in this chapter, you should be all set for this quiz!

The Ubuntu installer tries to detect your exact system setup and provides some simple options:

- If your entire hard drive is currently used for Windows, the Ubuntu installer will offer to shrink the partition to make room for an Ubuntu partition and create a dual-boot environment.

- If you've already shrunk your existing Windows partition manually, the Ubuntu installer will offer to install Ubuntu on the available empty partition and create a dual-boot environment.

- If you have a previous version of Ubuntu already installed, the Ubuntu installer will offer to upgrade only the operating system and leave your data intact if possible.

- If you have a second hard drive in your workstation the Ubuntu installer will offer to use it for Ubuntu, leaving your existing hard drive alone, and creating a dual-boot environment.

- If you have a single hard drive that already contains an existing Windows or Linux partition, the Ubuntu installer will offer to erase the entire partition and just install Ubuntu.

- If you're an experienced Linux expert and you prefer to do your own disk partitioning, there's an option to manually partition your hard drive to create your own partitions.

The option you select depends on what type of setup you want to try. If you want to run an Ubuntu-only workstation, the option to erase the existing operating system is the quickest and easiest way to go.

**WARNING**

Even if you select one of the options to keep the existing operating system, it's a very good idea to back up any important files contained in that operating system. Mistakes can (and often do) happen when working with hard drives.

If you select an option to keep an existing operating system on your hard drive, the Ubuntu installer allows you to select how much disk space to allocate for the new Ubuntu partition. You can drag the partition separator to redistribute disk space between the original operating system and the new Ubuntu partition.

If you select the manual partition process, Ubuntu turns control of the partition process over to you. It does provide a great partition utility, similar to the GParted utility, for you to use to create, edit, or delete hard-drive partitions.

The manual partition utility displays the current hard drives, along with any existing partitions configured in them. You can manually remove, modify, or create individual partitions on any hard drives installed on the system.

If you're new to this Linux stuff, I recommend just using one of the automatic options and letting the Ubuntu installer do the driving for you. When you're more comfortable with Linux, you can try your hand at customizing your disks!

**7.** **Click Install Now to accept the proposed hard-drive partition changes and continue with the installation.**

**WARNING**

Up until this point, you could change your mind about the hard-drive changes. But after you click Install Now, you're committed to those changes and there's no going back.

**8.** **Select your location, and click Continue.**

Because Ubuntu is in use worldwide, you'll need to manually select just where in the world you're located so Ubuntu can assign the correct time zone and locale settings.

**9.** **Create a Login ID, and click Continue.**

Up next in the installation process is the Login ID window. The login ID you create in this process is somewhat important. Unlike some other Linux distributions, the Ubuntu distribution doesn't use an administrator login account (usually called *root* in the Unix/Linux world). Instead, Ubuntu provides the ability for normal user accounts to belong to an administrators group. Members in the administrators group have the ability to become temporary administrators on the system (see Book 4, Chapter 3).

Having an account with administrative privileges is important, as the administrator is the only account that's allowed to perform most system functions, such as changing system features, adding new devices, and installing new software. Without an administrative account, you won't be able to do much of anything new on the system.

Besides identifying yourself, you'll also need to assign a name to the computer itself. Ubuntu uses this name when advertising its presence on the network, as well as when referencing the system in log files. You should select a computer name that's unique on your network.

One final setting — you must determine if you want the system to automatically log you into your desktop or prompt for your login password. If you'll be the only one using this workstation (and there aren't any nosy people around), you can utilize the automatic login feature to save some time. Otherwise, set it to prompt you for a password each time you log into your system.

**10.** **Sit back and enjoy the show!**

As the installation process proceeds, the installer presents a series of informational slides. Scan over these slides to learn about the features available in your new Ubuntu system. I cover each of these features in greater depth in the upcoming chapters.

After the Ubuntu system is installed on the hard drive, the installation program prompts you to reboot. The next time your system boots, you'll be in Ubuntu-land!

# Your First Ubuntu Boot

After Ubuntu reboots, it will either take you directly to your desktop, or you'll be greeted by a login window, depending on the setting you chose during installation. If you're greeted by a login window, click your user account, and then enter your password in the password text box.

The first time you get to your user desktop in Ubuntu, there are a few housekeeping questions it needs to ask. Follow these steps to make your way to your desktop:

1. **If you have a network account from Ubuntu, Google, Nextcloud, or Microsoft, select the appropriate icon from the menu; if you don't have a network account, or choose not to use it, click Skip.**

   Ubuntu can sync many of your network account features such as your desktop calendar, along with any files you have stored in common cloud accounts from any of the listed providers. Just select the account type you have from the menu, enter your login information, and select the items you want to sync.

2. **If you want to use the Ubuntu Livepatch feature, click Setup Livepatch; otherwise, click Next.**

   The Ubuntu Livepatch feature allows you to link multiple computers to the Canonical cloud network. You can link up to three workstations for free, or pay to become an Advantage member to link more. If you participate in the Livepatch feature, Ubuntu will automatically install all updates on your system without your having to do anything!

TIP

   If you prefer to not have information about your Ubuntu setup stored in the cloud, you can skip this step and just handle the updates yourself.

3. **Select whether to send Ubuntu a report on your installation experience; after you've made your selection, click Next.**

   Ubuntu developers use this information to determine what hardware was or wasn't detected properly on your system during installation, as well as what additional software you've installed after the installation. This information helps developers determine what to include or leave out in future versions.

4. **Select whether to enable location services, and click Next.**

   Location services allow applications to determine your location automatically without having to prompt you.

**5.** **Take a quick scan of the additional software available to install in the Ready to Go window, and click Done.**

This is just a small sample of the software available for you to install. The Ubuntu software repositories contain hundreds of open-source applications ready for you to install and use. I walk you through the software installation process in Book 1, Chapter 5.

Congratulations! You've made it through all the installation and post-installation prompts! By now, your head is probably spinning a bit, so take some time to collect yourself, and then continue on in the book to learn more about your Linux system.

**IN THIS CHAPTER**

» **Getting acquainted with virtual servers**

» **Installing Linux in VirtualBox**

» **Creating a Linux virtual machine and installing Linux on a virtual machine**

# Chapter **3**

# Living in a Virtual World

Although the term *virtual server* sounds an awful lot like *air guitar*, virtual servers are actually a good thing. They allow you to support multiple guest systems on a single physical machine, saving both space and money. Virtual servers are quickly becoming all the rage in the corporate world, but they can also have a place in the home environment. With virtual servers, you can now install more than one Linux distribution on a single Windows PC, making it a breeze to experiment with Linux distributions!

## What Are Virtual Servers?

In this fast-paced world of changing technology, nothing is taken for granted. In the old days, if you needed to run ten separate servers on your network, you had to go out and purchase ten separate hardware systems and place them in a huge data center taking up space.

Nowadays, you have another tool at your disposal: virtual servers. With virtual servers, you can run all ten separate systems on one large hardware server. This saves not only hardware costs, but also space in your data center, electricity and cooling costs, and perhaps even costs in terms of the people needed to support the servers.

Running virtual servers requires a special software package that allows you to create guest systems (often called *virtual machines*) within a single virtual server host operating system (OS). The host OS takes care of interfacing with the hardware, and the virtual server software plays the middleman between the host system and the virtual machines.

Each virtual machine has its own area, called a *sandbox*, to run in. The host server gives the virtual machine memory and CPU time to use just as if it were running directly on the underlying hardware.

The trick in virtual servers is all in the virtual server software. There are a few different virtual server packages around. The most popular are the following:

>> **KVM:** An open-source project that plugs directly into the Linux kernel. It only runs on systems that have a CPU that supports virtualization.

>> **VirtualBox:** A project sponsored by Oracle that installs in any Linux distribution, as well as in Windows and Intel-based macOS environments.

>> **Parallels:** A virtual server package for macOS environments, including the newer Apple silicon Macs.

>> **VMware Server:** A software package provided by VMware with both free and commercial versions that run on Windows, macOS, and Linux hosts.

The beauty of these virtual server packages is that after you install them on a host, you can run one or more guest virtual machines on top of them, and the guest OS doesn't have to be the same as the host OS. That makes for an excellent way of experimenting with different Linux distributions without interfering with your existing Windows or macOS installation.

In this chapter, I walk you through installing and using the Oracle VirtualBox virtual server package in Windows, and then running the Ubuntu 22.04 LTS workstation distribution as a virtual machine inside the Windows virtual server.

# Installing VirtualBox

The first step is to install the VirtualBox software package in Windows. You can download it directly from the VirtualBox website and install it from the download package. The VirtualBox website provides installation packages for Windows,

Intel-based macOS, and many common Linux distributions (yes, you can even run Windows inside a Linux virtual server!).

Here are the steps for downloading and installing the VirtualBox package from the website:

1. **Open a web browser and go to** www.virtualbox.org.

   Although the VirtualBox project is sponsored by Oracle, it has its own website, which includes the download files, documentation, and a community forum area.

2. **Select the Downloads link on the left side of the main web page.**

3. **Select the link for your OS.**

   This is the host OS, not the guest virtual machine OS. If you're installing VirtualBox on your Windows desktop, select the Windows Hosts link.

4. **When the download starts, make sure you select the option to save the package on your hard drive.**

   The installation process is a bit lengthy and can crash. It's a good idea to just download the entire package to your hard drive and perform the installation from there.

5. **Find the location of the VirtualBox installation package file using File Manager, and double-click the package file.**

6. **Go through the VirtualBox installation wizard.**

   As you walk through the installation wizard, you'll have the option to not install specific features (such as network or USB support). Unless you're an expert and you need to customize the installation, you'll want to just use all the default options as you go through the wizard.

After you install VirtualBox, it appears as an icon on your desktop, as well as in the Programs menu. Double-click the desktop icon to start it. Figure 3-1 shows what the main VirtualBox window looks like after it starts.

After you've gotten to the main window, you're ready to start creating some virtual machines!

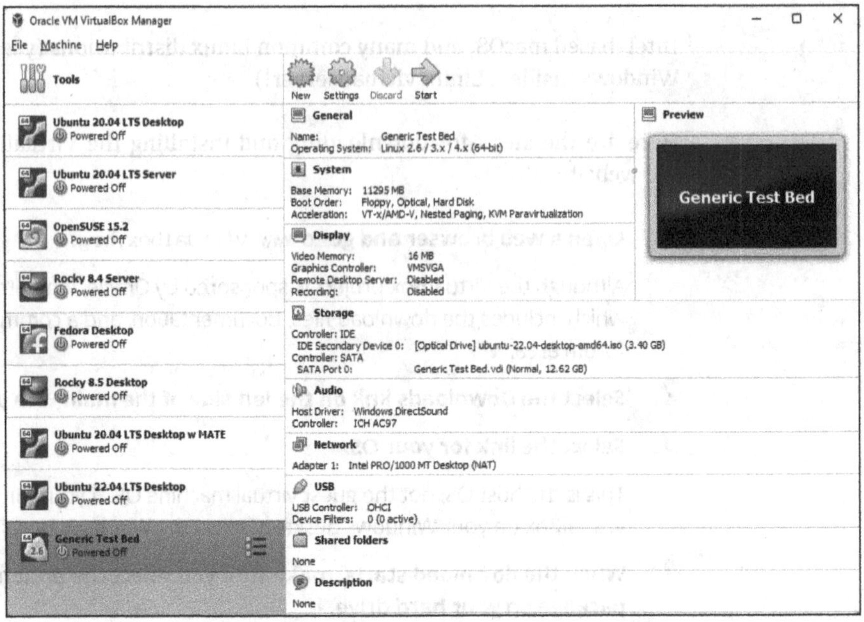

FIGURE 3-1:
The VirtualBox
main window.

# Creating a Linux Virtual Machine

The next step in the process is to build a sandbox for your Linux system to run. In this process, you'll need to tell VirtualBox the size of the sandbox to play in. You'll need to select the amount of disk space to allocate for the virtual machine and the amount of memory to use. Both of these items are shared with the host system, so be careful how much you dedicate to the virtual machine.

Follow these steps to create your first virtual server sandbox:

1. **Open the VirtualBox main window.**

2. **Click the New icon in the VirtualBox toolbar area.**

    This starts a wizard to walk you through creating the virtual server sandbox.

3. **Assign a name to the sandbox area, select the operating system you plan on installing in the virtual server area, and click the Next button.**

    As you can tell from the drop-down menu, you have lots of choices for the types of virtual server operating systems you can install in the virtual server area.

**4.** **Select the operating system you're going to install, as shown in Figure 3-2.**

The VirtualBox software package provides a way to run multiple operating systems from inside a host system, but it doesn't provide any licenses for those operating systems. It's your responsibility to obtain a proper license for any operating system software that you install in VirtualBox.

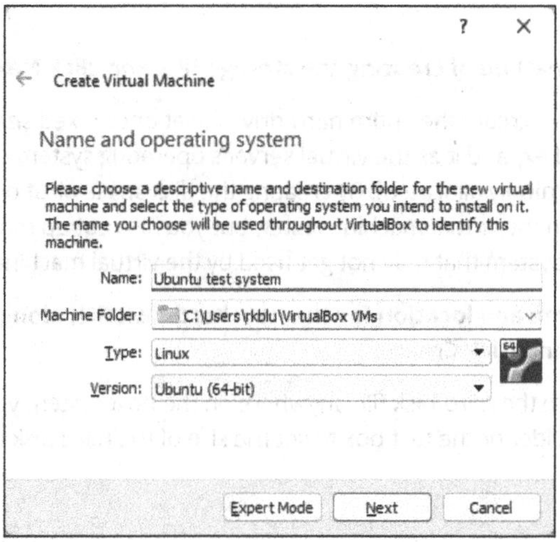

---

? ☓

← Create Virtual Machine

Name and operating system

Please choose a descriptive name and destination folder for the new virtual machine and select the type of operating system you intend to install on it. The name you choose will be used throughout VirtualBox to identify this machine.

Name: Ubuntu test system

Machine Folder: 📁 C:\Users\rkblu\VirtualBox VMs ▾

Type: Linux ▾

Version: Ubuntu (64-bit) ▾

Expert Mode    Next    Cancel

---

**FIGURE 3-2:**
The first dialog box in the VirtualBox new server wizard.

**5.** **Select the amount of memory to dedicate to the virtual server, and click the Next button.**

VirtualBox provides a recommended amount of memory to select, based on the operating system you selected and the amount of memory installed on the host system. You can increase or decrease that amount by using the slider or typing the amount into the text box.

The amount of memory you dedicate to the virtual server will be taken from the amount of memory available to the host server while the virtual server is running.

**6.** **Select Hard Disk Emulation for the virtual server, and click Next.**

VirtualBox emulates a hard drive by creating a large file on the host system. The amount of disk space you select for the hard drive is created inside the file, so it can't be larger than the disk space available on the host system.

**7.** **Select the Create a Virtual Hard Disk Now radio button to create a new hard drive file.**

If you happen to have an existing hard-drive file, select the Use an Existing Virtual Hard Disk File radio button instead, and then browse to its location using the file browser.

Living in a Virtual World

If you selected to create a new hard-disk file, the next dialog box asks you to select a storage type.

8. **Select the storage type, and click Next.**

The VirtualBox Disk Image (VDI) is a proprietary format that can't be read by other virtual server systems. However, it provides the best performance within VirtualBox. Select that option if you plan on running your virtual server only in VirtualBox.

9. **Select the method of creating the storage file, and click Next.**

VirtualBox can create the entire hard-drive file at once (fixed size) or create a base file and expand it as the virtual server's operating system uses more disk space (dynamically allocated). By creating the disk space all at once, you make disk access in the virtual machine faster, but you also eat up more disk space on the host system that may not get used by the virtual machine.

10. **Select a name and location for the new hard-disk file, along with the size of the file, and click Create.**

You can place the hard-disk file anywhere on the host system you have access to. Use the slider or the text box to set the size of the hard disk file, as shown in Figure 3-3.

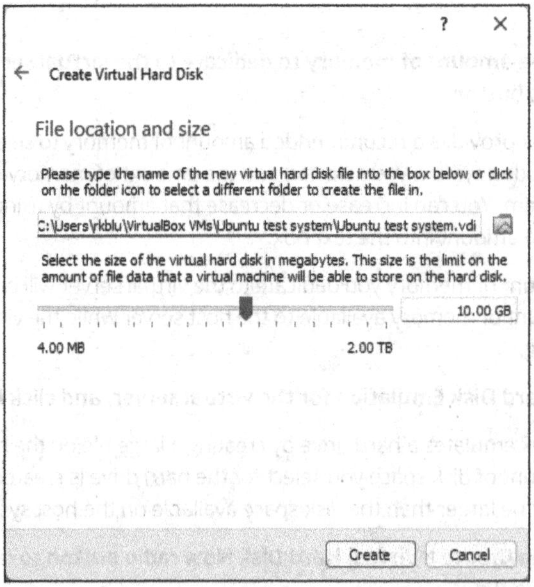

? X

← Create Virtual Hard Disk

File location and size

Please type the name of the new virtual hard disk file into the box below or click on the folder icon to select a different folder to create the file in.

C:\Users\rkblu\VirtualBox VMs\Ubuntu test system\Ubuntu test system.vdi

Select the size of the virtual hard disk in megabytes. This size is the limit on the amount of file data that a virtual machine will be able to store on the hard disk.

10.00 GB

4.00 MB                                    2.00 TB

Create        Cancel

**FIGURE 3-3:**
Setting the virtual server hard disk file location and size.

When you finish the wizard, your new virtual server entry appears on the main VirtualBox window.

Now that you have a virtual machine sandbox created, you're ready to start playing!

# Installing Linux on a Virtual Machine

Before you can start entering your virtual world, you'll need to do a little more setup of your sandbox. The new virtual server wizard sets up a generic sandbox environment, so you'll want to spruce things up a bit first. This section walks you through how to customize the virtual server sandbox and how to load your virtual server operating system.

## Changing settings

Let's first take a look at what VirtualBox has set up. Then you can do some tweaking. Each virtual server you create in VirtualBox has its own set of configuration settings. These configuration settings determine just what VirtualBox emulates in the sandbox.

To get to the configuration settings, select the virtual machine entry on the left side (refer to Figure 3-1), and click the Settings icon in the toolbar. The Settings dialog box, shown in Figure 3-4, appears.

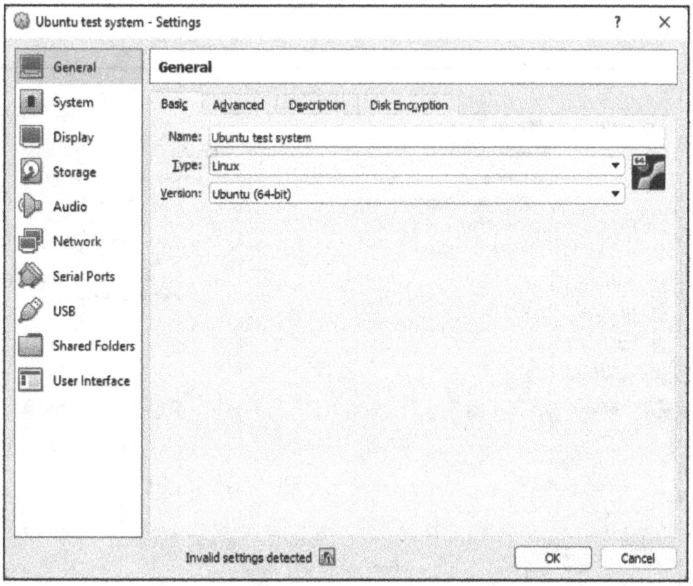

**FIGURE 3-4:** The VirtualBox Settings dialog box.

The Settings dialog box has various setting categories, which are shown as icons with text on the left side:

>> **General:** Sets the virtual server name and operating system type. The Advanced tab allows you to enable the clipboard so you can copy and paste text, files, and folders between the host and the guest systems.

>> **System:** Sets the CPU and memory allocated for the virtual machine.

>> **Display:** Manages the video memory and virtual displays allocated to the virtual machine.

>> **Storage:** Defines the virtual hard drives and DVD drive emulation access. You should see the virtual hard drive you created listed here, but you can add additional drives if needed. This is where you can also allow the virtual machine access to the DVD drive on the host system. Another cool feature of VirtualBox is that you can directly mount an ISO image file directly on the guest virtual machine. This way you can install Linux distributions directly from the ISO image file without having to burn them onto DVD. Figure 3-5 shows what this section looks like.

TIP

If you're going to install the virtual server operating system from a DVD, you'll want to make sure you mount the drive in the DVD section. Unfortunately that's not selected by default.

>> **Audio:** Manages access to the sound card on the host system. You can use both the speakers and the microphone from the host system in the virtual machine.

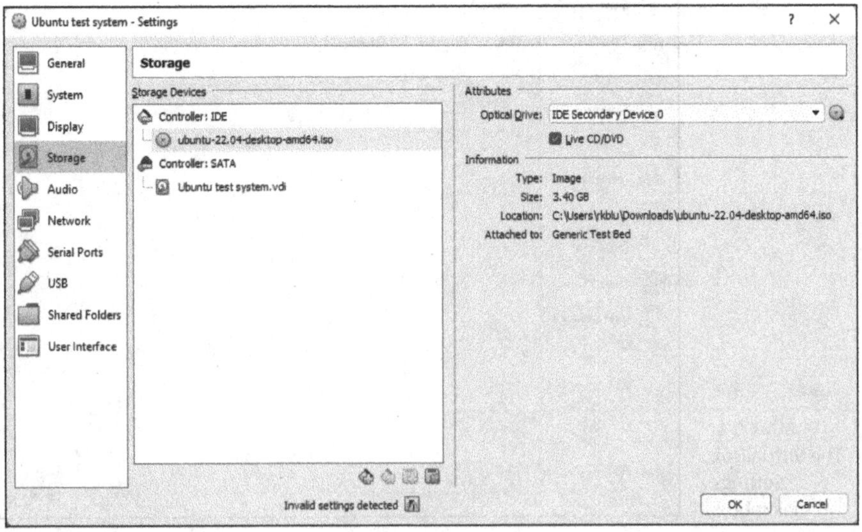

**FIGURE 3-5:**
The Storage section of the Settings dialog box.

>> **Network:** The virtual machine can tap into the network connection of the host system, and here's where you can configure that feature. The default NAT feature allows the host to act as a Dynamic Host Configuration Protocol (DHCP) server and creates an internal network between the virtual machine and the host. You can then access the host system's network using the network interface on the virtual server. The bridged networking option allows your virtual machine to connect directly to the local network, without using the NAT feature.

>> **Serial Ports:** Manages access to the serial communication ports on the host system if available.

>> **USB:** Lists which USB devices on the host system you want to allow on the guest virtual machine.

>> **Shared Folders:** Allows you to create a folder that both the host system and the virtual machine can access. This makes a convenient pipeline for moving files between the two environments.

>> **User Interface:** Defines which menu bar features you want activated for controlling the virtual machine.

After you have your settings customized, click OK to save them and return to the main VirtualBox window. Now you're ready to install some software!

## Loading the operating system

With the virtual machine sandbox all customized for your new operating system, you're all set to go! First, before you get started, make sure you have the bootable DVD, USB, or ISO image file required for the installation (see Book 1, Chapter 2). After you have that in hand, you can follow these steps to get it installed:

**1.** Insert the operating system installation DVD into the CD/DVD player on the host system, or point the virtual machine's DVD drive to the ISO image file.

There's no need to burn the Linux distribution onto a DVD — just copy the ISO image file onto your host system's drive and point to it!

**2.** Select the virtual machine icon you want to install the operating system on from the listing on the left.

**3.** Click the Start toolbar icon.

This "powers up" the virtual machine, just as if you had turned on the power switch on the hardware. You should see a new window open. This is the VirtualBox console emulation window. Anything that would normally appear on the monitor will appear inside this window. You can see this in Figure 3-6.

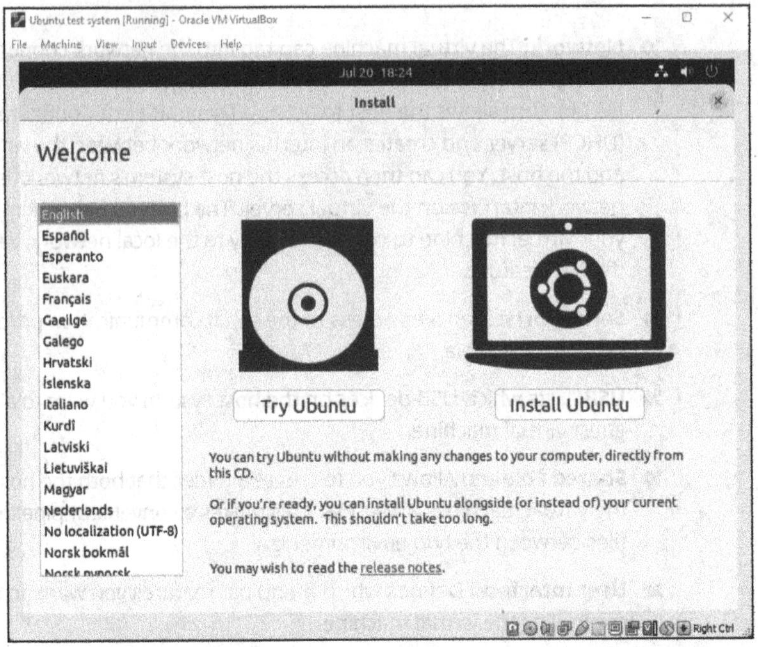

FIGURE 3-6:
The VirtualBox
console
emulation
window.

Also, you'll notice a set of icons at the bottom of the window (see Figure 3-7), that indicate when the virtual server is accessing hardware on the system:

- The hard disk
- The DVD drive
- The audio input/output
- The network interface
- The USB interface
- The shared folder
- Video memory
- Recording
- CPU status

You'll also notice in the lower-right corner of the window a mouse icon, a down-arrow icon, and the words *Right Ctrl*. When you start the virtual machine, VirtualBox takes control of the keyboard and mouse on the host system and turns them over to the virtual machine. If at any time you want to release control back to the host system (such as if you want to run another application at the same time), press the Ctrl key on the right side of the keyboard. To gain control back in the virtual machine, just place the mouse anywhere inside the console emulation window and press the right Ctrl key again.

4. **Proceed through the installation process of the operating system you're installing.**

   The virtual machine should have booted from the DVD or ISO file installed (if not, refer back to the General section of the Settings dialog box). Just follow the normal installation process for the operating system. The operating systems should detect all the emulated hardware you configured in the virtual server.

5. **Reboot the virtual server when the installation is complete.**

   Most operating system installations automatically reboot the system. If this happens, you'll notice that the VirtualBox console emulation window detects the reboot and stays open, allowing you to watch the reboot process.

**WARNING**

You may need to remove the Storage pointer to the DVD or ISO file in the Settings section before you reboot the virtual machine. Otherwise, the virtual machine will continue to boot from it rather than the hard drive.

The final results should be a perfectly working operating system running inside your sandbox, as shown in Figure 3-7.

When you tell the virtual machine's operating system to shut down, VirtualBox will automatically close the console emulation window.

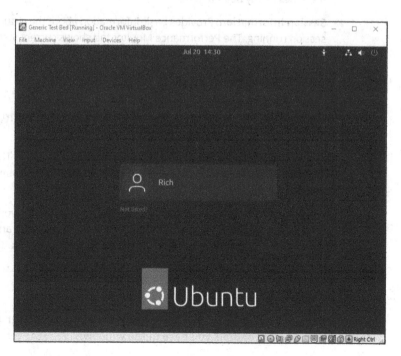

FIGURE 3-7:
Running Ubuntu
in a Windows
VirtualBox
window.

# Working with the sandbox

When you have your virtual machine running, there are a few VirtualBox commands you'll need to become familiar with. You've already seen the importance of the right-side Ctrl button. That's how you grab and release control over the keyboard and mouse in your virtual server.

There are also four menu bar items that can help you in your virtual server environment: Machine, View, Input, and Devices. The following sections give you a tour through the options available in those menus.

## The Machine menu

The Machine menu provides easy access to several common functions you may want to perform with you virtual server:

>> **Settings:** Displays the Settings dialog box for the virtual server, allowing you to make changes to the virtual server environment. Some of the settings won't take effect until the next time you start the virtual server.

>> **Take Snapshot:** This isn't related to taking a screen capture of the window. A snapshot in VirtualBox allows you to save a copy of the virtual disk file as it exists at the time. This provides a great way to perform backups of virtual machines at any point in time!

>> **Session Information:** Provides basic information about the virtual server session running. The Performance Monitor tab shows current statistics on the CPU load, memory usage, network rate, and disk I/O rate.

>> **File Manager:** Provides a graphical interface for viewing the host and virtual machine file systems, allowing you to copy files from one to the other.

>> **Pause:** Places the virtual server in a suspended mode but doesn't send any signals to the guest operating system to shut it down.

>> **Reset:** Emulates pressing the Reset button on the workstation. This usually sends a shutdown signal to the guest operating system and restarts the virtual server.

>> **ACPI Shutdown:** Emulates pressing the power button on the workstation. This usually sends a shutdown signal to the guest operating system and stops the virtual server when the guest operating system has finished shutting down.

## The View menu

The View menu allows you to control just how the virtual server appears on your desktop and what options you have in the window:

- >> **Fullscreen Mode:** Enlarges the virtual server console emulation window to take the full size of the host screen. To return to windows mode, press the Ctrl+F key combination.

- >> **Seamless Mode:** A special feature available with certain guest operating systems. VirtualBox allows you to install a video driver on the guest operating system, which allows VirtualBox to display and control the guest operating system as a normal window on the host.

- >> **Scaled Mode:** Adjusts the console emulation window based on the resolution of the guest desktop.

- >> **Adjust Window Size:** Changes the size of the VirtualBox console emulation window on the host.

- >> **Take Screenshot:** Takes a picture of the current console area.

- >> **Recording:** Starts a video recording of all activity in the console area.

- >> **Menu bar:** Changes the settings for what's available in the menu bar.

- >> **Status bar:** Changes the settings for what's available in the status bar.

- >> **Virtual Screens:** Controls the virtual displays assigned to the guest system. If more than one display is assigned, you can enable or disable them from here, as well as scale them as needed.

## The Input menu

The Input menu allows you to create keyboard shortcuts or remap common key combinations. There's also a quick menu that sends specific key combinations to the virtual machine so you don't have to enter them on the keyboard. This is especially helpful to send key combinations that the host system may normally intercept (such as the Windows Ctrl+Alt+Del combination).

## The Devices menu

The Devices menu allows you to control the status of the hardware devices being used in the virtual server. The options available in this section depend on which hardware devices you selected when you created the virtual server sandbox. The available options are as follows:

- >> **Mount Optical Drives:** Allows you to connect the virtual server to the host system's DVD drive or to an ISO image of a DVD stored on the host system. The latter feature is great for easily installing Linux distributions from ISO images without having to burn them onto a physical disc!

- » **Audio:** Controls the audio output (speakers) or input (microphone) of the guest system.

- » **Network Adapters:** Provides access to the emulated network adapters on the virtual server. You can either enable or disable the network adapter from this interface. A check mark next to the adapter means it's enabled.

- » **USB Devices:** If you selected allowing the virtual server to access your USB devices during the virtual server setup, this menu option will appear. When you plug a USB device into the host system, VirtualBox should automatically detect the new device and pass it on to the guest operating system. After you've inserted the device, you shouldn't remove it until you disable the entry in this menu.

- » **Shared Folders:** If you selected creating shared folders for the virtual server during the setup, use this area to enable and disable access to the shared folders.

- » **Shared Clipboard:** Controls how the host clipboard can be shared with the guest system.

- » **Drag and Drop:** Controls how you can move objects between the host and the guest system.

- » **Install Guest Additions:** You can download the VirtualBox Guest Additions CD from this menu entry. The Guest Additions CD contains specialized drivers that you can install on guest operating systems to allow customized video and mouse interaction (see "The Machine menu," earlier in this chapter).

With VirtualBox, you can run multiple desktop operating systems from the comfort of your own desktop, allowing you to easily explore various Linux distributions with ease.

# Chapter **4**

# Trying Out Linux

You're sitting in front of your PC, about to turn it on. You know that the PC has Linux installed. (Maybe you did the installing yourself, but who's keeping track?) You're wondering what to expect when you turn it on and what you do afterward. Not to worry. If you're using Linux for the first time, this chapter shows you how to log in, check out the graphical desktops, try some cryptic Linux commands, and (finally) shut down the PC.

If you're trying one of the Live distributions, all you have to do is boot from the bootable media (flash drive/DVD/CD), as explained in Book 1, Chapter 2, and you can try that distribution without installing or overwriting your existing operating system.

For those of you who already know something about Linux, flip through this chapter to see whether anything looks new. You never know what you don't know!

## Starting Linux

When you turn on the PC, it goes through the normal power-up sequence and loads the Linux bootloader, which for most Linux distributions is the Grand Unified Bootloader program (called GRUB for short). The *bootloader* (once known as the bootstrap loader) is a tiny computer program that loads the rest of the operating system from the hard drive into the computer's memory. The entire process of starting a computer is called *booting*.

**TIP**

For Live distributions, the bootloader typically is ISOLINUX, a bootloader designed to work from an ISO 9660 CD-ROM.

By default, the GRUB bootloader displays a graphical screen with the names of the operating systems that the bootloader can load. If your PC has Windows and Linux, you see both names listed, and you can use the up- and down-arrow keys to select the operating system you want to use. If the PC is set up to just load Linux, some distributions hide the boot menu and just proceed to boot Linux. Others will still show a boot menu, and there may be a couple of different options for loading a backup or emergency Linux kernel. Either way, when you select to boot Linux, the bootloader loads the *Linux kernel* — the core of the Linux operating system — into the PC's memory.

Other bootloaders, such as ISOLINUX, may display a text boot: prompt at which you can type boot commands to load specific operating systems and to pass options to whichever operating system you load.

While the Linux kernel starts, you may see a long list of opening messages, often referred to as the *boot messages.* Some Linux distributions (such as Ubuntu) hide those messages in a separate virtual console window. To see them, press the Escape key. You'll see a series of entries as the Linux kernel loads each program, as shown in Figure 4-1.

```
            Starting Tool to automatically collect and submit kernel crash signatures...
            Starting NFS Mount Daemon...
            Starting Samba NMB Daemon...
            Starting Postfix Mail Transport Agent (instance -)...
            Starting NFS status monitor for NFSv2/3 locking...
[  OK  ] Started crash report submission.
whoopsie.service
[  OK  ] Started NFS Mount Daemon.
nfs-mountd.service
[  OK  ] Started NFS status monitor for NFSv2/3 locking.
rpc-statd.service
            Starting NFS server and services...
[  OK  ] Started Tool to automatically collect and submit kernel crash signatures.
kerneloops.service
[  OK  ] Started Samba NMB Daemon.
nmbd.service
            Starting Samba SMB Daemon...
nfs-server.service
[  OK  ] Finished NFS server and services.
            Starting Notify NFS peers of a restart...
[  OK  ] Started Notify NFS peers of a restart.
rpc-statd-notify.service
[  OK  ] Started Samba SMB Daemon.
smbd.service
[  OK  ] Started MariaDB 10.6.7 database server
mariadb.service
tmp-syscheck\x2dmountpoint\x2d736847485.mount
postgresql@14-main.service
[  OK  ] Started PostgreSQL Cluster 14-main.
            Starting PostgreSQL RDBMS...
[  OK  ] Finished PostgreSQL RDBMS.
postgresql.service
[  OK  ] Started Snap Daemon.
snapd.service
            Starting Wait until snapd is fully seeded...
            Starting Time & Date Service...
```

**FIGURE 4-1:**
The Ubuntu boot screen after pressing the Escape key.

You should see [ OK ] appear on each line, indicating that the program loaded successfully. If you don't, you can jump to Book 1, Chapter 5 and walk through some of the suggested troubleshooting techniques.

After Linux boots, you typically get a graphical login screen. For some distributions, such as KNOPPIX and some of the other Live distributions, you get the desktop without having to log in as a user. The system automatically logs you in as a guest account. Among the distributions that use a graphical login screen, some prompt you to enter the user account, while others provide a list of existing user accounts to choose from. Figure 4-2 shows the Ubuntu 22.04LTS login window.

**FIGURE 4-2:**
The Ubuntu
login window.

**WARNING**

Every distribution contains a user account named root, which happens to be the *superuser* (the administrator account). You shouldn't normally log in as root. When you log in as root, you have full permissions to everything, providing you the opportunity to accidentally damage your system. Always log in as a normal user. When you need to perform any task as root, type **su -** in a terminal window and then enter the root password. The default password for root is the one you gave during the installation of the operating system.

**TIP**

In the Ubuntu installation process, you create only a normal user account; Ubuntu doesn't give you the opportunity to set a password for the root user account. Whenever you want to perform any tasks that require you to be root, you have to use the sudo command (an abbreviation for *superuser do*).

Trying Out Linux

To log in as user spiderman, for example, either select the spiderman icon on the login window, or type **spiderman** in the Username text field, and press Enter. (Move the cursor to the login dialog box before you begin typing.) Then type spiderman's password and press Enter. You see the initial graphical user interface (GUI). What you get depends on your choice of GUI: GNOME or KDE Plasma. If someone made the choice for you, don't worry; GNOME and KDE Plasma are both quite good and versatile.

Chapters 1 and 2 in Book 2 explore the GUI desktops — first GNOME and then KDE Plasma. The following section focuses on the command line, which is the only interface you'll have access to if you experience problems loading a graphical desktop.

# Playing with the Shell

Linux is basically Unix, and Unix just doesn't feel like Unix unless you can type cryptic commands in a text terminal. Although GNOME and KDE Plasma do a lot to bring you into the world of windows, icons, mouse, and pointer (affectionately known as *WIMP*), sometimes, you're stuck with nothing but a plain-text screen with a prompt that looks something like this (when you log in as spiderman):

```
spiderman@ubuntu22:~$
```

You see the text screen most often when something is wrong with the X Window System, which is the machinery that runs the windows and menus that you normally see. In those cases, you have to work with the shell and know some cryptic Linux commands.

You can prepare for unexpected encounters with the shell by trying some Linux commands in a terminal window while you're in the GNOME or KDE Plasma GUI. After you get the hang of using the terminal, you might even keep a terminal window open so that you can use one of those cryptic commands, simply because using a command is faster than pointing and clicking. Those two-letter commands do pack some punch!

## Starting the bash shell

Simply put, the *shell* is the Linux *command interpreter* — a program that reads what you type, interprets that text as a command, and does what the command is supposed to do.

Before you can start playing with the shell, you'll need to open a terminal window. In either GNOME or KDE Plasma, the panel typically includes an icon that looks like a monitor. When you click that icon, you see a window with a prompt, like the one shown in Figure 4-3. That window is a terminal window, and it works like an old-fashioned terminal. A shell program is running and ready to accept any text that you type. Type text and press Enter, and something happens (depending on what you typed).

spiderman@Ubuntu22: ~

spiderman@Ubuntu22: $

**FIGURE 4-3:**
The terminal
window in
Ubuntu awaits
your input.

**TIP**

If the GNOME or KDE Plasma panel on your desktop doesn't seem to have an icon that starts a terminal or shell window, search the Main menu hierarchy; you should be able to find an item labeled Console or Terminal. Choosing that item should open a terminal window.

The prompt that you see depends on the shell that runs in that terminal window. The default Linux shell is bash (which stands for *Bourne-Again Shell*, a play on the name of the original author of the Unix shell, Stephen Bourne).

bash understands a host of standard Linux commands, which you can use to look at files, go from one directory to another, see what programs are running (and who else is logged in), and do a whole lot more.

In addition to the Linux commands, bash can run any program stored in an executable file. bash can also execute *shell scripts* — text files that contain Linux commands.

# Understanding shell commands

Because a shell interprets what you type, knowing how the shell figures out the text that you enter is important. All shell commands have this general format:

```
command option1 option2 ... optionN
```

Such a single line of commands is commonly called a *command line*. On a command line, you enter a command followed by one or more optional parameters (or *arguments*). Such command-line options (or arguments) help you specify what you want the command to do.

One basic rule is that you have to use a space or a tab to separate the command from the options and to separate options from one another. If you want to use an option that contains embedded spaces, you have to put that option within quotation marks. To search for two words of text in the password file, for example, enter the following grep command. (grep is one of those cryptic commands used to search for text in files.)

```
grep "WWW daemon" /etc/passwd
```

When grep prints the line with those words, it looks like the following. (What you see on your system may differ from what I show.)

```
wwwrun:x:30:8:WWW daemon apache:/var/lib/wwwrun:/bin/false
```

If you created a user account in your name, go ahead and type the grep command with your name as an argument but remember to enclose the name in quotes if it includes spaces.

# Trying a few Linux commands

While you have the terminal window open, try a few Linux commands just for fun. I'll guide you through some examples to give you a feel for what you can do at the shell prompt.

To see how long the Linux PC has been up since you last powered it up, type the following. (*Note:* I show the typed command in bold, followed by the output from that command.)

```
uptime
12:06:34 up 59 days, 16:23, 4 users, load average: 0.56, 0.55, 0.37
```

The part up 59 days, 16:23 tells you that this particular PC has been up for nearly two months. Hmmm . . . can Windows do that?

To see what version of Linux kernel your system is running, use the uname command:

```
uname -srv
```

This code runs the uname command with three options: -s, -r, and -v (which can be combined as -srv, as this example shows). The -s option causes uname to print the name of the kernel; -r prints the kernel release number; and -v prints the kernel version number. The command generates the following output on one of my Linux systems:

```
spiderman@Ubuntu22:~/Desktop$ uname -srv
Linux 5.15.0-37-generic #39-Ubuntu SMP Wed Jun 1 19:16:45 UTC 2022
spiderman@Ubuntu22:~/Desktop$
```

In this case, the system is running Linux kernel version 5.15.0-37.

To read a file, use the more command. Type **more /etc/passwd** to read the /etc/passwd file, for example. The resulting output looks similar to the following:

```
root:x:0:0:root:/root:/bin/bash
bin:x:1:1:bin:/bin:/bin/bash
daemon:x:2:2:Daemon:/sbin:/bin/bash
lp:x:4:7:Printing daemon:/var/spool/lpd:/bin/bash
mail:x:8:12:Mailer daemon:/var/spool/clientmqueue:/bin/false
news:x:9:13:News system:/etc/news:/bin/bash
uucp:x:10:14:Unix-to-Unix Copy system:/etc/uucp:/bin/bash
... lines deleted ...
```

To see a list of all the programs currently running on the system, use the ps command, like this:

```
ps ax
```

The ps command takes many options, which you can provide without the usual dash prefix. This example uses the a and x options. The a option lists all processes that you're running, and the x option displays the rest of the processes. The result is that ps ax prints a list of all processes running on the system, as shown in the following sample output of the ps ax command:

```
spiderman@Ubuntu22:~/Desktop$ ps ax
    PID TTY      STAT   TIME COMMAND
```

```
    1 ?         Ss      0:04 /sbin/init splash
    2 ?         S       0:00 [kthreadd]
    3 ?         I<      0:00 [rcu_gp]
    4 ?         I<      0:00 [rcu_par_gp]
    5 ?         I<      0:00 [netns]
    7 ?         I<      0:00 [kworker/0:0H-events_highpri]
   10 ?         I<      0:00 [mm_percpu_wq]
...
41064 ?         S       0:00 /usr/bin/python3 /usr/bin/gnome-terminal --wait
41065 ?         Sl      0:00 /usr/bin/gnome-terminal.real --wait
41070 ?         Ssl     0:00 /usr/libexec/gnome-terminal-server
41088 pts/0     Ss      0:00 bash
41123 pts/0     R+      0:00 ps ax
spiderman@Ubuntu22:~/Desktop$
```

It's amazing how many programs can run on a system even when only you are logged in as a user, isn't it? Notice that at the end of the listing is the ps command that you just typed and, before that, the bash shell program that's running in your Terminal window.

As you can guess, you can do everything from a shell prompt, but the procedure does take some getting used to. Book 4, Chapter 1 takes you through using the Bash shell to complete many common functions in Linux — all without using the GUI.

# Shutting Down

When you're ready to shut down Linux, you must do so in an orderly manner. Even if you're the sole user of a Linux PC, several other programs usually run in the background. Also, operating systems such as Linux try to optimize the way that they write data to the hard drive. Because hard-drive access is relatively slow (compared with the time needed to access memory locations), data generally is held in memory and written to the hard drive in large chunks. Therefore, if you simply turn off the power, you run the risk that some files won't be updated properly.

Any user can shut down the system from the desktop or from the graphical login screen without even being logged in, although some distributions, such as Debian, prompt for the root password. Typically, you should look for a Log Out option on the main menu or submenus. When you choose this option, a Log Out dialog box appears, providing options for logging out immediately or waiting 60 seconds. More detailed menu options can include rebooting or halting the system in addition to simply logging out. To shut down the system, choose Shutdown and then click OK. The system shuts down in an orderly manner.

If the logout menu doesn't have a shutdown option, first log out and then select Shutdown on the graphical login screen. You can also shut down a Linux computer from a terminal with the command init 0. This method is sometimes required if you're running the operating system within a virtual software manager such as VMware.

While the system shuts down, you see messages about processes shutting down. You may be surprised by how many processes there are even when no one is explicitly running any programs on the system. If your system doesn't automatically power off on shutdown, you can turn off the power manually.

**WARNING**

Shutting down or rebooting the system may *not* require root access, so it's important to make sure that physical access to the console is protected adequately. You don't want just anyone to be able to simply walk up to the console and shut down your system.

**TIP**

You don't always need to shut down when you're finished with a session; instead, you may choose to log out. To log out of KDE Plasma, choose Main Menu⇨Logout. You can also right-click an empty area of the desktop and choose Logout from the contextual menu that appears. To log out from GNOME, choose System⇨Log Out. Click OK when a dialog box asks whether you really want to log out. (In some GNOME desktop distributions, the logout menu option is the second or third menu button from the left on the top panel.)

Chapter **5**

# Troubleshooting and Customizing Linux

D uring the installation of Linux, the installer attempts to detect key hardware components, such as the network card and any installed peripherals. According to what it detects, the installer takes you through a sequence of installation steps. If the installer can't detect the network card, for example, it usually skips the network configuration step. This omission is okay if you don't in fact have a network card, but if you do have one and the installer mistakenly insists that you don't, you have an installation problem on your hands.

Another installation problem can occur when you restart the PC and see a text terminal instead of the graphical login screen. This error means that something is wrong with the X Window System configuration.

In addition, the Linux installation typically doesn't include configuration procedures for every piece of hardware on your PC system. Most installations don't set up printers during installation, for example.

In this chapter, I show you some ways to troubleshoot installation problems. You find out how to use Linux log files to investigate issues and see what their cause might be. The chapter also explains how to handle printers and different types of removable media, such as DVDs and USB sticks, from your graphical desktop. Finally, I show you how to keep your Linux installation up-to-date by installing software updates and security patches and adding new software.

# Using Text Mode Installation

Most Linux installers attempt to use the X Window System (X) to display the graphical installation screens. If the installer fails to detect a video card, for example, X doesn't start. If (for this or any other reason) the installer fails to start X, you can always fall back on text mode installation. Then you can specify the video card manually or configure X later by using a separate configuration program. You can also configure X by editing its text configuration file.

Table 5-1 lists how you can get to the text mode installation screen. Typically, the text mode installation sequence is similar to that of the graphical installation outlined in Book 1, Chapter 2. You respond to the prompts and perform the installation.

**TABLE 5-1**     **Text Mode Installation in Some Linux Distributions**

| Distribution | How to Get to the Text Mode Installer |
|---|---|
| Debian | Runs in text mode by default. |
| Fedora | Type **text** at the boot: prompt after you start the PC from the Fedora CD or DVD. |
| KNOPPIX | Start KNOPPIX in text mode by typing **knoppix 2** at the boot: prompt (because KNOPPIX is a Live distribution, you don't have to install it). |
| SUSE | At the first installation screen, press F3, use the arrow keys to select the text mode option, and then press Enter. |
| Ubuntu | Runs in text mode by default. |

# Lookin' for Trouble

If your Linux system doesn't boot correctly or doesn't detect your network card, graphics card, or any other hardware device correctly, you'll need to explore the *log files* to see just what went wrong. As Linux performs operations, it logs events in files that you can peruse to see what happened on the system.

There are three basic ways to view log files in Linux:

>> Use the dmesg command to view the kernel ring buffer.

>> View events logged in the system log files.

>> Use the journalctl command to view journaled messages.

The following sections take a look at how to use each of these methods.

## Using the kernel ring buffer

As the Linux system boots, each program the kernel starts will display its startup status on the main console. You can often see when hardware detection fails or application servers fail to start by watching the boot messages. Unfortunately, most Linux distributions hide the main console from view by switching to a graphical window during boot-up. However, you can view those messages after the fact by using the dmesg command.

Linux logs all messages sent to the main console in what's called the *kernel ring buffer.* The kernel ring buffer is a set place in memory where Linux stores kernel messages. As the name suggests, the memory buffer acts as a ring — when the memory area fills up, as new messages are placed in the buffer old messages are removed.

You can use the more command to pause the output of the dmesg command to help you walk through the messages:

```
rich@ubuntu22:~$ sudo dmesg | more
[sudo] password for rich:
[    0.000000] Linux version 5.15.0-41-generic (buildd@lcy02-amd64-105) (gcc
(Ubuntu 9.4.0-1ubuntu1~20.04.1) 9.4.0, GNU ld (GNU Binutils for Ubuntu) 2.34)
#44~20.04.1-Ubuntu SMP Fri Jun 24 13:27:29 UTC 2022 (Ubuntu
    5.15.0-41.44~20.04.1-gene
ric 5.15.39)
[    0.000000] Command line: BOOT_IMAGE=/boot/vmlinuz-5.15.0-41-generic
  root=UUID=5423117e-4aaf-4416-ada7-01e07073b2e1 ro quiet splash
[    0.000000] KERNEL supported cpus:
[    0.000000]   Intel GenuineIntel
[    0.000000]   AMD AuthenticAMD
[    0.000000]   Hygon HygonGenuine
[    0.000000]   Centaur CentaurHauls
[    0.000000]   zhaoxin   Shanghai
[    0.000000] x86/fpu: Supporting XSAVE feature 0x001: 'x87 floating point
  registers'
[    0.000000] x86/fpu: Supporting XSAVE feature 0x002: 'SSE registers'
```

```
[    0.000000] x86/fpu: Supporting XSAVE feature 0x004: 'AVX registers'
[    0.000000] x86/fpu: xstate_offset[2]:  576, xstate_sizes[2]:   256
[    0.000000] x86/fpu: Enabled xstate features 0x7, context size is 832 bytes,
  using 'standard' format.
[    0.000000] signal: max sigframe size: 1776
[    0.000000] BIOS-provided physical RAM map:
[    0.000000] BIOS-e820: [mem 0x0000000000000000-0x000000000009fbff] usable
[    0.000000] BIOS-e820: [mem 0x000000000009fc00-0x000000000009ffff] reserved
...
```

Often just looking through the kernel ring buffer for error messages can help you narrow down hardware or software issues on the system.

## Using log files

Most Linux distributions maintain both system and application log files in the /var/log directory. Check in here for any log files that can help you troubleshoot problems. For Ubuntu systems, check out the /var/log/syslog file to look for system-related issues:

```
root@ubuntu22:/var/log# cat syslog | more
Jul 22 18:00:43 ubuntu22 rsyslogd: [origin software="rsyslogd" swVersion="8.2001
.0" x-pid="610" x-info="https://www.rsyslog.com"] rsyslogd was HUPed
Jul 22 18:00:43 ubuntu22 systemd[1]: Started OpenBSD Secure Shell server.
Jul 22 18:00:43 ubuntu22 systemd[1]: logrotate.service: Succeeded.
Jul 22 18:00:43 ubuntu22 systemd[1]: Finished Rotate log files.
Jul 22 18:00:43 ubuntu22 accounts-daemon[591]: started daemon version 0.6.55
Jul 22 18:00:43 ubuntu22 systemd[1]: Started Accounts Service.
Jul 22 18:00:43 ubuntu22 systemd[1]: Started Modem Manager.
Jul 22 18:00:43 ubuntu22 systemd[1]: Started Disk Manager.
Jul 22 18:00:43 ubuntu22 udisksd[615]: Acquired the name org.freedesktop.UDisks2
  on the system message
 bus
Jul 22 18:00:43 ubuntu22 dbus-daemon[598]: [system] Successfully activated
  service
'org.freedesktop.hostname1'
Jul 22 18:00:43 ubuntu22 systemd[1]: Started Hostname Service.
Jul 22 18:00:43 ubuntu22 NetworkManager[599]: <info>  [1658491243.6176]
  hostname: hostname: using
hostnamed
Jul 22 18:00:43 ubuntu22 NetworkManager[599]: <info>  [1658491243.6176]
  hostname: hostname changed from
(none) to "ubuntu22"
Jul 22 18:00:43 ubuntu22 NetworkManager[599]: <info>  [1658491243.6179]
  dns-mgr[0x556f9e07e290]: init:
dns=systemd-resolved rc-manager=symlink, plugin=systemd-resolved
```

```
Jul 22 18:00:43 ubuntu22 NetworkManager[599]: <info>  [1658491243.6181]
    manager[0x556f9e097030]:
rfkill: Wi-Fi hardware radio set enabled
Jul 22 18:00:43 ubuntu22 NetworkManager[599]: <info>  [1658491243.6181]
    manager[0x556f9e097030]:
rfkill: WWAN hardware radio set enabled
...
```

The great thing about these log files is that they're stored in plain text, so you can use your favorite text editor program (see Book 2, Chapter 6) to view them. However, log files are usually protected so that only users with administrative privileges on the system can view them. For this reason, you may need to either log in as the root user account or obtain root user privileges using the sudo command (explained in Book 4, Chapter 3).

**TIP**

Debian-based Linux distributions such as Ubuntu use the /var/log/syslog file to log system and application messages, but Red Hat–based Linux distributions such as CentOS and Fedora commonly use the /var/log/messages file to log system and application messages. You can usually do some digging around in the /var/log directory to find the log files you need.

## Using the journal

Many people enjoy chronicling their life events in journals. Linux systems can do the same thing! Linux systems that use the Systemd startup method (see Book 4, Chapter 2) typically use the journald program to log startup and application messages in a journal file. The downside to journald is that it stores messages in the journal file using a nontext format. To read those messages, you can't use a text editor but instead need to use the journalctl program:

```
rich@ubuntu22:~$ sudo journalctl -r
-- Logs begin at Tue 2020-09-22 15:00:13 EDT, end at Fri 2022-07-22 19:08:54 ED>
Jul 22 19:08:54 ubuntu22 sudo[2844]: pam_unix(sudo:session): session opened for>
Jul 22 19:08:54 ubuntu22 sudo[2844]:     rich : TTY=pts/0 ; PWD=/home/rich ; US>
Jul 22 19:08:36 ubuntu22 sudo[2824]: pam_unix(sudo:session): session closed for>
Jul 22 19:08:27 ubuntu22 sudo[2824]: pam_unix(sudo:session): session opened for>
Jul 22 19:08:27 ubuntu22 sudo[2824]:     rich : TTY=pts/0 ; PWD=/home/rich ; US>
Jul 22 19:08:18 ubuntu22 systemd[1747]: Started VTE child process 2811 launched>
Jul 22 19:08:18 ubuntu22 systemd[1747]: Started GNOME Terminal Server.
Jul 22 19:08:18 ubuntu22 dbus-daemon[1762]: [session uid=1000 pid=1762] Success>
Jul 22 19:08:18 ubuntu22 gnome-terminal-server[2806]: Display does not support >
Jul 22 19:08:18 ubuntu22 systemd[1747]: Starting GNOME Terminal Server...
Jul 22 19:08:18 ubuntu22 systemd[1747]: Created slice apps-org.gnome.Terminal.s>
Jul 22 19:08:18 ubuntu22 systemd[1747]: Created slice apps.slice.
Jul 22 19:08:18 ubuntu22 dbus-daemon[1762]: [session uid=1000 pid=1762] Activat>
```

```
Jul 22 19:08:16 ubuntu22 gnome-shell[1899]: ../clutter/clutter/clutter-actor.c:>
Jul 22 19:07:16 ubuntu22 systemd[1747]: Started Virtual filesystem metadata ser>
Jul 22 19:07:16 ubuntu22 dbus-daemon[1762]: [session uid=1000 pid=1762] Success>
Jul 22 19:07:16 ubuntu22 systemd[1747]: Starting Virtual filesystem metadata se>
Jul 22 19:07:16 ubuntu22 dbus-daemon[1762]: [session uid=1000 pid=1762] Activat>
Jul 22 19:07:07 ubuntu22 systemd[1]: geoclue.service: Succeeded.
Jul 22 19:07:07 ubuntu22 geoclue[1573]: Service not used for 60 seconds. Shutti>
Jul 22 19:06:52 ubuntu22 systemd[1747]: tracker-store.service: Succeeded.
Jul 22 19:06:52 ubuntu22 tracker-store[2124]: OK
...
```

**TIP**

By default, the `journalctl` command displays the oldest messages first. To see the newest messages first and work backward, use the `-r` option.

# Resolving Other Installation Problems

I'm sure that I haven't exhausted all the installation problems lurking out there. No one can. So many components in Intel x86 PCs exist that Murphy's Law practically requires there to be some combination of hardware that the installation program can't handle. In this section, I list a few known problems. For other problems, I advise you to go to Google (https://www.google.com) and type some of the symptoms of the trouble. Assuming that others are running into similar problems, you can get some indication of how to troubleshoot your way out of your particular predicament.

## Using KNOPPIX boot commands

The KNOPPIX Live CD can be a great troubleshooting tool because KNOPPIX is good at detecting hardware and can be run directly from the boot medium (CD/DVD/USB).

**TIP**

If you have trouble starting KNOPPIX, try entering KNOPPIX boot commands at the `boot:` prompt. If KNOPPIX seems to hang when trying to detect a SCSI card, for example, you can disable SCSI probing by typing **knoppix noscsi** at the `boot:` prompt. Or, if you want the X server to load the *nv module* (for graphics cards based on the NVIDIA chipset), you can type **knoppix xmodule=nv** at the `boot:` prompt.

Table 5-2 lists some commonly used KNOPPIX boot commands.

**TABLE 5-2**     ## Some Common KNOPPIX Boot Commands

| Boot Command | What It Does |
|---|---|
| expert | Starts in *expert mode,* which enables the user to interactively set up and configure KNOPPIX. |
| failsafe | Boots without attempting to detect hardware (except for the bare minimum needed to start Linux). |
| fb1280x1024 | Uses fixed framebuffer graphics at the specified resolution. (Specify the resolution you want, such as 1024 x 768 or 800 x 600.) |
| knoppix 1 | Starts KNOPPIX in run level 1 (single-user mode), which you can use to perform rescue operations. |
| knoppix 2 | Starts at run level 2, which provides a text-mode shell prompt only. |
| knoppix acpi=off | Disables ACPI (Advanced Configuration and Power Interface). |
| knoppix atapicd | Uses the ATAPI CD-ROM interface instead of emulating a SCSI interface for IDE CD-ROM drives. |
| knoppix desktop=*wmname* | Uses the specified Window Manager instead of the default KDE desktop=*wmname* (where *wmname* is kde, gnome, icewm, fluxbox, openbox, larswm, evilwm, or twm). |
| knoppix dma | Enables direct memory access (DMA) for all IDE drives. |
| knoppix floppyconfig | Runs the shell script named knoppix.sh from a floppy. (The shell script contains Linux commands that you want to run.) |
| knoppix fromhd=/dev/hda1 | Boots from a previously copied image of Live CD that's in the specified hard drive partition. |
| knoppix hsync=80 | Uses an 80 kHz horizontal refresh rate for X. (Enter the horizontal refresh rate you want X to use.) |
| knoppix lang=*xx* | Sets the keyboard language as specified by the two-letter code *xx* (where *xx* is cn = Simplified Chinese, de = German, da = Danish, es = Spanish, fr = French, it = Italian, nl = Dutch, pl = Polish, ru = Russian, sk = Slovak, tr = Turkish, tw = Traditional Chinese, or us = U.S. English). |
| knoppix mem=256M | Specifies that the PC has the stated amount of memory (in megabytes). |
| knoppix myconf=/dev/hda1 | Runs the shell script knoppix.sh from the /dev/hda1 partition. (Enter the partition name where you have the knoppix.sh file.) |
| knoppix myconf=scan | Causes KNOPPIX to search for the file named knoppix.sh, scan, and execute the commands in that file, if it exists. |
| knoppix noeject | Doesn't eject the Live CD after you halt KNOPPIX. |
| knoppix noprompt | Doesn't prompt you to remove the Live CD after you halt KNOPPIX. |

*(continued)*

**TABLE 5-2** *(continued)*

| Boot Command | What It Does |
|---|---|
| `knoppix nowheel` | Forces the PS/2 protocol for a PS/2 mouse or touchpad (as opposed to the mouse being detected automatically). |
| `knoppix noxxx` | Causes KNOPPIX to skip specific parts of the hardware detection (where *xxx* identifies the hardware or server that shouldn't be probed: `apic` = Advanced Programmable Interrupt Controller, `agp` = Accelerated Graphics Port, `apm` = Advanced Power Management, `audio` = sound card, `ddc` = Display Data Channel, `dhcp` = Dynamic Host Configuration Protocol, `fstab` = file system table, `firewire` = IEEE 1394 high-speed serial bus, `pcmcia` = PC Card, `scsi` = Small Computer System Interface, `swap` = hard drive space used for virtual memory, `usb` = Universal Serial Bus). |
| `knoppix pci=bios` | Uses BIOS directly for bad PCI controllers. |
| `knoppix pnpbios=off` | Skips the plug-and-play (PnP) BIOS initialization. |
| `knoppix screen=resolution` | Sets the screen resolution in pixels (where *resolution* is the resolution you want, such as 1024x768, 800x600, 640x480, and so on). |
| `knoppix testcd` | Checks the data integrity of the Live CD by using the MD5 sum. |
| `knoppix tohd=/dev/hda1` | Copies the Live CD to the specified hard drive partition and runs from there (requires 1GB of free space on the partition). A performance boost can be obtained by changing `tohd` to `toram` and utilizing RAM. |
| `knoppix toram` | Copies the Live CD to RAM (memory) and runs from there (requires 1GB of RAM). |
| `knoppix vga=ext` | Uses a 50-line text mode display. |
| `knoppix vsync=60` | Uses a vertical refresh rate of 60 Hz for X. (Enter the vertical refresh rate you want X to use.) |
| `knoppix wheelmouse` | Enables the IMPS/2 protocol for wheel mice. |
| `knoppix xmodule=modname` | Causes the X server to load the module specified by *modname* so that X works on your video card (where *modname* is `ati`, `fbdev`, `i810`, `mga`, `nv`, `radeon`, `savage`, `svga`, or `s3`). |
| `knoppix xserver=progname` | Starts the X server specified by *progname* (where *progname* is XFree86 or XF86_SVGA). |

TIP

When you want to issue multiple KNOPPIX boot commands, simply combine them in a single line. To specify that you want to skip the SCSI autodetection, turn off ACPI, use the U.S. keyboard, use a wheel mouse, and require the X server to load the nv module, enter the following at the `boot:` prompt:

```
knoppix noscsi acpi=off lang=us wheelmouse xmodule=nv
```

## Handling the fatal signal 11 error

During installation, some people get a fatal signal 11 error message, which stops the process cold. This error usually happens past the initial boot screen as the installer is starting its GUI or text interface. The most likely cause of a signal 11 error during installation is a hardware error related to memory or the cache associated with the CPU (microprocessor).

**TECHNICAL
STUFF**

A signal 11, or SIGSEGV (short for Segment Violation Signal), error can occur in Linux applications. A *segment violation* occurs when a process tries to access a memory location that it's not supposed to access. The operating system catches the problem before it happens and stops the offending process by sending it a signal 11. During installation, a signal 11 means that the installer made an error while accessing memory and that the most likely reason is a hardware problem. A commonly suggested cure for the signal 11 problem is to turn off the CPU cache in the BIOS. To do so, you have to enter Setup while the PC boots (by pressing a function key, such as F2) and turn off the CPU cache from the BIOS Setup menu.

If the problem is due to a hardware error in memory (in other words, the result of bad memory chips), you can try swapping the memory modules around in their slots. You might also consider replacing an existing memory module with another memory module if you have one handy.

You can read more about the signal 11 problem at www.bitwizard.nl/sig11.

## Getting around the PC reboot problem

On some PCs, when you press Enter at the boot prompt, the initial Linux kernel loads and immediately reboots the PC. This situation could be due to a bad implementation of ACPI in the PC's BIOS. To bypass the problem, type **linux acpi=off** at the boot prompt to turn off ACPI. If that method doesn't work, consult Table 5-3 for other boot options to try.

## Using Linux kernel boot options

When you boot the PC for Linux installation from the CD/DVD or a USB stick, you get a text screen with the boot: prompt. Typically, you press Enter at that prompt or do nothing and installation begins shortly. You can specify a variety of options at the boot: prompt, however. The options control various aspects of the Linux kernel startup, such as disabling support for troublesome hardware or starting the X server with a specific X driver module. Some of these boot options can be helpful in bypassing problems that you may encounter during installation.

**TABLE 5-3**     Some Linux Boot Options

| Boot Option | What It Does |
|---|---|
| allowcddma | Enables DMA for CD/DVD drive. |
| apic | Works around a bug commonly encountered in the Intel 440GX chipset BIOS and executes only with the installation program kernel. |
| acpi=off | Disables ACPI in case problems with it occur. |
| dd | Prompts for a driver disk during the installation of Red Hat Linux. |
| display=IP_address:0 | Causes the installer GUI to appear on the remote system identified by the IP address. (Make sure that you run the command xhost +*hostname* on the remote system, where *hostname* is the host where you run the installer.) |
| driverdisk | Prompts for a driver disk during installation of Red Hat Linux. |
| enforcing=0 | Turns off Security Enhanced Linux (SELinux) mandatory access control. |
| expert | Enables you to partition removable media and prompts for a driver disk. |
| ide=nodma | Disables DMA on all IDE devices and can be useful when you're having IDE-related problems. |
| ks | Configures the Ethernet card using DHCP and runs a kickstart installation by using a kickstart file from an NFS server identified by the boot server parameters provided by the DHCP server. |
| ks=*kickstartfile* | Runs a kickstart installation by using the kickstart file, specified by *kickstartfile*. (The idea behind kickstart is to create a text file with all the installation options and then kickstart the installation by booting and providing the kickstart file as input.) |
| lowres | Forces the installer GUI to run at a lower resolution (640 x 480). |
| mediacheck | Prompts you to check the integrity of the CD image (also called the ISO image). The image is checked by computing the MD5 checksum and comparing that with the official Fedora value. Checking a CD-ROM can take a few minutes. |
| mem=*xxx*M | Overrides the amount of memory that the kernel detects on the PC. (Some older machines could detect only 16MB of memory, and on some new machines, the video card may use a portion of the main memory.) Make sure to replace *xxx* with the number representing the megabytes of memory on your PC. |
| nmi_watchdog=1 | Enables the built-in kernel deadlock detector that makes use of Non-Maskable Interrupt (NMI). |
| noapic | Prevents the kernel from using the Advanced Programmable Interrupt Controller (APIC) chip. (You can use this command on motherboards known to have a bad APIC.) |
| nofirewire | Doesn't load support for FireWire. |

| Boot Option | What It Does |
|---|---|
| noht | Disables *hyperthreading*, which is a feature that enables a single processor to act as multiple virtual processors at the hardware level. |
| nomce | Disables self-diagnosis checks performed on the CPU by using Machine Check Exception (MCE). On some machines, these checks are performed too often and need to be disabled. |
| nomount | Doesn't automatically mount any installed Linux partitions in rescue mode. |
| nopass | Doesn't pass the keyboard and mouse information to stage 2 of the installation program. |
| nopcmcia | Ignores any PCMCIA controllers in the system. |
| noprobe | Disables automatic hardware detection, and prompts the user for information about SCSI and network hardware installed on the PC. You can pass parameters to modules by using this approach. |
| noshell | Disables shell access on virtual console 2 (the one you get by pressing Ctrl+Alt+F2) during installation. |
| nousb | Disables the loading of USB support during the installation. (Booting without USB support may be useful if the installation program hangs early in the process.) |
| nousbstorage | Disables the loading of the usbstorage module in the installation program's loader. This option may help with device ordering on SCSI systems. |
| reboot=b | Changes the way that the kernel tries to reboot the PC so that it can reboot even if the kernel hangs during system shutdown. |
| pci=noacpi | Causes the kernel to not use ACPI to route interrupt requests. |
| pci=biosirq | Causes the kernel to use BIOS settings to route interrupt requests (IRQs). |
| rescue | Starts the kernel in rescue mode, where you get a shell prompt and can try to fix problems. |
| resolution=*HHHxVVV* | Causes the installer GUI to run in the specified video mode (where *HHH* and *VVV* are standard resolution numbers, such as 640x480, 800x600, or 1024x768). |
| selinux=0 | Disables the SELinux kernel extensions. |
| serial | Turns on serial console support during installation. |
| skipddc | Skips the Display Data Channel (DDC) probe of monitors. (This option is useful if probing causes problems.) |
| vnc | Starts a VNC (Virtual Network Computing) server so that you can control the GUI installer from another networked system that runs a VNC client. |

To use these boot options, you typically type **linux** followed by the boot options. To perform text mode installation and tell the kernel that your PC has 512MB of memory, you type the following at the boot: prompt:

```
linux text mem=512M
```

Consult Table 5-3 earlier in this chapter for a brief summary of some of the Linux boot options. You can use these commands to turn certain features on or off.

**TIP**

Although I mention these Linux kernel boot commands in the context of trouble-shooting installation problems, you can use many of these commands any time you boot a PC with any Linux distribution and want to turn specific features on or off.

# Setting Up Printers

In most Linux distributions, you can set up printers only after you install the distribution. The following sections outline the printer configuration steps for Ubuntu and are similar for all distributions.

To set up a printer, follow these steps:

**1.** **From the desktop system menu, click the reboot options icon, and then choose the Settings option.**

This displays the Settings dialog box, allowing you to check on various settings in the Ubuntu system.

**2.** **Click the Printers icon from the left side of the Settings dialog box.**

This displays the list of currently installed printers.

**3.** **Click the Add button to configure a new printer.**

If the device can be identified, it appears in the list. If the device can't be identified, you can still continue with the installation and manually add the drivers and configuration data needed. Figure 5-1 shows that the Epson network printer was detected after I entered its IP address in the Search text box.

**TIP**

Some network printers support multiple protocols for connecting to the printer. When the Linux system detects these printers, it may think there are actually multiple printers available (see Figure 5-1). Just select the icon for the protocol you prefer to use to connect with the printer. If Ubuntu autodetects the actual printer model (as shown by the ET-3750 entry in Figure 5-1), it's usually best to use that entry, because Ubuntu will load the correct drivers for that specific printer model.

4.  **Click the icon for the printer you want to install, and then click the Add button to continue.**

    The system searches for drivers, and if more than one is available for that printer type, it offers choices based on what it thinks you're installing. If necessary, select the appropriate driver and then click Forward.

5.  **Enter the printer name and description variables, and then click Apply.**

    Both the description and location variables are optional but are helpful if you are configuring this for access by others across the network. Identifying the location can help users know where to pick up the reports they print.

6.  **After you install the new printer, it will appear in the Printers list (see Figure 5-2).**

7.  **Print a test page to make sure that everything is working as it should.**

    Make any modifications to the settings as needed, using the configuration options, which are shown in Figure 5-3.

8.  **When the printer is configured as it should be, exit the printer configuration tool.**

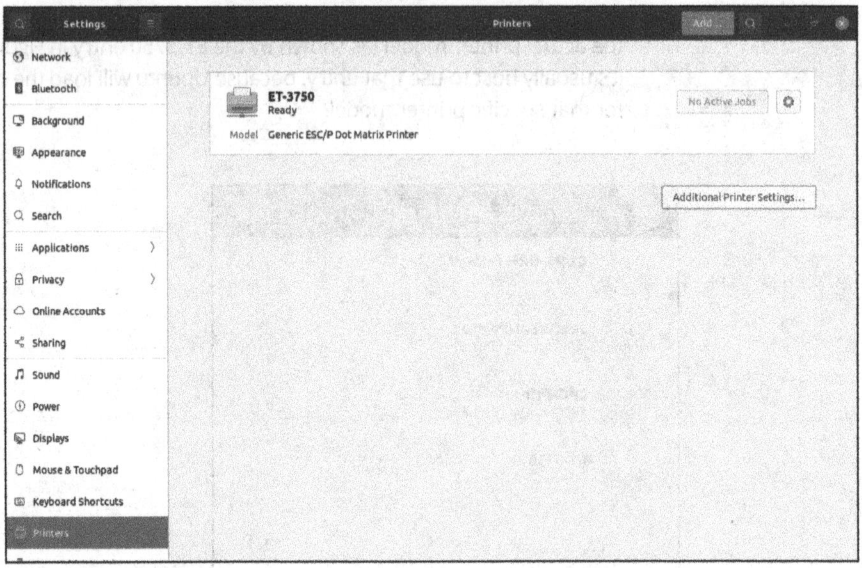

**FIGURE 5-2:**
The new printer
displayed in the
Printers list.

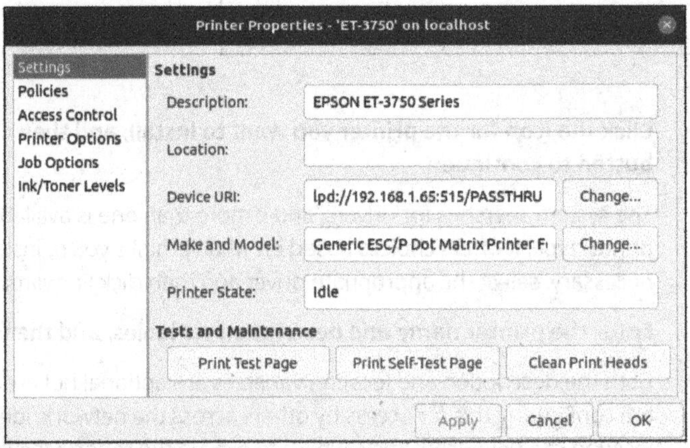

**FIGURE 5-3:**
Edit the printer
settings with
the printer
configuration
tool.

# Managing DVDs, CD-ROMs, and Flash Drives

The GUI desktop makes using DVDs, CD-ROMs, and flash drives in Linux easy. Just place the external media in the drive, and an icon appears on the desktop. Then you can access the media by double-clicking the icon on the desktop.

In some Linux distributions, the GUI automatically opens the contents of the media in a file-manager window soon after you insert the CD or DVD in the drive.

To access the files and folders, simply double-click the icons that appear in the GUI file manager window.

If you see an icon for the drive, right-click that icon to display a context menu. From that menu, you can eject the media when you're finished.

# Updating the Operating System

A vital feature of any operating system is the ability to quickly and easily update it. There are always new features, security fixes, and software bug fixes that you should try to install to keep things running smoothly.

Most Linux distributions include a program for automatically updating the installed software on your system via an Internet connection. If your PC is connected to the Internet, you can receive daily updates and be up to the minute with all the latest patches! The following sections walk you through how each of these programs works on your desktop system.

The following sections show how to handle updates in the Ubuntu and openSUSE Linux distributions.

## Updating Ubuntu

The Ubuntu distribution runs the Software Updater program in the background to regularly check for updates. If a new update is available, a notification appears on your desktop. You can also run the Software Updater program manually at any time:

1. **Select Software Updater from the Application Launcher menu.**

   The main Update Manager window, shown in Figure 5-4, appears.

2. **If you want to disable automatic update checks or just change how they occur, click the Settings button.**

   The Settings button in the Software Updater window allows you to customize how Ubuntu handles updates, such as enabling automatic installation of security updates but notifying you of application updates.

3. **If you want information on individual updates, select the > to the left of Details of Updates drop-down, select the update from the list, and click the Technical Description arrow under the listing.**

   The information about the update appears below the update list.

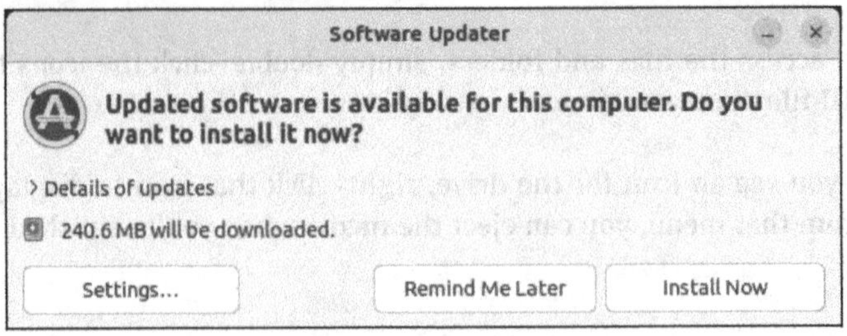

Software Updater

Updated software is available for this computer. Do you want to install it now?

> Details of updates

240.6 MB will be downloaded.

Settings...     Remind Me Later     Install Now

**FIGURE 5-4:**
The Ubuntu
Software Updater
window.

4. **Click the Install Now button to begin installing the updates.**

   You'll be asked for your password to ensure that you have the proper privileges to add updates.

5. **Click the Close button to exit the Software Updater dialog box.**

Now your Ubuntu system should be current with all the available patches!

## Updating openSUSE

Similar to Ubuntu, openSUSE runs an updater program in the background, and when updates are available, the Notifications widget in the system tray produces a pop-up notification. When you see the notification, click the Software Updates icon in the system tray, and then click the Install button to install them. It's that easy!

If you'd like to manually check for updates, you do that using the Discover program. Just follow these steps:

1. **Click the KDE menu and choose Applications⇨System⇨Discover.**

   Discover automatically checks for updates.

2. **When Discover finishes checking for updates, click the Updates button in the lower-left corner.**

   The Updates page appears, as shown in Figure 5-5.

3. **Click the Update All button.**

And just like that, your openSUSE system should be current with all the available patches!

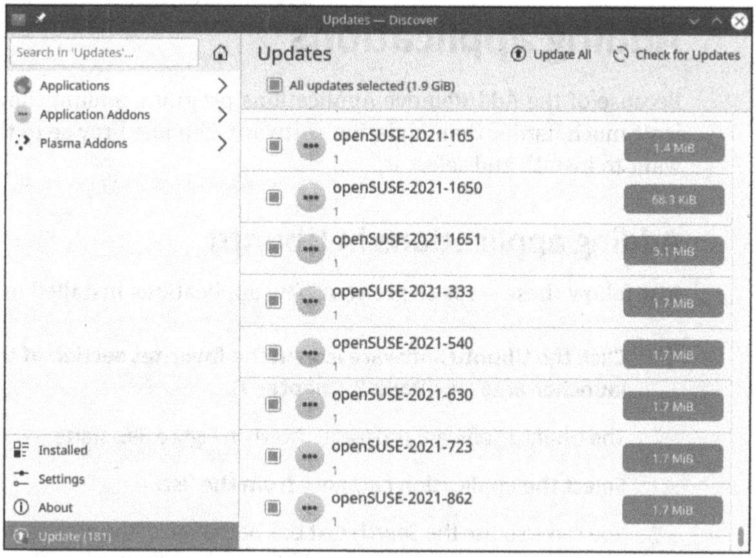

**FIGURE 5-5:**
The openSUSE
Discover window
showing available
updates.

# Installing New Software

Besides updating existing software packages, I'm sure you'll want to install new ones. There are two ways to add new software in both Ubuntu and openSUSE:

>> The Add/Remove Applications program

>> The Package Manager program

The Add/Remove Applications program allows you to add new software based on a complete application name. Often an application consists of several different components, called *packages.* Instead of having to install the individual packages one by one, you can just install the complete application. This method is commonly used for larger applications, such as LibreOffice or Firefox.

However, there are times when you just want to install an individual package, either because you just need part of a complete application or because a program is not large enough to get its own entry in the Add/Remove Applications program. This is where the Package Manager comes in.

This section walks you through using both of these tools to get new software on your system.

# Adding applications

Because of the Add/Remove Applications program, adding complete applications isn't much harder than updating software. You just browse to the application you want to install, and select it.

## Adding applications in Ubuntu

Just follow these steps to get your new applications installed in Ubuntu:

1. **Click the Ubuntu Software icon in the favorites section of the Application launcher area (see Book 2, Chapter 1).**

   The Ubuntu Software program, shown in Figure 5-6, starts.

2. **Select the application category from the list.**

   You can also use the Search text box at the top of the window to search for a specific application or a keyword within an application.

3. **Select the application to install from the icons that appear in the window.**

   A description of the application appears.

4. **Click the Install button to install the application.**

5. **Repeat the process for any other applications you want to install.**

   The new application is available on your system. Most of the time applications are automatically added to the Applications menu.

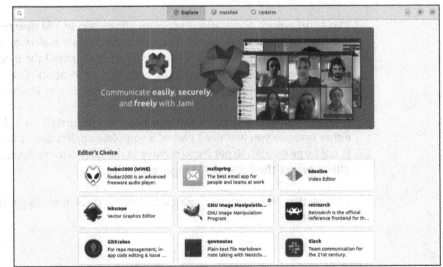

**FIGURE 5-6:** The Ubuntu Software program in Ubuntu.

## Adding applications in openSUSE

The Discover program (called Software Center in the menu) not only handles the update process but also handles installing new applications. To install a new application, follow these steps:

**1.** **From the K menu, choose Applications⇨System⇨Discover (see Book 2, Chapter 2).**

The Discover main window (refer to Figure 5-5) appears.

**2.** **Select the application category from the left.**

You can also use the Search text box above the category list to search for a specific application or a keyword within an application.

**3.** **Select the application to install from the list in the upper-right windowpane.**

A description of the application appears in the lower windowpane.

**4.** **Click the Install button.**

# Adding packages

Ubuntu and openSUSE use separate programs to install individual packages on the system. This section walks you through installing individual packages in your Linux system.

## The Synaptic Package Manager

Ubuntu uses the Synaptic Package Manager to manage packages. This tool allows you to add, remove, and update packages manually from the same interface. Unfortunately, later versions of Ubuntu don't install it by default, but you can use the Ubuntu Software program to do that.

After you install Synaptic Package Manager, to add a new package, follow these steps:

**1.** **Start Synaptic from the Application Launcher menu.**

The Synaptic Package Manager starts, displaying the main window (see Figure 5-7).

**2.** **Select the category of the package in the filter list on the left, or type the package in the Search text box at the top.**

Packages matching the filter category or search keyword appear in the list on the right.

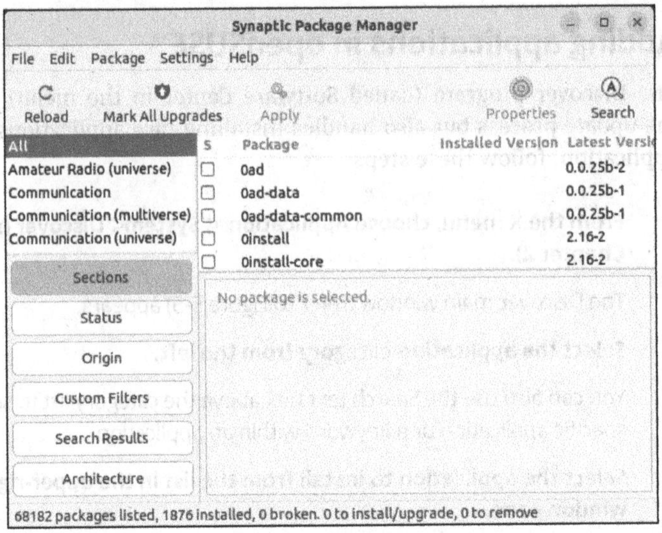

FIGURE 5-7:
The Synaptic
Package Manager
in Ubuntu.

3. **Select a package from the list to view the details.**

   The details for the package appear in the lower window pane.

4. **Click the check box and select Mark for Installation from the pop-up menu.**

5. **Click the Apply button to install the selected packages.**

## Installing with YaST2

The openSUSE distribution uses the Yet another Setup Tool, version 2 (YaST2) program to install individual packages. Follow these steps to look for packages using YaST2:

1. **Select KDE⇨Applications⇨System⇨YaST Software.**

   Because installing and removing software requires root privileges, you'll be prompted for your password. After you enter your password, the main YaST2 window appears, as shown in Figure 5-8.

2. **Enter the package you want in the Search text box and click Search.**

   YaST2 allows you to specify what fields to search in, such as the package name, description, or keywords. This can help limit the results returned.

3. **Click a package to display information about the package.**

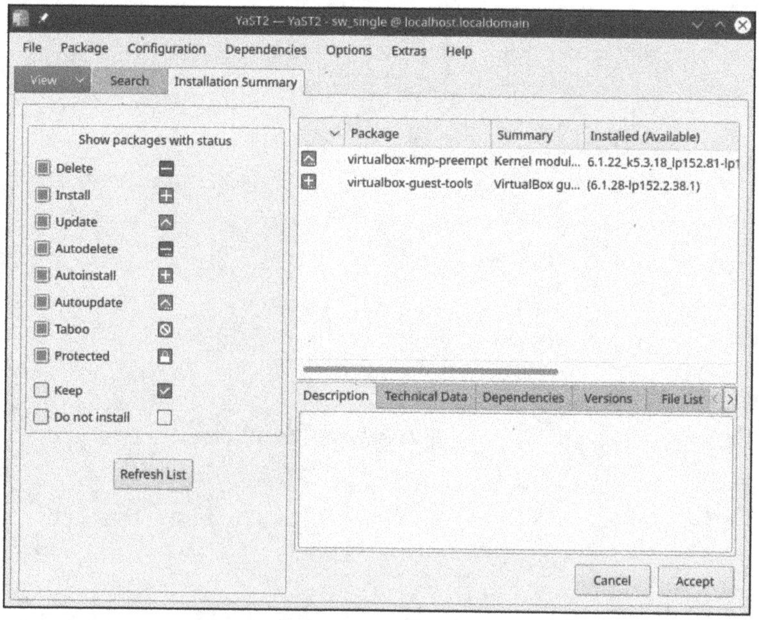

FIGURE 5-8:
The YaST2
package manager
in openSUSE.

4. **Click the check box on the package(s) you want to install.**

When you click the check box, a plus sign appears in the box indicating that package has been selected for installation. Click the check box again to remove it from the installation list.

5. **Click the Accept button to start the installation.**

YaST2 will download and install all the packages you selected.

# 2

# Linux Desktops

# Contents at a Glance

# Chapter **1**

# The GNOME Desktop

S ome people like to characterize Linux as being an operating system built *by* nerds, exclusively *for* nerds. This idea instills visions of having to type cryptic commands to get anything done on your computer. However, that can't be further from the truth! Linux supports several graphical desktop environments that provide some of the most user-friendly interfaces available for desktop computers.

What can be a bit confusing, though, is that, unlike Windows and macOS, there's no *one* standard Linux graphical desktop. Linux is full of choices, and nowhere is that more evident than in the graphical desktop world. In this chapter and the next two chapters, I cover the most common Linux graphical desktop environments used by the popular Linux distributions. This chapter starts out the discussion by examining the GNOME desktop.

## Looking at the History of GNOME

The GNU Network Object Model Environment (GNOME) desktop is (as you may suspect from its name) part of the GNU project, popular for creating and supporting many open-source packages used in Linux (see Book 1, Chapter 1). The initial version of GNOME became popular as the default desktop used by the popular Red Hat Linux distribution, one of the first commercial Linux distributions. It has since been adopted by many other Linux distributions, including Ubuntu.

However, GNOME's history hasn't been all rosy. The original version of GNOME was popular, but in 2011 the GNOME development team made a major change in version 3, which took the Linux community by surprise. Instead of the standard graphical desktop environment that most people had grown to love and been comfortable with, GNOME 3 incorporated a completely new paradigm for graphical desktops — using a consistent interface among different devices, such as laptops, tablets, and mobile phones. No matter what type of device you use the GNOME 3 desktop on, your user experience should be the same.

The new design places less emphasis on user interface elements that are awkward to use on mobile devices (such as selecting items using long drop-down menus) and more emphasis on user interface elements that you can scroll and click through (such as selecting items from a list of icons). Although this made things easier for tablet and mobile phone users, it was perceived as an inconvenience by desktop and laptop users. The new version of GNOME sent the Linux world into a tizzy, and even produced some new graphical desktop environments based on the original GNOME version (see Book 2, Chapter 3).

However, over time, people have become more comfortable with the desktop paradigm behind GNOME 3, and it's now become (mostly) accepted in the Linux world. The following sections walk you through the major points of the GNOME 3 desktop and how you can customize things to your liking.

**TECHNICAL STUFF**

The user interface of the GNOME 3 graphical desktop is now referred to as the *GNOME Shell*. This gets somewhat confusing, and you may see GNOME 3 and GNOME Shell used interchangeably in documentation and books. I prefer to just use *GNOME 3* so as not to confuse it with the original GNOME desktops or the command-line shell, and that's what I do in this chapter.

# Breaking Down the GNOME Desktop

Simplicity has become the hallmark of the GNOME 3 desktop environment. There aren't any long menus from which you need to select things, nor do you need to go digging through folders looking for files, but getting comfortable with the new interface may take some time. This section walks you through the basic features of the GNOME 3 desktop so you can maneuver your way around.

## Menu, please!

At the top of the GNOME 3 desktop is a panel (called the *top bar*) that when the desktop first opens, contains just three menu selections, as shown in Figure 1-1:

» **Activities:** Where you get to your applications and see the status of any running applications

» **Calendar and notifications:** Displays a calendar and any calendar and system notifications

» **System menu:** Displays icons showing the status of several features on your system, such as network connection status, sound card status, battery status (if applicable), and reboot options

Activities

Application menu          Calendar and notifications          System menu

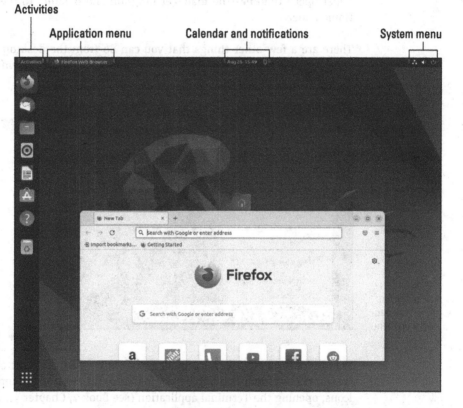

**FIGURE 1-1:**
The default
GNOME 3
desktop as
used in Ubuntu.

**TIP**

I mentioned that, by default, there are only three menus visible in the top bar but a fourth menu appears at times. When you launch an application in the GNOME 3 desktop, a separate menu appears in the top bar, called the *application menu.* The application menu contains options related to the application. Instead of placing the application menu in the application's window title bar, GNOME 3 has it in the top bar, separate from the application window. This can take some getting used to.

## The desktop

The GNOME 3 desktop paradigm has changed how you interact with the desktop a bit. Desktop icons are no longer the preferred way to launch applications, store files, or access removable media. In fact, many Linux distributions don't even bother creating icons on the desktop at all by default! However, for those of us who have trouble breaking old habits, GNOME 3 does still allow us to create and use icons on the desktop.

The Ubuntu Linux distribution just creates a single icon by default. The Home folder opens the Files file manager program and defaults to the user account's Home folder.

There are a few other things that you can do from the desktop. Right-click an empty area on the desktop and you see a pop-up menu, as shown in Figure 1-2.

**FIGURE 1-2:**
The GNOME 3 desktop pop-up menu.

The desktop pop-up menu provides you with a few different choices, such as creating new folders, copying files or folders to the desktop, arranging the desktop icons, opening the Terminal application (see Book 2, Chapter 5), or changing the background or display settings.

**TIP**

Many graphical desktops allow you to create new files by right-clicking the desktop. Unfortunately, GNOME 3 isn't one of them. If you want to create an icon for a file on your desktop, you'll need to store the file in the Desktop folder, located in your Home folder, using the Files file manager program (see Book 2, Chapter 5).

# Exploring the Activities Overview

The Activities overview area is what has replaced the application menu system used in older versions of GNOME, and it's what has made GNOME 3 so controversial. Although it was designed to be easy to navigate, the overall structure and layout can be confusing, especially if you're already comfortable using the old menu system. There are three features you'll want to explore in the Activities overview section:

>> **The dash:** A set of applications icons that appear on the left-hand side of the Activities overview by default. They provide quick access to favorite applications, removable media, and any running applications. At the bottom of the dash is the Application overview icon (the grid). Clicking this icon displays the Application overview, which displays icons for all the currently installed desktop applications.

>> **Windows overview area:** Provides quick access to managing active applications on the desktop.

>> **Workspace selector:** Allows you to switch between virtual desktop areas.

Figure 1-3 shows where each of these sections appears on the desktop.

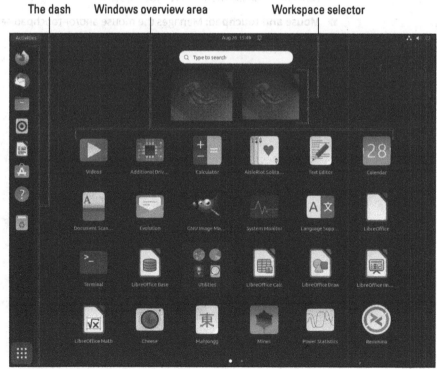

**FIGURE 1-3:** The Ubuntu Activities overview area.

# Customizing Your Ride

At the beginning of this chapter, I mention that Linux is well known for providing choices when it comes to graphical desktops. What I didn't mention is that even after you choose a specific desktop to use, you still have lots of choices available to customize your desktop experience.

This is done with the desktop settings options in the general Settings tool for GNOME 3. You can get to the Settings tool either by right-clicking an empty area on the desktop and selecting Settings, or by selecting the Settings option in the system menu discussed in the "Menus, please" section.

There are four things you can customize with the Settings tool:

>> **Background:** You can choose from a wide variety of custom backgrounds or even use your own images.

>> **Appearance:** Allows you to alter the color schemes used in application windows.

>> **Displays:** Changes the monitor orientation, resolution, and refresh rate, or configure multiple monitors for your system.

>> **Mouse and touchpad:** Manages the mouse and/or touchpad settings for your system.

IN THIS CHAPTER

» Walking you through KDE Plasma

» Playing with widgets

» Setting up your workspace

# Chapter 2

# The KDE Plasma Desktop

I n Book 2, Chapter 1, you see how the GNOME 3 desktop works. This chapter discusses the other popular desktop in the Linux world: KDE Plasma. The KDE Plasma desktop environment provides a graphical user interface (GUI) to your Linux distribution using features commonly found in Microsoft Windows systems. It's available as a software package in Fedora, openSUSE, and Ubuntu, and is the main desktop used in Kubuntu, a Linux distribution based on Ubuntu but focused on the KDE Plasma desktop. This chapter walks you through the KDE Plasma desktop features, showing you how to work your way around the desktop and get the most from your workspace.

## The KDE Plasma Desktop

KDE desktop was first released in 1996 as the Kool Desktop Environment, but these days it tries to be a little more sophisticated and prefers to be called just the K Desktop Environment (but it is still pretty cool). It quickly became popular among Linux beginners because it provides a Windows-like interface for your Linux desktop.

Besides the graphical desktop, the KDE community releases lots of other software applications, so to avoid confusion, starting with version 4.4 the KDE desktop has been called the KDE Plasma desktop, or just *Plasma*, to distinguish it from the other software projects the KDE organization produces. Figure 2-1 shows the Plasma desktop used in the openSUSE Leap 15.4 Linux distribution.

Application launcher

The desktop

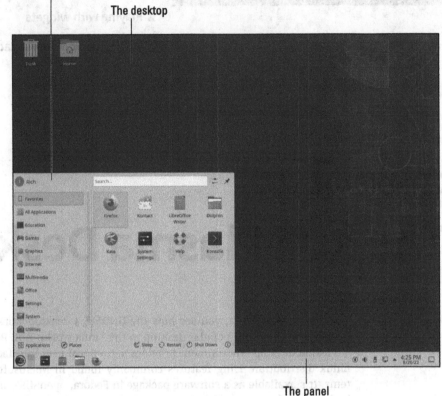

**FIGURE 2-1:**
The openSUSE
15.4 KDE Plasma
desktop.

The panel

To find out more about the KDE project, take a look at the KDE website (https://kde.org).

**REMEMBER**

As with everything else in Linux, the Plasma desktop layout is highly customizable, so what you have on your system may vary from what you see in the figures in this chapter. Don't panic — all these features are there, and I show you just how to customize your desktop to suit your needs and desires!

The Plasma desktop contains three main components that you should become familiar with:

>> The Application Launcher

>> The panel

>> The desktop

In the following sections, I walk you through each of these components and show you what they look like.

## The Application launcher

You access the Application Launcher from a single icon on the far-left side at the bottom of the panel. Clicking the icon produces the entire Application Launcher layout.

Along the bottom of the Launcher are six entries:

>> **Applications tab:** Contains submenus of program icons to launch applications on your system

>> **Places tab:** Contains shortcuts to special locations on your computer and the network in the Computer tab, a set of icons of recently run applications in the History tab, and a set of icons for frequently used applications in the Frequently Used tab

>> **Sleep:** Locks the desktop and suspends running applications

>> **Restart:** Brings up a menu allowing you to restart, shut down, sleep, or log out

>> **Shutdown:** Brings up a menu allowing you to restart, shut down, sleep, or log out

>> **Leave:** Gives you options for exiting (logging out from) the current desktop session

TIP

With all these different menu options, it can be cumbersome to find what you're looking for. To help out, the Application Launcher also provides a quick search tool. It's located at the top of the menu next to your username. Just click the text box and type in your search. You can search for just about anything — a file, an application, a command-line program, or even a website. The Application Launcher quickly returns any items on the system that match the search term. Then just click the menu item from the search results.

TIP

If you find that you're really not a fan of the Application Launcher format, you have more choices! Right-click the Application Launcher icon and select Alternatives. You're presented with other application launching menu systems, such as the Application menu, which provides a more old-fashioned menu system, and the Application Dashboard, which looks a lot like the GNOME 3 application overview system.

# The panel

At the bottom of your Plasma desktop you'll see a line with a bunch of icons. This is called the *panel.* The panel contains *widgets* (small programs that run on the panel to provide functions directly on the panel).

The layout of the Plasma panel is another feature that can be easily changed, so it often looks different in different Linux distributions. Usually, it's common for distributions to place the icon for the Application Launcher on the far-left side of the panel (which just so happens to be the same place that Microsoft Windows places its Start icon — I told you Plasma was kind to ex–Microsoft Windows users!).

On the openSUSE Plasma desktop (refer to Figure 2-1), after the Application Launcher icon, the following widgets appear on the panel:

>> **Pager:** Allows you to switch between different virtual desktop workspaces. Virtual desktop workspaces allow you to group running applications onto separate desktops and then use the Pager to switch between them.

>> **System Settings:** Opens the System Settings dialog box.

>> **Discover:** Opens the Software Center application to manage installed applications.

>> **Dolphin:** Opens the Dolphin file manager application.

>> **Firefox:** Opens the Firefox web browser application.

>> **Task Bar:** Displays icons for each of the currently running applications.

>> **System Tray:** Contains icons for utilities and system applications that run in background mode, such as the sound system, the Network Manager, the software updater, and the clipboard.

>> **Digital Clock:** Displays the current date and time.

>> **Show Desktop:** Minimizes all open windows to show the desktop.

You can easily modify the panel layout to suite your likes. Just right-click anywhere on the panel and select Enter Edit Mode to put the panel and desktop both in Edit Mode. Edit Mode allows you to edit the desktop layout as well. The next section describes the features available in the Plasma desktop.

# The desktop

The desktop is possibly the most controversial feature in Plasma. It behaves significantly different from other desktop environments you may be used to.

The desktop in Plasma works more like an extension of the panel rather than a desktop. Besides being able to place files, folders, or application icons in the Plasma desktop, you can also place widgets, just like in the panel. This basically allows you to have applications running directly on your desktop.

The default desktop in openSUSE 15.4 shows just two icons:

>> **Trash:** Opens the user's Trash folder

>> **Home:** Opens Dolphin in the user's Home folder

Right-clicking any open area in the desktop produces the desktop context menu, as shown in Figure 2-2.

| | |
|---|---|
| 🖼 Configure Desktop and Wallpaper... | Alt+D, Alt+S |
| 🖵 Configure Display Settings... | |
| 🗋 Create New | > |
| ⬚ Icons | > |
| 📋 Paste | Ctrl+V |
| ↺ Undo: Trash | Ctrl+Z |
| 🖵 Refresh Desktop | F5 |
| 🗑 Empty Trash | |
| + Add Widgets... | Alt+D, A |
| + Add Panel | > |
| 🎛 Show Activity Switcher | Alt+D, Alt+A |
| ✎ Enter Edit Mode | Alt+D, E |
| 🔒 Lock Screen | Meta+L |
| ‹ Leave... | Ctrl+Alt+Del |

**FIGURE 2-2:** The KDE Plasma desktop context menu.

The desktop context menu provides several options:

>> **Configure Desktop and Wallpaper:** Changes the look and feel of the desktop.

>> **Configure Display Settings:** Sets the resolution, orientation, and scaling of the active monitors on your system.

>> **Create New:** Creates a new folder, file, LibreOffice document, or link to an application.

>> **Icons:** Sorts the desktop icons in a specified order.

>> **Paste:** Pastes material from the clipboard onto the desktop.

- » **Undo:** Undoes the previous command.
- » **Refresh Desktop:** Repaints the desktop environment.
- » **Empty Trash:** Removes any files or folders placed in the special Trash folder.
- » **Add Widgets:** Adds or removes widgets from the desktop.
- » **Add Panel:** Adds a new panel to the desktop. You can have a panel on each side of the desktop — top, bottom, left, and right.
- » **Show Activity Switcher:** The Activity Switcher allows you to group applications running on a virtual desktop into a single area, within the same virtual desktop. This allows you to sort your active applications into separate groups without using additional virtual desktops.
- » **Enter Edit Mode:** Places the Plasma panel and desktop in Edit Mode.
- » **Lock Screen:** Activates the screen-lock feature.
- » **Leave:** Allows you to log out, restart, shut down, or lock the desktop.

The Plasma desktop and panel both use the same widgets, so I take a closer look at the widgets next.

# Using Widgets

The keys to the Plasma desktop environment are the widgets, small applications that run on the desktop. Each widget provides a different utility or small program to use in your desktop. There are widgets available to display the date and time in lots of different formats, quickly bring up a small calculator, view system performance, and even display your favorite Internet cartoon strip. This section walks you through how to add, remove, and get new widgets in your Plasma environment.

## Adding widgets

The Plasma package provides lots of different widgets for you to use in both your panel and desktop. Clicking the Add Widgets button from the panel or desktop editor produces a list of the widgets. At the top you can select whether to show just the currently running widgets or a list of all available widgets.

Widgets that are already active on your desktop or panel have a mark next to them. Adding a new widget is as easy as selecting the desired widget and clicking the Add Widget button.

## Getting more widgets

Besides all the standard widgets, you can even download more! Clicking the Get New Widgets button in the Add Widgets dialog box produces a drop-down menu with two options:

>> **Download New Plasma Widgets:** Browse the online repositories for new widget packages.

>> **Install Widgets from Local File:** Browse to a location on your workstation to install a new widget package from a file already on your computer.

After you've installed the new widget on your desktop or panel, you can access the control menu to manage the widget.

# Plasma System Settings

With Plasma you can configure just about every feature in your desktop environment to your liking. The Plasma System Settings utility provides quick access to all your configuration needs.

You start the Plasma System Settings utility from the Applications Launcher. In openSUSE, just select the System Settings menu item from the Favorites or Settings tab. The main System Settings dialog box, shown in Figure 2-3, appears.

The KDE Plasma Desktop

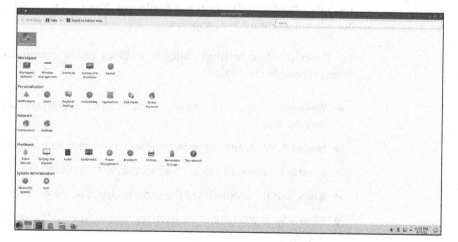

**FIGURE 2-3:**
The Plasma System Settings dialog box.

The dialog box contains six separate areas:

>> **Appearance:** Accesses most of the common "look and feel" features of the desktop

>> **Workspace:** Manages how windows appear and how you control windows on the desktop

>> **Personalization:** Sets custom actions for your user account, such as setting accessibility features, notifications, and connecting with online accounts

>> **Network:** Controls how your system connects to the network (see Book 3, Chapter 4)

>> **Hardware:** Defines new hardware devices such as monitors, keyboards, mice, and printers

>> **System Administration:** Manages high-level features such as creating new user accounts, managing network services, and software repositories

As you can see, there are lots of things that you can customize in your Plasma desktop environment. However, oddly enough, there's one more place where you can tweak things on your desktop: the Desktop Folder Settings dialog box.

# Desktop Settings

To access the desktop folder settings, right-click an empty space in your desktop and select Configure Desktop and Wallpaper. The Desktop Folder Settings dialog box, shown in Figure 2-4, appears.

The Desktop Folder Settings dialog box allows you to customize a few different things related to the desktop:

>> **Wallpaper:** Lets you choose what appears as the background of the desktop area

>> **Mouse Actions:** Allows you to set what actions each mouse button takes

>> **Location:** Determines what directory the desktop Folder View displays

>> **Icons:** Sets the properties of the icons displayed on the desktop

>> **Filter:** Allows you to filter out icons for specific types of files from the desktop display

>> **About:** Displays information about the current version of the KDE Plasma desktop

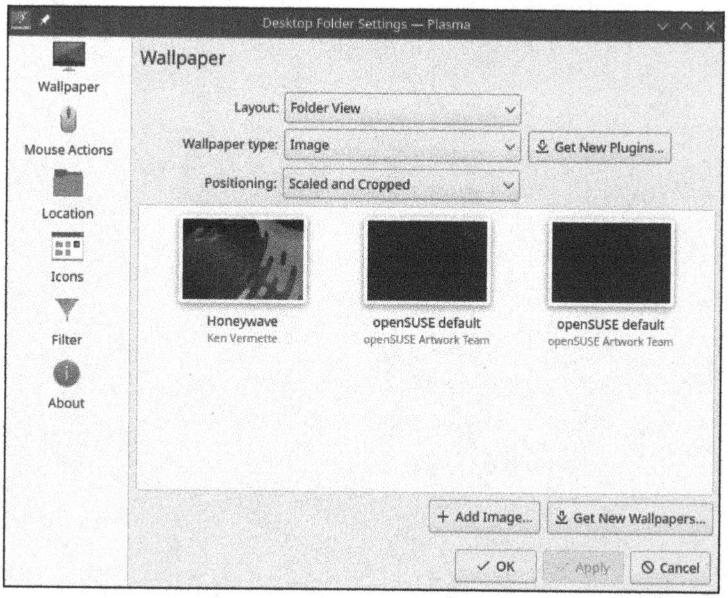


**FIGURE 2-4:** The Desktop Folder Settings dialog box.

Chapter **3**

# Other Popular Desktops

C hapters 1 and 2 of this minibook walk you through the GNOME 3 and KDE Plasma desktops, respectively. Although these are the two most popular desktops used in Linux systems, they're not the only games in town. There are lots of graphical desktops to choose from in Linux, and just because the Linux distribution you selected uses a particular desktop by default that doesn't mean you're stuck with it. Every Linux distribution allows you to install an alternative desktop, providing you with a wealth of options for how to interact with your Linux system.

This chapter walks you through the basics of three additional graphical desktops you'll come across in the Linux world: Cinnamon, MATE, and Xfce. This will give you an idea of how other desktops work within Linux.

## Spicing Things Up with Cinnamon

In Book 2, Chapter 1, I mention that there was great angst in the Linux world with the release of the GNOME 3 desktop. Many hard-core Linux users were perfectly comfortable with the look and feel of GNOME 2, and the desktop paradigm change introduced by GNOME 3 upset their worlds. The GNOME 2 desktop very much resembled the desktop interface used by the popular macOS computers, easing the transition into the Linux world for macOS users

This gave rise to some new desktops that were spinoffs from the original GNOME desktop, keeping the same macOS-like desktop interface. Cinnamon is one of those spinoffs. This section walks you through the basics of the Cinnamon desktop.

## Reviewing the history of Cinnamon

The Cinnamon desktop project was initiated in 2011 by the developers of the Linux Mint distribution as an alternative to GNOME 3. It uses much of the same background code as the GNOME 3 desktop project but keeps the original look and feel of the GNOME 2 desktop, as shown in Figure 3-1.

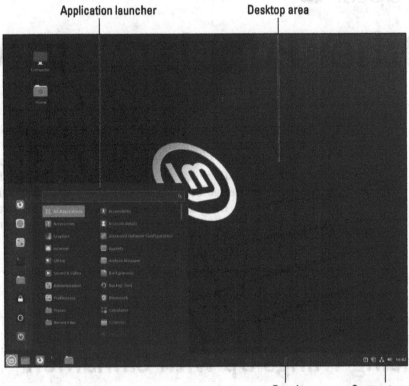

As you can see in Figure 3-1, the Cinnamon desktop in Linux Mint has many similar features to the Windows desktop:

» A single panel at the bottom of the desktop

» An application launcher at the left-hand edge of the panel

» A system tray at the right-hand edge of the panel

» A desktop area where you can save folders and files

The Cinnamon application launcher was designed to be similar to the old GNOME 2 menu system, which may feel somewhat familiar to macOS desktop users.

**TIP**

Your specific Linux distribution's Cinnamon desktop may vary slightly from what you see in Figure 3-1. With Cinnamon, you can move the panel to any side of the desktop, and you can even have multiple panels. Just right-click an empty place on the panel and select the Move option to move the panel, or select the Add Panel option to create additional panels.

## Looking at the menu

The Cinnamon application launcher, called simply the Cinnamon menu, provides quick access to applications and directories on the system.

There are four main sections contained in the Cinnamon menu:

» A list of favorites on the left-hand side

» A list of categories in the middle

» A detailed list of applications that match the category selected from the middle

» A Search text box at the top to help search for files, directories, or applications

**TIP**

Each Linux distribution that uses Cinnamon sets its own default Favorites icons. Plus, you can add your own at any time.

Next to the Favorites icons are the application categories. As you hover your mouse pointer over each category, the list of applications shown in the right-hand column changes appropriately. Just click the icon that you need to launch the application.

You can modify the Cinnamon menu layout by right-clicking the menu icon in the panel and then selecting Configure. In the Configuration dialog box, click the Menu button at the top to alter the menu behavior and menu items. You can add and remove menu items, as well as set whether icons are displayed in the menu.

## Changing settings

The Cinnamon desktop allows you to customize lots of features from the System Settings dialog box (see Figure 3-2), accessed from the Application Launcher.

Other Popular Desktops

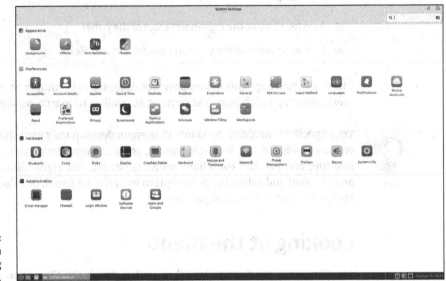

**FIGURE 3-2:**
The System
Settings dialog
box in Cinnamon.

There are four sections in the dialog box:

>> **Appearance:** Controls how the desktop looks, such as the background, fonts, and window themes

>> **Preferences:** Allows you to set the features of the desktop, such as accessibility features, how the panel looks, and the use of hot corners

>> **Hardware:** Allows you to set the display, printer, and network features

>> **Administration:** Lets you manage user accounts, software sources, and the firewall

The Preferences section is where you can really go to town customizing your desktop environment. There are plenty of things you can fine-tune to customize your Cinnamon experience.

## Adding more spice

The Cinnamon desktop and panel both allow you to add widgets (called *spices*) to provide additional functionality to your desktop. For the desktop, these are called *desklets*; for the panel, they're called *applets*.

To add spices to the desktop, click the Desklets icon in the Settings dialog box. You see a list of currently available desklet spices as well as a tab that allows you to download even more. There are desklets to provide easy access to common functions, such as monitoring disk space or CPU usage, as well as novelty desklets that let you view the weather, watch your stock or cryptocurrency prices, or check in on your favorite Internet cartoons.

Similarly, for applets just click the Applets icon in the System Settings dialog box. You see a selection of applets that you can add to your panel(s). Applets tend to be somewhat smaller programs than desklets, but you'll still see some useful utilities, such as searching for files, listing recently accessed documents, or listing open windows.

Applets that appear with a check mark are already installed. Some applets allow you to configure their behavior, as indicated by the gear icon next to them.

# Working with MATE

Another popular GNOME spinoff is the MATE desktop environment. It has many of the same features as Cinnamon but with some twists. This section walks you through the components of MATE and how to customize them to your liking.

## The history of MATE

The MATE (pronounced mah-*tay*, after the South American plant) desktop was also created in 2011 as a result of the GNOME project's switch to GNOME 3. It was created by a developer for the Arch Linux distribution, but it has also gained popularity as a desktop alternative in other Linux distributions. The MATE Desktop retains almost all of the original GNOME 2 desktop features (even more so than Cinnamon), so GNOME purists often prefer MATE. Figure 3-3 shows the default MATE desktop in the Fedora 36 MATE spin.

In many ways, the MATE desktop keeps the basic GNOME 2 desktop layout:

>> Two panels — one at the bottom of the desktop and one at the top

>> A menu system at the upper-left corner of the desktop that supports multiple top-level menus

>> A system tray at the upper-right corner of the desktop

>> A desktop area where you can save folders and files

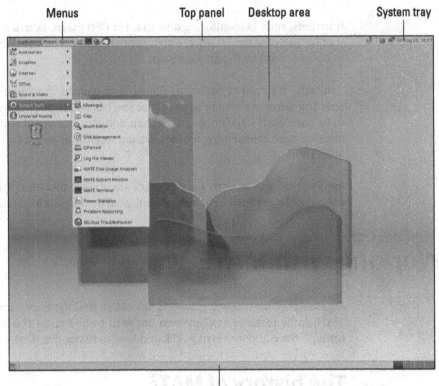

Menus      Top panel   Desktop area     System tray

**FIGURE 3-3:**
The default
MATE desktop in
Fedora 36 MATE.

Bottom panel

The Fedora MATE spin uses three separate menus in the top panel instead of just one:

>> **Applications:** Provides access to all the installed graphical applications on the system

>> **Places:** Provides access to various directories, such as Home, Documents, Downloads, and any network drives

>> **System:** Provides access to system preferences, administration, and shut-down features

After the menus, you see several icons for favorite applications. These menus provide quick access to often-used applications. On the far right side of the top menu is the system tray, which includes icons for the time and date, network status, and sound card status.

At the bottom of the desktop is the second panel, which includes three main sections:

>> **Show Desktop icon:** When clicked, minimizes all open windows

>> **Running applications:** Displays icons and titles of all open windows on the desktop

>> **Workspace Switcher:** Allows you to change the active workspace area displayed on the desktop

The desktop area itself allows you to create icons for files, directories, and applications, just like the old GNOME 2 desktop did.

## Looking at the menu

As discussed in the previous section, the default menu setup used in Fedora MATE creates three menu entries on the top panel.

The Applications menu provides quick access for launching any graphical application installed. The default Application menu in Fedora MATE breaks the applications into seven categories, including Accessories, Graphics Programs, Internet Applications, Office Tools, Sound and Video applications, system-related utilities, and accessibility options. As you add new software packages using the software manager (see Book 1, Chapter 5), they automatically appear in the Application menu.

## Changing desktop settings

As with any other graphical desktop environment in Linux, you can change just about everything in the MATE desktop layout. To do that, you need to go to the Control Center. You can get there from the System menu. The main Control Center dialog box is shown in Figure 3-4.

The Control Center divides the settings into six main sections:

>> **Administration:** For setting features such as software management, printing, firewall, and login window

>> **Hardware:** For managing hardware features such as the sound card and power management

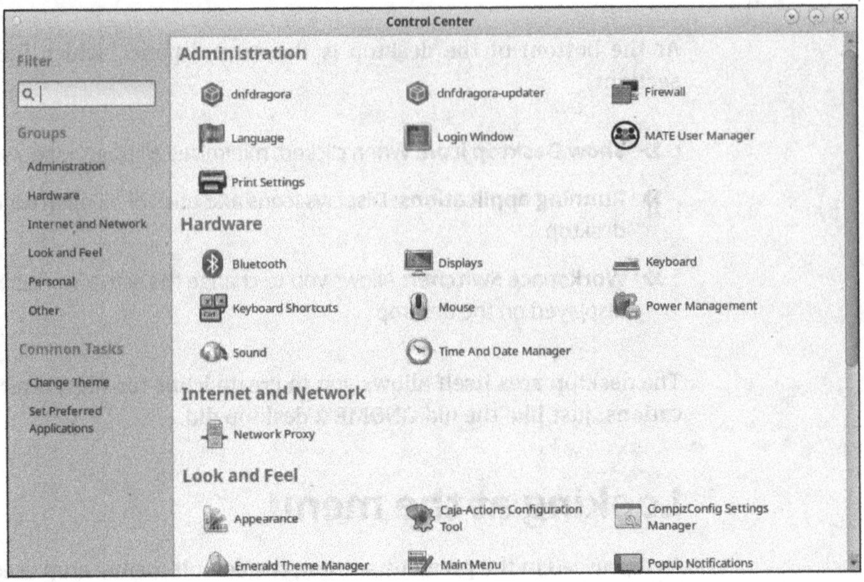

**FIGURE 3-4:**
The MATE
Control Center.

>> **Internet and Network:** For advanced network configuration

>> **Look and Feel:** For setting the appearance of windows, pop-up windows, and the screensaver

>> **Personal:** For enabling accessibility features, preferred applications, and applications to run at startup

>> **Other:** For setting character display for special characters

**TIP**
The Appearance settings in the Look and Feel category allow you to change the background and theme of the desktop. You can also get to this location directly by right-clicking an empty place on the desktop and selecting Change Desktop Background.

## Applets

Similar to Cinnamon, MATE also provides applets that you can add to any of the panels on the desktop. Right-click in a panel and select Add to Panel to see a list of applets currently installed.

# The Xfce Desktop Interface

The GNOME 3, KDE Plasma, Cinnamon, and MATE desktops are very fancy, but they all require quite a bit of computing resources to operate. One of the original selling points of Linux is that it could run on just about any old PC you had lying around. Unfortunately, with those desktops, that's not always the case.

However, there are other graphical desktop environments that are less resource-intensive and can, indeed, run on just about anything. The Xfce desktop is one such desktop. This section explores the features of the Xfce desktop and shows how you can customize it.

## The history of Xfce

The Xfce desktop is actually one of the older desktop packages in the Linux world, created in 1996 by Olivier Fourdan as an open-source replacement of the then commercial Common Desktop Environment (CDE) used in Unix. Because it was created at a time when x486 computers ruled the world, it didn't take many resources to run Xfce — and that's still true today.

Because of its lightweight requirements, the Xfce desktop is popular in Linux distributions oriented toward older or less-powerful hardware such as devices that use the ARM processor chip. Figure 3-5 shows the default Xfce desktop used in the MX Linux distribution.

**FIGURE 3-5:**
The Xfce desktop
in MX Linux.

The key to Xfce is simplicity. The desktop contains two elements: a single panel (in MX Linux it defaults to the left side of the desktop) and the desktop area. The Xfce panel uses applets to provide different features. The default panel setup in MX Linux contains several applets by default:

>> **Action button:** Provides a pop-up window to log out, restart, or shut down the system

>> **Digital clock:** When clicked, brings up the Orage calendar application

>> **Favorites:** Displays icons for quickly launching favorite applications

>> **Active windows area:** Displays icons for open application windows on the desktop

>> **Notification area:** Displays icons for showing the status of various applications, such as the network, sound, and software update applications

>> **Pager:** Allows you to switch between workspaces

>> **Whisker menu:** Provides access to applications

You'll notice that many of the same features found in the "big name" graphical desktops are available in Xfce. It's amazing what they can do with a minimal amount of memory requirements.

## The Whisker menu

The Whisker menu (named because the mascot for Xfce is a mouse) provides quick access to all the graphical applications on the system.

At the top of the menu, you see the user account that you're logged in as, along with four icons:

>> **Settings Manager:** Brings up the Settings Manager dialog box (see the "Changing Xfce settings" section, next)

>> **Lock:** Locks the desktop with a screensaver

>> **Switch user:** Keeps the current user account logged in and allows another user to log in

>> **Log out:** Displays a dialog box to log out, restart, or shut down the system

Under the user account is a search text box, allowing you to enter the name of an application to quickly display matching application icons. Just click the application icon to launch the program.

At the bottom of the Whisker menu, you see the applications menu area. Similar to other menu systems, there are two sections. On the right side is a list of categories, and on the left side is a list of programs within the selected category. You can customize the Whisker menu by right-clicking the menu icon and selecting Edit Applications. This allows you to change existing entries and add new ones.

**TIP**

You can also quickly access the Whisker applications menu by right-clicking in the desktop area and selecting Applications.

## Changing Xfce settings

As you would expect, the Xfce desktop allows you to customize things to your liking. To do that select Settings Manager from the Settings area of the Whisker menu. This opens the Settings dialog box, as shown in Figure 3-6. From here you can set desktop, hardware, and system preferences to your liking.

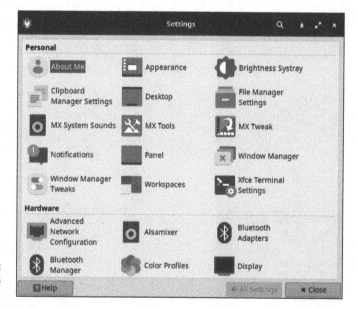

**FIGURE 3-6:**
The Xfce Settings dialog box.

**TIP**

Notice that in Xfce you set the accessibility features in the System section of the Settings dialog box. That's somewhat different from most graphical desktops.

## Applets

A surprise feature of the Xfce panel is the ability to add applets. You wouldn't expect such a feature from a bare-bones graphical desktop environment, but Xfce

Other Popular Desktops

provides quite a few fancy applets that you can add to the panel. Just right-click the panel, select Panel, and then select Add New Items. One of my favorites is the Notes applet, which allows me to place sticky-style notes on my desktop to remind me of things.

Before long, you can have your Xfce desktop customized to look and behave just like the fancier GNOME 3 or KDE Plasma desktop environments.

# Chapter 4

# Linux Desktop Applications

Having a shiny new Linux system installed on your desktop or laptop is great, but now what? Obviously, you'll want to actually be able to do things other than just stare in amazement at it. Fortunately, many very talented people have created lots of great applications for us to use in our Linux desktops. In this chapter, I cover some of the more popular ones available, but there are plenty more that you can download and play with. I hope this batch will help get you started and keep you busy on your new Linux system.

## The LibreOffice Suite

These days, just about everyone who has a computer has at least one office suite at their fingertips. For Microsoft Windows users, this suite is probably Microsoft Office, although it may be another worthy contender, such as Corel WordPerfect Office, or if your PC is connected to the Internet, the Google Workspace suite of programs. In Linux, typically the suite is LibreOffice, which has separate programs for word processing, spreadsheets, presentations, and even working with databases.

After you figure out how to use one of the programs in this suite, you may be happy to find that the others are designed to look and work in very similar ways. You can even open and save files in Microsoft Office format, if you need to share them with people who are using it — and you can edit the Office files people send you, too.

The full LibreOffice suite includes six separate programs:

» **Writer** for word processing

» **Calc** for spreadsheets

» **Impress** for presentation graphics

» **Draw** for drawing graphics

» **Base** for creating and using databases

» **Math** for creating complex mathematical formulas

However, not all Linux distributions install all these pieces. For example, Ubuntu doesn't install the Base package by default.

If you chose not to install the LibreOffice productivity software at installation time, or you need to install one of the packages that wasn't installed by default in your Linux distribution, don't sweat it — you can do that now without having to completely reinstall your Linux distribution. Just see Book 1, Chapter 5 to find how to add the LibreOffice packages from the software package manager used in your distribution.

After you've installed the LibreOffice packages, most of them are listed in the GNOME 3 or KDE Plasma application menus. The two oddballs are the Draw and Math packages, which unfortunately often don't rate a listing of their own.

To access either of these packages, you need to start one of the other LibreOffice packages (such as Writer), and then choose File⇔New. The New menu area contains the options for creating a new Drawing (which starts Draw) or a new Formula (which starts Math).

In some Linux distributions, the Writer package even has its own quick-launch icon on the panel. Just a single click of the icon launches Writer with a blank document.

# Browsing the Web with Firefox

Many people attribute the explosive growth of the Internet to the graphical web browser. The Internet has been around for much longer than the invention of the browser. It's just that most of the work done on the Internet was in plain old text, which held little attraction for those people who like pretty pictures.

In the world of Linux, the most popular browser is arguably Firefox (www.mozilla. org/products/firefox), which is based on Mozilla — essentially Firefox is just the web browser portion of Mozilla, whereas Mozilla can also handle email and news browsing. Just about every Linux distribution installs the Firefox browser by default, so most likely it's already an icon on your desktop or in your Applications menu.

## Configuring Firefox

You can start surfing right now, if you want. You don't need to customize your browser. However, you may want to take a moment to tell Firefox your preferences, such as the default website to show when it starts, what font sizes to use by default, what colors to use, and many other options.

The following steps introduce you to the Preferences window, where all the Firefox configuration parameters are stored:

1. **Start Firefox.**

   There's usually more than one way to start Firefox. Linux distributions that use the GNOME 3 desktop often provide an Application Launcher icon in the Dash favorites (see Book 2, Chapter 1). Distributions that use the KDE Plasma desktop often include Firefox as a favorite either in the panel or in the Applications menu (see Book 2, Chapter 2).

2. **Click the Firefox menu button and select Settings.**

   The Settings window appears, as shown in Figure 4-1. This window contains all the settings you need to play with to modify your web browsing experience.

3. **Click the entries along the left side of the Settings window to access the various categories.**

   Some categories have subcategories of settings listed as separate sections.

4. **If you get tired of reading through menus, just click Close to close the Settings window and get back to surfing.**

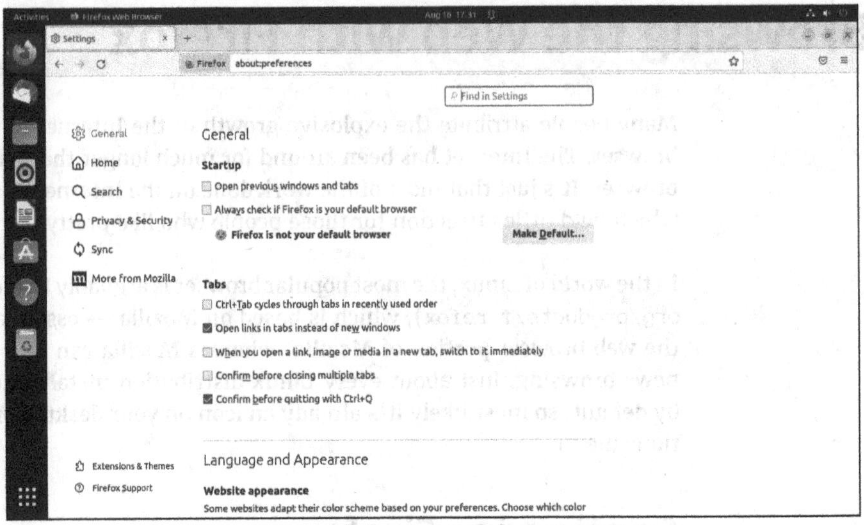

**FIGURE 4-1:**
The Firefox
Settings window
in Ubuntu.

There are several settings categories to work with:

>> **General:** Determines the look and feel of Firefox.

>> **Home:** Sets the content Firefox displays as your initial web page.

>> **Search:** Provides options to customize the built-in search features of the browser.

>> **Privacy & Security:** Sets how cookies, logins, form data, browsing history, and site data are handled.

>> **Sync:** If you're using Firefox on more than one device, use this feature to synchronize your bookmarks, browsing history, tabs, passwords, add-ons, and preferences across all your devices.

>> **More from Mozilla:** Accesses other Mozilla products, such as the Mozilla VPN service.

>> **Extensions and Themes:** Manages the extensions, themes, and plug-ins installed in your Firefox browser. These allow you to install additional capabilities for your browsing experience, such as installing ad blockers or listing all the tabs in a single menu.

# Communicating with Email

Before you start hacking away at trying to set up your email package, you need to grab some information about the Internet service provider (ISP) that supports your email address. Most of this information you should be able to obtain either from the information you received from your ISP with your email account or by calling the help desk at your ISP and asking a few simple questions.

Here are the items you need to have handy before you start:

» **Your email address:** This should be assigned by your ISP, with a format such as me@myhost.com. You need to remember to enter this in your email package exactly as it appears in your email or people won't be able to respond to your messages!

» **The type of email server your ISP uses for incoming mail:** ISP email servers use several different methods to communicate with email clients. The two most popular are POP (also called POP3 to refer to the version) and IMAP.

The main difference between these two protocols is that POP usually requires you to download all your incoming messages from the ISP server to your local workstation. After the messages are downloaded to your PC, the ISP deletes them from the server.

IMAP allows you to create folders on the ISP server and store all your messages on the server. IMAP servers usually allow you a specific amount of storage space on the server, so you must be careful how much mail you accumulate. One nice feature of an IMAP mailbox is that you can access your email from multiple devices, since all the mail is on the server and not downloaded to individual devices.

» **The hostname or IP address of your ISP incoming mail server:** Your ISP should provide a hostname or IP address for you to receive your mail, such as pop.isp.com.

» **The type of email server your ISP uses for outbound mail:** Sending outbound email requires a different protocol than retrieving inbound email. Most ISP email servers use SMTP for sending email to clients.

» **The hostname or IP address of your ISP outbound mail server:** Some ISPs use a separate server for outbound mail than inbound mail. Check with your ISP for the outbound server host name, such as smtp.isp.com.

» **Any special ports or passwords needed for authentication in an encrypted session**

Nowadays many ISPs require that you log in using your email account credentials to establish an encrypted connection for both inbound and outbound emails. If this isn't a requirement on your ISP server, you should still consider using it if your ISP supports it.

After you have all that information in hand, you're ready to configure your email package. The three main email client software packages you run across in the Linux world are

>> GNOME Evolution

>> KDE KMail

>> Mozilla Thunderbird

The following sections walk you through the basics of how to use any one of these packages.

## Evolving into email

If you're using the GNOME 3 desktop, the default email package is called Evolution. Evolution should remind you very much of Microsoft Outlook. If you like being able to integrate your calendar, address book, task manager, and email, you'll feel right at home with Evolution.

TIP

Not all Linux distributions that use the GNOME 3 desktop install the Evolution email software by default (such as Ubuntu), but it's easy to install from the distribution repository because it's a standard GNOME application. (See Book 1, Chapter 5 for how to do that.)

When you start Evolution for the first time, the Evolution Setup Assistant launches. Click Next to proceed past the Welcome screen, after which the Restore from Backup window appears. If you've previously saved a backup copy of your Evolution setup, you can quickly and easily restore it from this window. Click Next if this is just the first time you've used Evolution.

A series of wizard dialog boxes begins, walking you through the email configuration:

>> **Identity:** Provide your real name the way you want it to appear in your outbound email messages.

>> **Receiving Email:** Provide your email server information, including your email address. If you select the Look Up Mail Server Details check box, Evolution will try to contact your email provider and determine the correct entries for you.

>> **Receiving Options:** Set how frequently you want Evolution to check for new email messages, and set any filters needed to block spam messages.

>> **Sending Email:** Enter your email provider's information for sending outbound messages, such as the server name, protocol used (usually SMTP), and whether they utilize encryption.

After you complete all the steps in the wizard, the Evolution program opens, as shown in Figure 4-2.

**FIGURE 4-2:**
The Evolution application window.

**TIP**

Evolution enables you to check multiple email accounts at once. To add an email account, just click the down-arrow button next to the New button and select Mail Account.

## Working with KMail

Linux distributions that use the KDE Plasma desktop often provide the KMail application for email access. KMail is another all-in-one package similar to

Evolution. It provides an email client, calendar, and task scheduler all in one window.

This section walks you through the steps you need to take to get your KMail software working with your ISP. Then it walks you through using it to send and receive email.

## Setting up KMail

You can usually find the KMail application in the Internet group of the Applications menu section (see Book 2, Chapter 2). The first time you start KMail, you're greeted by the KMail Wizard.

**TIP**

If you previously opened KMail and didn't create an account, you won't be greeted by the wizard. Just choose Settings⇨Add Account to start the wizard to add a new account.

Click the Next button to get the configuration process started. Before you can start sending and receiving email, you need to tell KMail how to interact with your ISP's email server. Unlike the monolithic Evolution setup wizard, KMail's wizard is a little more compact. Fill out the required information and the main KMail window opens, as shown in Figure 4-3.

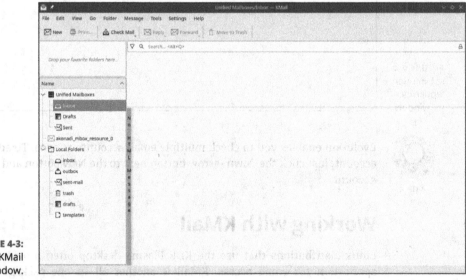

**FIGURE 4-3:**
The main KMail window.

After you create a new account you'll go to the main KMail window. The main KMail window is divided into four sections:

>> **Favorite folders:** Allows you to quickly access popular folders if you have more than one email account configured.

>> **Folder:** Displays all the folders used in KMail for the account. Each email account has a separate group of folders.

>> **Message list:** Displays your messages, sorted by any of the columns (just click a column heading to sort by it).

>> **Preview pane:** Displays the currently selected email message.

From the main KMail window, you can view your inbox by simply selecting the inbox entry in the Folders section. Click the Check Mail icon in the toolbar to manually connect with your ISP server to check your mailbox.

Sending email messages is as easy as clicking the New button in the toolbar.

## The amazing Thunderbird

Evolution is built for the GNOME desktop, and KMail is built for the KDE Plasma desktop, but you can use one email client package, Thunderbird, in any desktop environment. Thunderbird is part of the Firefox family of software packages from Mozilla. It looks and feels very similar to Evolution.

Due to its popularity, you can find Thunderbird in the software installation repository of most Linux distributions (see Book 1, Chapter 5), and it's now even the default email client package installed in Ubuntu.

After you have Thunderbird installed, you need to go through the configuration wizard to get things set up. Just start Thunderbird (it should be located in the Internet group of your menu system) and the wizard appears. You can also select from other wizards to help set up your calendar, address book, chat, and other Internet resources, as shown in Figure 4-4.

After you get your account set up, the Thunderbird main window shows all your email, calendar items, address book, chats, and newsfeeds in one easy-to-access area.

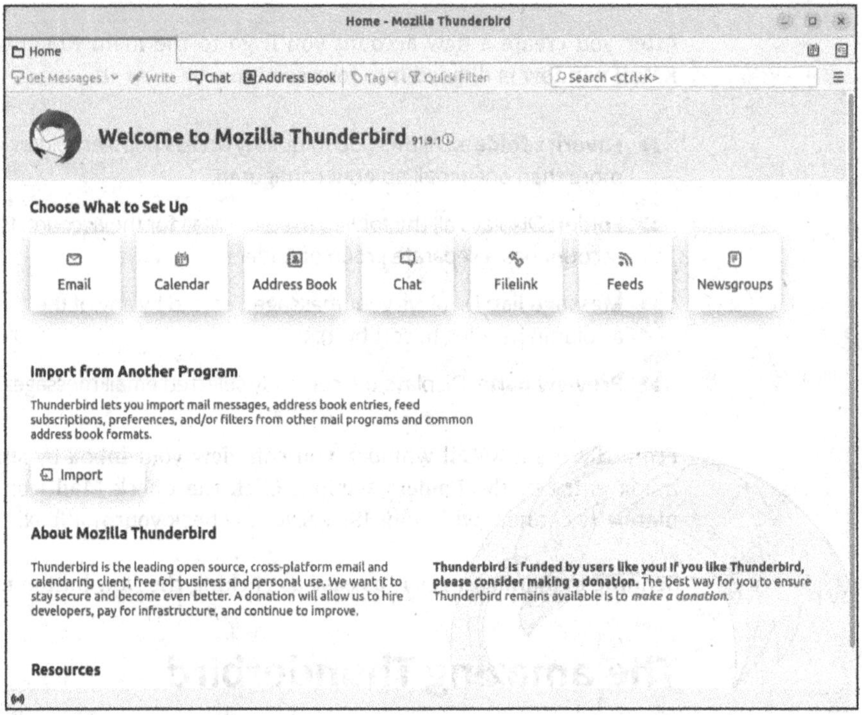

FIGURE 4-4:
The Thunderbird
wizard page.

# Listening to Audio

These days, just about every workstation and laptop comes with a built-in sound card or chip, and most Linux distributions do a great job of automatically detecting those during the installation process. If for some reason your sound setup failed the test, or you try playing sound by using one of the options in this chapter and it doesn't work, use this section to diagnose and fix your problem.

First, start with a sound setup that, although it passed the test, for some reason you can't hear anything. Check and make sure that your speakers or headphones are hooked up correctly. Many modern laptops use a single audio port for both a microphone and headset connection, and it can be tricky making sure that you have the correct connector. Consult your hardware user manual for those requirements.

Next, it's possible that your audio settings got turned down to zero, or muted. Both the GNOME 3 and KDE Plasma desktops have an icon in the system tray that allows you to immediately access the volume control for the sound system. Just look for the speaker icon on your panel. Left-clicking the icon produces a simple slider bar that you can drag up or down with your mouse to increase or decrease the volume level, or click the speaker icon to mute or unmute the output.

For more detailed volume adjustments, you need to go to the system settings for your desktop. In GNOME 3 desktops, just click the system tray area, select Settings, and look for the Sound option in the left-hand menu; see Figure 4-5 for the Sound options.

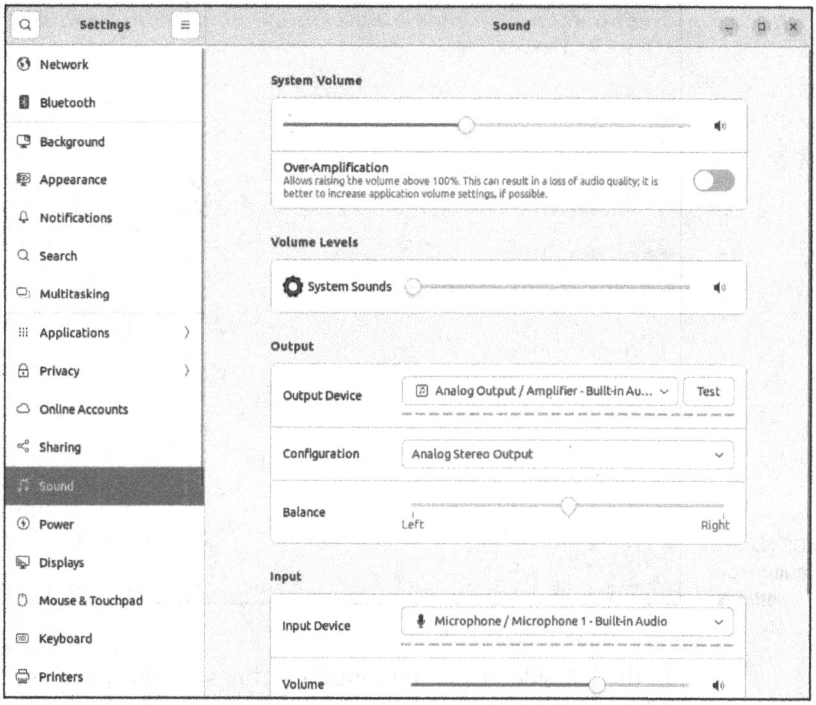

**FIGURE 4-5:**
The GNOME 3
Sound options in
Settings.

When this pane is open, it helps to understand the terms you're about to see:

>> **System Volume:** The main volume control for the sound card. You can mute and unmute the sound by clicking the speaker icon.

>> **Volume Levels:** Controls the volume for individual audio applications. By default, it shows a control for sounds generated by the operating system.

>> **Output:** Controls the output card used if multiple options are available, as well as the audio method used.

>> **Input:** Controls the microphone input used, along with its sensitivity.

>> **Alert Sound:** Selects the sound played when the operating system is trying to get your attention.

If you're working on the KDE Plasma desktop, after you open the Configure Desktop icon from the System Settings app, select the Multimedia icon in the Hardware settings section to access the audio settings. The multimedia settings are shown in Figure 4-6.

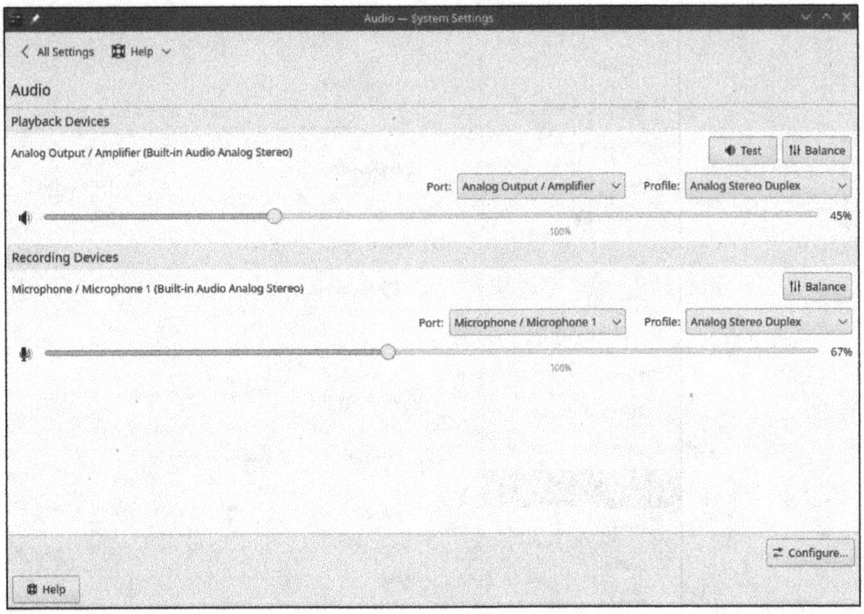

**FIGURE 4-6:**
The KDE Plasma multimedia settings.

On the left side of the multimedia settings window, you see separate icons for different elements:

>> **Audio CDs:** Controls options for how KDE Plasma handles playing audio CDs, such as how much CPU to spend on encoding the data while playing, and what informational data to extract from the encoded CD

>> **Audio Volume:** Selects the audio input and output methods, default volumes, and operating system notification volume

>> **Audio and Video:** Manages the physical hardware devices used for audio and video playback and recording

Now that you know what you're looking at in this dialog box, look for one of these two major clues as to what might be wrong:

>> **Are any of the items you see muted?** You can tell by looking for a red X on top of the volume icon for each section. Is the one you see muted responsible for your problem? For example, if you had headphones hooked up to your

audio jack and the port was muted, you would put on your headphones and hear nothing. To unmute, click the X to get rid of it.

>> **Are any of the volume sliders all the way down?** Even if the audio port isn't muted, you would hear nothing because the sliders are down. Slide them up and see whether you can hear anything.

When you get the basic sound and volume issues fixed, you're ready to start listening to your music!

## Listening to downloaded music

Downloading music from the Internet is fun. However, these days it has become mired in a web of copyright and license complexities. Many people like to pretend that it's both legal and ethical to download any music files they find on the Internet, when in fact it's often theft, depending on where you grabbed the music. I'll leave the ethics to you.

One source of legal songs is artists' websites. Many popular artists offer free samples of their songs, and many new artists offer their entire songs free to download in the hopes of gaining a following. In these situations, you're more than welcome to download and listen!

## THE OTHER MP3 CONTROVERSY

Depending on where you live, you may also have to worry about the legality of being able to process the MP3 file itself without a license. The MP3 audio file format is a standard that was created by several developers over the course of several years. Because of that odd process, multiple companies filed, and were granted, patents on the MP3 technology in various countries at various times. Over time, each of the different companies has successfully enforced those patents in court, suing any software package that used MP3 technology without a license.

Because of this, most Linux distributions didn't allow MP3 libraries or players in standard software repositories. However, those patents have (mostly) expired, and in most countries (including the United States) it's legal to read and process an MP3 file without a license. Because of that, some Linux distributions now install MP3 libraries by default, while others provide the option to add them during the installation process (see Book 1, Chapter 2). Today, most software packages that play audio files check whether the MP3 libraries are installed, and if they aren't, they won't provide the option to read MP3 audio files.

As you probably know by now, the program used to listen to downloaded music depends on your desktop. This section takes a look at Amarok for the KDE Plasma desktop, and sees how Rhythmbox can help you out on a GNOME 3 desktop.

## Amarok

In the KDE Plasma desktop world, the king of audio file playing is the Amarok package. Many Linux distributions install it by default, and if they don't, it's usually available in the distribution software repository (see Book 1, Chapter 5) for easy installation.

When you first launch Amarok, it asks to scan the Music folder in your Home folder hierarchy by default, looking for audio files to add to your playlist library. If you have other locations where you've stored your music files, use the Settings menu to point Amarok to the locations.

Along the left side of the Amarok window is a collection of tabs. What you see and what I see may be different, depending on what audio files Amarok found on your system. Each tab offers a certain segment of functionality and may change the interface to the left of the playlist. No matter how you get music over into the playlist, when it's there you can click the Play button at the upper-left side of the pane to play the entire playlist of songs, or double-click a specific track in the playlist to play it. Adjust the volume with the slider on the upper-right side of the pane.

TIP

If you listen to your digital audio files using a mobile digital audio player (which smartphones now do), you may be able to use Amarok to interface with your digital player. Amarok can detect digital players plugged into the USB port and create a Device tab in that tab section. Select the tab to see whether Amarok can interact with your mobile digital audio player.

## Rhythmbox

The most popular tool for playing audio files in the GNOME 3 desktop is Rhythmbox. It's somewhat multitalented in that it can play those old-fashioned CDs as well as audio files.

By default, the main Rhythmbox library area is the Music folder under your home folder. When you select the Music link in the Library section of the main page, Rhythmbox displays the files it finds in your library. Just as with Amarok, you can create playlists to group specific files.

## STREAMING VERSUS DOWNLOADING

Due to the popularity of home broadband Internet, Internet radio stations and music streaming services have exploded in popularity. With services from Amazon, Google, Pandora, Spotify, and many others, you can (legally) have an entire library of music available at your fingertips. However, you only have the right to listen to the music via the stream, or possibly temporarily download the music file to a specific player, not export the music file for use in other programs. Services that allow you to purchase and download music files save those files as true audio files, which you can then use in any player. Be careful what type of streaming service you sign up for!

**WARNING**

If you try to play an audio file that your Linux distribution doesn't have a codec for (such as MP3 files), it displays a warning message and may provide a link for you to download and install a codec for that music file type.

# Viewing Movie Files

With the popularity of digital video recorders, it's not uncommon to receive a video clip of your niece's ballet recital in an email or from a file-sharing site (just be careful that the file-sharing site is legal). These files are stored in a variety of video formats:

>> **AVI:** Audio Visual Interleave format, a standard video format supported by most video software packages.

>> **DivX:** A proprietary AVI video compression format that must be licensed to work in Linux.

>> **MPG:** Moving Pictures Experts Group standard format. This includes both MPEG and MPG formats.

>> **WMV:** Windows Media Video format, a proprietary Microsoft format.

>> **RM:** The RealNetworks proprietary video format. You need the RealOne video player to play these files.

>> **MOV and QT:** The proprietary Apple QuickTime video formats.

To watch these movies, you need a video player application. A few different video players are available in Linux. Which player your Linux distribution uses by default depends mostly on your desktop, although there are some great video players that have versions for all desktops. Here's a rundown of the most popular ones:

>> **GNOME Videos:** The default video player in the GNOME 3 desktop environment. In Ubuntu, you can start Videos either by double-clicking a saved video file, or start it from the Application Launcher.

>> **KDE Dragon:** The flagship video player application for the KDE Plasma desktop. You can start Dragon from the Applications menu by choosing Applications⇨Multimedia⇨Dragon. You can change what controls display in the playback toolbar by choosing Settings⇨Configure Toolbars.

>> **VLC:** The VLC player is the Swiss army knife of multimedia in Linux. It can play both audio and video files, both saved locally and stored remotely. The VLC project has created versions that work in just about every Linux graphical desktop environment, so it's common to see it used across many Linux distributions. If it's not installed by default in your Linux distribution, you'll probably find it in your distribution's software repository (see Book 1, Chapter 5).

# Creating and Modifying Graphics

The GIMP software package is a graphics program that's considered to be equivalent in many ways to Adobe Photoshop. Many people don't consider GIMP the friendliest program on the planet, but at the very least, it has enough features to keep you busy experimenting for weeks! Because of its size and specialty use, most Linux distributions don't install GIMP by default. You need to use one of the methods outlined in Book 1, Chapter 5 to install GIMP in your Linux distribution.

After you start GIMP, a collection of one or more items pops up for the GIMP application (see Figure 4-7). There's a main application window, plus two additional tool windows. You can close the right-hand window that contains the Paintbrush selector and Layers sections. The Toolbox window on the left side and the main window are somewhat incorporated together.

GIMP is an incredibly complex program, with entire books written for the people who really want to use it heavily. In a nutshell, just about everything you can do in Photoshop you can do in GIMP.

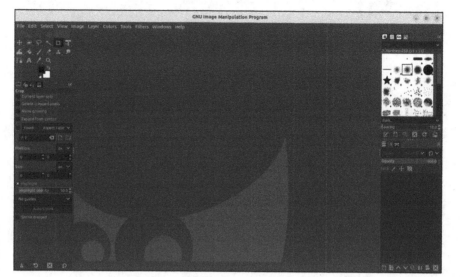

**FIGURE 4-7:**
The GIMP main
window in
Ubuntu.

# Chapter **5**

# The Linux File System

One of the most frustrating things about mastering a new operating system can be figuring out where it keeps files. Instead of keeping all important system files in a single directory, such as the C:\Windows directory in Microsoft Windows, Linux follows the lead of its Unix cousins and spreads things out a bit more. Although the Linux and Windows setups involve different methods, they're both logical (although it may not feel that way until you understand where to look).

After taking you on a tour of where to find things, this chapter shows you how to work in your file system on the command line. Reading this section isn't mandatory if typing commands gives you heart palpitations, but it can be handy if you need to fix something later, and some people just like to know how to do these things.

## Pieces of the Puzzle

It helps to understand the lingo before getting started. A lot of this will be familiar to you from other operating systems such as Microsoft Windows, but there are some differences that you'll need to get used to as well. To start, the term *file system* is actually used in more than one way. The general use (and what I typically refer to throughout the book when I use the term) means "the files and directories (or folders) you have access to right now."

The first major difference to be aware of is that Linux uses a forward slash (/) between directories, not the backslash (\) that Windows does. So, the file hosts in the directory etc is /etc/hosts. Files and directories can have names up to 256 characters long, and these names can contain underscores (_), dashes (-), and dots (.) anywhere within, even more than one. So, my.big.file or my.big_file or my-big-file are all valid filenames.

In Linux, uppercase and lowercase in filenames also matter quite a bit: They have to match exactly. The files hosts and Hosts are not the same as far as Linux is concerned. Finally, the same file system can span multiple partitions, hard drives, and removable media, such as DVD drives and USB sticks. You just keep going down through subdirectories, not having to care if something is on disk A, B, or whatever. I expand on this a little more in the "Where removable media lives" section, later in this chapter.

# Touring the Linux File System

In this section, I take a look at the contents of the typical Linux file system. Being at least a bit familiar with it will help you track things down later and know where it's safe to mess with things and where you need to be very careful.

## The root of the tree

Everything in the Linux file system is relative to the *root directory*, which is referred to as /. Don't confuse this with the system Administrator, who is the root user, or the /root directory assigned to the root user. (I'm not sure why Unix and Linux geeks like the word *root* so much!) The root directory is the file system base — a doorway into all your files. The root directory contains a mostly predictable set of subdirectories. Each distribution varies slightly, but certain standards exist to which they all conform. The standards keep the Linux world somewhat sane.

**TIP**

In the early days of Linux, different distributions used different places to store files. Thankfully, a standard has evolved, called the *Filesystem Hierarchy Standard* (FHS), which has made life much easier. If you're interested in the FHS, go to https://refspecs.linuxfoundation.org/fhs.shtml and look at the latest version of the rules.

Table 5-1 lists what you might find in the base directories, meaning the items you find in /. (This list can vary depending on what you installed.) A Yes in the Important column indicates that you shouldn't mess with this directory unless you have a *really good reason* because it contains files that are *very important* to the functioning of your system. Really, most of the base directories should be left alone. It's the sections inside them that are safe to change.

**TABLE 5-1** **Standard / Contents in Linux**

| Directory | Important | Contains |
|---|---|---|
| /bin | Yes | Essential commands that everyone needs to use at any time. |
| /boot | Yes | The information that boots the machine, including your kernel. |
| /dev | Yes | The device drivers for all the hardware that your system needs to interface with. |
| /etc | Yes | The configuration files for your system. |
| /home | No | The home directories for each of your users. |
| /lib | Yes | The *libraries* or code that many programs (and the kernel) use. |
| /media | No | A spot where you add temporary media, such as DVDs and USB sticks; not all distributions have this directory. |
| /mnt | No | A spot where you add extra file system components such as networked drives and items you aren't permanently adding to your file system but that aren't as temporary as DVDs and USB sticks. |
| /opt | No | The location that some distributions use for installing new software packages, such as word processors and office suites. |
| /proc | Yes | Current settings for your kernel (operating system). |
| /root | No | The superuser's (root user's) home directory. |
| /sbin | Yes | The commands the system Administrator needs access to. |
| /srv | Yes | Data for your system's *services* (the programs that run in the background). |
| /sys | Yes | Kernel information about your hardware. |
| /tmp | No | The place where everyone and everything stores temporary files. |
| /usr | No | A complex hierarchy of additional programs and files. |
| /var | No | The data that changes frequently, such as log files and your mail. |

Some of these directories have some equally important subdirectories. For example, while the /etc directory contains primarily configuration files, many applications create a subdirectory under the /etc directory to help keep their own configuration files separate.

## Where removable media lives

One of the more confusing things for people moving from Windows to Linux is how Linux handles removable media, such as DVDs and USB sticks. Windows assigns different drive letters to removable media devices, but in most Linux distributions, when you insert a removable media drive, Linux automatically places it within the root file system structure for you (called *mounting*).

Typically, Linux creates a subdirectory in the /media directory using your user ID, followed by another subdirectory under that, which is a unique identifier for the media, such as the DVD label or USB unique identifier number. For example, after I plugged a USB stick into my PC, Ubuntu created the new directory named /media/rich/88CE-4A75 where I can access all the files on the USB stick.

In the "Managing Your File System without a Net (or Mouse)" section, later in this chapter, I show you how to find these items using the command line. In the "Clicking Your Way through the File System" section, you find out how to find them using the handier point-and-click method in the graphical desktop.

# Managing Your File System without a Net (or Mouse)

In this section, I take a look at how to use the command-line tools to find your way around the file system. It isn't vital for you to know this, but it could certainly prove useful someday.

## Viewing information about files on the command line

If you decide to do any serious work in Linux, you'll want to become familiar with the *command line interface* (CLI). The CLI allows you to submit commands directly to Linux without a graphical go-between, and see the results immediately.

If you're in the older generation, the CLI may remind you of the early days of MS-DOS. You just get a prompt to enter a text command, and you see the text response on your monitor — boring, but efficient!

In the graphical user interface (GUI) world, you can get to the CLI by using the Terminal program, as shown in Figure 5-1.

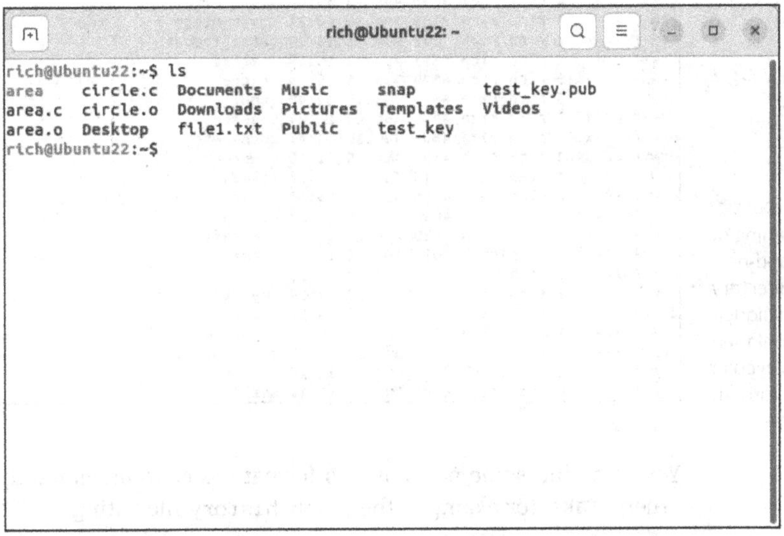

```
rich@Ubuntu22:~$ ls
area     circle.c   Documents   Music      snap        test_key.pub
area.c   circle.o   Downloads   Pictures   Templates   Videos
area.o   Desktop    file1.txt   Public     test_key
rich@Ubuntu22:~$
```

**FIGURE 5-1:**
The Terminal
program in
Ubuntu.

The Terminal program provides a graphical window that displays the CLI, allowing you to enter commands and view the results.

To view files and directories, you want to use the ls command. Just by itself, it shows you the names of the nonhidden files and directories that you ask for; Figure 5-1 shows an example.

The ls command shows everything in the requested location except for *hidden files*, which start with a dot. To see the hidden files, too, type **ls -a.**

So far, all you've done is look at files and find out a little about them from the colors you see. The next section shows you how to discover more.

## Understanding file listing information

To see more information than just names and vague types, you'll want a long format file listing. You get this listing with the command ls –l (if you want long format and hidden files, you would type **ls -la**). Figure 5-2 shows a sample of what you might see with the -la options.

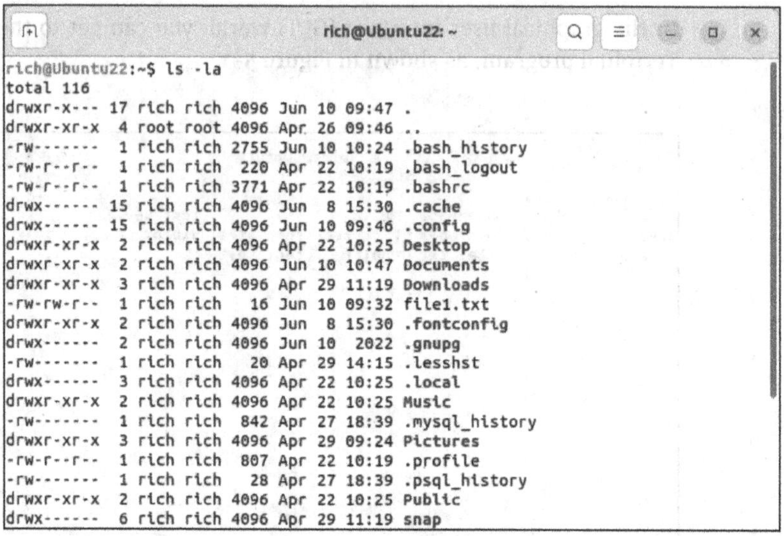

**FIGURE 5-2:**
The beginning of the brand-new home directory with both hidden and nonhidden files displayed in long format.

```
rich@Ubuntu22:~$ ls -la
total 116
drwxr-x--- 17 rich rich 4096 Jun 10 09:47 .
drwxr-xr-x  4 root root 4096 Apr 26 09:46 ..
-rw-------  1 rich rich 2755 Jun 10 10:24 .bash_history
-rw-r--r--  1 rich rich  220 Apr 22 10:19 .bash_logout
-rw-r--r--  1 rich rich 3771 Apr 22 10:19 .bashrc
drwx------ 15 rich rich 4096 Jun  8 15:30 .cache
drwx------ 15 rich rich 4096 Jun 10 09:46 .config
drwxr-xr-x  2 rich rich 4096 Apr 22 10:25 Desktop
drwxr-xr-x  2 rich rich 4096 Jun 10 10:47 Documents
drwxr-xr-x  3 rich rich 4096 Apr 29 11:19 Downloads
-rw-rw-r--  1 rich rich   16 Jun 10 09:32 file1.txt
drwxr-xr-x  2 rich rich 4096 Jun  8 15:30 .fontconfig
drwx------  2 rich rich 4096 Jun 10  2022 .gnupg
-rw-------  1 rich rich   20 Apr 29 14:15 .lesshst
drwx------  3 rich rich 4096 Apr 22 10:25 .local
drwxr-xr-x  2 rich rich 4096 Apr 22 10:25 Music
-rw-------  1 rich rich  842 Apr 27 18:39 .mysql_history
drwxr-xr-x  3 rich rich 4096 Apr 29 09:24 Pictures
-rw-r--r--  1 rich rich  807 Apr 22 10:19 .profile
-rw-------  1 rich rich   28 Apr 27 18:39 .psql_history
drwxr-xr-x  2 rich rich 4096 Apr 22 10:25 Public
drwx------  6 rich rich 4096 Apr 29 11:19 snap
```

You may find some parts of this format easier to understand, at a glance, than others. Take, for example, the .bash_history file listing:

```
-rw-------  1 rich rich 2755 Jun 10 10:24 .bash_history
```

The first item in each listing (the part with the letters and dashes) is the *permission set* assigned to the item. Briefly, permissions define who can read the file, change it, or run it if it's a program. You can read more about permissions in "A Permissions Primer," later in this chapter. The second item in the first line is the number of hard links to the item. A hard link is a pointer to the same file, but it uses a separate filename.

The third item (rich for the .bash_history file) is the file's *owner*, and the fourth (rich) is the *group* — depending on which version of Linux you're using, both these items may or may not be identical. You can find out more about both of these in "A Permissions Primer," later in this chapter. The fifth item is the file's size in bytes. All directories show up as 4,096 bytes; everything else has its own size. You can tell an empty file from the size of 0 bytes.

The sixth, seventh, and eighth entries are all related to the last time the file was changed: for the .bash_history file, the month (Jun), the date (10), and the time in 24-hour format (10:24). Finally, the ninth item is the filename (for example, .bash history).

## Comprehending file types

The first letter in any long format file listing tells you which type of file you're dealing with. In Table 5-2, I list the types you're likely to run into. Some of these may seem familiar after examining the file listing color scheme.

**TABLE 5-2**

### Linux File Types

| Label | Type | Description |
|---|---|---|
| – | Regular file | The item is an everyday file, such as a text file or program. |
| B | Block device | The item is a *driver* (control program) for a *storage medium*, such as a hard drive or DVD drive. |
| C | Character device | The item is a *driver* (control program) for a piece of hardware that transmits data, such as a modem. |
| D | Directory | The item is a container for files, also referred to as a *folder* in some operating systems' lingo. |
| L | Link | The item is a *link* to another file. The item doesn't exist as a separate file but is a pointer to another file. |

In addition to those mentioned in Table 5-2, you find lots more different file types out there in the Linux world. By types, I'm not referring to extensions, such as .exe or .doc. Linux sees everything within its file system — even directories and hardware like your monitor — as "files." As a result, assigning a type to a file is merely a Linux machine's way of keeping track of what's what.

The main thing Windows users in particular want to know when they move to Linux is how to recognize programs. Instead of looking for files with particular extensions (like .exe), programs have (or need to have) an *executable permission* set so the system knows they're allowed to run.

**TIP**

On the command line, try the file command, such as file Desktop, to find out more about what a particular file contains.

# Navigating the file system in Linux

In case you're enjoying playing around on the command line, here's a short primer on some other commands you'll find useful when it comes to wandering through your file system.

To move, you can use cd to change from one directory to another. For example, to go from /home/rich to /home/rich/Documents, you could type one of the following:

```
cd /home/rich/Documents
cd Documents
```

Either of those commands gets you there. Then to go back to /home/rich from /home/rich/Documents, you could type one of the following:

```
cd /home/rich
cd ..
```

Again, either of these commands works for the purpose. In both cases, the first commands are referred to as *absolute* navigation ("I want to go to exactly this address") and the other is called *relative* ("I want to go three houses down from here"). The .. backs you up one directory in the tree. If you get lost and can't figure out which branch of the tree you're on, type **pwd** (which may seem like an odd command but is short for "print working directory") to find out what directory you're in right now.

Now some quick commands to work with files. To work with their contents, see Book 2, Chapter 6 about using text editors in Linux. However, just to copy files at the command line, use the cp command, such as the following, to copy file1 to a new file named file2:

```
cp file1 file2
```

If you want to rename a file, use the mv (move) command in the same format, or use this same command to move a file from one location to another. To create a directory, use the mkdir command, such as the following, to create a Documents directory in the current directory:

```
mkdir Documents
```

To delete files, use the rm (remove) command, such as this format, to delete file1 from the directory /home/rich:

```
rm /home/rich/file1
```

Finally, to remove a directory, with the special `rmdir` command, first you have to delete all the files inside it, and then you can delete it.

```
cd /home/rich/notes
rm *
cd ..
rmdir notes
```

To remove all the files in the directory /home/rich/notes and delete it at the same time (make sure that you really want to do this!), you can just use the `-rf` options of the `rm` command:

```
rm -rf /home/rich/notes
```

This should be enough to get you started. Happy exploring!

# A Permissions Primer

If you find yourself scratching your head when looking at parts of that long format file listing in Figure 5-2, don't worry. It's just code that describes the permissions assigned to the file. Linux was created as a multiuser operating system — meaning that it assumes more than one person is using the system, and it also assumes you'll want some type of security on who can (or can't) mess with your files.

The "Comprehending file types" section, earlier in this chapter, gives you a feeling for the first letter on each line, but nine more characters are attached to that item before you get to the next column. This group of nine is the set of *permissions* (also called a *permission set*) for the file or directory. Linux uses these permissions as a way of providing file and directory security by giving you the means to specify exactly who can look at your files, who can change them, and even who can run your programs. You need this capability when you have a bunch of different users on the same machine, networked to the world.

## Checking out the triplets

Each permission set consists of three triplets. Each of the triplets has the same basic structure but controls a different aspect of who can use what. Consider the long format listing for /home/rich in the following code:

```
total 464
drwx------ 23 rich  rich  4096 Dec 15 05:01 .
```

```
drwxr-xr-x  3 root  root  4096 Dec  3 06:27 ..
-rw-------  1 rich  rich     5 Dec  3 07:07 .bash_history
-rw-r--r--  1 rich  rich    24 Jun 12 00:11 .bash_logout
-rw-r--r--  1 rich  rich   176 Jun 12 00:11 .bash_profile
-rw-r--r--  1 rich  rich   124 Jun 12 00:11 .bashrc
```

As you've already seen, the first character in the permission set refers to the type of file. For a directory, the character is shown as a d, as you see here for the first two items in the preceding list; files are designated with a dash (–) instead. Each file or directory's permission set is a group of nine characters — that is, the nine characters that follow the first character (for a total of ten). But this group of nine is really three groups of three, as shown in Figure 5-3.

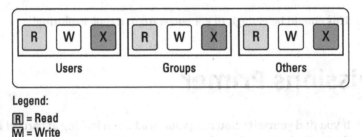

**FIGURE 5-3:**
Breakdown of the
nine permission
characters.

Legend:
R = Read
W = Write
X = Execute

The three triplets are read as follows:

>> **The first triplet consists of the second, third, and fourth characters in the long format file listing.** This triplet sets the permissions for the user, or *owner*, of the file. (Owners are discussed in the "Beware of owners" section, later in this chapter.)

>> **The second triplet consists of the fifth, sixth, and seventh characters in the long format file listing.** This triplet sets the permissions for the *group* that is assigned to the file. (Groups are discussed in the "Hanging out in groups" section, later in this chapter.)

>> **The third triplet consists of the eighth, ninth, and tenth characters in the long format file listing.** This triplet sets the permissions for *other*, or everyone who isn't the file's owner or a member of the owning group.

Although each triplet is often different from the others, the internal structure of each one is made up in the same way. Focus specifically on how to read one triplet before looking at the set of them together. Each triplet includes three characters:

>> **The first character is either an** r **or a dash.** The r stands for *read* permission. If r is set, the triplet allows the entity it stands for (user, group, or other) to view the directory or file's contents.

>> **The second character is either a** w **or a dash.** The w stands for *write* permission. If w is set, the triplet allows the entity it stands for to add, delete, or edit items in this directory or file.

>> **The third character is either an** x **or a dash.** The x stands for *execute* permission. If x is set, the triplet allows the entity it stands for to access the files contained in this directory or to run the particular program in this file.

TIP

In all cases, if the dash sits in place of r, w, or x, the triplet doesn't allow the entity the read, write, or execute permission.

The following sections describe owners and groups in more detail.

## Beware of owners

You may have noticed by now that I talk a great deal about owners (users) and groups in Linux. Every file and directory has both of these components: a user from the /etc/passwd file that's assigned as its owner and a group from /etc/group that's assigned as the group.

Although an everyday user probably doesn't need to change file ownerships often, the root user does so regularly. If you add the file comments, for example, to /home/rich while you're logged on as the *superuser* (another term for the Administrator, who is the person who owns the root account), root owns that file. The user rich can't do anything with it unless you've set the last triplet's permissions to allow the *other* folks (those who aren't the file's owner or in the specified group) to read and write to the file. But this method is a pretty sloppy way of doing things because the whole idea of permissions is to reduce access, not to give everyone access. Instead, remember to change the file's owner to the user rich. You do this with the chown (*change owner*) command. For example, by typing chown rich comments, root changes the ownership over to rich. Then rich can work with this file and even change its permissions to something he prefers.

## Hanging out in groups

Groups are more interesting to work with than owners. You use groups to allow the root user to assign to multiple users the ability to share certain file system areas. For example, in many versions of Linux, all users are added to a group named *users* (openSUSE does this, for example). Then rather than a long format file list-ing, such as the one shown earlier in this chapter, you may see the following:

```
total 20
drwx------ 2 rich   users 4096 Jun 29 07:48 .
drwxr-xr-x 5 root   root  4096 Jun 27 11:57 ..
-rw-r--r-- 1 rich   users   24 Jun 27 06:50 .bash_logout
-rw-r--r-- 1 rich   users  230 Jun 27 06:50 .bash_profile
-rw-r--r-- 1 rich   users  124 Jun 27 06:50 .bashrc
-rw-rw-r-- 1 rich   users    0 Jun 29 07:48 lsfile
```

Everyone in the users group has read access to the files. In other distributions (such as Ubuntu), a unique group is created for every user, so one user can't access the files created by another user by default. This is why the earlier listing showed the owner and group items as identical (rich rich).

Now that you've seen the basics of how Linux handles files, continue to the next section to see how to use the graphical tools available in Linux desktops to maneu-ver your way around the Linux system with the greatest of ease.

# Clicking Your Way through the File System

The key to managing files and directories from your graphical desktop is the *file manager* program. The file manager program provides a nice graphical interface to the mess of files and directories present on your system. Instead of having to dig through command-line commands, you just point and click your way to a man-aged file system.

However, as with just about everything else in the Linux world, you can choose from several different file manager programs. The default one available in your Linux distribution mostly depends on which desktop you're using. The main players are

>> **Files:** The default file manager used in the GNOME 3 desktop

>> **Dolphin:** The default file manager used in the KDE Plasma desktop

>> **Thunar:** The default file manager used in the Xfce desktop

Of course, just because a file manager is the default for a desktop doesn't mean that you're stuck having to use it! Any of the file manager programs work just fine in the other desktop environments. In fact, if you install the KDE Plasma desktop in Ubuntu the Files file manager still stays as the default.

The following sections walk you through the features of each of these popular file manager programs, allowing you to get comfortable maneuvering around.

## Using files

In the GNOME 3 desktop environment, the default file manager is Files. Moving through the file system in Files involves a couple of skills that are different from using the command line. You may know exactly where in the file system you want to go but not what to click to get there. In the first place, you need to know where you want to begin. This decision isn't as difficult as it sounds.

**REMEMBER**

In the earlier versions of GNOME, the file manager program was called Nautilus. In GNOME 3, it's the same program, but the name changed to Files. To make things even more confusing, internally in GNOME it's still referred to as the Nautilus project. You often see the two names used interchangeably in documentation and help files. I do my best to remember to call it Files in this book!

There are usually a few different ways to start Files from the GNOME 3 desktop:

» **Click the Files icon in the dash.** Most Linux distributions include the Files icon (the picture of the folder) as a favorite in the dash.

» **Double-click your desktop's Home icon.** Ubuntu (and many other GNOME-based distributions) includes the Home icon on the default desktop. This opens Files to the user's Home directory.

» **Open the Application Launcher, and then select the Files icon.** Files is installed by default in all Linux distributions that use the GNOME 3 desktop. Just open the Application Launcher and click the Files icon that appears.

Regardless of how you start the program, Files opens using your Home folder as the default location, as shown in Figure 5-4.

The Files window consists of four main sections:

» **Toolbar:** The toolbar is located at the top of the window. It contains back and forward buttons for directory navigation, a path bar to identify where in the directory structure you currently are, a search button for finding files, a button that allows you to change the layout and behavior of the content area, and the application menu button.

» **Sidebar:** The sidebar allows you to navigate to common directories in your Home folder, as well as quickly navigate to installed removable media drives and network drives. If you prefer, you can hide the sidebar by pressing the F9 key.

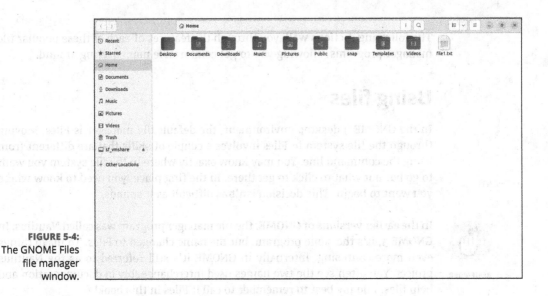

FIGURE 5-4:
The GNOME Files
file manager
window.

>> **Context area:** The main area of Files, it displays the files and directories contained in the selected directory. You can customize how much information Files displays in the context area.

>> **Status bar:** When you select a file or directory, a floating status bar appears at the bottom of the window, showing some information about the file or directory.

The context area is where the action occurs. You can take a few actions on the items you see in the context area:

>> **To open the file using the default application, double-click a file icon.** For application files, the application opens. For text files, the standard GNOME text editor opens for you to view the file. If a default application isn't assigned for the file, you're prompted for how to open the file. Proceed to the section "Opening files and running programs," later in this chapter, for more information on that.

>> **To open a directory, you have a few options:**

- Double-click the directory icon to open it in the existing context area.

- Middle-click the directory icon to open it in a new tab in the Files window. If you don't have a three-button mouse, the middle click feature is often emulated by clicking both the left and right mouse buttons at the same time.

- Right-click the directory icon to view a context menu. You can select to then open the directory in a new tab or a new window, along with performing other operations, such as changing the directory permissions.

» To close the Files window, choose Files⇨Quit from the panel applications menu, or click the X in the window's upper-right corner.

You can click any of the directory buttons in the path bar to jump directly to that directory. This allows you to walk your way down or up a directory structure.

**TIP**

Often it's easier to drag and drop files between tabs in the same window instead of trying to switch between separate windows.

## Creating new directories

You can use the graphical interface in Files to create a new directory. Just right-click an empty spot inside the directory window and select New Folder.

That's a lot easier than messing around with the cryptic mkdir command in the command line!

## Opening files and running programs

To open a file or run a program in Files, just double-click it. That's it! Well, not entirely. You can also right-click a file to open a context menu that provides a few more options, such as allowing you to open the file with an alternative program.

Most common file types already have a default application defined in Files that's used to open the file, such as text files, multimedia files, and LibreOffice documents, spreadsheets, and presentation files.

## Copying and moving files

You can copy and move items using two different methods in Files:

» **Use the method you're probably familiar with from Windows or macOS — click and grab a file or directory and then drag it where you want it to go.** You can click and drag between directory windows anywhere on the desktop, even into specific directory icons within Files.

» **Right-click the file or directory icon and select the Cut or Copy action from the context menu.**

**TIP**

If you only have one Files window open, it can be difficult trying to navigate around to other directories to cut or copy a file. If you select the Copy To or Move To options, a new window appears, allowing you to navigate to the directory where you want the file to go.

## Deleting files and directories

To use Files to delete either a file or a directory from the file system, you can either select the file or directory to delete and press the Delete key, or right-click the icon and choose Move to Trash.

**REMEMBER**

These deleted items are, in fact, sitting in the trash can, so they aren't really deleted from your hard drive. You can move these files out of the trash and back into your file system if you want to.

## Taking out the trash

You can permanently delete the contents of your Trash folder by right-clicking the Trash icon and choosing Empty Trash. Click Empty in the confirmation dialog box to permanently delete the contents of the Trash folder.

## Viewing and changing permissions

In the "A Permissions Primer" section, you see that every file and directory in Linux has a set of *permissions* that govern who is allowed to view it, run it, delete it, and so on. These permissions are used to make sure that people can't mess with the system's or each other's files, so they're pretty important. In this section, I focus on how to work with files in the GUI.

To view and change a file or directory's permissions in Files, follow these steps:

1.  **Open a Files window to the folder that contains the file or directory.**

2.  **Right-click the file or directory and choose Properties.**

    The Properties dialog box appears with the Basic tab open.

3.  **Select the Permissions tab.**

    The Permissions portion of the Properties dialog box appears, as shown in Figure 5-5.

4.  **Set the new permissions and ownerships.**

    Notice that the GUI has the user, group, and "others" broken down into separate drop-down list boxes. Unless you're familiar with SELinux, leave the Context option alone.

5. **Click Close to close the dialog box.**

   The file's permissions are now changed.

**FIGURE 5-5:**
The Files file
manager's
Properties dialog
box with the
Permissions tab
displayed.

That pretty much covers the basics of everything you'd want to do with the file system in Files. In the next section, you take a look at the KDE Dolphin package.

# Swimming with Dolphin

If you're using a new Linux distribution with the KDE Plasma desktop, most likely you're using the Dolphin file manager program. Dolphin works very much like Files, allowing you to easily browse through directories in the file system from a single window.

To open a Dolphin window, the Plasma menu system (see Book 2, Chapter 2) provides links under the Computer tab to specific locations on your workstation. You can view your Home folder, remote shared folders found on the network, the entire file system starting at the root folder, or the special Trash directory. Figure 5-6 shows the main Dolphin window layout.

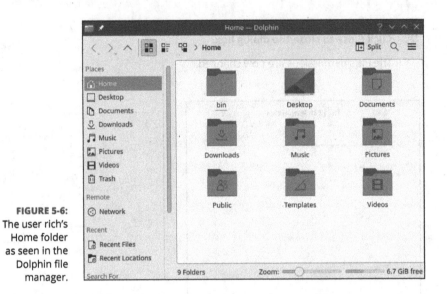

Taking a look at the default Dolphin window, you see that it has many of the same features as Files:

>> **The toolbar:** Provides buttons for quick access to commonly used menu features

>> **The location bar:** The area under the toolbar that displays the current directory name, as well as any directories higher in the directory structure

>> **The Places panel:** Provides easy access to drives and bookmarked directories

>> **The status bar:** Displays the number of files and folders in the currently viewed folder, along with the current amount of free space available on the disk

When you single-click a directory icon in the view window, the folder opens in the same window and the path to the folder appears above the location bar. That's called a *breadcrumb*. Just like leaving breadcrumbs in the forest to find your way back, you can click anywhere along the breadcrumb pathname to find your way back to the folder you started in.

Creating, copying, and renaming files and folders in Dolphin works exactly as in Files. Right-clicking a file or directory icon produces a shortcut menu, which allows you to cut or copy the file, or move it to the Trash folder for removal.

**WARNING**

Be careful when working in Dolphin; by default, it uses the KDE Plasma single-click method of activating an icon. That means if you just single-click an icon, Dolphin tries to display the file using the default application for the file. That's somewhat annoying for those coming from a Microsoft Windows environment. You can change that behavior using the System Settings feature (see Book 2, Chapter 2). In the Workspace section of the System Settings window, select the Workspace Behavior icon. Within the General Behavior section, you'll see the place to change the click behavior from single-click to double-click.

## Don't forget Xfce!

With the low-power requirements of the Xfce desktop, you wouldn't expect anything too fancy in the way of a default file manager. However, you're in for a surprise! The Thunar file manager program is a gem of a tool that works well in underpowered PCs.

To start Thunar, click the File Manager icon (the file cabinet) in the panel favorites. The main Thunar window, shown in Figure 5-7, appears.

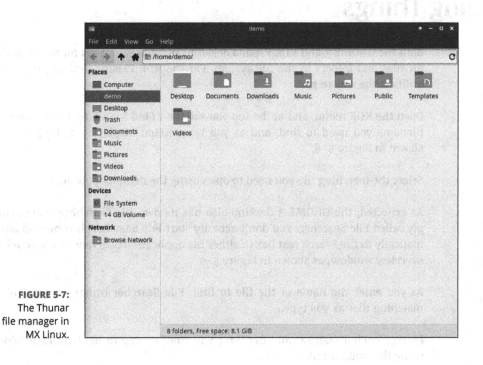

**FIGURE 5-7:**
The Thunar file manager in MX Linux.

Look a little familiar? Despite its small size, Thunar has many of the same features as Files and Dolphin. The side pane displays a list of common locations, divided into three sections:

>> **Devices:** Lists the devices, such as hard drives and removable media

>> **Places:** Lists common directories within your Home folder

>> **Network:** Allows you to easily browse the network for shared drives

The main area in the window displays the file and directory icons contained in the selected directory. To change the layout, click the View option in the menu bar; then select the icon, detailed list, or compact list view. To customize the fields in detailed list view, select the Configure Columns option.

With the power of Thunar, you'd never know you were operating in a low-power computing environment!

# Finding Things

Both the GNOME 3 and KDE Plasma desktops provide easy ways for you to search for files and folders in the file system. For the KDE Plasma desktop, the KFind utility is the way to go.

Open the KDE menu, and at the top you see the KFind Search text box. Enter the filename you need to find, and as you type, KFind displays matching files, as shown in Figure 5-8.

Select the matching file you need to open using the default application.

As expected, the GNOME 3 desktop also has its own file searching utility, simply called File Searcher. You don't actually start File Searcher; it comes up automatically as the Search text box in either the application overview or the activities overview window, as shown in Figure 5-9.

As you enter the name of the file to find, File Searcher brings up a list of all matching files as you type.

Using the Find feature can often save you from having to hunt through folders using the standard file manager.

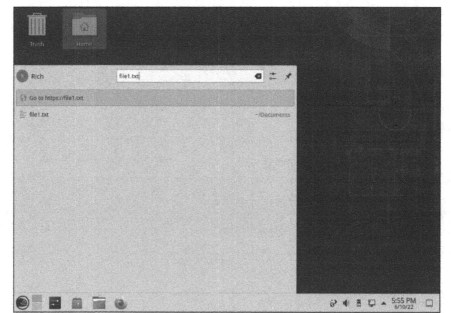

**FIGURE 5-8:**
The KFind
search window.

**FIGURE 5-9:**
The GNOME 3
File Searcher
dialog box.

IN THIS CHAPTER

» **Viewing the contents of text files**

» **Manipulating text files in nano**

» **Working with text files in gedit**

» **Editing text with KWrite and Kate**

» **Editing text using command-line tools**

# Chapter **6**

# Text Editors

From text editors to word processors, Linux offers a wide variety of options for working with words. These days, with software packages trying to incorporate multiple features, it can be difficult to tell the difference between a text editor and a word processor. By *text editor,* I mean a tool that's primarily used by programmers to create plain text files with no formatting. Word processors can do that, too, but their primary focus is on creating fancy documents that format text using different fonts and styles. In this chapter, I take a look at different ways to work with plain text files, using some simple text editors in both the graphical user interface (GUI) and non-GUI environments. In Book 2, Chapter 4, I take a look at office suites for those who would rather do word processing.

## Viewing the Contents of a Text File

Almost all configuration files in Linux are text files. In addition, many pseudo-programs (called *shell scripts*), all HTML documentation, and many other items in your system are text files. Fortunately, if you just want to see what's in a text file and you don't want to do anything to its contents, you don't have to use an editor or word processor. You can use three command-line commands to view text files: cat, less, and more. I bet that you'll grow to love them.

Yes, that first command is cat, and it's taken from the word *concatenate*, which means to bring together end to end — you can use the cat command on multiple text files to have their text joined, one file's contents directly after another's. Typically, you use this command in the Linux world in the format cat *filename*, where the contents of the file *filename* are displayed on the screen. For example, if you create the short text file greetings and then type **cat greetings**, you see the following:

```
$ cat greetings
These are the contents of the greetings file.
Hello!
$ _
```

Of course, if the file contains more than a screen's worth of information, cat spews it all out at one time, and all but the last screen of text scrolls off the screen. It's a good thing that you have some other choices.

The one you're likely to choose is less, which displays the contents of a file one full screen at a time. Then you press the spacebar to continue to the next screen or the B key to scroll backward one screen. You can also use the arrow keys to move up and down one line at a time if you want.

An alternative to less is more. The main difference between the two is that with more, you can only move forward through the file and only see a screen's worth of information at a time. You can't back up.

To use either less or more, the format is similar to the format used with the cat command: less *filename* or more *filename*. When you finish reading the document, press Q to exit (remember, you can't change any of the text in the document with less or more).

# Editing Text Files with nano

If you aren't using (or can't use) the GUI, numerous text editors are available. The most powerful of these are vi and ed, which you'll hear more about later in this chapter. However, both these programs have a learning curve. For beginners who just want to edit the file and move on, I recommend nano, which offers a friendly, menu-driven interface.

To open a file in nano, type **nano** *filename*, such as **nano file1**. The file opens in the nano editor, as shown in Figure 6-1.

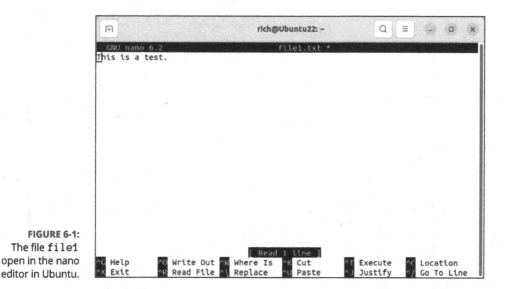

FIGURE 6-1:
The file file1
open in the nano
editor in Ubuntu.

You can then edit or type in that file as much as you need to. At the bottom of the editor window, nano shows the different Ctrl key combinations required to save files and exit the editor.

# Going with gedit

You're not stuck with just command-prompt-based text editors in Linux. Lots of graphical options are available. In this section, I cover gedit (see Figure 6-2) because it's the default GUI text editor for the GNOME 3 desktop.

**TIP**

If you're looking for the gedit application in the Application Launcher, GNOME just calls it Text Editor.

gedit is strictly a text editor, in that you use it to generate raw text, whereas a word processor creates marked-up text that can be opened only by programs that can read that word processor's file formatting. If you want to add bold, italics, underlines, or any other special features to your document, look in Book 2, Chapter 4 for the LibreOffice Writer application.

To enter text in gedit, just click in the big white space and start typing. You have access to the standard collection of editing tools, such as Cut, Paste, and Copy. To use these, select the text you want to work with and then right-click and choose the appropriate command from the context menu.

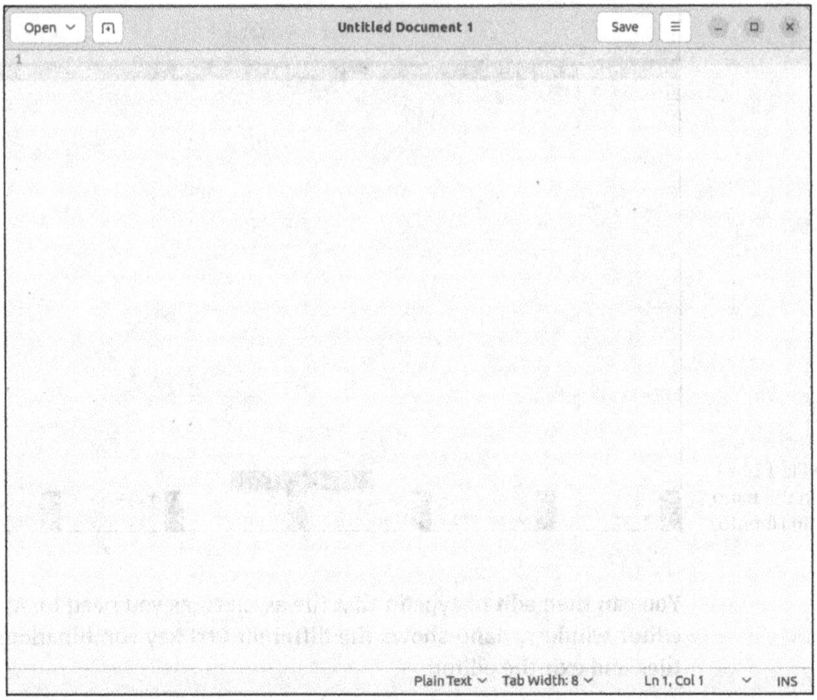

Open ✕   ⌷            Untitled Document 1            Save   ≡   —  ☐  ✕

1

Plain Text ∨   Tab Width: 8 ∨        Ln 1, Col 1    ∨   INS

**FIGURE 6-2:**
The gedit window
with a blank file,
in Ubuntu.

The gedit editor utilizes plug-ins to perform specialized functions to help out as you type. Two of my favorites are the Date/Time plug-in, which automatically enters the current date and time for you, and the Snippet plug-in, which can automatically complete common words for you. Just start typing a word and press the Tab key to see the possible ways to complete it. Check out the plug-in section for details on how to install new plug-ins.

The application menu contains a Preferences item. This allows you to set the look and feel of gedit.

TIP

# Editing Text in the KDE Plasma Desktop

Not to be left out, the KDE Plasma environment also provides a way to graphically edit text files. In fact, it offers two different packages, KWrite and Kate. If you do your work in the KDE Plasma world, you'll want to get familiar with at least one of them. In this section, I explain how they both work.

**TIP**

Some Linux distributions install only one of the two editors, while others install both of them. If your Linux distribution installs only one, it's easy to use the software installation tool (see Book 1, Chapter 5) to install the other, because both are part of the standard KDE project application suite.

## Writing with KWrite

The basic editor for the KDE Plasma environment is KWrite. It provides simple word processing–style text editing, along with support for code syntax highlighting and editing.

The default KWrite editing window is shown in Figure 6-3.

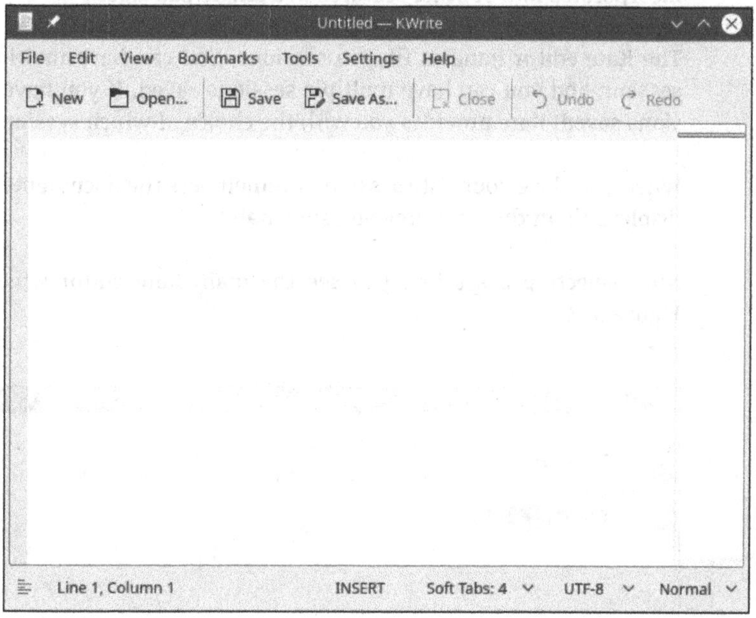

**FIGURE 6-3:**
The default
KWrite window in
openSUSE.

You can't tell from Figure 6-3, but the KWrite editor recognizes several types of programming languages and uses color coding to distinguish constants, functions, and comments. If you're a programmer (or an aspiring programmer), you'll love this feature!

The KWrite editing window provides full cut-and-paste capabilities using the mouse and the arrow keys. Just as in `gedit`, you can highlight and cut (or copy) text anywhere in the editor area and paste it in any other place.

To edit a file using KWrite, you can either select KWrite from the KDE menu system on your desktop (some Linux distributions even create a panel icon for it) or start it from the command-line prompt and specify the file you want to open:

```
$ kwrite factorial.sh
```

**TIP**

Choose Settings⇨Configure to open the Configuration Editor dialog box, which allows you to customize the various features in KWrite.

## Meet Kate

The Kate editor is the flagship editor for the KDE Project. It uses the same text editor as the KWrite application (so most of those features are the same), but it incorporates lots of other features in a single package.

The Kate editor handles files in sessions. You can have multiple files open in a session, and you can have multiple sessions saved. If you have one or more sessions saved, Kate provides you with the choice of which session to return to.

When you close your Kate session, it remembers the documents you had open and displays them the next time you start Kate!

After selecting a session, you see the main Kate editor window, as shown in Figure 6-4.

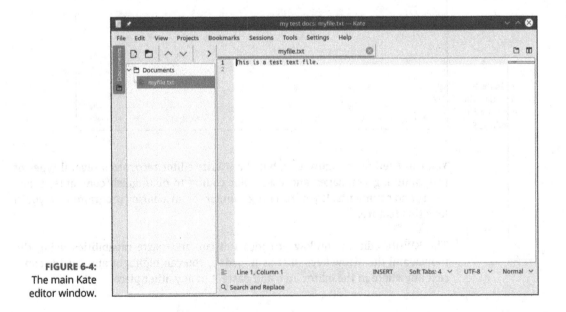

**FIGURE 6-4:**
The main Kate editor window.

The left frame shows the documents currently open in the session. You can switch between documents just by clicking the document name. If the frame gets in the way, you can remove it by choosing View➪Tools.

To start a new file, just click the Create New Document icon on the left side. To open an existing file, just click the Open an Existing Document icon. This allows you to graphically browse to locate your file.

Kate also supports multiple tabs, but with a twist. Choose View➪Split View to select how tab windows appear. You can

>> Split the current windows vertically.

>> Split the current windows horizontally.

>> Move the splitter up, down, left, or right.

>> Close the current window.

To set the configuration settings in Kate, choose Settings➪Configure Kate.

The Editor settings area is exactly the same as for KWrite. This is because the two editors share the same text editor engine. The Application settings area allows you to configure settings for the Kate items, such as controlling sessions, the documents list, and the editor appearance. Kate also supports external plug-in applications, which can be activated here.

# Text Editing with ed and vi

GUI text editors enable you to edit text files by using the mouse and keyboard much the same way as you would in any word processor. Text-mode editors are different beasts, however; you use only the keyboard and have to type cryptic commands to perform editing tasks, such as cutting and pasting text or entering and deleting text.

Most Linux distributions come with the following two text-mode text editors:

>> ed: A line-oriented text editor

>> vi: A full-screen text editor that supports the command set of an earlier editor named ex

The ed and vi editors are cryptic compared with the graphical text editors. You should still get to know the basic editing commands of ed and vi, however, because sometimes they're the only editors available. If Linux refuses to boot from the hard drive, for example, you may have to boot from a CD, DVD, or flash drive. In that case, you have to edit system files with the ed editor because that editor is small enough to fit on the boot medium.

In the following sections, I walk you through the basic text-editing commands of ed and vi, which aren't too hard.

# Using ed

Typically, you have to use ed only when you boot a minimal version of Linux (from the medium you've set up as a boot disk, for example) and the system doesn't support full-screen mode. In all other situations, you can use the vi editor, which works in full-screen text mode.

When you use ed, you work in command mode or text-input mode:

>> **Command mode:** This mode is the default. In command mode, anything you type is interpreted as a command. The ed text editor has a simple command set in which each command consists of one or more characters.

>> **Text-input mode:** This mode is for typing text. You can enter text-input mode with the commands a (append), c (change), and i (insert). After entering lines of text, you can leave text-input mode by entering a period (.) on a line by itself.

To practice editing a file, copy the /etc/fstab file to your home directory by issuing the following commands:

```
cd
cp /etc/fstab .
```

Now you have a file named fstab in your home directory. Type **ed -p: fstab** to begin editing a file in ed. The editor responds as follows:

```
878
:
```

This example uses the –p option to set the prompt to the colon character (:) and opens the fstab file (in the current directory, which is your home directory) for editing. The ed editor opens the file, reports the number of characters in the file (878), displays the prompt (:), and waits for a command.

**REMEMBER**

When you're editing with ed, make sure that you always turn on a prompt character (by using the –p option). Without the prompt, distinguishing whether ed is in text-input mode or command mode is difficult.

After ed opens a file for editing, the current line is the last line of the file. To see the current line number (the line to which ed applies your command), use the `.=` command, like this:

```
:.=
9
```

This output tells you that the fstab file has nine lines. (Your system's /etc/fstab file may have a different number of lines, in which case ed shows a different number.)

You can use the 1,$p command to see all lines in a file, as the following example shows:

```
:1,$p
# This file is edited by fstab-sync - see 'man fstab-sync' for details
/dev/VolGroup00/LogVol00 / ext3 defaults 1 1
LABEL=/boot /boot ext3 defaults 1 2
/dev/devpts /dev/pts devpts gid=5,mode=620 0 0
/dev/shm /dev/shm tmpfs defaults 0 0
/dev/proc /proc proc defaults 0 0
/dev/sys /sys sysfs defaults 0 0
/dev/VolGroup00/LogVol01 swap swap defaults 0 0
/dev/scd0 /media/cdrecorder auto pamconsole,exec,noauto,managed 0 0
/dev/hdc /media/cdrom auto pamconsole,exec,noauto,managed 0 0
:
```

To go to a specific line, type the line number:

```
:2
```

The editor responds by displaying that line:

```
/dev/VolGroup00/LogVol00 / ext3 defaults 1 1
:
```

Suppose you want to delete the line that contains cdrom. To search for a string, type a slash (/) followed by the string that you want to locate:

```
:/cdrom
/dev/hdc /media/cdrom auto pamconsole,exec,noauto,managed 0 0
:
```

The editor locates the line that contains the string and then displays it. That line becomes the current line.

To delete the current line, use the d command:

```
:d
:
```

To replace a string with another, use the s command. To replace cdrom with the string cd, for example, use this command:

```
:s/cdrom/cd/
:
```

To insert a line in front of the current line, use the i command:

```
:i
(type the line you want to insert)
. (type a single period to indicate you're done)
:
```

You can enter as many lines as you want. After the last line, enter a period (.) on a line by itself. That period marks the end of text-input mode, and the editor switches to command mode. In this case, you can tell that ed switches to command mode because you see the prompt (:).

When you're happy with the changes, you can write them to the file with the w command. If you want to save the changes and exit, type **wq** to perform both steps at the same time:

```
:wq
857
```

The ed editor saves the changes in the file, displays the number of saved characters, and exits. If you want to quit the editor without saving any changes, use the Q command.

These examples give you an idea of how to use ed commands to perform basic tasks in editing a text file. To see a complete listing of all the commands available in ed, check out the ed main page.

# Using vi

After you dabble with ed, you'll find that vi is a dream come true, even though it's still a command-line editor. The vi editor is a full-screen text editor, so you can view several lines at the same time. Most Unix systems, including Linux, come with vi. Therefore, if you know the basic features of vi you can edit text files on almost any Unix-based system.

When vi edits a file, it reads the file into a *buffer* (a block of memory) so you can change the text in the buffer. The vi editor also uses temporary files during editing, but the original file isn't altered until you save the changes.

To start the editor, type **vi** followed by the name of the file you want to edit, like this:

```
vi /etc/fstab
```

The vi editor loads the file into memory, displays the first few lines in a text screen, and positions the cursor on the first line (see Figure 6-5).

```
rich@Ubuntu22: ~                         Q  ≡  _  □  ✕

# /etc/fstab: static file system information.
#
# Use 'blkid' to print the universally unique identifier for a
# device; this may be used with UUID= as a more robust way to name devices
# that works even if disks are added and removed. See fstab(5).
#
# <file system> <mount point>   <type>  <options>       <dump>  <pass>
# / was on /dev/sda3 during installation
UUID=5cfa3b9b-29b5-4f3c-8e15-c77febd8c08d /            ext4    errors=remount
-ro 0       1
# /boot/efi was on /dev/sda2 during installation
UUID=8B9D-4521 /boot/efi        vfat    umask=0077      0       1
/swapfile                       none            swap    sw
  0       0
~
~
~
~
~
~
~
~
~
~
"/etc/fstab" [readonly] 12 lines, 665 bytes
```

**FIGURE 6-5:**
You can edit files with the vi full-screen text editor.

The last line shows the pathname of the file, as well as the number of lines (12) and the number of characters (665) in the file. In this case, the text [readonly] appears after the filename because I'm opening the /etc/fstab file while I'm logged in as a normal user (which means that I don't have permission to modify the file). Later, the last line in the vi display functions as a command entry area. The rest of the lines display the file. If the file contains fewer lines than the screen, vi displays the empty lines with a tilde (~) in the first column.

The current line is marked by the cursor, which appears as a small black rectangle. The cursor appears on top of a character.

When using vi, you work in one of three modes:

>> **Visual command mode:** This mode is the default. In this mode, anything you type is interpreted as a command that applies to the line containing the cursor. The vi commands are similar to the ed commands.

>> **Colon command mode:** You use this mode for reading or writing files, setting vi options, and quitting vi. All colon commands start with a colon (:). When you type the colon, vi positions the cursor on the last line and waits for you to type a command. The command takes effect when you press Enter.

>> **Text-input mode:** This mode is for typing text. You can enter text-input mode with the command a (insert after cursor), A (append at end of line), o (open a line below the current one), O (open a line above the current one), or i (insert after cursor). After entering lines of text, you have to press Esc to leave text-input mode and reenter visual command mode.

One problem with all these modes is that you can't easily tell the current mode that vi is in. You may begin typing only to realize that vi isn't in text-input mode, which can be frustrating.

TIP

If you want to make sure that vi is in command mode, press Esc a few times. (Pressing Esc more than once doesn't hurt.)

To view online help in vi, type **:help** while in colon command mode. When you're finished with help, type **:q** to exit the Help screen and return to the file that you're editing.

The vi editor initially positions the cursor on the first character of the first line. Use the arrow keys to move the cursor around in the file.

You can go to a specific line number at any time by using the handy colon command. To go to line 6, for example, type the following and then press Enter:

```
:6
```

When you type the colon, vi displays the colon on the last line of the screen. From then on, vi uses any text you type as a command. You have to press Enter to submit the command to vi. In colon command mode, vi accepts all commands that the ed editor accepts and then some.

To search for a string, first type a slash (/). The vi editor displays the slash on the last line of the screen. Type the search string and then press Enter. The vi editor locates the string and positions the cursor at the beginning of that string. To locate the string cdrom in the file /etc/fstab, type

```
/cdrom
```

To delete the line that contains the cursor, type **dd**. The vi editor deletes that line of text and makes the next line the current one.

To begin entering text in front of the cursor, type **i**. The vi editor switches to text-input mode. Now you can enter text. When you finish entering text, press Esc to return to visual command mode.

After you finish editing the file, you can save the changes in the file with the :w command. To quit the editor without saving any changes, use the :q! command. If you want to save the changes and exit, you can use the :wq command to perform both steps at the same time. The vi editor saves the changes in the file and exits. You can also save the changes and exit the editor by pressing Shift+ZZ (that is, hold Shift down and press Z twice).

vi accepts a large number of commands in addition to the commands I just mentioned. Table 6-1 lists some commonly used vi commands, organized by task.

**TABLE 6-1**     **Common vi Commands**

| Command | Does the Following |
| --- | --- |
| **Insert text** | |
| a | Inserts text after the cursor |
| A | Inserts text at the end of the current line |
| I | Inserts text at the beginning of the current line |
| i | Inserts text before the cursor |
| **Delete text** | |
| D | Deletes up to the end of the current line |
| dd | Deletes the current line |
| dG | Deletes from the current line to the end of the file |
| dw | Deletes the current word where the cursor presently resides |
| x | Deletes the character on which the cursor rests |

*(continued)*

**TABLE 6-1** *(continued)*

| Command | Does the Following |
|---|---|
| **Change text** | |
| C | Changes up to the end of the current line |
| cc | Changes the current line |
| J | Joins the current line with the next one |
| r$x$ | Replaces the character under the cursor with $x$ (where $x$ is any character) |
| **Move cursor** | |
| h or ← | Moves one character to the left |
| j or ↓ | Moves one line down |
| k or ↑ | Moves one line up |
| L | Moves to the end of the screen |
| l or → | Moves one character to the right |
| w | Moves to the beginning of the following word |
| b | Moves to the beginning of the previous word |
| **Scroll text** | |
| Ctrl+D | Scrolls forward through the file by half a screen |
| Ctrl+U | Scrolls backward through the file by half a screen |
| **Refresh screen** | |
| Ctrl+L | Redraws the screen |
| **Cut and paste text** | |
| yy | Yanks (copies) the current line to an unnamed buffer |
| P | Puts the yanked line above the current line |
| p | Puts the yanked line below the current line |
| **Colon commands** | |
| :!command | Executes a shell command |
| :q | Quits the editor |
| :q! | Quits without saving changes |
| :r filename | Reads the file and inserts it after the current line |

**TABLE 6-1** *(continued)*

| Command | Does the Following |
| --- | --- |
| :w filename | Writes a buffer to the file |
| :wq | Saves changes and exits |
| **Search text** | |
| /string | Searches forward for a string |
| ?string | Searches backward for a string |
| **Miscellaneous** | |
| u | Undoes the last command |
| Esc | Ends input mode and enters visual command mode |
| U | Undoes recent changes to the current line |

Text Editors

# 3

# Networking

# Contents at a Glance

# Chapter **1**

# Connecting to the Internet

G iven the prevalence and popularity of the Internet, it's a safe bet to assume that you will want to connect your Linux system not only to a network but also to the largest network of all: the Internet. In this chapter, I discuss how to connect to the Internet in several ways. The method you select mostly depends on your location and how much you want to pay for Internet service.

Most options for connecting to the Internet involve using a special router to connect your Linux system to the Internet service provider (ISP). In these cases, you have to set up Ethernet networking on your Linux system. (I explain wired networking in Book 3, Chapter 2, and wireless networking in Book 3, Chapter 3.) If your machine is nothing more than a client on a network that it connects to via a mobile/Wi-Fi connection and doesn't need its own dedicated connection, things couldn't be easier; you'll simply want to skim this chapter before moving on to subsequent chapters.

# Understanding the Internet

How you view the Internet depends on your perspective. Most people see the Internet in terms of the services they use. As a user, you might think of the Internet as an information-exchange medium with features such as

>> **Email:** Send email to any other user on the Internet, using addresses such as mom@home.net.

>> **Web:** Download and view documents from millions of servers throughout the Internet, connect on Facebook, search for information on Google, and so on.

>> **Information sharing:** Download software, music files, videos, and other valuable content. Reciprocally, you may provide files that users on other systems can download.

>> **Streaming:** On-demand playing of movies, TV programs, games, and music from providers is quickly replacing cable and satellite TV in providing entertainment content.

>> **Remote access:** Log in to another computer across the Internet, assuming that you have access to and permissions on that remote computer.

The techies say that the Internet is a worldwide *network of networks*. The term *internet* (without capitalization) is a shortened form of *internetworking* — the interconnection of networks. The Internet Protocol (IP) was designed with the idea of connecting many separate networks.

**TECHNICAL STUFF**

In terms of physical connections, the Internet is similar to a network of highways and roads. This similarity prompted the popular press to dub the Internet "the Information Superhighway." Just as the network of highways and roads includes some interstate highways, many state roads, and many more residential streets, the Internet has some very high-capacity networks (a 10-Gbps backbone can handle 10 billion bits per second) and many lower-capacity networks ranging from 56 Kbps dial-up connections to a high-speed cable connection of 1 Gbps or more. (*Kbps* is a thousand bits per second, and *Gbps* is a trillion bits per second.) The high-capacity network is the backbone of the Internet.

In terms of management, the Internet isn't run by a single organization; neither is it managed by any central computer. You can view the physical Internet as being a network of networks managed collectively by thousands of cooperating organizations. Yes, a collection of networks managed by *thousands* of organizations. It sounds amazing, but it works!

# Deciding How to Connect to the Internet

So you want to connect your Linux workstation to the Internet, but you don't know how? Let me count the ways. Nowadays, you have some popular options for connecting homes and small offices to the Internet (whereas huge corporations and governments have many other ways to connect):

>> **Fiber-optic:** Currently the fastest and most reliable Internet connectivity available is via fiber-optic cable. Fiber-optic cables utilize thin strands of glass or plastic to send data as pulses of light over long distances. Although fiber-optic connectivity was initially available only for businesses, its price point is continually getting lower, so homeowners can now enjoy high-speed connectivity (up to 5 Gbps). Because this method requires special cables, most ISPs are just getting started in building out their fiber-optic cable infrastructure, so this service may not be available yet in your area.

>> **Digital Subscriber Line (DSL):** Your local telephone company, as well as other telecommunications companies, may offer DSL. DSL provides a way to send high-speed digital data over a regular phone line. Typically, DSL offers data transfer rates of between 128 Kbps and 500 Mbps. (Usually, the higher the speed, the more you pay.) You can often download from the Internet at much higher rates than when you send data from your PC to the Internet *(upload)*. One caveat with DSL is that your home must be within a defined proximity to your local central office (the DSL provider's facility where your phone lines end up). The distance limitation varies from provider to provider and the DSL technology they use.

>> **Cable router:** If the cable television company in your area offers Internet access over cable, you can use that service to hook up your Linux system to the Internet. Typically, cable routers offer higher data-transfer rates than DSL — for about the same cost — but bandwidth may be shared with other subscribers. Downloading data from the Internet via cable router is much faster than sending data from your PC to the Internet.

>> **Wireless hot spot:** With the explosion of cell phone use came yet another method of connecting to the Internet. Most cell phones can act as a wireless hot spot, providing wireless Internet access to external devices via the cell tower data network. Additionally, many cell phone providers also offer custom wireless hot spot devices specifically made for sharing data with other devices. With the advent of the 5G network (with sustained download speeds of up to 1 Gbps), it's possible to provide Internet connectivity for an entire house with a single wireless hot spot.

>> **Satellite:** If your house is not serviced by fiber, DSL, or cable, and you can't connect to a cell tower, you may still be able to access higher-speed Internet connectivity through a satellite Internet service. Satellite Internet service just

requires a satellite dish mounted with an unobstructed view of the sky (such as from the roof of your house). Satellite speeds are not as fast as DSL or cable, but they're better than dial-up services.

>> **Dial-up:** In the early days of the Internet, dial-up services such as AOL and MSN ruled the roost. However dial-up speeds maxed out at 56 Kbps, so when cable and DSL Internet access became common, dial-up providers soon went out of business. If you're not able to utilize a high-speed Internet connection, though, there are still dial-up providers around who can connect you for basic email and browsing. Just don't expect to stream the latest episode of your favorite TV show!

For most residential customers, the easiest way to obtain Internet service is through a telephone company (which uses DSL) or a cable TV company. Because of that, I take a closer look at those two connectivity methods in the following sections.

# Connecting with DSL

DSL uses your existing phone line to send digital data in addition to normal analog voice signals. (*Analog* means continuously varying, whereas digital data is represented by 1s and 0s.) The phone line goes from your home to a central office, where the line connects to the DSL provider's network. By the way, the connection from your home to the central office is called the *local loop*.

When you sign up for DSL service, the DSL provider hooks up your phone line to some special equipment at the central office. That equipment can separate the digital data from voice. From then on, your phone line can carry digital data that is directly sent to an Internet connection at the central office.

## How DSL works

A special box called a *DSL modem* takes care of sending digital data from your PC to the DSL provider's central office over your phone line. Your PC can connect to the Internet with the same phone line that you use for your normal telephone calls; you can make voice calls even as the line is being used for DSL. Figure 1-1 shows a typical DSL connection to the Internet.

Your PC talks to the DSL modem through either a wired Ethernet connection or a wireless connection, which means that you need either an Ethernet card or a wireless card in your Linux system.

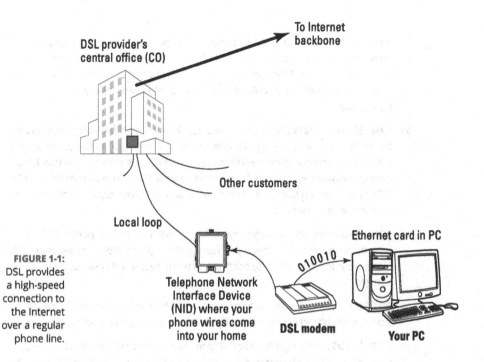

FIGURE 1-1:
DSL provides
a high-speed
connection to
the Internet
over a regular
phone line.

Your PC sends digital data to the DSL modem; then the DSL modem sends the digital data at different frequencies from those used by the analog voice signals. The voice signals occupy a small portion of all the frequencies that the phone line can carry. DSL uses the higher frequencies to transfer digital data, so both voice and data can travel on the same phone line.

**WARNING**

If you have a landline, you'll need to attach a small filter device to the phone line. This helps prevent interference between the analog phone signal and the digital DSL signal.

## DSL alphabet soup: ADSL, IDSL, SDSL

**WARNING**

I've been using the term *DSL* as though there were only one kind of DSL, but DSL has several variants, each with different features. Take a look at a few options:

>> **ADSL:** *Asymmetric DSL* is the most common form of DSL with much higher download speeds (from the Internet to your PC) than upload speeds (from your PC to the Internet). Most DSL providers can offer packages of 1.5 Mbps, 3 Mbps, or 6 Mbps download service, but only a max of 512 Kbps upload service. ADSL works best when your location is within about 2 to 2.5 miles (12,000 feet) of the central office. ADSL service is priced according to the download and upload speeds you want.

A newer version, ADSL2, made some improvements in the data rate and increased the distance from the telephone exchange that the line can run. After it, ADSL2+ doubled the downstream bandwidth and kept all the features of ADSL2. Both ADSL2 and ADSL2+ are compatible with legacy ADSL equipment.

>> **IDSL:** Short for *ISDN DSL* (ISDN is an older technology called *Integrated Services Digital Network*), *IDSL* is a special type of DSL that works at distances of up to 5 miles between your phone and the central office. The downside is that IDSL averages *downstream* (from the Internet to your PC) and *upstream* (from your PC to the Internet) speeds similar to what an old-fashioned modem could do over a dial-up connection.

>> **SDSL:** *Symmetric DSL* provides equal download and upload speeds. SDSL is priced according to the speed you want, with higher speeds costing more. The closer your location is to the central office, the faster the connection you can get.

>> **RADSL:** *Rate-adaptive DSL* is a variation on ADSL that can modify its transmission speeds based on signal quality. RADSL supports line sharing.

>> **VDSL/VHDSL:** *Very-high bit-rate DSL* is an asymmetric version of DSL, and as such, it can share a telephone line. VHDSL supports high-bandwidth applications such as Voice over Internet Protocol (VoIP) and high-definition television (HDTV). VHDSL can achieve data rates up to approximately 10 Mbps. To achieve high speeds, VHDSL uses fiber-optic cabling.

>> **VDSL2:** Very-high bit-rate DSL version 2 is compatible with ADSL2+ and can reach download speeds up to 500 Mbps using a combination of fiber-optic connections to the provider equipment and copper connections to homes.

>> **HDSL:** *High-bit-rate DSL* is a symmetric version of the technology that offers identical transmission rates in both directions. HDSL doesn't allow line sharing with analog phones.

**TECHNICAL STUFF**

Internet connection speeds are typically specified by two numbers separated by a slash, such as 1500/384. The numbers refer to data-transfer speeds in kilobits per second (that is, thousands of bits per second, abbreviated Kbps). The first number is the download speed; the second, the upload. Thus, 1500/384 means that you can expect to download from the Internet at a maximum rate of 1,500 Kbps (or 1.5 Mbps) and upload to the Internet at 384 Kbps. If your phone line's condition isn't perfect, you may not get these maximum rates; ADSL and SDSL adjust the speeds to suit existing line conditions.

The price of DSL service depends on which variant you select. For most home users, the primary choice is ADSL (or, more accurately, the G.lite form of ADSL).

# Typical DSL setup

To get DSL for your home or business, you must contact a DSL provider. You can find many DSL providers in addition to your phone company. No matter who provides the DSL service, some work has to be done at the central office — the place where your phone lines connect to the rest of the phone network. The work involves connecting your phone line to equipment that can work with the DSL modem at your home or office. Then the central office equipment and the DSL modem at your location can do whatever magic is needed to send and receive digital data over your phone line.

The distance between your home and the central office — the *loop length* — is a factor in DSL's performance. Unfortunately, the phone line can reliably carry the DSL signals over only a limited distance — typically 3 miles or less, which means that you can get DSL service only if your home (or office) is located within about 3 miles of the central office. Contact your DSL provider to verify. You may be able to check this availability on the web. Try typing into Google (www.google.com) the words **DSL availability** and then your provider's name. The search results will probably include a website where you can type your phone number to find out whether DSL is available for your home or office.

If DSL is available, you can look for types of service — ADSL versus VHDSL — and pricing. The price depends on what download and upload speeds you want. Sometimes, phone companies offer a simple residential DSL (basically, the G.lite form of ADSL) with a 1500/256 speed rating, meaning that you can download at up to 1,500 Kbps and upload at 256 Kbps. These ratings are the *maximums*; your mileage may vary. Many DSL modems have other features built into them beyond just modem capabilities: NAT (network address translation) routing, multiple Ethernet ports, and even Wi-Fi capabilities are common options.

After selecting the type of DSL service and provider you want, you can place an order and have the provider install the necessary equipment at your home or office. Figure 1-2 shows a sample connection diagram for typical residential DSL service.

Here are some key points to note in Figure 1-2:

>> Connect your DSL modem's data connection to the phone jack on a wall plate.

>> Connect the DSL modem's Ethernet connection to the Ethernet port on your PC or laptop.

>> When you connect other telephones or fax machines on the same phone line, install a microfilter between the wall plate and each of these devices.

Because the same phone line carries both voice signals and DSL data, you need the microfilter to protect the DSL data from possible interference. You can buy these filters at electronics stores or from the DSL provider.

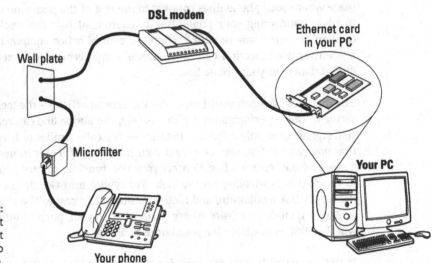

FIGURE 1-2:
You can connect a PC's Ethernet card directly to the DSL modem.

TIP

These days it's common for the telephone company to provide a DSL modem that includes a built-in wireless router and a Gigabit network switch — all in a single device. With this type of device, you can connect your Linux computer using either a wired Ethernet cable or a wireless signal (see Book 3, Chapter 3). The benefit of this method is that it also allows you to connect other wireless devices (such as phones, tablets, gaming systems, and laptops) to the DSL connection, providing easy Internet access for everything in your home.

# Connecting with a Cable Modem

Cable TV companies also offer high-speed Internet access over the same coaxial cable that carries television signals to your home. After the cable company installs the necessary equipment at its facility to send and receive digital data over the coaxial cables, customers can sign up for cable Internet service. Then you can get high-speed Internet access over the same line that delivers cable TV signals to your home.

# How a cable modem works

A box called a *cable modem* is at the heart of Internet access over the cable TV network (see Figure 1-3). The cable modem takes digital data from your PC's Ethernet card and puts it in an unused block of frequency. (Think of this frequency as being another TV channel, but instead of carrying pictures and sound this channel carries digital data.)

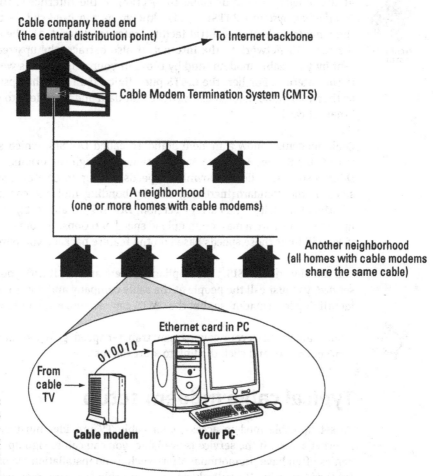

**FIGURE 1-3:** Cable modems provide high-speed Internet access over the cable TV network.

The cable modem places *upstream data* — data that's being sent from your PC to the Internet — in a different channel from that of the *downstream* data that's coming from the Internet to your PC. By design, the speed of downstream data transfers is much higher than that of upstream transfers. The assumption is that people download far more stuff from the Internet than they upload (which is probably true for most of us).

The coaxial cable that carries all those hundreds of cable TV channels to your home is a very capable signal carrier. In particular, the coaxial cable can carry signals covering a huge range of frequencies — hundreds of megahertz (MHz). Each TV channel requires 6 MHz, and the coaxial cable can carry hundreds of such channels. The cable modem places the upstream data in a small frequency band and expects to receive the downstream data in another frequency band.

At the other end of your cable connection to the Internet is the *Cable Modem Termination System* (CMTS) — also known as the *head end* — that your cable company installs at its central facility (refer to Figure 1-3). The CMTS connects the cable TV network to the Internet. It also extracts the upstream digital data sent by your cable modem (and by those of your neighbors as well) and sends it to the Internet. Further, the CMTS puts digital data into the upstream channels so that your cable modem can extract that data and provide it to your PC via the Ethernet card.

Cable modems follow a modem standard called DOCSIS, which stands for Data Over Cable Service Interface Specification. Although the original versions of the DOCSIS standard allowed download speeds only up to 40 Mbps, subsequent versions of the standard increased that by bonding multiple channels to provide additional capacity. The current version, DOCSIS 3.1, allows for download speeds up to 10 Gbps, with a maximum upload speed of 6 Gbps. Of course, your cable provider will limit those speeds based on the feature package you purchase.

You can buy any DOCSIS 3.1–compliant modem and use it with your cable Internet service; you just call the people at the cable company and give them the modem's identifying information so that the CMTS can recognize and initialize the modem.

If you want to check your downstream transfer speed, go to www.bandwidthplace.com/speedtest and click the link to start the test.

## Typical cable modem setup

To set up cable modem access, your cable TV provider must offer high-speed Internet access. If the service is available, you can call to sign up. The cable companies often have promotional offers such as no installation fee or a reduced rate for three months. If you're lucky, a local cable company may have a promotion going on just when you want to sign up.

The installation is typically performed by a technician, who splits your incoming cable in two; one side goes to the TV, and the other goes to the cable modem. The technician provides information about the cable modem to the cable company's head end for setup at its end. When that work is complete, you can plug your PC's

Ethernet port into the cable modem, and you'll be all set to enjoy high-speed Internet access. Figure 1-4 shows a typical cable modem hookup.

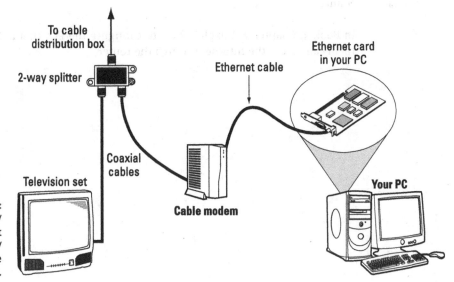

**FIGURE 1-4:** The cable TV signal is split between the TV and the cable modem.

The cable modem connects to an Ethernet port in your PC or laptop.

Here are some key points to note about the cable modem setup in Figure 1-4:

>> Split the incoming cable TV signal into two parts by using a two-way splitter. (The cable company technician installs the splitter.) The two-way splitter needs to be rated for 1 GHz; otherwise, it may not let the frequencies that contain the downstream data from the Internet pass through.

>> Connect one of the video outputs from the splitter to your cable modem's F-type video connector, using a coaxial cable.

>> Connect the cable modem's Gigabit Ethernet connection to the Ethernet card on your PC.

>> Connect your TV to the other video output from the two-way splitter. When you use a cable modem to connect your Linux PC directly to the Internet, the connection is always on, so you have more of a chance that someone may try to break into the PC. Linux includes the iptables packet filtering capability, which you may want to use to protect your PC from unwanted Internet connections.

**TIP**

Just as in the DSL world, most cable companies now provide cable modems that also contain wireless routers and Gigabit Ethernet switches, all in one device. This allows you to connect any device that requires Internet service to the cable modem connection.

In Book 3, Chapter 2, I explain how to configure the PCs in a LAN so that all of them can access the Internet through the router.

# Chapter **2**

# Setting Up a Local Area Network

L inux comes with built-in support for Transmission Control Protocol/Internet Protocol (TCP/IP) networking, as do most modern operating systems from Windows to macOS. You can have TCP/IP networking over many physical interfaces, such as Ethernet cards and USB ports.

Typically, you use an Ethernet network for your local area network (LAN) at your office or even your home (if you happen to have two or more systems at home), with wireless (see Book 3, Chapter 3) gaining in popularity in most locations.

This chapter describes how to set up an Ethernet network. Even if you have a single PC, you may need to set up an Ethernet network interface so that you can connect to high-speed Internet access (via a DSL or cable modem somewhere along the way).

## Understanding TCP/IP

You can understand TCP/IP networking best if you think in terms of a four-layer model, with each layer being responsible for performing a particular task. The layered model describes the flow of data between the physical connection to the network and the end-user application. Figure 2-1 shows the four-layer network model for TCP/IP.

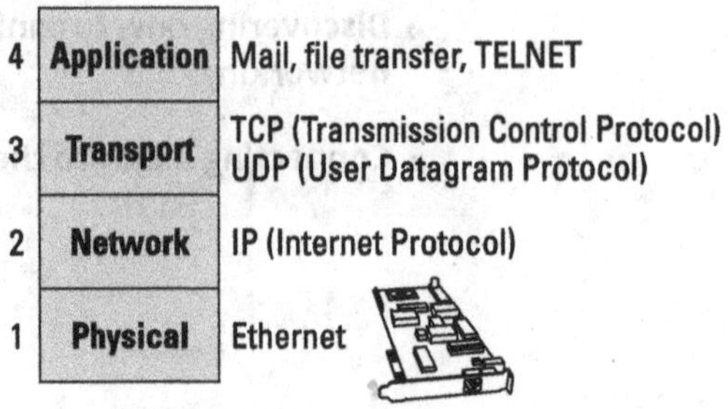

FIGURE 2-1:
You can
understand
TCP/IP by using
the four-layer
network model.

| 4 | Application | Mail, file transfer, TELNET |
| 3 | Transport | TCP (Transmission Control Protocol)<br>UDP (User Datagram Protocol) |
| 2 | Network | IP (Internet Protocol) |
| 1 | Physical | Ethernet |

In this four-layer model, information always moves from one layer to the next. When an application sends data to another application, for example, the data goes through the layers in this order: application⇨ transport⇨ network⇨ physical. At the receiving end, the data goes up from physical⇨ network⇨ transport⇨ application.

Each layer has its own set of *protocols* — conventions — for handling and formatting the data. If you think of sending data as being something akin to sending letters through the postal service, a typical protocol is a preferred sequence of actions for a task, such as addressing an envelope (first the name, then the street address, followed by the city, state, and zip or other postal code).

These four layers, depending on what reference you look at, may have different names. If you look at the old DOD model, for example, the transport layer is called host-to-host, the network layer is called internetwork or Internet, the application layer is called process/application, and the physical layer is called network access.

Here's what the four layers do, top to bottom:

>> **Application:** Runs the applications that users use, such as email readers, file transfers, and web browsers. Application-level protocols are Simple Mail Transfer Protocol (SMTP) and Post Office Protocol (POP) for email, Hypertext Transfer Protocol (HTTP) for the web, and File Transfer Protocol (FTP) for file transfers. Application-level protocols also have a *port number* that you can think of as being an identifier for a specific application. Port 80, for example, is associated with HTTP or a web server.

>> **Transport:** Sends data from one application to another. The two most important protocols in this layer are Transmission Control Protocol (TCP) and User Datagram Protocol (UDP). TCP guarantees delivery of data; UDP just sends the data without ensuring that it actually reaches the destination.

# TCP/IP AND THE INTERNET

TCP/IP has become the protocol of choice on the Internet — the network of networks that evolved from ARPANET. The U.S. government's Advanced Research Projects Agency (ARPA) initiated research in the 1970s on a new way of sending information, using packets of data sent over a network. The result was ARPANET: a national network of linked computers. Subsequently, ARPA acquired a Department of Defense prefix and became DARPA. Under the auspices of DARPA, the TCP/IP protocols emerged as a popular collection of protocols for *internetworking* — communication among networks.

TCP/IP has flourished because the protocol is *open,* which means that the technical descriptions of the protocol appear in public documents, so anyone can implement TCP/IP on specific hardware and software.

>> **Network:** Gets data packets from one network to another. If the networks are far apart, the data packets are routed from one network to the next until they reach their destinations. The primary protocol in this layer is Internet Protocol (IP).

>> **Physical:** Refers to the physical networking hardware (such as an Ethernet cable or wireless signal) that carries the data packets in a network.

The beauty of the layered model is that each layer takes care of only its specific task, leaving the rest to the other layers. The layers can mix and match; you can have TCP/IP network over any type of physical network medium, from Ethernet to radio waves (in a wireless network). The software is modular as well; each layer can be implemented in different modules. Typically, the transport and network layers already exist as part of the operating system, and any application can use these layers.

TCP/IP also made great inroads because stable, working software was available. Instead of a paper description of network architecture and protocols, the TCP/IP protocols started out as working software — and who can argue with what's already working? These days, as a result, TCP/IP rules the Internet.

## IP addresses

When you have many computers on a network, you need a way to identify each one uniquely. In TCP/IP networking, the address of a computer is the IP address. Because TCP/IP deals with internetworking, the address is based on the concepts of a network address and a host address. You may think of the idea of a network address and a host address as having to provide two addresses to identify a computer uniquely:

>> **Network address** indicates the network on which the computer is located.

>> **Host address** indicates a specific computer on that network.

The network and host addresses together constitute an *IP address*. There are two types of IP addresses you'll need to be aware of:

>> **IPv4:** The original version of IP addresses (and still often called just "IP") uses a 32-bit value (4 bytes) to represent the network and host addresses. The convention is to write each byte as a decimal value, and to put a dot (.) after each number. Thus, you see network addresses such as 192.168.1.10. This way of writing IP addresses is known as *dotted decimal notation* or *dotted quad notation*.

>> **IPv6:** IPv6 was created because the world was running out of available 32-bit addresses to assign to hosts on the Internet. It uses 128 bits for addresses, so there's no danger of running out of addresses anytime soon. Unlike IPv4, IPv6 addresses are commonly represented as eight groups of four hexadecimal digits, separated by colons. You'll see IPv6 addresses that look like this: 2600:1702:1ce0:eeb0:b23d:1c26:b444:e673.

Each device on a network must have a unique IPv4 or IPv6 address assigned to it (and some networks assign both types). For the average home Internet user, that could make things quite complicated. Fortunately, techies designed the Dynamic Host Configuration Protocol (DHCP), which allows network devices to query the network asking for a unique address. DHCP servers (often included as part of the local router software) can then assign a unique address to the device and keep track of which addresses it uses. If for some reason you do need to manually assign an IPv4 or IPv6 address to your Linux system, Book 3, Chapter 4 dives into how to do that.

TIP

Because it's difficult for people to remember IPv4 and IPv6 addresses, techies also created the Domain Name System (DNS). DNS provides a way to assign human-readable names to individual addresses. Thus, you can type www.linux.org into your browser instead of its IPv6 address, 2606:4700:3037:0000:ac43:943f, and your browser will magically take you there. Domain names are maintained by individual DNS servers, usually one for each network on the Internet. Through a complicated process of behind-the-scenes inter-server communication, all your Linux system needs to know is the address of your local DNS server and it can look up any domain name on the Internet.

# Internet services and port numbers

Although IPv4 and IPv6 addresses will connect your Linux system to a remote computer, they won't tell the remote computer which application you intend to connect with. It's sort of like finding the address of your friend's apartment building, but not knowing the apartment number.

To solve that problem, the Internet techies created *port numbers*. Each application running on a network server uses a unique port number, from 1 to 65,535. The port number is like the apartment number — your workstation just specifies the port number assigned to the application it wants to connect with on the server and the server connects you with that application.

Just like IP addresses, port numbers have been assigned names to make things easier for people. These names are called *service names*. There are many well-known service names in use, such as the following:

>> **DHCP** (Dynamic Host Configuration Protocol) is for dynamically configuring TCP/IP network parameters on a computer. DHCP is primarily used to assign dynamic IP addresses and other networking information (such as name server, default gateway, and domain names) needed to configure TCP/IP networks. The DHCP server listens on port 67.

>> **FTP** (File Transfer Protocol) is used to transfer files between computers on the Internet. FTP uses two ports: Data is transferred on port 20, and control information is exchanged on port 21.

>> **DNS** (Domain Name System) is used to translate domain names into IP addresses. This service runs on port 53.

>> **HTTP** (Hypertext Transfer Protocol) is a protocol for sending documents from one system to another. HTTP is the underlying protocol of the World Wide Web. By default, the web server and client communicate on port 80. When combined with the SSL/TLS protocols to encrypt the data as it's sent on the network, the protocol becomes HTTPS, and the port changes to 443.

>> **SMTP** (Simple Mail Transfer Protocol) is for exchanging email messages among systems. SMTP uses port 25 for information exchange.

>> **POP3** (Post Office Protocol version 3) is used by the client to receive mail, and it uses port 110. When combined with SSL/TLS for security, the port changes to 995.

>> **IMAP** (Internet Message Access Protocol) can also be used by clients to interact with mail (in place of POP3), and it uses port 143. When combined with SSL/TLS for security, the port changes to 993.

>> **NNTP** (Network News Transfer Protocol) is for distribution of news articles in a store-and-forward fashion across the Internet. NNTP uses port 119.

>> **NetBIOS** is used by Windows for networking, and it uses several ports for the session, the most common of which is 139.

>> **SSH** (Secure Shell) is a protocol for secure remote login and other secure network services over an insecure network. SSH uses port 22.

>> **Telnet** is used when a user on one system logs in to another system on the Internet. (The user must provide a valid user ID and password to log in to the remote system.) Telnet uses port 23 by default, but the Telnet client can connect to any port.

>> **SNMP** (Simple Network Management Protocol) is for managing all types of network devices on the Internet. Like FTP, SNMP uses two ports: 161 and 162.

>> **Rendezvous Directory Service** (used by Cisco) uses port 465.

>> **TFTP** (Trivial File Transfer Protocol) is for transferring files from one system to another. (It's typically used by X terminals and diskless workstations to download boot files from another host on the network.) TFTP data transfer takes place on port 69.

>> **NFS** (Network File System) is for sharing files among computers. NFS uses Sun's Remote Procedure Call (RPC) facility, which exchanges information through port 111.

A standard port number (often called a well-known port) is associated with each of these services. The TCP protocol uses each such port to locate a service on any system. (A *server process* — a special computer program running on a system — provides each service.)

# Setting Up an Ethernet LAN

Ethernet is a standard way to move packets of data among two or more computers connected to a single hub, router, or switch. (You can create larger networks by connecting multiple Ethernet segments with gateways.) To set up an Ethernet LAN, you need an Ethernet interface for each PC. These days, most PC and laptop devices include a built-in Ethernet interface (either a wired port or a wireless chip), but if you're working with older hardware, you may need to buy a separate Ethernet card. Linux supports a wide variety of Ethernet cards for the PC.

Ethernet is a good choice for the physical data-transport mechanism for the following reasons:

>> Ethernet is a proven technology that has been in use since the early 1980s.

>> Ethernet provides good data-transfer rates — typically, 100 million bits per second (100 Mbps), although Gigabit Ethernet (1,000 Mbps) is now common.

>> Ethernet hardware is often built into PCs or can be installed at a relatively low cost. (PC Ethernet cards cost about $10 to $20.)

>> With wireless Ethernet, you can easily connect laptop PCs to your Ethernet LAN without having to run wires all over the place. (See Book 3, Chapter 3 for information on wireless Ethernet.)

## How Ethernet works

What makes Ethernet tick? In essence, it's the same thing that makes any conversation work: listening and taking turns.

**TECHNICAL STUFF**

In an Ethernet network, all systems in a segment are connected to the same wire. A protocol is used for sending and receiving data because only one data packet can exist on the single wire at any time. An Ethernet LAN uses a data-transmission protocol known as *Carrier-Sense Multiple Access/Collision Detection* (CSMA/CD) to share the single transmission cable among all the computers. Ethernet cards in the computers follow the CSMA/CD protocol to transmit and receive Ethernet packets.

The way that the CSMA/CD protocol works is similar to the way in which you have a conversation at a party. You listen for a pause (that's sensing the carrier) and talk when no one else is speaking. If you and another person begin talking at the same time, both of you realize the problem (that's collision detection) and pause for a moment; then one of you starts speaking again. As you know from experience, everything works out.

In an Ethernet LAN, each Ethernet card checks the cable for signals; that's the carrier-sense part. If the signal level is low, the Ethernet card sends its packets on the cable; the packet contains information about the sender and the intended recipient. All Ethernet cards on the LAN listen to the signal, and the recipient receives the packet. If two cards send out a packet simultaneously, the signal level in the cable rises above a threshold, and the cards know that a collision has occurred. (Two packets have been sent out at the same time.) Both cards wait for a random amount of time before sending their packets again.

## WHAT IS ETHERNET?

Ethernet was invented in the early 1970s at the Xerox Palo Alto Research Center (PARC) by Robert M. Metcalfe. In the 1980s, Ethernet was standardized by the cooperative effort of three companies: Digital Equipment Corporation (DEC), Intel, and Xerox. Using the first initials of the company names, that Ethernet standard became known as the DIX standard. Later, the DIX standard was included in the 802-series standards developed by the Institute of Electrical and Electronics Engineers (IEEE). The final Ethernet specification is formally known as IEEE 802.3 CSMA/CD, but people continue to call it *Ethernet.*

Ethernet sends data in *packets* (discrete chunks also known as *frames*). You don't have to hassle much with the innards of Ethernet packets except to note the 6-byte source and destination addresses. Each Ethernet controller has a unique 6-byte (48-bit) address at the physical layer; every packet must have one.

## Ethernet cables

Any time you hear experts talking about Ethernet, you'll also hear some bewildering terms used for the cables that carry the data. Here's a quick rundown.

**TECHNICAL STUFF**

The original Ethernet standard used a thick coaxial cable nearly half an inch in diameter. This wiring is called *thicknet, thickwire,* or just *thick Ethernet* although the IEEE 802.3 standard calls it *10Base5.* That designation means several things: The data-transmission rate is 10 megabits per second (10 Mbps); the transmission is *baseband* (which simply means that the cable's signal-carrying capacity is devoted to transmitting Ethernet packets only), and the total length of the cable can be no more than 1,640 feet. Thickwire was expensive, and the cable was rather unwieldy. Unless you're a technology-history buff, you don't have to care one whit about 10Base5 cables.

**TECHNICAL STUFF**

Nowadays, several other forms of Ethernet cabling are more popular, and the days of thickwire, and even thinwire, have given way to Ethernet over unshielded twisted-pair cable (UTP), known as 1xxBaseT where the xx represents the speed such as 100BaseT4, 100BaseT2, and 100BaseTX for 100-Mbps Ethernet and 1000BaseT for Gigabit Ethernet. The Electronic Industries Association/Telecommunications Industries Association (EIA/TIA) defines the following categories of shielded and unshielded twisted-pair cables:

>> **Category 1 (Cat 1):** Traditional telephone cable.

>> **Category 2 (Cat 2):** Cable certified for data transmissions up to 4 Mbps.

» **Category 3 (Cat 3):** Cable that can carry signals up to a frequency of 16 MHz. Cat 3 was the most common type of wiring in old corporate networks, and it normally contains four pairs of wire. As network speeds pushed the 100 Mbps speed limit, Category 3 became ineffective; it's now considered to be obsolete.

» **Category 4 (Cat 4):** Cable that can carry signals up to a frequency of 20 MHz. Cat 4 wires aren't common and are now considered to be obsolete.

» **Category 5 (Cat 5):** Cable that can carry signals up to a frequency of 100 MHz. Cat 5 cables normally have four pairs of copper wire. Cat 5 UTP is the most popular cable used in new installations today. This category of cable was superseded by Category 5e (enhanced Cat 5).

» **Category 5e (Cat 5e):** Similar to Cat 5 but with improved technical parameters to mitigate communication problems. Cat 5e cables support 10BaseT, 100BaseT4, 100BaseT2, and 100BaseTX and 1000BaseT Ethernet.

» **Category 6 (Cat 6):** Similar to Cat 5e but capable of carrying signals up to a frequency of 250 MHz. Category 6 twisted-pair uses a longitudinal separator, which separates each of the four pairs of wires. This extra construction significantly reduces the amount of crosstalk in the cable and makes the faster transfer rates possible. Cat 6 cables can support all existing Ethernet standards as well as the Gigabit Ethernet standard 1000BaseTX.

» **Category 6a (Cat 6a):** Also called augmented 6. This category offers improvements over Category 6 by offering minimum 500 MHz of bandwidth. It specifies transmission distances up to 328 feet with 10 Gbps networking speeds.

» **Category 7 (Cat 7):** The big advantage to this cable is that shielding has been added to individual pairs and to the cable as a whole to greatly reduce crosstalk. Category 7 is rated for transmission of 600 MHz and is backward-compatible with Category 5 and Category 6. Category 7 differs from the other cables in this group in that it isn't recognized by the EIA/TIA and that it's shielded twisted-pair. (All others listed as exam objectives are unshielded.)

» **Category 7a (Cat 7a):** This category improves on Cat 7 by increasing the transmission rate to 1,000 MHz, but it's still not recognized by the EIA/TIA. This higher transmission rate allows it to carry a faster signal but for shorter distances. Cat 7a is rated at 40 Gbps for up to 164 feet.

» **Category 8 (Cat 8):** The newest category (as of this writing), Cat 8 is approved by the EIA/TIA and capable of handling up to 40 Gbps for 98 feet using a 2,000 MHz transmission rate.

To set up a Gigabit Ethernet network, you need an *Ethernet switch*, which is similar to a hub but helps segment traffic to help control congestion. You build the network by running twisted-pair wires (usually, Category 5e or 6 cables) from each

PC's Ethernet port to this switch. You can get an eight-port switch for about $40. Figure 2-2 shows a typical small Ethernet LAN that you might set up in a small office or your home.

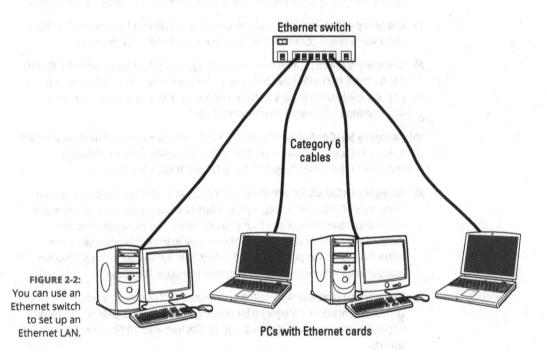

**Ethernet switch**

**Category 6 cables**

FIGURE 2-2:
You can use an Ethernet switch to set up an Ethernet LAN.

**PCs with Ethernet cards**

When you install most the Linux distributions on a PC connected with an Ethernet port, the Linux kernel automatically detects the Ethernet port and installs the appropriate drivers. The installer also lets you set up TCP/IP networking.

**TIP**

The Linux kernel loads the driver for the Ethernet port every time it boots. To verify that the Ethernet driver is loaded, type the following command in a terminal window as the root user account:

```
dmesg | grep eth0
```

On my Ubuntu Linux PC, I get the following output when I type that command:

```
$ sudo dmesg | grep eth0
[sudo] password for rich:
[    1.980430] e1000 0000:00:03.0 eth0: (PCI:33MHz:32-bit) 08:00:27:65:10:19
[    1.980437] e1000 0000:00:03.0 eth0: Intel(R) PRO/1000 Network Connection
[    1.982149] e1000 0000:00:03.0 enp0s3: renamed from eth0
$
```

You should see something similar showing the name of your Ethernet card and related information.

# Configuring TCP/IP Networking

When you set up TCP/IP networking during Linux installation, the installation program prepares all appropriate configuration files by using the information you provide. As a result, you rarely have to configure the network manually. Most Linux distributions, however, come with graphic user interface (GUI) tools for configuring the network devices, just in case something needs changing. For all distributions, the steps are similar.

In Ubuntu, for example, you can use the graphical network configuration tool. To start the GUI network configuration tool, choose Settings ⇨ Network. The network configuration tool displays a dialog box, as shown in Figure 2-3. Then you can configure your network through the choices that appear in the dialog box, including settings for wired and wireless.

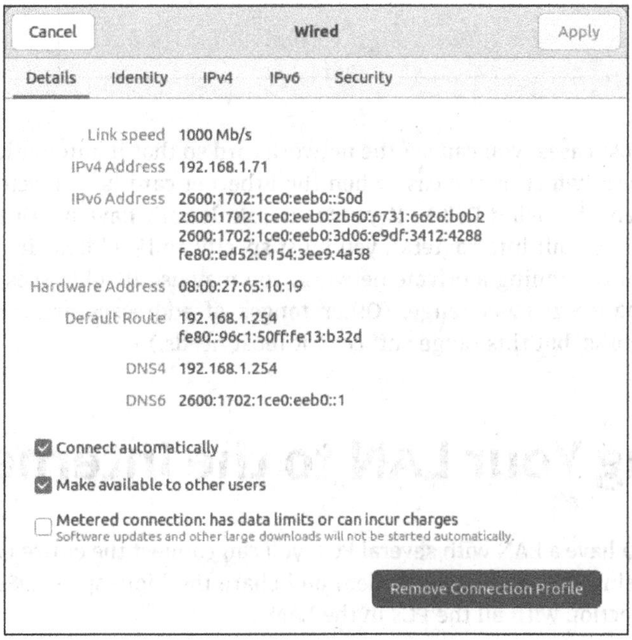

| Cancel | Wired | Apply |

Details    Identity    IPv4    IPv6    Security

Link speed    1000 Mb/s

IPv4 Address    192.168.1.71

IPv6 Address    2600:1702:1ce0:eeb0::50d
2600:1702:1ce0:eeb0:2b60:6731:6626:b0b2
2600:1702:1ce0:eeb0:3d06:e9df:3412:4288
fe80::ed52:e154:3ee9:4a58

Hardware Address    08:00:27:65:10:19

Default Route    192.168.1.254
fe80::96c1:50ff:fe13:b32d

DNS4    192.168.1.254

DNS6    2600:1702:1ce0:eeb0::1

☑ Connect automatically

☑ Make available to other users

☐ Metered connection: has data limits or can incur charges
Software updates and other large downloads will not be started automatically.

Remove Connection Profile

**FIGURE 2-3:**
Move through the dialog-box choices to configure the connection.

Clicking the Security tab displays a dialog box similar to the one shown in Figure 2-4. From there, you can specify whether to use 802.1x security and what level of authentication users can use to log in.

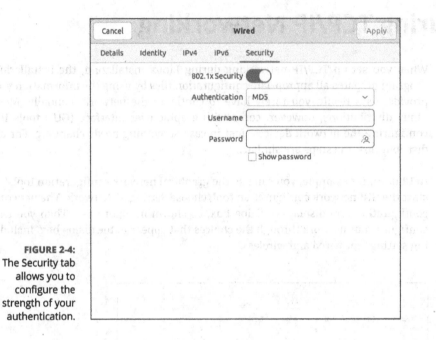

**TIP**

In most cases, you can set the network card so that it automatically obtains an IP address (which is the case when the Ethernet card is connected to DSL or cable modem) by using DHCP. If your network doesn't have a DHCP server (which is typically built into routers), you must specify an IP address for the network card. If you're running a private network, you may use IP addresses in the 192.168.0.0 to 192.168.255.255 range. (Other ranges of addresses are reserved for private networks, but this range suffices for most needs.)

# Connecting Your LAN to the Internet

If you have a LAN with several PCs, you can connect the entire LAN to the Internet by using DSL or a cable modem and share the high-speed DSL or cable modem connection with all the PCs in the LAN.

Book 3, Chapter 1 explains how to set up a DSL or cable modem. In this section, I briefly explain how to connect a LAN to the Internet so that all the PCs can access the Internet.

The most convenient way to connect a LAN to the Internet via DSL or cable modem is to buy a hardware device called a *DSL/cable modem NAT router* with a four-port or eight-port Ethernet switch. *NAT* stands for *Network Address Translation*, and the NAT router can translate many private IP addresses into a single, externally known IP address. The Ethernet switch part appears to you as a series of RJ-45 Ethernet ports where you can connect the PCs to set up a LAN. In other words, you need only one extra box besides the DSL or cable modem.

Figure 2-5 shows how you might connect your LAN to the Internet through a NAT router with a built-in Ethernet switch. You need a DSL or cable modem hookup for this scenario to work, and you must sign up with a DSL provider (for DSL service) or with a cable provider for cable Internet service.

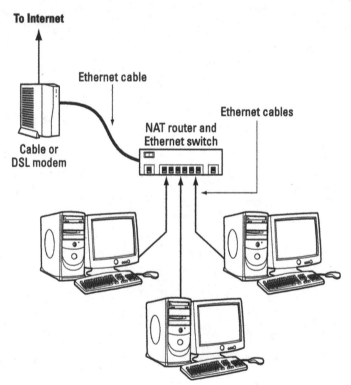

**FIGURE 2-5:** Connect your LAN to the Internet through a NAT router with a built-in Ethernet hub.

When you connect a LAN to the Internet, the NAT router acts as a gateway for your LAN. The NAT router also dynamically provides IP addresses to the PCs in your LAN. Therefore, on each PC, you have to set up the networking options to obtain the IP address dynamically.

If you're using DSL and incurring speeds slower than you should be (2 Mbps when it should be 5 Mbps, for example), try a different phone cord. Make sure that the phone cord that runs from the modem to the wall jack is no longer than 10 feet and doesn't go through a filter, surge protector, or splitter (which can attenuate the signal). All other phone devices (such as fax machines) should go through a filter or surge protector.

These days, most DSL and cable companies provide modems that have a wireless NAT router and a Gigabit Ethernet switch built into a single device. This allows you to connect either using wires or wireless signals to the modem, providing Internet connectivity to phones, tablets, laptops, gaming systems, and wired desktop computers.

# Chapter **3**

# Going Wireless

I f you have laptop computers on your local-area network (LAN), or if you don't want to run a rat's nest of wires to connect a PC to the LAN, you have the option of using a wireless Ethernet network. In a typical scenario, you have a cable modem or DSL connection to the Internet, and you want to connect one or more laptops with wireless network cards to access the Internet through the cable or DSL modem. This chapter shows you how to set up wireless networking for connecting to an Ethernet LAN and accessing the Internet.

## Understanding Wireless Ethernet Networks

*Wi-Fi* stands for *Wireless Fidelity* — a short-range wireless network similar to wired Ethernet networks. Standards from an organization known as IEEE (Institute of Electrical and Electronics Engineers) define the technical details of how Wi-Fi networks work. Manufacturers use these standards to build the components that you can buy to set up a wireless local-area network (WLAN).

The standard governing Wi-Fi networks has evolved swiftly. What started as 802.11a gave birth to 802.11b, and the two combined to make up 802.11g, which was superseded by 802.11n. But the purpose of every one of these standards was the same: to specify how the wireless Ethernet network works at the physical layer. You don't have to fret about the details of all those standards to set up a wireless network, but knowing some pertinent details is good so that you can buy the right kind of equipment for your wireless network.

The wireless Ethernet standards you'll likely encounter today have the following key characteristics:

» **802.11b:** Operates in the 2.4 GHz radio band (2.4 GHz to 2.4835 GHz) in up to three non-overlapping frequency bands or channels and supports a maximum bit rate of 11 Mbps per channel. One disadvantage of 802.11b is that the 2.4 GHz frequency band is crowded. Many devices (such as microwave ovens, cordless phones, medical and scientific equipment, and Bluetooth devices) work within the 2.4 GHz frequency band. Nevertheless, 802.11b is popular in corporate and home networks. Because of this and the slower speeds associated with it, the 802.11b standard isn't used these days except in older systems.

» **802.11a:** Operates in the 5 GHz radio band (5.725 GHz to 5.850 GHz) in up to eight non-overlapping channels and supports a maximum bit rate of 54 Mbps per channel. The 5 GHz band isn't as crowded as the 2.4 GHz band, making it a more popular choice these days. Products that conform to the 802.11a standard are on the market, and some wireless access points are designed to handle both 802.11a and 802.11b connections.

» **802.11g:** Supports up to a 54 Mbps data rate in the 2.4 GHz band (the same band that 802.11b uses). 802.11g achieves the higher bit rate by using a technology called OFDM (orthogonal frequency-division multiplexing), which is also used by 802.11a. Equipment that complies with 802.11g is on the market. 802.11g has generated excitement by working in the same band as 802.11b but promising much higher data rates — and by being backward-compatible with 802.11b devices. Vendors currently offer access points that can support both the 802.11b and 802.11g connection standards.

» **802.11n:** Approved in 2008, the goal of this standard is to significantly increase throughput in both the 2.4 GHz and the 5 GHz frequency range. The baseline goal was to reach speeds of 100 Mbps, but in theoretical conditions it can reach 600 Mbps. This became known as Wi-Fi 4 to avoid confusion with the previous 802.11 versions, which then started a trend of referring to wireless standards by their generational number rather than by the standard number.

» **802.11ac:** Also known as Wi-Fi 5, 802.11ac was approved as a standard in 2014. In essence, it is an extension of 802.11n but is a 5 GHz–only technology.

» **802.11ax:** Known as Wi-Fi 6, 802.11ax was approved in 2019 for both the 2.4 GHz and 5 GHz frequencies and can support data rates up to 9.6 Gbps. An additional standard, Wi-Fi 6e, includes support for the 6GHz frequency.

>> **802.11be:** At the time of this writing, 802.11be hasn't been officially approved yet, but it's expected to be the next standard, named Wi-Fi 7. It uses the 2.4 and 5.6 GHz frequencies and is expected to support data rates of up to 40 Gbps.

In all cases, the maximum data throughput that a user sees is much less than the channel's total capacity because all users of that radio channel share this capacity. Also, the data-transfer rate decreases as the distance increases between the user's PC and the wireless access point and when there are obstacles between the device and the wireless access point.

To play it safe, though, go with 802.11ac, with its supported data rates five times the existing throughput and double the range of previous standards.

**TIP**

An 802.11g access point can communicate with older (and slower) 802.11b devices. You can also consider a MIMO (multiple-input-multiple-output) access point, which supports multiple 802.11 standards and implements techniques for getting higher throughputs and better range.

**REMEMBER**

To find out more about wireless Ethernet, visit www.wi-fi.org, the home page of the Wi-Fi Alliance, which is the not-for-profit international association formed in 1999 to certify interoperability of wireless LAN products based on IEEE 802.11 standards.

## Understanding infrastructure and ad hoc modes

The 802.11 standard defines two modes of operation for wireless Ethernet networks: ad hoc and infrastructure. *Ad hoc* mode is simply two or more wireless Ethernet cards communicating with one another without an access point.

*Infrastructure* mode refers to the approach in which all the wireless Ethernet cards communicate with one another and with the wired LAN through an access point. For the discussions in this chapter, I assume that you set your wireless Ethernet card to infrastructure mode. In the configuration files, this mode is referred to as *managed*.

## Understanding wireless security

As you would expect, sending data through the air does come with risks. Anyone with an antenna and the proper listening equipment (which is easy to obtain) can intercept wireless radio signals and snoop on data traffic. For this reason, including some type of encryption of the data with wireless transmissions is essential. This section walks you through the more common encryption methods you'll run into.

## Wired Equivalent Privacy (WEP)

The 802.11 standard includes Wired Equivalent Privacy (WEP) for protecting wireless communications from eavesdropping. WEP relies on a 40-bit or 104-bit secret key that's shared between a mobile station (such as a laptop with a wireless Ethernet card) and an access point (also called a *base station*). The secret key is used to encrypt data packets before they're transmitted, and an integrity check is performed to ensure that packets aren't modified in transit.

The 802.11 standard doesn't explain how the shared key is established. In practice, most wireless LANs use a single key that's shared by all its mobile stations and access points. Such an approach, however, doesn't scale up very well to an environment such as a college campus, because the keys are shared with all users — and you know how it is if you share a secret with hundreds of people. For that reason, WEP typically isn't used on large wireless networks, such as the ones at universities. In such wireless networks, you have to use other security approaches, such as SSH (Secure Shell) to log in to remote systems.

**WARNING**

With the increase in attacks and vulnerabilities with WEP, it's no longer recommended to use in wireless networks today.

## Wi-Fi Protected Access (WPA)

In 2003 the Wi-Fi Alliance published a specification called Wi-Fi Protected Access (WPA), which replaced the existing WEP standard and improved security by making some changes. Unlike WEP, which uses fixed keys, the WPA standard uses Temporal Key Integrity Protocol (TKIP), which generates new keys for every 10 KB of data transmitted over the network and makes WPA more difficult to break.

In 2004, the Wi-Fi Alliance introduced a follow-up called Wi-Fi Protected Access 2 (WPA2), the second generation of WPA security. WPA2 is based on the final IEEE 802.11i standard, which uses public key encryption with digital certificates and an authentication, authorization, and accounting RADIUS (Remote Authentication Dial-In User Service) server to provide better security for wireless Ethernet networks. WPA2 uses the Advanced Encryption Standard (AES) for data encryption.

In 2018, the Wi-Fi Alliance announced WPA3 as the official replacement for WPA2. It utilizes a 192-bit cryptographic algorithm and replaces the pre-shared keys (PSKs) used in WPA2 with the Simultaneous Authentication of Equals (SAE) exchange. Most Linux distributions support the WPA3 standards, so if your wireless equipment supports WPA3, it's a good idea to use it.

# Setting Up Wireless Hardware

To set up the wireless connection, you need a wireless access point (either connected to your Internet service device — such as a DSL or cable modem — or built into your Internet service device) and a wireless network interface in each PC. You can also set up an ad hoc wireless network among two or more PCs with wireless network cards. In this section, I focus on the scenario in which you want to set up a wireless connection to an established LAN that has a wired Internet connection through a cable modem or DSL.

In addition to the wireless access point, you need a cable modem or DSL connection to the Internet, along with a Network Access Translation (NAT) router and hub, as described in Book 3, Chapters 1 and 2. Figure 3-1 shows a typical setup for wireless Internet access through an existing cable modem or DSL connection.

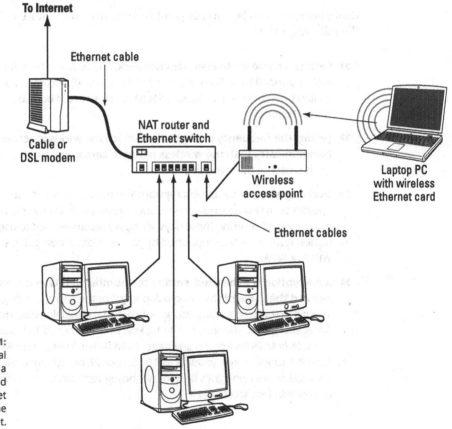

**FIGURE 3-1:** Typical connection of a mixed wired and wireless Ethernet LAN to the Internet.

As Figure 3-1 shows, the LAN has both wired and wireless PCs. In this example, a cable or DSL modem connects the LAN to the Internet through a NAT router and switch. Laptops with wireless network cards connect to the LAN through a wireless access point attached to one of the RJ-45 ports on the switch. To connect desktop PCs to this wireless network, you can use a USB wireless network card (which connects to a USB port).

TIP

These days, most DSL and cable companies provide modems that have a wireless router and Gigabit Ethernet switch built into a single device. Check with your Internet service provider (ISP) to see what your options are when connecting to their service.

# Configuring the Wireless Access Point

Configuring the wireless access point (commonly called an AP or WAP) involves the following tasks:

>> **Setting a name for the wireless network:** The technical term for this name is the Extended Basic Service Set ID (ESSID), but WAP documentation and utilities often refer to it as Service Set ID (SSID), because both identify the same network.

>> **Setting the frequency or channel on which the wireless access point communicates with the wireless network cards:** The access point and the cards must use the same channel.

>> **Deciding whether to use encryption:** You usually have a number of options and can even choose to go without any encryption at all or implement one or more levels of security. These days, it's highly recommended to use the highest level of security supported by your wireless access point, such as WPA3 or WPA2.

>> **If encryption is to be used, setting the number of bits in the encryption key and the value of the encryption key:** For the encryption key, 24 bits are internal to the access point; you specify only the remaining bits. Thus, for 64-bit encryption, you specify a 40-bit key, which comes to 10 hexadecimal digits. (A *hexadecimal digit* is an integer from 0–9 or a letter from A–F.) For a 128-bit encryption key, you specify 104 bits, or 26 hexadecimal digits. This is yet another area where it's best to use the highest level of security supported by your wireless access point.

>> **Setting the access method that wireless network cards must use when connecting to the access point:** You can opt for the open-access or shared-key method. The open-access method is typical (even when encryption is used).

>> **Setting the wireless access point to operate in infrastructure (managed) mode:** You use this mode to connect wireless network cards to an existing Ethernet LAN.

**REMEMBER**

The exact method of configuring a wireless access point depends on the device's make and model; the vendor provides instructions for configuring the wireless access point. Typically, you work through a graphical client application on a Windows PC to do the configuration or a web-based interface for WAP. If you enable encryption, make note of the encryption key; you must specify that same key for each wireless network card on your laptop or desktop computers.

# Configuring Wireless Networks

For most Linux desktops, connecting to a wireless network couldn't be easier. Thanks to the NetworkManager application (which most Linux distributions use these days), all you need to know is your Wi-Fi name, and the user ID/password combination required to connect to it.

For example, in Ubuntu, the wireless icon appears in the upper-right corner of the desktop in the system tray. When you click it, a dialog box appears, showing all the wireless networks the wireless card detects, as shown in Figure 3-2.

After you select the appropriate wireless network, a dialog box appears prompting you for the user ID and password to connect (you did remember to enable encryption on your wireless access point, didn't you?). After you're connected, you can use the NetworkManager application to view the wireless settings or make any changes, as shown in Figure 3-3.

With NetworkManager, connecting to any wireless network is a breeze!

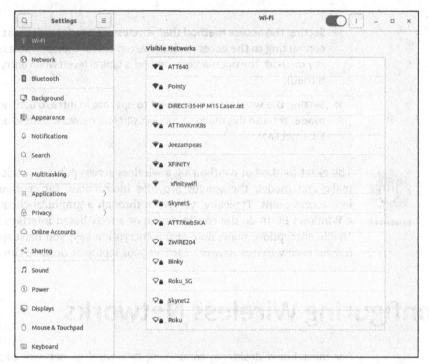

**FIGURE 3-2:**
The wireless
network list
dialog box
in Ubuntu.

**FIGURE 3-3:**
The Ubuntu
NetworkManager
wireless
connections
dialog box.

# Chapter **4**

# Managing the Network

These days, it's almost a necessity to have your Linux system connected to some type of network. Whether it's because of the need to share files and printers on a local network or the need to connect to the Internet to download updates and security patches, most Linux systems have some type of network connection. This chapter looks at how to configure your Linux system to connect to a network, as well as how to troubleshoot network connections if things go wrong.

## Configuring Network Features

There are five main pieces of information you need to configure in your Linux system to interact on a network:

» The host address

» The network subnet address

» The default router (sometimes called the *gateway*)

» The system hostname

» A Domain Name System (DNS) server address for resolving hostnames

That's a lot of information to handle, and to top it off, there are three different ways to configure this information in Linux systems:

>> Manually editing network configuration files

>> Using a graphical tool included with your Linux distribution

>> Using command-line tools

The following sections walk you through each of these methods.

## Manually editing network configuration files

Every Linux distribution uses network configuration files to define the network settings required to communicate on the network. Unfortunately, there's not a single standard configuration file that all distributions use. Instead, different distributions use different configuration files to define the network settings.

Table 4-1 shows the most common network configuration files that you'll run into.

**TABLE 4-1** **Linux Network Configuration Files**

| Distribution | Network Configuration Location |
| --- | --- |
| Debian based | /etc/network/interfaces file |
| Red Hat based | /etc/sysconfig/network-scripts directory |
| openSUSE | /etc/sysconfig/network file |

Each of the Linux distributions uses a different method of defining the network settings, but they all have similar features. Most configuration files define each of the required network settings as separate values in the configuration file. Here's an example from a Debian-based system:

```
auto eth0
iface eth0 inet static
    address 192.168.1.77
    netmask 255.255.255.0
    gateway 192.168.1.254
iface eth0 inet6 static
```

```
address 2003:aef0::23d1::0a10:00a1
netmask 64
gateway 2003:aef0::23d1::0a10:0001
```

In this example, the configuration assigns both an Internet Protocol (IP) and an Internet Protocol version 6 (IPv6) address to the wired network interface designated as eth0.

If your network uses the Dynamic Host Configuration Protocol (DHCP) to automatically assign IP addresses to devices, the configuration gets a lot simpler:

```
auto eth0
iface eth0 inet dhcp
iface eth0 inet6 dhcp
```

**TIP** Since version 17.04, the Ubuntu distribution has deviated from the standard Debian method and has utilized the Netplan tool to manage network settings. Netplan uses simple YAML text files in the /etc/netplan folder to define the network settings for each network interface installed on the system. By default, Netplan just passes the network settings off to the NetworkManager tool, so you don't need to worry about how the Netplan configuration files are set.

For Red Hat–based systems, you'll need to define the network settings in multiple files, one for each network interface. The format of each filename is

```
ifcfg-interface
```

where *interface* is the device name for the network adapter, such as ifcfg-enp0s3. Here's an example from a Rocky Linux system:

```
TYPE=Ethernet
PROXY_METHOD=none
BROWSER_ONLY=no
BOOTPROTO=dhcp
DEFROUTE=yes
IPV4_FAILURE_FATAL=no
IPV6INIT=yes
IPV6_AUTOCONF=yes
IPV6_DEFROUTE=yes
IPV6_FAILURE_FATAL=no
IPV6_ADDR_GEN_MODE=stable-privacy
NAME=enp0s3
UUID=c8752366-3e1e-47e3-8162-c0435ec6d451
DEVICE=enp0s3
```

```
ONBOOT=yes
IPV6_PRIVACY=no
```

This configuration indicates that the workstation is using the DHCP process to automatically retrieve network information from a network server. For static IP addresses, you can set the IP address, default gateway, and subnet mask in the configuration file.

Most Linux distributions use the `/etc/hostname` file to store the local hostname of the system but some use `/etc/HOSTNAME` instead. You also need to define a DNS server so the system can resolve DNS hostnames. Fortunately, this is a standard that all Linux systems follow and is handled in the `/etc/resolv.conf` configuration file:

```
domain mydomain.com
search mytest.com
nameserver 192.168.1.1
```

The domain entry defines the domain name assigned to the network. By default, the system will append this domain name to any hostnames you specify. The search entry defines any additional domains used to search for hostnames. The `nameserver` entry is where you specify the DNS server assigned to your network. Some networks can have more than one DNS server; just add multiple `nameserver` entries in the file.

**TIP**

For systems using the Systemd startup method, you can use the `hostnamectl` command to view or change the hostname information. Also, to help speed up connections to commonly used hosts, you can manually enter their hostnames and IP addresses into the `/etc/hosts` file on your Linux system. The `/etc/nsswitch.conf` file defines whether the Linux system checks this file before or after using DNS to look up the hostname.

## Using a graphical tool

If the configuration files in the preceding section look like gibberish to you, don't run away screaming just yet — life can be easier! The NetworkManager tool is a popular program used by many Linux distributions to provide a graphical user interface (GUI) for defining network connections. The NetworkManager tool starts automatically at boot time and appears in the system tray area of the desktop as an icon.

If your system detects a wired network connection, the icon appears as a mini network with blocks connected together. If your system detects an available wireless network connection, the icon appears as an empty radio signal.

To view or edit the network connection settings for the system, follow these steps:

1. **Click the NetworkManager icon in the system tray.**

   You see a list of the available wireless networks detected by the network card (see Figure 4-1).

2. **Click your wireless network to select it from the list.**

   If your wireless network is using encryption, you'll be prompted to enter the password to gain access to the network.

   When your system is connected to a wireless network, the NetworkManager icon appears as a radio signal.

   TIP

3. **Whether you're connected to a wired or wireless network, click the Settings entry in the system menu.**

4. **Select the Network tab, and then click the gear icon to view or edit the network connection settings for the system (see Figure 4-2).**

5. **Select the network connection you want to configure (either wireless or wired), and then click the Edit button to change the current configuration.**

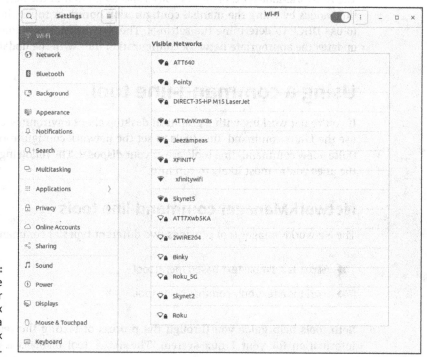

**FIGURE 4-1:**
The NetworkManager dialog box showing a wireless network connection.

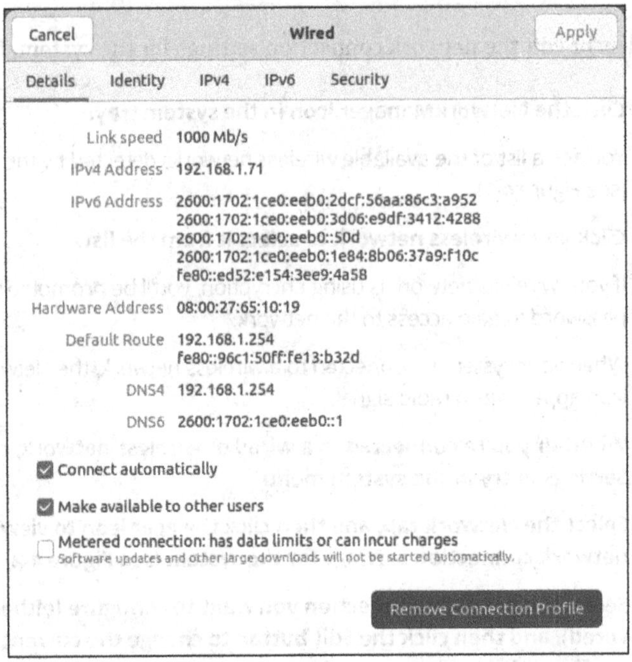

| Cancel | **Wired** | Apply |

Details    Identity    IPv4    IPv6    Security

Link speed    1000 Mb/s

IPv4 Address    192.168.1.71

IPv6 Address    2600:1702:1ce0:eeb0:2dcf:56aa:86c3:a952
2600:1702:1ce0:eeb0:3d06:e9df:3412:4288
2600:1702:1ce0:eeb0::50d
2600:1702:1ce0:eeb0:1e84:8b06:37a9:f10c
fe80::ed52:e154:3ee9:4a58

Hardware Address    08:00:27:65:10:19

Default Route    192.168.1.254
fe80::96c1:50ff:fe13:b32d

DNS4    192.168.1.254

DNS6    2600:1702:1ce0:eeb0::1

☑ Connect automatically

☑ Make available to other users

☐ Metered connection: has data limits or can incur charges
Software updates and other large downloads will not be started automatically.

Remove Connection Profile

**FIGURE 4-2:**
The Network
Connections
dialog box.

The NetworkManager tool allows you to specify all four of the network configuration values by using the manual configuration option or to set the configuration to use DHCP to determine the settings. The NetworkManager tool automatically updates the appropriate network configuration files with the updated settings.

## Using a command-line tool

If you're not working with a graphical desktop client environment, you'll need to use the Linux command-line tools to set the network configuration information. Quite a few command-line tools are at your disposal. The following sections cover the ones you're most likely to run into.

### NetworkManager command-line tools

The NetworkManager tool provides two different types of command-line tools:

» nmtui is a simple text-based menu tool.

» nmcli is a text-only command-line tool.

Both tools help guide you through the process of setting the required network information for your Linux system. The nmtui tool displays a stripped-down version of the graphical tool where you can select a network interface and assign network properties to it, as shown in Figure 4-3.

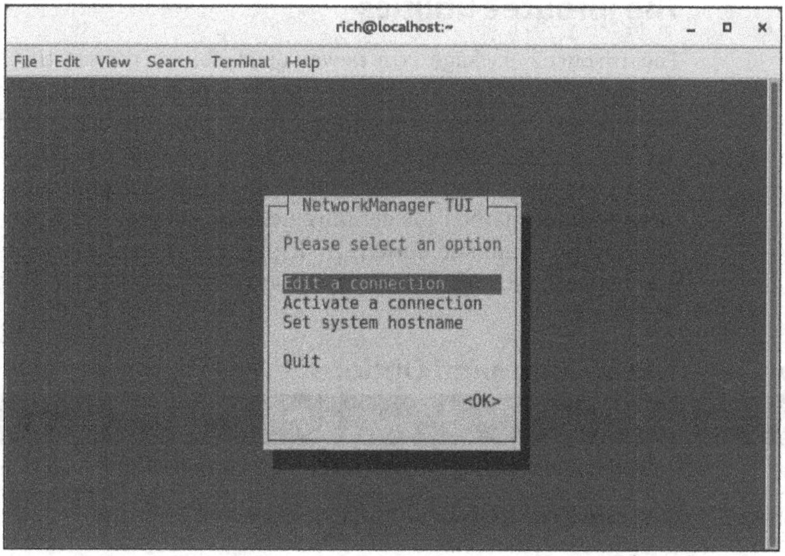

Managing the Network

FIGURE 4-3:
The
NetworkManager
nmtui
command-line
tool.

The nmcli tool doesn't use any type of graphics capabilities; it just has a command-line interface where you can view and change the network settings. By default, the command displays the current network devices and their settings, as follows:

```
$ nmcli
enp0s3: connected to enp0s3
        "Intel 82540EM Gigabit Ethernet Controller (PRO/1000 MT Desktop Adapter)
        ethernet (e1000), 08:00:27:73:1C:6D, hw, mtu 1500
        ip4 default
        inet4 10.0.2.15/24
        route4 0.0.0.0/0
        route4 10.0.2.0/24
        inet6 fe80::5432:eddb:51ea:fb44/64
        route6 ff00::/8
        route6 fe80::/64
        route6 fe80::/64
```

The nmcli command uses command-line options to allow you to set the network settings:

```
# nmcli con add type ethernet conname eth1 ifname enp0s3 ip4
10.0.2.10/24 gw4 192.168.1.254
```

This allows you to set all the necessary network configuration features in a single nmcli command.

## The iproute2 utilities

The iproute2 package is a newer open-source project that contains a set of command-line utilities for managing network connections. Although the package contains several different programs, the ip program is the most used.

The ip command is the Swiss army knife of network programs. It's becoming the more popular method for defining network settings from the command line. It uses several command options to display the current network settings or define new network settings. Table 4-2 shows these commands.

**TABLE 4-2**   The ip **Command Options**

| Parameter | Description |
|---|---|
| address | Display or set the Internet Protocol version 4 (IPv4) or IPv6 address on the device. |
| addrlabel | Define configuration labels. |
| l2tp | Tunnel Ethernet over IP. |
| link | Define a network device. |
| maddress | Define a multicast address for the system to listen to. |
| monitor | Watch for netlink messages. |
| mroute | Define an entry in the multicast routing cache. |
| mrule | Define a rule in the multicast routing policy database. |
| neighbor | Manage Address Resolution Protocol (ARP) or IPv6 Neighbor Discovery (NDISC) cache entries. |
| netns | Manage network namespaces. |
| ntable | Manage the neighbor cache operation. |
| route | Manage the routing table. |
| rule | Manage entries in the routing policy database. |
| tcpmetrics | Manage Transmission Control Protocol (TCP) metrics on the interface. |
| Token | Manage tokenized interface identifiers. |
| Tunnel | Tunnel over IP. |
| Tuntap | Manage tunneled or tapped (TUN/TAP) devices. |
| xfrm | Manage Internet Protocol Security (IPSec) policies for secure connections. |

Each command option utilizes parameters to define what to do, such as display network settings or modify existing network settings. This example demonstrates how to display the current network settings using the show parameter:

```
$ ip address show
1: lo: <LOOPBACK,UP,LOWER_UP> mtu 65536 qdisc noqueue state UNKNOWN group
default qlen 1000
    link/loopback 00:00:00:00:00:00 brd 00:00:00:00:00:00
    inet 127.0.0.1/8 scope host lo
       valid_lft forever preferred_lft forever
    inet6 ::1/128 scope host
       valid_lft forever preferred_lft forever
2: enp0s3: <BROADCAST,MULTICAST,UP,LOWER_UP> mtu 1500 qdisc pfifo_fast
state UP group default qlen 1000
    link/ether 08:00:27:73:1c:6d brd ff:ff:ff:ff:ff:ff
    inet 10.0.2.15/24 brd 10.0.2.255 scope global noprefixroute dynamic
enp0s3
       valid_lft 84411sec preferred_lft 84411sec
    inet6 fe80::5432:eddb:51ea:fb44/64 scope link noprefixroute
       valid_lft forever preferred_lft forever
$
```

This example shows two network interfaces on the Linux system:

>> lo: The local loopback interface. lo is a special virtual network interface. Any local program can use it to communicate with other programs on the system just as if they were across a network, which can simplify transferring data between programs.

>> enp0s3: A wired network interface. The enp0s3 network interface is the wired network connection for the Linux system. The ip command shows the IP address assigned to the interface (there's both an IP and an IPv6 link local address assigned), the netmask value, and some basic statistics about the packets on the interface.

If the output doesn't show a network address assigned to the interface, you can use the ip command with the add parameter to specify the host address and netmask values for the interface:

```
# ip address add 10.0.2.15/24 dev enp0s3
```

Then use the ip command with the route option to set the default router for the network interface:

```
# ip route add default via 192.168.1.254 dev enp0s3
```

Finally, make the network interface active by using the `link` option:

```
# ip link set enp0s3 up
```

With the single `ip` command you can manage just about everything you need for your network connections.

# Basic Network Troubleshooting

After you have your Linux network setting configured, there are a few things you can do to check to make sure things are operating properly. The following sections walk through the commands you should know to monitor the network activity, including watching what processes are listening on the network and what connections are active from your system.

One way to test network connectivity is to send test packets to known hosts. Linux provides the `ping` and `ping6` commands to do that. The `ping` and `ping6` commands send Internet Control Message Protocol (ICMP) packets to remote hosts using either the IPv4 (`ping`) or IPv6 (`ping6`) protocol. ICMP packets work behind the scenes to track connectivity and provide control messages between systems. If the remote host supports ICMP, it will send a reply packet back when it receives a ping packet.

**WARNING**

Unfortunately, these days, many hosts don't support ICMP packets because they can be used to create a denial-of-service (DoS) attack against the host. Don't be surprised if you try to ping a remote host and don't get any response. Usually, pinging a big-name website such as www.google.com will provide a response.

The basic format for the `ping` command is to specify the IP address of the remote host:

```
$ ping 10.0.2.2
PING 10.0.2.2 (10.0.2.2) 56(84) bytes of data.
64 bytes from 10.0.2.2: icmp_seq=1 ttl=63 time=14.6 ms
64 bytes from 10.0.2.2: icmp_seq=2 ttl=63 time=3.82 ms
64 bytes from 10.0.2.2: icmp_seq=3 ttl=63 time=2.05 ms
64 bytes from 10.0.2.2: icmp_seq=4 ttl=63 time=0.088 ms
64 bytes from 10.0.2.2: icmp_seq=5 ttl=63 time=3.54 ms
64 bytes from 10.0.2.2: icmp_seq=6 ttl=63 time=3.97 ms
```

```
64 bytes from 10.0.2.2: icmp_seq=7 ttl=63 time=0.040 ms
^C
--- 10.0.2.2 ping statistics ---
7 packets transmitted, 7 received, 0% packet loss, time 6020ms
rtt min/avg/max/mdev = 0.040/4.030/14.696/4.620 ms
$
```

The ping command continues sending packets until you press Ctrl+C. You can also use the –c command-line option to specify a set number of packets to send and then stop.

For the ping6 command, things get a little more complicated. If you're using an IPv6 link local address, you also need to tell the command which interface to send the packets out on:

```
$ ping6 –c 4 fe80::c418:2ed0:aead:cbce%enp0s3
PING fe80::c418:2ed0:aead:cbce%enp0s3(fe80::c418:2ed0:aead:cbce)
56 data bytes
64 bytes from fe80::c418:2ed0:aead:cbce: icmp_seq=1 ttl=128 time=1.47 ms
64 bytes from fe80::c418:2ed0:aead:cbce: icmp_seq=2 ttl=128 time=0.478 ms
64 bytes from fe80::c418:2ed0:aead:cbce: icmp_seq=3 ttl=128 time=0.777 ms
64 bytes from fe80::c418:2ed0:aead:cbce: icmp_seq=4 ttl=128 time=0.659 ms

--- fe80::c418:2ed0:aead:cbce%enp0s3 ping statistics ---
4 packets transmitted, 4 received, 0% packet loss, time 3003ms
rtt min/avg/max/mdev = 0.478/0.847/1.475/0.378 ms
$
```

The %enp0s3 part tells the system to send the ping packets out on the enp0s3 network interface for the link local address.

Yet another useful tool is the traceroute command, which utilizes a feature of ICMP packets that restrict the number of network "hops" they can make. By manipulating that value in the packet, the traceroute command allows you to see the network routers used to get the packets from the client to the server.

Finally, the mtr program is a package that utilizes data retrieved from ping and traceroute commands to document network availability and latency in a real-time chart. Figure 4-4 shows the output of the mtr command tracing the connectivity to the linux.org server.

```
┌─┐                          rich@localhost:~                              ×
File  Edit  View  Search  Terminal  Help
                         My traceroute  [v0.92]
localhost.localdomain (10.0.2.15)
Keys:  Help   Display mode   Restart statistics   Order oт гieιds   quit
                                      Packets                Pings
Host                                 Loss%   Snt   Last   Avg  Best  Wrst StDev
 1. _gateway                          0.0%    47    0.7   0.9   0.4   6.9   1.0
 2. homeportal                        4.3%    47    5.0  69.3   3.8 2398. 357.1
 3. 75-27-164-1.lightspeed.iplsin.sb  4.3%    47   21.7  27.5  20.9  91.4  15.8
 4. 71.152.230.45                     4.3%    47   22.7  24.0  20.6  48.9   4.5
 5. ???
 6. 32.130.17.213                     4.3%    47   33.5  32.7  27.7  42.7   2.9
 7. ae16.cr7-chi1.ip4.gtt.net         8.5%    47   46.3  35.5  26.5  58.8   8.3
 8. ae21.cr9-chi1.ip4.gtt.net         6.4%    47   29.5  30.9  26.8  44.7   4.5
 9. ip4.gtt.net                       8.5%    47   78.9  49.6  27.2 127.9  25.9
10. 141.101.73.22                     6.4%    47   73.3  80.7  30.0 223.8  45.2
11. 172.67.201.246                    6.4%    47   29.4  37.9  27.4 192.0  28.5
```

**FIGURE 4-4:**
Using `mtr` to monitor network connectivity to a server.

# Advanced Network Troubleshooting

Besides the simple network tests shown in the preceding section, Linux has some more advanced programs that can provide more detailed information about the network environment. Sometimes it helps to be able to see just what network connections are active on a Linux system. The `netstat` command is a popular tool used by Linux system administrators to get a handle on what network connections are live on the Linux system.

The `netstat` command is part of the `net-tools` package and can provide a wealth of network information for you. By default, it lists all the open network connections on the system:

```
# netstat
Active Internet connections (w/o servers)
Proto Recv-Q Send-Q Local Address          Foreign Address         State
Active UNIX domain sockets (w/o servers)
Proto RefCnt Flags       Type       State         I-Node  Path
unix  2      [ ]         DGRAM                     10825
   @/org/freedesktop/systemd1/notify
unix  2      [ ]         DGRAM                     10933
   /run/systemd/shutdownd
unix  6      [ ]         DGRAM                     6609
   /run/systemd/journal/socket
unix  25     [ ]         DGRAM                     6611    /dev/log
unix  3      [ ]         STREAM     CONNECTED      25693
```

```
unix  3      [ ]           STREAM     CONNECTED     20770
  /var/run/dbus/system_bus_socket
unix  3      [ ]           STREAM     CONNECTED     19556
unix  3      [ ]           STREAM     CONNECTED     19511
unix  2      [ ]           DGRAM                    24125
unix  3      [ ]           STREAM     CONNECTED     19535
unix  3      [ ]           STREAM     CONNECTED     18067
  /var/run/dbus/system_bus_socket
unix  3      [ ]           STREAM     CONNECTED     32358
unix  3      [ ]           STREAM     CONNECTED     24818
  /var/run/dbus/system_bus_socket
...
```

The netstat command produces lots of output because there are normally lots of programs that use network services on Linux systems. You can limit the output to just TCP or User Datagram Protocol (UDP) connections by using the –t command-line option for TCP connections or –u for UDP connections:

```
$ netstat -t
Active Internet connections (w/o servers)
Proto Recv-Q Send-Q Local Address         Foreign Address          State
tcp   1      0 10.0.2.15:58630            productsearch.ubu:https  CLOSE_WAIT
tcp6  1      0 ip6-localhost:57782        ip6-localhost:ipp        CLOSE_WAIT
$
```

You can also get a list of which applications are listening on which network ports by using the –l option:

```
$ netstat -l
Active Internet connections (only servers)
Proto Recv-Q Send-Q Local Address         Foreign Address      State
tcp   0      0 ubuntu02:domain           *:*                  LISTEN
tcp   0      0 localhost:ipp             *:*                  LISTEN
tcp6  0      0 ip6-localhost:ipp         [::]:*               LISTEN
udp   0      0 *:ipp                     *:*
udp   0      0 *:mdns                    *:*
udp   0      0 *:36355                   *:*
udp   0      0 ubuntu02:domain           *:*
udp   0      0 *:bootpc                  *:*
udp   0      0 *:12461                   *:*
udp6  0      0 [::]:64294                [::]:*
udp6  0      0 [::]:60259                [::]:*
udp6  0      0 [::]:mdns                 [::]:*
...
```

As you can see, just a standard Linux workstation can have lots of services running in the background, waiting for connections.

Yet another great feature of the `netstat` command is that the `-s` option displays statistics for the different types of packets the system has used on the network:

```
# netstat -s
Ip:
    240762 total packets received
    0 forwarded
    0 incoming packets discarded
    240747 incoming packets delivered
    206940 requests sent out
    32 dropped because of missing route
Icmp:
    57 ICMP messages received
    0 input ICMP message failed.
    ICMP input histogram:
        destination unreachable: 12
        timeout in transit: 38
        echo replies: 7
    7 ICMP messages sent
    0 ICMP messages failed
    ICMP output histogram:
        echo request: 7
IcmpMsg:
        InType0: 7
        InType3: 12
        InType11: 38
        OutType8: 7
Tcp:
    286 active connections openings
    0 passive connection openings
    0 failed connection attempts
    0 connection resets received
    0 connections established
    239933 segments received
    206091 segments send out
    0 segments retransmited
    0 bad segments received.
    0 resets sent
Udp:
    757 packets received
    0 packets to unknown port received.
    0 packet receive errors
    840 packets sent
    0 receive buffer errors
    0 send buffer errors
UdpLite:
TcpExt:
    219 TCP sockets finished time wait in fast timer
```

```
    15 delayed acks sent
    26 delayed acks further delayed because of locked socket
    Quick ack mode was activated 1 times
    229343 packet headers predicted
    289 acknowledgments not containing data payload received
    301 predicted acknowledgments
    TCPRcvCoalesce: 72755
IpExt:
    InNoRoutes: 2
    InMcastPkts: 13
    OutMcastPkts: 15
    InOctets: 410722578
    OutOctets: 8363083
    InMcastOctets: 2746
    OutMcastOctets: 2826
#
```

The netstat statistics output can give you a rough idea of how busy your Linux system is on the network or if there's a specific issue with one of the protocols installed.

# 4

# Administration

# Contents at a Glance

# Chapter **1**

# Working with the Shell

Sometimes, things don't work perfectly and problems pop up. What do you do if, because of those problems, the graphical user interface (GUI) desktop stops responding to your mouse clicks? What do you do if the GUI won't start at all? All is not lost: You can still tell your Linux system what to do, but you have to do so by typing commands in a text screen. In these situations, you work with the shell — the Linux command interpreter. This chapter introduces the Bash shell, the default shell in most Linux distributions.

After you figure out how to work with the shell, you may even begin to like the simplicity and power of the Linux commands. Then, even if you're a GUI aficionado, someday soon you may find yourself firing up a terminal window and making the system sing and dance with two- or three-letter commands strung together by strange punctuation characters. (Hey, I can dream, can't I?)

## Opening Terminal Windows and Virtual Consoles

First things first. If you're working in a GUI desktop, such as GNOME or KDE Plasma, where do you type commands for the shell? Good question.

The easiest way to get to the shell is to open a *terminal* (also called *console*) window. The terminal application you use depends, of course, on your desktop:

>> **Terminal:** The default terminal program used in the GNOME 3 desktop

>> **Konsole:** The default terminal program used in the KDE Plasma desktop

To start Terminal from the GNOME 3 application launcher, select the Terminal icon, or if you don't see it, type **Terminal** in the search textbox (in Ubuntu you can also right-click anywhere on the desktop and select Open Terminal). Once you start Terminal you'll see an interface, as shown in Figure 1-1.

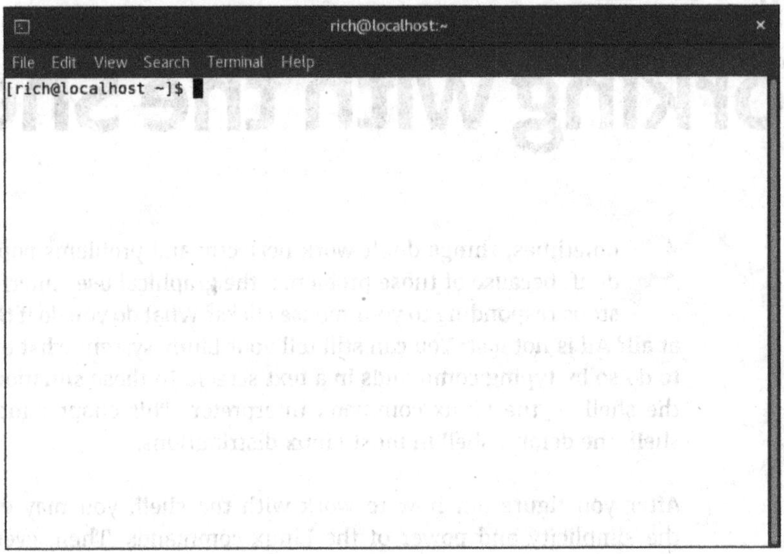

```
                          rich@localhost:~                           ×
  File  Edit  View  Search  Terminal  Help
[rich@localhost ~]$
```

**FIGURE 1-1:**
The GNOME
Terminal window.

Notice the prompt in the upper-left corner of the window. That's the shell command prompt, waiting for you to enter shell commands.

In the KDE Plasma world, choose K menu⇨Applications⇨System⇨Konsole. The Konsole interface is shown in Figure 1-2.

Again, you'll see the shell command prompt in the upper-left corner of the window. Besides just allowing you to type commands, both Terminal and Konsole have a few additional cool features that can come in handy, such as cutting and pasting text and changing the color of the text and background.

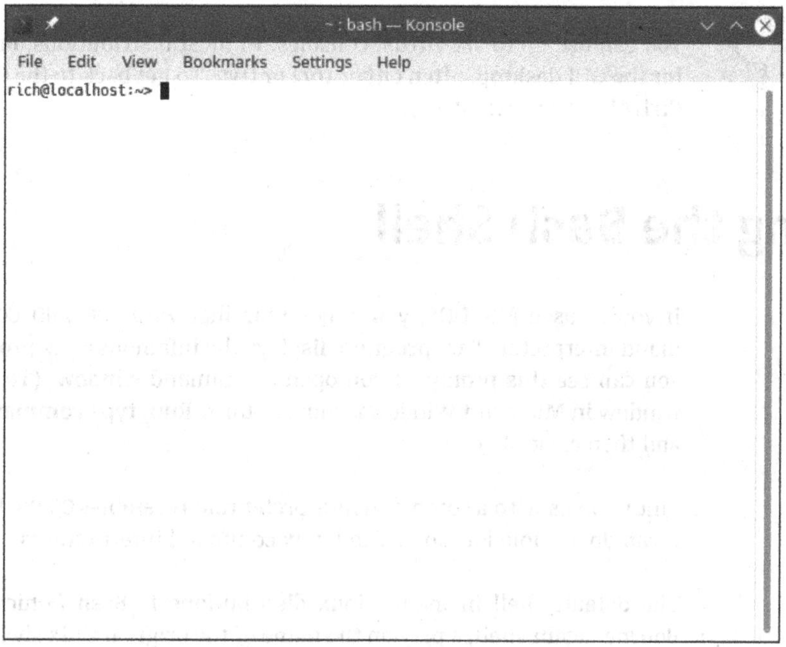

**FIGURE 1-2:**
The KDE Plasma Konsole window.

If for some reason the GUI seems to be *hung* (you click and type, but nothing happens), you can turn to the virtual consoles. (The physical console is the monitor-and-keyboard combination.) Virtual consoles enable you to switch among several text consoles even though you have only one physical console. Whether or not you're running a GUI, you can use different text consoles to type different commands.

To get to the first virtual console from the GNOME or KDE Plasma desktop, press Ctrl+Alt+F3. This produces a simple text-only window with a login prompt:

```
Ubuntu 22.04 LTS testbox tty3

testbox login:
```

Just type your user ID, press Enter, type your password when prompted, and press Enter. After you log in, you'll see the familiar shell command prompt:

```
rich@testbox:~$
```

Most Linux distributions include six virtual consoles, which you can access by pressing Ctrl+Alt+F#, where the # is the console number from 3 to 8. Each virtual console is a text screen where you can log in and type Linux commands to perform various tasks. When you're finished, type **exit** to log out.

**TIP**

You can use up to six virtual consoles. In most distributions, one console is used for the GUI desktop, often either tty2 or tty7. To get back to the GUI desktop, press Ctrl+Alt+F2 or Ctrl+Alt+F7.

# Using the Bash Shell

If you've used MS-DOS, you may be familiar with COMMAND.COM, the DOS command interpreter. That program displays the infamous C:\> prompt. In Windows, you can see this prompt if you open a command window. (To open a command window in Microsoft Windows, choose Start➪ Run, type **command** in the text box, and then click OK.)

Linux comes with a command interpreter that resembles COMMAND.COM in DOS, but it can do a whole lot more. The Linux command interpreter is called a *shell*.

The default shell in many Linux distributions is Bash (which is short for the Bourne-again shell, a play on the name of the original Unix shell's creator). When you open a terminal window or log in at a text console, the Bash shell is what prompts you for commands. Then, when you type a command, the shell executes your command.

**TECHNICAL STUFF**

Just as multiple GUIs (GNOME or KDE Plasma) are available for Linux, you have a choice of shells other than Bash. Some people prefer the C shell, for example as it supports many programming features found in the C language. You can easily change your default shell by using the chsh command (although you may need to install the other shells from your distribution's software repository first).

In addition to executing the standard Linux commands, Bash can execute any computer program. Type the name of an application at the shell prompt and the shell starts that application.

## Understanding the syntax of shell commands

Because a shell interprets what you type, knowing how the shell processes the text you enter is important. All shell commands have the following general format (but some commands have no options):

```
command [option1] [option2] ... [optionN]
```

Issuing such a command is a process commonly referred to as a *command line*. On a command line, you enter a command, followed by zero or more options (or *arguments*). These strings of options — the *command-line options* (or command-line arguments) — modify the way the command works so that you can get it to do specific tasks such as change the format of an output listing.

The shell uses a blank space or a tab to distinguish between the command and options, so you must use a space or a tab to separate the command from the options and the options from one another.

If an option contains spaces, you put that option inside quotation marks. To search for a name in the password file, for example, enter the following grep command (grep is used for searching for text in files):

```
grep "Ima Test" /etc/passwd
```

When grep prints the line with the name, it looks like this:

```
imatest:x:1001:1001:Ima Test,,,:/home/imatest:/bin/bash
```

If you create a user account with your username, type the grep command with your username as an argument to look for that username in the /etc/passwd file.

**TECHNICAL STUFF**

In the output from the grep command, you see the name of the shell (/bin/bash) following the last colon (:). Because the Bash shell is an executable file, it resides in the /bin directory where Linux stores most program files; you must provide the full path to it.

The number of command-line options and their format depend on the actual command. Typically, these options look like –X, where X is a single character. You can use the –l option with the ls command, for example. The command lists the contents of a directory, and the option provides additional details. Here's a result of typing **ls -l** in a user's home directory:

```
$ ls -l
total 36
drwxr-xr-x 2 imatest imatest 4096 Apr 26 19:48 Desktop
drwxr-xr-x 2 imatest imatest 4096 Apr 26 19:48 Documents
drwxr-xr-x 2 imatest imatest 4096 Apr 26 19:48 Downloads
drwxr-xr-x 2 imatest imatest 4096 Apr 26 19:48 Music
drwxr-xr-x 2 imatest imatest 4096 Apr 26 19:48 Pictures
drwxr-xr-x 2 imatest imatest 4096 Apr 26 19:48 Public
drwx------ 3 imatest imatest 4096 Apr 26 19:48 snap
drwxr-xr-x 2 imatest imatest 4096 Apr 26 19:48 Templates
```

```
drwxr-xr-x 2 imatest imatest 4096 Apr 26 19:48 Videos
$
```

If a command is too long to fit on a single line, you can allow the command to automatically wrap to the next line, or if you prefer, you can press the backslash key (\) followed by Enter and then continue typing the command on the next line. Type the following command, pressing Enter after each line:

```
cat \
/etc/passwd
```

The cat command displays the contents of the /etc/passwd file.

You can *concatenate* (string together) several shorter commands on a single line by separating the commands with semicolons (; ). The command

```
cd; ls -l; pwd
```

changes the current directory to your home directory, lists the contents of that directory, and then shows the name of that directory.

## Working with files

You can use the fancy graphical tools to copy, move, and delete files, but sometimes it's faster using shell commands — especially if you have lots of files to work with. For example, to copy a file, just use the cp command:

```
cp file1.txt file2.txt
```

This creates a copy of file1.txt and names it file2.txt. If you just want to rename a file, use the mv command (for move):

```
mv file2.txt file3.txt
```

This renames file2.txt to file3.txt. To delete a file, use the rm command (for remove):

```
rm file3.txt
```

This information may seem trivial when working with just a single file, but later on in the "Going wild with asterisks and question marks" section, I show you how to use wildcard characters in the filenames to help make copying or deleting lots of files a breeze.

# Combining shell commands

You can combine simple shell commands to create a more sophisticated command. Suppose that you want to find out whether a device file named cdrom resides in your system's /dev directory, because some programs automatically look for that generic device name rather than where the CD-ROM device is actually located. You can use the ls /dev command to get a directory listing of the /dev directory and then browse it to see whether that listing contains cdrom.

Unfortunately, the /dev directory has a great many entries, so you may find it hard to find any item with cdrom in its name. You can combine the ls command with grep, however, and come up with a command line that does exactly what you want. Here's that command line:

```
ls /dev | grep cdrom
```

The shell sends the output of the ls command (the directory listing) to the grep command, which searches for the string cdrom. That vertical bar ( | ) is known as a *pipe* because it acts as a conduit (think of a water pipe) between the two programs. The output of the first command is fed into the input of the second one.

# Controlling command input and output

Most Linux commands have a common feature: They always read from the *standard input* (usually, the keyboard) and write to the *standard output* (usually, the screen). Error messages are sent to the *standard error* (usually, to the screen as well). These three devices are often referred to as stdin, stdout, and stderr.

You can make a command get its input from a file and then send its output to another file. Just so you know, the highfalutin term for this feature is *input and output (I/O) redirection*.

Table 1-1 shows the syntax of common I/O redirection commands, and the next few sections explain how to use some of these commands.

## Getting command input from a file

If you want a command to get its instructions by reading from a file, you can redirect the standard input to come from that file instead of from the keyboard. The command

```
sort < /etc/passwd
```

**TABLE 1-1**

## Common Standard I/O Redirections

| Task | Command Syntax |
| --- | --- |
| Send stdout to a file. | *command > file* |
| Send stderr to file. | *command 2> file* |
| Send stdout and stderr to file. | *command > file 2>&1* |
| Read stdin from a file. | *command < file* |
| Read stdin from file.in and send stdout to file.out. | *command < file.in > file.out* |
| Append stdout to the end of a file. | *command >> file* |
| Append stderr to the end of a file. | *command 2>> file* |
| Append stdout and stderr to the end of a file. | *command >> file 2>&1* |
| Read stdin from the keyboard until the character c. | *command <<c* |
| Pipe stdout to command2. | *command | command2* |
| Pipe stdout and stderr to command2. | *command 2>&1 | command2* |

displays a sorted list of the lines in the /etc/passwd file (sorted in alphabetical order based on the text in each line). In this case, the less-than sign (<) redirects stdin so that the sort command reads its input from the /etc/passwd file.

## Saving command output in a file

To save the output of a command in a file, redirect the standard output to a file. Type **cd** to change to your home directory and then type the following command:

```
grep typedef /usr/include/* > typedef.out
```

This command searches all files in the /usr/include directory for the occurrence of the text typedef and then saves the output in a file called typedef.out. The greater-than sign (>) redirects stdout to a file. This command also illustrates another feature of Bash: When you use an asterisk (*), Bash replaces the asterisk with a list of all filenames in the specified directory. Therefore, /usr/include/* means all the files in the /usr/include directory.

TIP

If you want to append a command's output to the end of an existing file instead of saving the output in a new file, use two greater-than signs (>>), like this:

```
command >> filename
```

**TIP**

Another interesting way to send stdout to a file is to use the `cat` command to prepare small text files quickly. Suppose that you want to create a new text file to store lines of text you type until you type **ZZ** and press Enter. Here's how you can accomplish that task:

```
cat <<ZZ > input.txt
```

After you type this command, you can keep typing lines and then type **ZZ** on a line when you finish. Everything you type is saved in the file input.txt.

### Saving error messages in a file

Sometimes, when you type a command, it generates a lot of error messages that scroll by so fast that you can't tell what's going on. One way to see all the error messages is to save them in a file so that you can see what the heck happened. You can do that by redirecting stderr to a file.

Type the following command:

```
find / -name COPYING -print 2> finderr
```

This command looks through the file system for files named COPYING and saves all the error messages (if any) in the finderr file. The number 2 followed by the greater-than sign (2>) redirects stderr to a file.

**TIP**

If you want to discard the error messages instead of saving them in a file, use /dev/null as the filename, like this:

```
find / -name COPYING -print 2> /dev/null
```

**TECHNICAL STUFF**

That /dev/null is a special file (often called the *bit bucket* and sometimes glorified as the *Great Bit Bucket in the Sky*) that simply discards whatever it receives. Now you know what it means when you hear a phrase such as "Your mail probably ended up in the bit bucket."

## Going wild with asterisks and question marks

You have another way to avoid typing long filenames. (After all, making less work for users is why we use computers, isn't it?)

This particular trick involves using the asterisk (*) and question mark (?). These special characters are *wildcards* because they match zero or more characters in a line of text.

If you know MS-DOS, you may have used commands such as COPY *.* A: to copy all files from the current directory to the A: drive. Bash accepts similar wildcards in filenames. As you might expect, Bash provides many more wildcard options than the MS-DOS command interpreter does. Newer computers (particularly notebook computers and especially netbooks) don't have A and B drives anymore, of course, which deprives an entire generation of the fun of trying to copy a large file to floppy disks!

You can use three types of wildcards in Bash:

>> **Asterisk (*):** Matches zero or more characters in a filename. The asterisk denotes all files in a directory.

>> **Question mark (?):** Matches any single character. If you type **test?**, Bash matches any five-character text that begins with *test*.

>> **Set of characters in brackets:** Matches any single character from that set. The string [aB], for example, matches only files named a or B. The string [aB]*, though, matches any filename that starts with a or B.

Wildcards are handy when you want to do something to many files. To copy all the files from the /media/cdrom directory to the current directory, for example, type the following:

```
cp /media/cdrom/* .
```

Bash replaces the wildcard character * with the names of all the files in the /media/cdrom directory. The period at the end of the command represents the current directory.

You can use the asterisk with other parts of a filename to select a more specific group of files. Suppose that you want to use the grep command to search for the text typedef struct in all files of the /usr/include directory that meet the following criteria:

>> The filename starts with s.
>> The filename ends with .h.

The wildcard specification s*.h denotes all filenames that meet these criteria. Thus, you can perform the search with the following command:

```
grep "typedef struct" /usr/include/s*.h
```

The string contains a space that you want the grep command to find, so you have to enclose that string in quotation marks. That way, Bash doesn't try to interpret each word in that text as a separate command-line argument.

The question mark (?) matches a single character. Suppose that you have four files in the current directory: image1.pcx, image2.pcx, image3.pcx, and image4.pcx. To copy these files to the /personal/calendar directory, use the following command:

```
cp image?.pcx /personal/calendar
```

Bash replaces the single question mark with any single character and copies the four files to /personal/calendar.

The third wildcard format — [ ... ] — matches a single character from a specific set of characters enclosed in square brackets. You may want to combine this format with other wildcards to narrow the matching filenames to a smaller set. To see a list of all filenames in the /etc/X11/xdm directory that start with x or X, type the following command:

```
ls /etc/X11/xdm/[xX]*
```

# Discovering and Using Linux Commands

You type Linux commands at the shell prompt. By *Linux commands*, I mean some of the commands that the Bash shell understands as well as the command-line utilities that come with Linux. In this section, I introduce a few major categories of Linux commands.

I can't cover every single Linux command in this chapter, but I want to give you a feel for the breadth of the commands by showing you common Linux commands. Table 1-2 lists common Linux commands by category. Before you start memorizing any Linux commands, browse this table.

**TABLE 1-2    Essential Linux Commands**

| Command Name | Action |
|---|---|
| **Finding help and abbreviations** | |
| apropos | Finds online manual pages for a specified keyword. |
| info | Displays online help information about a specified command. |
| man | Displays online help information. |
| whatis | Searches for complete words only and finds the online manual pages. |
| alias | Defines an abbreviation for a long command. |
| type | Shows the type and location of a command. |
| unalias | Deletes an abbreviation defined with alias. |
| **Managing files and directories** | |
| cd | Changes the current directory. |
| chmod | Changes file permissions. |
| chown | Changes the file owner and group. |
| cp | Copies files. |
| ln | Creates symbolic links to files and directories. |
| ls | Displays the contents of a directory. |
| mkdir | Creates a directory. |
| mv | Renames a file and moves the file from one directory to another. |
| rm | Deletes files. |
| rmdir | Deletes directories. |
| pwd | Displays the current directory. |
| touch | Updates a file's time stamp. |
| **Finding files** | |
| find | Finds files based on specified criteria, such as name and size. |
| locate | Finds files by using a periodically updated filename database. (The database is created by the updatedb program.) |

| Command Name | Action |
|---|---|
| whereis | Finds files based in the typical directories where *executable* (also known as *binary*) files are located. |
| which | Finds files in the directories listed in the PATH environment variable. |
| **Processing files** | |
| cat | Displays a file in standard output (can be used to concatenate several files into one big file). |
| cut | Extracts specified sections from each line of text in a file. |
| dd | Copies blocks of data from one file to another (used to copy data from devices). |
| diff | Compares two text files and finds any differences. |
| expand | Converts all tabs to spaces. |
| file | Displays the type of data in a file. |
| fold | Wraps each line of text to fit a specified width. |
| grep | Searches for regular expressions in a text file. |
| less | Displays a text file one page at a time. (Go backward by pressing **b**.) |
| lpr | Prints files. |
| more | Displays a text file one page at a time. (Goes forward only.) |
| nl | Numbers all nonblank lines in a text file and prints the lines to standard output. |
| paste | Concatenates corresponding lines from several files. |
| patch | Updates a text file by using the differences between the original and revised copies of the file. |
| sed | Copies a file to standard output while applying specified editing commands. |
| sort | Sorts lines in a text file. |
| split | Breaks up a file into several smaller files with specified sizes. |
| tac | Reverses a file (last line first and so on). |
| tail | Displays the last few lines of a file. |
| tr | Substitutes one group of characters for another throughout a file. |
| uniq | Eliminates duplicate lines from a text file. |

*(continued)*

**TABLE 1-2** *(continued)*

| Command Name | Action |
| --- | --- |
| wc | Counts the number of lines, words, and characters in a text file. |
| zcat | Displays a compressed file (after decompressing). |
| zless | Displays a compressed file one page at a time. (Go backward by pressing **b**.) |
| zmore | Displays a compressed file one page at a time. |
| **Archiving and compressing files** | |
| compress | Compresses files. |
| cpio | Copies files to and from an archive. |
| gunzip | Decompresses files compressed with GNU Zip (gzip). |
| gzip | Compresses files by using GNU Zip. |
| tar | Creates an archive of files in one or more directories (originally meant for archiving on tape). |
| uncompress | Decompresses files compressed with compress. |
| **Managing files** | |
| bg | Runs an interrupted process in the background. |
| fg | Runs a process in the foreground. |
| free | Displays the amount of free and used memory in the system. |
| halt | Shuts down Linux and halts the computer. |
| kill | Sends a signal to a process (usually to terminate the process). |
| ldd | Displays the shared libraries needed to run a program. |
| nice | Runs a process with a lower priority (referred to as nice mode). |
| ps | Displays a list of running processes. |
| printenv | Displays the current environment variables. |
| pstree | Shows parent–child process relationships. |
| reboot | Shuts down Linux and then restarts the computer. |
| shutdown | Shuts down Linux. |
| top | Displays a list of the most processor- and memory-intensive processes. |
| uname | Displays information about the system and the Linux kernel. |

| Command Name | Action |
|---|---|
| **Managing users** | |
| chsh | Changes the shell (command interpreter). |
| groups | Prints the list of groups that include a specified user. |
| id | Displays the user and group ID for a specified username. |
| passwd | Changes the password. |
| su | Starts a new shell as another user. (The other user is assumed to be root when the command is invoked without any argument.) |
| **Managing the file system** | |
| df | Summarizes free and available space in all mounted storage devices. |
| du | Displays disk-use information. |
| fdformat | Formats a floppy disk. |
| fdisk | Partitions a hard drive. |
| fsck | Checks and repairs a file system. |
| mkfs | Creates a new file system. |
| mknod | Creates a device file. |
| mkswap | Creates a swap space for Linux in a file or a hard drive partition. |
| mount | Mounts a device (such as a CD-ROM) on a directory in the file system. |
| swapoff | Deactivates a swap space. |
| swapon | Activates a swap space. |
| sync | Writes *buffered* (saved in memory) data to files. |
| tty | Displays the device name for the current terminal. |
| umount | Unmounts a device from the file system. |
| **Displaying dates and times** | |
| cal | Displays a calendar for a specified month or year. |
| date | Displays the current date and time or sets a new date and time. |

# Becoming root (superuser)

When you want to do anything that requires a high privilege level, such as administering your system, you must become root. Normally, you log in as a regular user with your everyday username. When you need the privileges of the superuser, there are two ways to do that:

>> Use the su command to become root and run multiple commands

>> Use the sudo command to run a single command with the root user's privileges

When you type the su command followed by a space and a hyphen, the shell prompts you for the root user account's password. Type the password and press Enter. You get a new prompt:

```
rich@testbox: ~$ su -
Password:
root@testbox: ~#
```

The command prompt shows that the root user account is now logged in, and that the shell has administrator privileges (indicated by the pound sign prompt). You can now perform any administrator command as the root user account.

When you finish whatever you want to do as root (and you have the privilege to do anything as root), type **exit** to return to your normal username.

Though it is convenient, using the su command to become the root user account can be just as dangerous as logging in directly as the root user. Because of that, some Linux distributions (such as Ubuntu) disable this feature and, instead, force you to use the sudo command to run individual commands with root user privileges:

```
rich@Ubuntu22:~$ cat /etc/shadow
cat: /etc/shadow: Permission denied
rich@testbox:~$ sudo cat /etc/shadow
[sudo] password for rich:
root:!:19104:0:99999:7:::
daemon:*:19101:0:99999:7:::
bin:*:19101:0:99999:7:::
sys:*:19101:0:99999:7:::
...
rich@testbox:~$
```

Notice that the prompt is for your password, not the root user account's password. To use this feature, your user account must be listed as an authorized user in the /etc/sudoers file. When the command completes, you're returned to your normal user account, indicated by the command prompt.

## Managing processes

Every time the shell executes a command that you type, it starts a process. The shell itself is a process, as are any scripts or programs that the shell runs.

Use the ps ax command to see a list of processes. When you type **ps ax**, Bash shows you the current set of processes. Here are a few lines of output that appeared when I typed **ps ax --cols 132**. (I include the –cols 132 option to ensure that you see each command in its entirety.)

```
PID   TTY    STAT TIME  COMMAND
1     ?      S    0:01  init [5]
2     ?      SN   0:00  [ksoftirqd/0]
3     ?      S<   0:00  [events/0]
4     ?      S<   0:00  [khelper]
9     ?      S<   0:00  [kthread]
19    ?      S<   0:00  [kacpid]
75    ?      S<   0:00  [kblockd/0]
115   ?      S    0:00  [pdflush]
116   ?      S    0:01  [pdflush]
118   ?      S<   0:00  [aio/0]
117   ?      S    0:00  [kswapd0]
711   ?      S    0:00  [kseriod]
1075  ?      S<   0:00  [reiserfs/0]
2086  ?      S    0:00  [kjournald]
2239  ?      S<s  0:00  /sbin/udevd -d
... lines deleted ...
6374  ?      S    1:51  /usr/X11R6/bin/X :0 -audit 0 -auth /var/lib/gdm/:0.Xauth
-nolisten tcp vt7
6460  ?      Ss   0:02  /opt/gnome/bin/gdmgreeter
6671  ?      Ss   0:00  sshd: imatest [priv]
6675  ?      S    0:00  sshd: imatest@pts/0
6676  pts/0  Ss   0:00  -bash
14702 ?      S    0:00  pickup -l -t fifo -u
14752 pts/0  R+   0:00  ps ax --cols 132
```

**TIP**

In this listing, the first column has the heading PID and shows a number for each process. *PID* stands for *process ID* (identification), which is a sequential number assigned by the Linux kernel. If you look through the output of the ps ax command, you see that the init command is the first process and has a PID of 1. For that reason, init is called the mother of all processes.

The COMMAND column shows the command that created each process, and the TIME column shows the cumulative processor time used by the process. The STAT column shows the state of a process: S means that the process is sleeping, and R means that it's running. The symbols following the status letter have further meanings. < indicates a high-priority process, and + means that the process is running in the foreground. The TTY column shows the terminal, if any, associated with the process.

The process ID, or process number, is useful when you have to forcibly stop an errant process. Look at the output of the ps ax command, and note the PID of the offending process. Then use the kill command with that process number to stop the process. To stop process number 8550, start by typing the following command:

```
kill 8550
```

If the process doesn't stop after 5 seconds, repeat the command. The next step in stopping a stubborn process is typing **kill -INT***pid*, where *pid* is the process number. If that command doesn't work, try the following command as a last resort:

```
kill -9 8550
```

The –9 option sends signal number 9 to the process. Signal number 9 is the KILL signal, which should cause the process to exit. You could also type this command as **kill -KILL***pid*, where *pid* is the process ID.

## Working with date and time

You can use the date command to display the current date and time or set a new date and time. Type **date** at the shell prompt and you get a result like the following:

```
Tue Apr 26 20:26:24 PM EDT 2022
```

As you see, issuing the date command alone displays the current date and time.

To set the date, log in as root and then type **date** followed by the date and time in the MMDDhhmmYYYY format, where each character is a digit. To set the date and time to December 31, 2023, and 9:30 p.m., type

```
date 123121302023
```

The MMDDhhmmYYYY date and time format is similar to the 24-hour military clock and has the following meaning:

>> MM is a two-digit number for the month (01 through 12).

>> DD is a two-digit number for the day of the month (01 through 31).

>> hh is a two-digit hour in 24-hour format (00 is midnight, and 23 is 11 p.m.).

>> mm is a two-digit number for the minute (00 through 59).

>> YYYY is the four-digit year (such as 2023).

The other interesting date-related command that may be installed by default in your Linux distribution is cal (for Ubuntu, you'll need to install the ncal package first). If you type **cal** without any options, it prints a calendar for the current month. If you type **cal** followed by a number, cal treats the number as the year and prints the calendar for that year. To view the calendar for a specific month in a specific year, provide the month number (1 = January, 2 = February, and so on) followed by the year. If you type **cal 12 2023**, you get the calendar for December 2023, as follows:

```
    December 2023
Su Mo Tu We Th Fr Sa
                1  2
 3  4  5  6  7  8  9
10 11 12 13 14 15 16
17 18 19 20 21 22 23
24 25 26 27 28 29 30
31
```

# Processing files

Not only does the Bash shell include commands for working with files but there are also commands available to help you process text data inside the files. This is one of the greatest features of working from the shell.

You can search a text file with grep and view a text file, a screen at a time, with more. To search for a username in the /etc/passwd file, use

```
grep imatest /etc/passwd
```

To view the /etc/services file a screen at a time, type

```
more /etc/services
```

As each screen pauses, press the spacebar to go to the next page.

Many more Linux commands work on files, mostly on text files, but some commands also work on any file. The following sections describe a few file-processing tools.

## Counting words and lines in a text file

I'm always curious about the sizes of files. For text files, the number of characters is the size of the file in bytes (because each character takes up 1 byte of storage space). What about words and the number of lines, though?

The Linux wc command comes to the rescue. The wc command displays the total number of lines, words, and characters in a text file. Type **wc /etc/services**, and you see output similar to the following:

```
417   1994 14464 /etc/services
```

In this case, wc reports that 417 lines, 1994 words, and 14,464 characters are in the /etc/services file. If you want to see the number of lines in a file, use the –1 option, and type **wc -1 /etc/services**. The resulting output should be similar to the following:

```
417 /etc/services
```

As you can see, with the –1 option, wc simply displays the line count.

If you don't specify a filename, the wc command expects input from the standard input. You can use the pipe feature (|) of the shell to feed the output of another command to wc, which can be handy sometimes.

Suppose that you want a rough count of the processes running on your system. You can get a list of all processes with the ps ax command, but instead of counting lines manually, pipe the output of ps to wc to get a rough count automatically:

```
ps ax | wc -1
86
```

Here, the ps command produces 86 lines of output. Because the first line shows the headings for the tabular columns, you can estimate that about 85 processes are running on your system. (This count probably includes the processes used to run the ps and wc commands as well.)

## Sorting text files

You can sort the lines in a text file by using the sort command. To see how the sort command works, first type **more /etc/passwd** to see the current contents of the /etc/passwd file. Then type **sort /etc/passwd** to see the lines sorted alphabetically. If you want to sort a file and save the sorted version in another file, you must use the Bash shell's output redirection feature, like this:

```
sort /etc/passwd > ~/sorted.text
```

This command sorts the lines in the /etc/passwd file and saves the output in a file named sorted.text in your home directory.

## Substituting or deleting characters from a file

Another interesting command is tr, which substitutes one group of characters for another (or deletes a selected character) throughout a file. Suppose that you have to occasionally use MS-DOS text files on your Linux system. Although you may expect to use a text file on any system without any problems, you find one catch: DOS uses a carriage return followed by a line feed to mark the end of each line, whereas Linux uses only a line feed.

**TIP**

On your Linux system, you can get rid of the extra carriage returns in the DOS text file by using the tr command with the –d option. Essentially, to convert the DOS text file named filename.dos to a Linux text file named filename.linux, type the following:

```
tr -d '\015' < filename.dos > filename.linux
```

In this command, '\015' denotes the code for the carriage-return character in octal notation.

## Splitting a file into several smaller files

The split command is handy for those times when you want to copy a file but the file is too large to send as one email attachment. You can use the split command to break the file into smaller files.

By default, split puts 1,000 lines into each file. The new split files are named by groups of letters: aa, ab, ac, and so on. You can specify a prefix for the filenames. To split a large file called hugefile.tar into smaller files, use split as follows:

```
split -b 9999k hugefile.tar part.
```

This command splits the hugefile.tar file into 9999KB chunks. The command creates files named part.aa, part.ab, part.ac, and so on.

To recombine the split files into a single file, use the `cat` command as follows:

```
cat part.?? > hugefile.tar
```

In this case, the two question marks (??) match any two-character extension in the filename. In other words, the filename `part.??` matches all filenames, such as `part.12`, `part.aa`, `part.ab`, and `part.2b`.

# Writing Shell Scripts

If you've ever used MS-DOS, you may remember MS-DOS *batch files,* which are text files with MS-DOS commands. Similarly, *shell scripts* are text files with a bunch of shell commands.

If you aren't a programmer, you may feel apprehensive about programming, but shell programming can be as simple as storing a few commands in a file. Right now, you may not be up to writing complex shell scripts, but you can certainly try a simple shell script.

To try your hand at a little shell programming, type the following text at the shell prompt exactly as shown, and press Ctrl+D when you finish:

```
cd
cat > simple
#!/bin/sh
echo "This script's name is: $0"
echo Argument 1: $1
echo Argument 2: $2
```

Press Ctrl+D.

The `cd` command changes the current directory to your home directory — the default for `cd` if you do not specify an option. Then the `cat` command displays the next line and any other lines you type before pressing Ctrl+D. In this case, you use `> simple` to send the output to a file named `simple`. After you press Ctrl+D, the `cat` command ends and you see the shell prompt again. You created a file named `simple` that contains the following shell script:

```
#!/bin/sh
echo "This script's name is: $0"
echo Argument 1: $1
echo Argument 2: $2
```

The first line causes Linux to run the Bash shell program (of the name /bin/bash). Then the shell reads the rest of the lines in the script.

Just as most Linux commands accept command-line options, a Bash script accepts command-line options. Inside the script, you can refer to the options as $1, $2, and so on. The special name $0 refers to the name of the script itself.

To run this shell script, first make the file executable (that is, turn it into a program) with the following command:

```
chmod +x simple
```

Type **./simple one two** to run the script, which displays the following output:

```
This script' name is: ./simple
Argument 1: one
Argument 2: two
```

The ./ prefix in the script's name indicates that the simple file is in the current directory.

This script prints the script's name and the first two command-line options that the user types after the script's name.

Next, try running the script with a few arguments, as follows:

```
./simple "This is one argument" second-argument third
This script's name is: ./simple
Argument 1: This is one argument
Argument 2: second-argument
```

The shell treats the entire string in the double quotation marks as a single argument. Otherwise, the shell uses spaces to separate arguments on the command line. The "third" text is assigned to the third argument ($3) but isn't displayed by the script.

Most useful shell scripts are more complicated than this simple script, but this exercise gives you a rough idea of how to write shell scripts. In the first two chapters of Book 7, I explore this a bit further.

**REMEMBER**

Place Linux commands in a file and use the chmod command to make the file executable. Voilà — you've created a shell script.

IN THIS CHAPTER

» Knowing how to become root

» Understanding the system startup process

» Viewing system information through the /proc file system

» Monitoring system performance

» Managing devices and scheduling jobs

» Using GUI system administration tools

# Chapter **2**

# Introducing Basic System Administration

*S*ystem administration refers to whatever must be done to keep a computer system up and running. That system could be just a stand-alone client machine, a network server that an organization depends on for its livelihood, and almost anything in between the two extremes. The *system administrator* is whoever is in charge of taking care of these tasks and making the system perform as needed.

If you're running Linux at home or in a small office, you're most likely the only one who can do it; thus, you're the system administrator for your systems. Or maybe you're the system administrator for an entire local-area network (LAN) full of Linux servers running an e-commerce site. Regardless of your position or title, this chapter introduces you to some of the basic system administration procedures and shows you how to perform common tasks.

# Taking Stock of System Administration Tasks

What are system administration tasks? An off-the-cuff reply is "Anything you have to do to keep the system running well." More accurately, though, a system administrator's duties include

>> **Adding and removing user accounts:** You have to add new user accounts and remove unnecessary user accounts. If a user forgets the password, you have to change the password.

>> **Managing the printing system:** You have to turn the print queue on or off, check the print queue's status, and delete print jobs if necessary.

>> **Installing, configuring, and upgrading the operating system and various utilities:** You have to install or upgrade parts of the Linux operating system and other software that's part of the operating system.

>> **Installing new software:** You have to install software that comes in various package formats, such as RPM or DEB. You also have to download and unpack software that comes in source-code form and then build executable programs from the source code.

>> **Managing hardware:** Sometimes, you have to add new hardware and install drivers so that the devices work properly.

>> **Making backups:** You have to back up files, whether to an optical drive, a USB memory stick, a network server, or an external hard drive.

>> **Mounting and unmounting file systems:** When you want to access the files on a USB memory stick, for example, you have to mount that stick's file system on one of the directories in your Linux file system. You may also have to mount such things as external or network hard drives that were created in both Linux format and DOS format.

>> **Automating tasks:** You have to schedule Linux tasks to take place automatically (at specific times) or periodically (at regular intervals).

>> **Monitoring the system's performance:** You may want to keep an eye on system performance to see where the processor is spending most of its time and to see the amount of free and used memory in the system.

>> **Starting and shutting down the system:** Although starting the system typically involves nothing more than powering up the PC, you do have to take some care when you shut down your Linux system. If your system is set up for a graphical login screen, you can perform the shutdown operation by choosing a menu item from the login screen. Otherwise, use the shutdown command to stop all programs before turning off your PC's power switch.

>> **Monitoring network status:** If you have a network presence (whether a LAN, a DSL line, or a cable modem connection), you may want to check the status of various network interfaces and make sure that your network connection is up and running.

>> **Setting up host and network security:** You have to make sure that system files are protected and that your system can defend itself against attacks over the network.

>> **Monitoring security:** You have to keep an eye on any intrusions, usually by checking the log files.

That's a long list of tasks! Not all these items are covered in this chapter, but the rest of Book 4 describes most of these tasks. The focus of this chapter is on some of the basics, such as becoming root (the superuser), identifying the system configuration files, monitoring system performance, managing devices, setting up periodic jobs, and using the graphic user interface (GUI) tools.

# Becoming root

You have to log in as root to perform system administration tasks. The root user is the superuser and the only account with all the privileges needed to do anything in the system.

**WARNING**

Common wisdom says you should *not* normally log in as root. When you're root, you can easily delete all the files with one misstep — especially when you're typing commands. You type the command rm *.html to delete all files that have the .html extension, for example. But what if you accidentally press the spacebar after the asterisk (*)? The shell takes the command to be rm * .html and — because * matches any filename — deletes everything in the current directory. This scenario seems implausible until it happens to you!

If you're logged in as a normal user, how do you do any system administration chores? There are two ways to do that: the su – command and the sudo command.

## Using the su - command

One method is to temporarily become the root user account while you're still logged in as your normal user account. If you're working at a terminal window or console, type

```
su -
```

Then enter the root password in response to the prompt. From this point, you're root. Do whatever you have to do. To return to your usual self, type

```
exit
```

That's it! The process is easy and a lot safer than logging in and having an entire session as the root user.

## Using the sudo command

Some distributions (such as Ubuntu) have disabled the ability to use the su-command to become the root user account. To perform any task that requires root privileges in these distributions, you must type **sudo** followed by the command and then provide your normal user password when prompted. This only allows you to submit one command at a time as the root user account, hopefully minimizing the damage you can accidentally do to the system. I address this issue in more detail in Book 6, but you can control who can use sudo through configuration files.

# Understanding How Linux Boots

Knowing the sequence in which Linux starts processes as it boots is important. You can use this knowledge to start and stop services, such as the web server and Network File System (NFS). Linux distributions currently use two common methods for starting and stopping services:

>> The SysVinit method

>> The Systemd method

The original Linux startup method was based on the Unix System V operating system. That system used the init program to start services, which became commonly called SysVinit. The SysVinit program uses a series of shell scripts, divided into separate runlevels, to determine what programs run at what times. Each program uses a separate shell script to start and stop the program. The system administrator sets which runlevel the Linux system starts in, which in turn determines which set of programs are running. The system administrator can also change the runlevel at any time while the system is running.

The SysVinit program served the Linux community well for many years, but as Linux systems became more complicated and required more services, the runlevel shell scripts became more complicated. This caused Linux developers to look for other solutions.

The Systemd method was developed by the Red Hat Linux distribution to handle dynamic Linux environments. Instead of runlevels, it uses targets and units to control which applications run at any time on the system. It uses separate configuration files that determine this behavior.

To find out which method your Linux system uses, use the ps command to display the program assigned process ID (PID) 1:

```
$ ps -p 1
    PID TTY          TIME CMD
      1 ?        00:00:01 systemd
$
```

The output from this Rocky Linux system shows that it's running the systemd program. If your Linux system is using the SysVinit method, the program assigned to PID 1 would be init.

The following sections take a closer look at each of these initialization process methods to help you get comfortable working with startup scripts in any Linux environment.

## Understanding the SysVinit method

When a Linux system boots, it loads and runs the kernel from the hard drive. The kernel is designed to run other programs. For systems that use the SysVinit startup method, the very first program it runs is the special init program. The init program then starts all the other service programs required by the system. What the init process starts depends on

>> **The runlevel,** an identifier that identifies a system configuration in which only a selected group of processes can exist.

>> **The contents of the** /etc/inittab **file,** a text file that specifies which processes to start at different runlevels.

>> **Shell scripts that are executed at specific runlevels,** some of which are located in the /etc/init.d directory and subdirectories of /etc. (These subdirectories have names that begin with rc.)

TIP

Most Linux distributions use seven runlevels: 0 through 6. The meaning of the runlevels differs from one distribution to another. Table 2-1 shows the meanings of the runlevels and points out some of the actions specific to Fedora, Debian, SUSE, and Ubuntu.

TABLE 2-1

## Runlevels in Linux

| Runlevel | Meaning |
| --- | --- |
| 0 | Shut down the system. |
| 1 | Run in single-user stand-alone mode. (No one else can log in; you work at the text console.) |
| 2 | Run in multiuser mode. (Debian and Ubuntu use runlevel 2 as the default runlevel.) |
| 3 | Run in full multiuser mode (for text-mode login in Fedora and SUSE). |
| 4 | Run in full multiuser mode (unused in Fedora and SUSE). |
| 5 | Run in full multiuser mode (the default runlevel with graphical login in Fedora and SUSE). |
| 6 | Reboot the system. |

The current runlevel together with the contents of the /etc/inittab file control which processes init starts in Linux. For most Linux desktop systems that use a graphical desktop, the default runlevel is 5. For Linux server systems that just use a command-line interface, the default runlevel is often 2 or 3. You can change the default runlevel by editing a line in the /etc/inittab file.

To check the current runlevel, type the following command in a terminal window:

```
/sbin/runlevel
```

In Ubuntu, the runlevel command prints an output like this:

```
N 5
```

The first character of the output shows the previous runlevel (N means no previous runlevel), and the second character shows the current runlevel (5). In this case, the system started at runlevel 5.

## Examining the /etc/inittab file

The /etc/inittab file is the key to understanding the processes that init starts at various runlevels. You can look at the contents of the file by using the more command, as follows:

```
more /etc/inittab
```

**REMEMBER**

To see the contents of the /etc/inittab file with the more command, you don't have to log in as root.

To interpret the contents of the /etc/inittab file, follow these steps:

**1.** **Look for the line that contains the phrase** initdefault.

Here's that line from the /etc/inittab file in a SysVinit system:

```
id:2:initdefault:
```

That line shows the default runlevel (in this case, 2).

**2.** **Find all the lines that specify what** init **runs at runlevel 2.**

Look for a line that has a 2 between the first two colons (:):

```
l2:2:wait:/etc/init.d/rc 2
```

This line specifies that init executes the file /etc/init.d/rc with 2 as an argument.

If you look at the file /etc/init.d/rc in a SysVinit system, you find that it's a shell script. You can study this file to see how it starts various processes for runlevels 1 through 5.

**TECHNICAL
STUFF**

Each entry in the /etc/inittab file tells init what to do at one or more runlevels; you simply list all runlevels at which the process runs. Each inittab entry has four fields, separated by colons, in the following format:

```
id:runlevels:action:process
```

Table 2-2 shows what each field means.

## Trying a new runlevel with the init command

To try a new runlevel, you don't have to change the default runlevel in the /etc/inittab file. If you log in as root, you can change the runlevel (and, consequently, the processes that run in Linux) by typing **init** followed by the runlevel.

To put the system in single-user mode, for example, type the following:

```
init 1
```

**TABLE 2-2**

## Fields in Each inittab Entry

| Field | Meaning |
|---|---|
| id | A unique one- or two-character identifier. The init process uses this field internally. You can use any identifier you want as long as you don't use the same identifier on more than one line. |
| runlevels | A sequence of zero or more characters, each denoting a runlevel. For example, if the runlevels field is 12345, that entry applies to each of the runlevels (1 through 5). This field is ignored if the action field is set to sysinit, boot, or bootwait. |
| action | What the init process will do with this entry. If this field is initdefault, for example, init interprets the runlevels field as the default runlevel. If this field is set to wait, init starts the program or script specified in the process field and waits until that process exits. |
| process | Name of the script or program that init starts. Some settings of the action field require no process field. When the action field is initdefault, for example, there's no need for a process field. |

Thus, if you want to try runlevel 3 without changing the default runlevel in the /etc/inittab file, enter the following command at the shell prompt:

```
init 3
```

The system ends all current processes and enters runlevel 3. By default, the init command waits 20 seconds before stopping all current processes and starting the new processes for runlevel 3.

**TIP**

To switch to runlevel 3 immediately, type the command init -t0 3. The number after the -t option indicates the number of seconds init waits before changing the runlevel.

You can also use the telinit command, which is simply a symbolic link (a shortcut) to init. If you make changes in the /etc/inittab file and want init to reload its configuration file, use the command telinit q.

## Understanding the Linux startup scripts

With the SysVinit method, the init process runs several scripts at system startup. Most Linux distributions that use the SysVinit method follow the same script format but the names and locations of the scripts may vary.

**TIP**

If you look at the /etc/inittab file in a SysVinit system, you find the following lines near the beginning of the file:

```
# Boot-time system configuration/initialization script.
si::sysinit:/etc/init.d/rcS
```

The first line is a comment line. The second line causes init to run the /etc/
init.d/rcS script, which is the first Linux startup script that init runs. The rcS
script performs many initialization tasks, such as mounting the file systems, setting the clock, configuring the keyboard layout, starting the network, and loading
many other driver modules. The rcS script performs these initialization tasks by
calling many other scripts and reading configuration files located in the /etc/
rcS.d directory.

After executing the /etc/init.d/rcS script, the init process runs the /etc/
init.d/rc script with the runlevel as an argument. For runlevel 2, the following
line in /etc/inittab specifies what init executes:

```
12:2:wait:/etc/init.d/rc 2
```

This example says that init executes the command /etc/init.d/rc 2 and waits
until that command completes.

The /etc/init.d/rc script is somewhat complicated. Here's how it works:

>> It executes scripts in a directory corresponding to the runlevel. For example,
for runlevel 2, the /etc/init.d/rc script runs the scripts in the /etc/rc2.d
directory.

>> In the directory that corresponds with the runlevel, /etc/init.d/rc looks for
all files that begin with K and executes each of them with the stop argument,
which kills any currently running processes. Then it locates all files that begin
with S and executes each file with a start argument, which starts the
processes needed for the specified runlevel.

To see what happens if the script is executed at runlevel 2, type the following
command:

```
ls -1 /etc/rc2.d
```

In the resulting listing, the K scripts — the files whose names begin with K — stop
(or *kill*) servers, whereas the S scripts start servers. The /etc/init.d/rc script
executes these files in the order in which they appear in the directory listing.

## Manually starting and stopping servers

In Linux, the server startup scripts reside in the /etc/init.d directory. You
can manually invoke scripts in this directory to start, stop, or restart specific

processes — usually, servers. To stop the FTP server, for example (the server program is vsftpd), type the following command:

```
/etc/init.d/vsftpd stop
```

If vsftpd is already running and you want to restart it, type the following command:

```
/etc/init.d/vsftpd restart
```

You can enhance your system administration skills by familiarizing yourself with the scripts in the /etc/init.d directory. To see that directory's listing, type the following command:

```
ls /etc/init.d
```

The script names give you some clue about which server the scripts can start and stop. The samba script, for example, starts and stops the processes required for Samba Windows networking services. At your leisure, you may want to study some of these scripts to see what they do. You don't have to understand all the shell programming; the comments help you discover the purpose of each script.

## Automatically starting servers at system startup

You want some servers to start automatically every time you boot the system. The exact commands to configure the servers vary from one distribution to another.

TIP

Use the chkconfig command to set up a server to start whenever the system boots into a specific runlevel. If you start the Secure Shell (SSH) server, for example, you want the sshd server to start whenever the system starts. You can make that startup happen by using the chkconfig command. To set sshd to start whenever the system boots into runlevel 3, 4, or 5, type the following command (while logged in as root):

```
chkconfig --level 345 sshd on
```

TIP

You can also use the chkconfig command to check which servers are turned on or off. To see the complete list of all servers for all runlevels, type the following command:

```
chkconfig --list
```

**TIP**

For some Linux distributions, you use the `update-rc.d` command to enable a server to start automatically at system startup. To set `sshd` to start automatically at the default runlevels, for example, type **update-rc.d sshd defaults** in a terminal window while logged in as `root`. You can also specify the exact runlevels and the sequence number (the order in which each server starts). To find out more about the `update-rc.d` command, type **man update-rc.d** in a terminal window.

# Understanding the Systemd method

The Systemd initialization process method quickly gained popularity in the Linux world, and it's now the default used by most of the mainstream Linux distributions, such as Debian, Red Hat, and openSUSE. The Systemd initialization process introduced a major paradigm shift in how Linux systems handle services, which has also caused some controversy in the Linux world. Instead of lots of the small initialization shell scripts that the SysVinit method uses, the Systemd method uses one monolithic program that reads individual configuration files for each service. This is somewhat of a departure from the earlier Linux philosophy of keeping things small and orderly, upsetting many of the Linux purists.

This section walks through the basics of how the Systemd initialization process works.

## Units and targets

Instead of using shell scripts and runlevels, the Systemd method uses units and targets. A unit defines a service or action on the system. It consists of a name, a type, and a configuration file. There are currently 12 different types of Systemd units:

>> automount

>> device

>> mount

>> path

>> scope

>> service

>> slice

>> snapshot

>> socket

>> swap

>> target

>> timer

The systemd program identifies units by their name and type using the format name.type. You use the systemctl command when working with units. To list the units currently loaded in your Linux system, use the list-units parameter:

```
# systemctl list-units
UNIT                    LOAD    ACTIVE SUB      DESCRIPTION
...
crond.service           loaded active running  Command Scheduler
cups.service            loaded active running  CUPS Printing Service
dbus.service            loaded active running  D-Bus System Message
...
multi-user.target       loaded active active   Multi-User System
network.target          loaded active active   Network
paths.target            loaded active active   Paths
remote-fs.target        loaded active active   Remote File Systems
slices.target           loaded active active   Slices
sockets.target          loaded active active   Sockets
...
218 loaded units listed. Pass --all to see loaded but inactive units, too.
To show all installed unit files use 'systemctl list-unit-files'.
#
```

Linux distributions can have hundreds of different units loaded and active at any given time, this listing shows just a few from the output to show you what they look like. The Systemd method uses service type units to manage the daemons on the Linux system. The target type units are important in that they group multiple units together so that they can be started at the same time. For example, the network.target unit groups all the units required to start the network interfaces for the system.

The Systemd initialization process uses targets similar to the way SysVinit uses runlevels. Each target represents a different group of services that should be running on the system. Instead of changing runlevels to alter what's running on the system, you just change targets.

To make the transition from SysV to Systemd smoother, there are targets that mimic the standard 0 through 6 SysVinit runlevels, called runlevel0.target through runlevel6.target.

## Configuring units

Each unit requires a configuration file that defines what program it starts and how it should start the program. The Systemd system stores unit configuration files in the /usr/1ib/systemd/system folder. Here's an example of the cron.service unit configuration file used in Ubuntu:

```
$ cat cron.service
[Unit]
Description=Regular background program processing daemon
Documentation=man:cron(8)
After=remote-fs.target nss-user-lookup.target

[Service]
EnvironmentFile=-/etc/default/cron
ExecStart=/usr/sbin/cron -f $EXTRA_OPTS
IgnoreSIGPIPE=false
KillMode=process
Restart=on-failure

[Install]
WantedBy=multi-user.target

$
```

The cron.service configuration file defines the program to start (/usr/sbin/cron), along with some other features, such as what services should run before the cron service starts (the After line), what target level the system should be in (the WantedBy line), and when to reload the program (the Restart line).

Target units also use configuration files. They don't define programs; instead, they define which service units to start. Here's an example of the graphical.target unit configuration file used in Rocky Linux:

```
$ cat graphical.target
#  SPDX-License-Identifier: LGPL-2.1+
#
#  This file is part of systemd.
#
#  systemd is free software; you can redistribute it and/or modify it
#  under the terms of the GNU Lesser General Public License as published by
#  the Free Software Foundation; either version 2.1 of the License, or
#  (at your option) any later version.

[Unit]
Description=Graphical Interface
```

```
Documentation=man:systemd.special(7)
Requires=multi-user.target
Wants=display-manager.service
Conflicts=rescue.service rescue.target
After=multi-user.target rescue.service rescue.target display-manager.service
AllowIsolate=yes
$
```

The target configuration defines which targets should be loaded first (the After line), which targets are required for this target to start (the Requires line), which targets conflict with this target (the Conflicts line), and which targets or services the target requires to be running (the Wants line).

## Setting the default target

The default target used when the Linux system boots is defined as the file default.target, located in the /usr/lib/systemd/system folder. This file is what the systemd program looks for when it starts up. The file is normally set as a link to a standard target file also in the /usr/lib/systemd/system folder:

```
$ ls -al default*
lrwxrwxrwx 1 root root 16 Sep  7 14:37 default.target -> graphical.target
$
```

On this Ubuntu system, the default target is set to the graphical.target unit.

You can also see the default target for the system by using the systemctl command:

```
$ systemctl get-default
graphical.target
$
```

This again shows that the graphical.target target is the default.

## The systemctl program

You use the systemctl program to also control services and targets. The systemctl program uses options to define what action to take, as shown in Table 2-3.

**TABLE 2-3**

# The systemctl Commands

| Command name | Explanation |
|---|---|
| get-default | Displays the default target configured for the system. |
| list-units | Displays the current status of all configured units. |
| default *name* | Changes to the default target unit. |
| isolate *name* | Starts the named unit and stops all others. |
| start *name* | Starts the named unit. |
| stop *name* | Stops the named unit. |
| reload *name* | Causes the named unit to reload its configuration file. |
| restart *name* | Causes the named unit to shut down and restart. |
| status *name* | Displays the status of the named unit. (You can pass a PID value rather than a name, if you like.) |
| enable *name* | Configures the unit to start when the computer next boots. |
| disable *name* | Configures the unit to not start when the computer next boots. |

Instead of using shell scripts to start and stop services, you use the start and stop commands in systemctl:

```
$ sudo systemctl stop cron.service
$ systemctl status cron.service
 cron.service - Regular background program processing daemon
     Loaded: loaded (/lib/systemd/system/cron.service; enabled; vendor
preset: enabled)
     Active: inactive (dead) since Sat 2021-10-23 08:51:01 EDT; 3s ago
       Docs: man:cron(8)
    Process: 585 ExecStart=/usr/sbin/cron -f $EXTRA_OPTS (code=killed,
signal=TERM)
   Main PID: 585 (code=killed, signal=TERM)

Apr 23 08:19:28 ubuntu20 systemd[1]: Started Regular background program
   processing daemon.
Apr 23 08:19:28 ubuntu20 cron[585]: (CRON) INFO (pidfile fd = 3)
Apr 23 08:19:28 ubuntu20 cron[585]: (CRON) INFO (Running @reboot jobs)
Apr 23 08:30:01 ubuntu20 CRON[2882]: pam_unix(cron:session): session opened for
   user root by (uid=0)
Apr 23 08:30:01 ubuntu20 CRON[2882]: pam_unix(cron:session): session closed for
   user root
Apr 23 08:51:01 ubuntu20 systemd[1]: Stopping Regular background program
   processing daemon...
```

```
Apr 23 08:51:01 ubuntu20 systemd[1]: cron.service: Succeeded.
Apr 23 08:51:01 ubuntu20 systemd[1]: Stopped Regular background program
    processing daemon.
$
```

To change the target that is currently running, you must use the isolate command. For example, to enter single-user mode, you'd use:

```
# systemctl isolate rescue.target
```

To go back to the default target for the system, you just use the default command.

TIP

Yet another of the more controversial features of the systemd initialization
process is that it doesn't use the standard Linux syslogd log file system. Instead,
it has its own log files, and those log files are not stored in text format. To view
the systemd log files you need to use the journalctl program.

# Monitoring System Performance

When you're the system administrator, you must keep an eye on how well your
Linux system is performing. You can monitor the overall performance of your
system by looking at information such as

>> Central processing unit (CPU) usage

>> Physical memory usage

>> Virtual memory (swap-space) usage

>> Hard drive usage

Linux comes with utilities that you can use to monitor these performance parameters. The following sections introduce a few of these utilities and show you how
to understand the information presented by said utilities.

## Using the top utility

To view the top CPU processes — the ones that use most of the CPU time — you
can use the text mode top utility. To start that utility, type **top** in a terminal
window (or text console). The top utility displays a text screen listing the
current processes, arranged in the order of CPU usage, along with various other
information, such as memory and swap-space usage. Figure 2-1 shows typical
output from the top utility.

```
┌─────────────────────────────────────────────────────────────────────────┐
│ ⊠                            rich@localhost:~                          × │
├─────────────────────────────────────────────────────────────────────────┤
│ File   Edit   View   Search   Terminal   Help                            │
│ top - 08:32:47 up 1 min,   1 user,  load average: 2.69, 1.07, 0.39       │
│ Tasks: 221 total,    1 running, 220 sleeping,   0 stopped,   0 zombie    │
│ %Cpu(s): 12.2 us,   1.7 sy,   0.0 ni, 85.1 id,   0.0 wa,   1.0 hi,   0.0 si,   0.0 st │
│ MiB Mem :  10821.8 total,    8443.2 free,    1180.9 used,    1197.7 buff/cache │
│ MiB Swap:   1728.0 total,    1728.0 free,       0.0 used.    9352.2 avail Mem │
│                                                                           │
│   PID USER     PR  NI    VIRT    RES    SHR S  %CPU  %MEM     TIME+ COMMAND │
│  2515 rich     20   0 2985464 340652 119572 S  12.9   3.1   0:08.07 gnome-shell │
│  3088 rich     20   0  729776  41320  28812 S   1.7   0.4   0:00.53 gnome-terminal- │
│  1038 root     20   0  703404  31916  15668 S   0.3   0.3   0:00.75 tuned │
│  2541 rich     20   0  576480  57248  45304 S   0.3   0.5   0:00.31 Xwayland │
│  2917 rich     20   0  386700   2676   2308 S   0.3   0.0   0:00.06 VBoxClient │
│  3131 rich     20   0  275324   5152   4300 R   0.3   0.0   0:00.11 top │
│     1 root     20   0  241280  14012   9008 S   0.0   0.1   0:01.54 systemd │
│     2 root     20   0       0      0      0 S   0.0   0.0   0:00.00 kthreadd │
│     3 root      0 -20       0      0      0 I   0.0   0.0   0:00.00 rcu_gp │
│     4 root      0 -20       0      0      0 I   0.0   0.0   0:00.00 rcu_par_gp │
│     5 root     20   0       0      0      0 I   0.0   0.0   0:00.02 kworker/0:0-ata_sff │
│     6 root      0 -20       0      0      0 I   0.0   0.0   0:00.00 kworker/0:0H-events_high+ │
│     7 root     20   0       0      0      0 I   0.0   0.0   0:00.05 kworker/0:1-events │
│     8 root     20   0       0      0      0 I   0.0   0.0   0:00.00 kworker/u2:0-events_unbo+ │
│     9 root      0 -20       0      0      0 I   0.0   0.0   0:00.00 mm_percpu_wq │
│    10 root     20   0       0      0      0 S   0.0   0.0   0:00.09 ksoftirqd/0 │
│    11 root     20   0       0      0      0 I   0.0   0.0   0:00.11 rcu_sched │
└─────────────────────────────────────────────────────────────────────────┘
```

**FIGURE 2-1:**
You can see
the top CPU
processes
by using the
top utility.

**TIP**

The top utility updates the display every 5 seconds. If you keep top running in a window, you can continually monitor the status of your Linux system. To quit top, press Q, press Ctrl+C, or close the terminal window.

The first five lines of the output screen (refer to Figure 2-1) provide summary information about the system, as follows:

>> The first line shows the current time, how long the system has been up, how many users are logged in, and three *load averages* — the average number of processes ready to run during the past 1, 5, and 15 minutes.

>> The second line lists the total number of processes/tasks and the status of these processes.

>> The third line shows CPU usage — what percentage of CPU time is used by user processes, what percentage by system (kernel) processes, and the percentage of time during which the CPU is idle.

>> The fourth line shows how the physical memory is being used — the total amount, how much is used, how much is free, and how much is allocated to buffers (for reading from the hard drive, for example).

>> The fifth line shows how the virtual memory (or swap space) is being used — the total amount of swap space, how much is used, how much is free, and how much is being cached.

The table that appears below the summary information (refer to Figure 2-1) lists information about the current processes, arranged in decreasing order by amount of CPU time used. Table 2-4 summarizes the meanings of the column headings in the table that top displays.

**TABLE 2-4** **Column Headings in top Utility's Output**

| Heading | Meaning |
| --- | --- |
| PID | Process ID of the process. |
| USER | Username under which the process is running. |
| PR | Priority of the process. |
| NI | Nice value of the process. The value ranges from –20 (highest priority) to 19 (lowest priority), and the default is 0. (The *nice value* represents the relative priority of the process: The higher the value, the lower the priority and the nicer the process, because it yields to other processes.) |
| VIRT | Total amount of virtual memory used by the process, in kilobytes. |
| RES | Total physical memory used by a task (typically shown in kilobytes, but an m suffix indicates megabytes). |
| SHR | Amount of shared memory used by the process. |
| S | State of the process (S for sleeping, D for uninterruptible sleep, R for running, Z for zombies — processes that should be dead but are still running — and T for stopped). |
| %CPU | Percentage of CPU time used since the last screen update. |
| %MEM | Percentage of physical memory used by the process. |
| TIME+ | Total CPU time the process has used since it started. |
| COMMAND | Shortened form of the command that started the process. |

## Using the uptime command

You can use the uptime command to get a summary of the system's state. Just type the command like this:

```
uptime
```

It displays output similar to the following:

```
15:03:21 up 32 days, 57 min, 3 users, load average: 0.13, 0.23, 0.27
```

This output shows the current time, how long the system has been up, the number of users, and (finally) the three load averages — the average number of processes that were ready to run in the past 1, 5, and 15 minutes. Load averages greater than 1 imply that many processes are competing for CPU time simultaneously.

The load averages give you an indication of how busy the system is.

# Using the vmstat utility

You can get summary information about the overall system usage with the vmstat utility. To view system usage information averaged over 5-second intervals, type the following command (the second argument indicates the total number of lines of output vmstat displays):

```
vmstat 5 8
```

You see output similar to the following listing:

```
procs -----------memory---------- ---swap-- -----io---- --system-- -----cpu-----
 r  b   swpd  free  buff  cache   si  so    bi   bo    in   cs  us sy id wa
 0  0  31324  4016 18568 136004    1   1    17   16     8  110  33  4 61  1
 0  1  31324  2520 15348 139692    0   0  7798  199  1157  377   8  8  6 78
 1  0  31324  1584 12936 141480    0  19  5784  105  1099  437  12  5  0 82
 2  0  31324  1928 13004 137136    7   0  1586  138  1104  561  43  6  0 51
 3  1  31324  1484 13148 132064    0   0  1260   51  1080  427  50  5  0 46
 0  0  31324  1804 13240 127976    0   0  1126   46  1082  782  19  5 47 30
 0  0  31324  1900 13240 127976    0   0     0    0  1010  211   3  1 96  0
 0  0  31324  1916 13248 127976    0   0     0   10  1015  224   3  2 95  0
```

The first line of output shows the averages since the last reboot. After that line, vmstat displays the 5-second average data seven more times, covering the next 35 seconds. The tabular output is grouped as six categories of information, indicated by the fields in the first line of output. The second line shows further details for each of the six major fields. You can interpret these fields by using Table 2-5.

**TECHNICAL
STUFF**

In the vmstat utility's output, continued high values in the si and so fields indicate too much swapping. (*Swapping* refers to the copying of information between physical memory and the virtual memory on the hard drive, so the numbers may be high for one or two samples but shouldn't stay that way for very long under normal circumstances.) Continued high numbers in the bi and bo fields indicate too much continual disk activity.

# Checking disk performance and disk usage

Linux comes with the /sbin/hdparm program to control IDE or ATAPI hard drives, which are common on PCs. One feature of the hdparm program allows you to use the -t option to determine the rate at which data is read from the disk into a buffer in memory. Here's the result of typing **/sbin/hdparm -t /dev/sdb** on one system:

```
[rich@localhost ~]$ sudo hdparm -t /dev/sdb

/dev/sdb:
```

```
Timing buffered disk reads: 1024 MB in  2.09 seconds = 488.94 MB/sec
[rich@localhost ~]$
```

**TABLE 2-5**  ## Meaning of Fields in the vmstat Utility's Output

| Field Name | Description |
|---|---|
| procs | Number of processes and their types: r = processes waiting to run, b = processes in uninterruptible sleep, and w = processes swapped out but ready to run. |
| memory | Information about physical memory and swap-space usage (all numbers in kilobytes): swpd = virtual memory used, free = free physical memory, buff = memory used as buffers, and cache = virtual memory that's cached. |
| swap | Amount of swapping (the numbers are in kilobytes per second): si = amount of memory swapped in from disk, and so = amount of memory swapped to disk. |
| io | Information about input and output. (The numbers are in blocks per second, where the block size depends on the disk device.) bi = rate of blocks sent to disk, and bo = rate of blocks received from disk. |
| system | Information about the system: in = number of interrupts per second (including clock interrupts), and cs = number of context switches per second — how many times the kernel changed which process was running. |
| cpu | Percentages of CPU time used: us = percentage of CPU time used by user processes, sy = percentage of CPU time used by system processes, id = percentage of time CPU is idle, and wa = time spent waiting for input or output (I/O). |

Because the hdparm program requires root privileges, you must either log in as the root user account or use the su or sudo commands to run in from your normal user account. The command requires the drive's device name (/dev/sda for the first hard drive and /dev/sdb for the second hard drive) as an argument. You can try this command to see how fast data is read from your system's disk drive.

To display the space available in the currently mounted file systems, use the df command. If you want a more readable output from df, type the following command:

```
df -h
```

Here's typical output from this command:

```
[rich@localhost ~]$ df -h
Filesystem            Size  Used Avail Use% Mounted on
devtmpfs              5.3G     0  5.3G   0% /dev
tmpfs                 5.3G   16K  5.3G   1% /dev/shm
tmpfs                 5.3G  9.3M  5.3G   1% /run
tmpfs                 5.3G     0  5.3G   0% /sys/fs/cgroup
/dev/mapper/rl-root   15G   8.5G  5.8G  60% /
/dev/sda1            1014M  439M  576M  44% /boot
vmshare               476G  258G  219G  55% /media/sf_vmshare
tmpfs                 1.1G   28K  1.1G   1% /run/user/1000
[rich@localhost ~]$
```

As this example shows, the –h option causes the df command to display the sizes in gigabytes (G) and megabytes (M).

To check the disk space being used by a specific directory, use the du command. You can specify the –h option to view the output in kilobytes (K) and megabytes (M), as shown in the following example:

```
du -h /var/log
```

Here's the typical output from that command:

```
[rich@localhost ~]$ sudo du -h /var/log
0    /var/log/private
0    /var/log/samba/old
0    /var/log/samba
7.1M  /var/log/audit
0    /var/log/glusterfs
0    /var/log/chrony
0    /var/log/speech-dispatcher
0    /var/log/libvirt/qemu
0    /var/log/libvirt
0    /var/log/swtpm/libvirt/qemu
0    /var/log/swtpm/libvirt
0    /var/log/swtpm
460K  /var/log/sssd
12K   /var/log/cups
0    /var/log/gdm
80K   /var/log/tuned
0    /var/log/qemu-ga
5.2M  /var/log/anaconda
```

```
12K   /var/log/mariadb
22M   /var/log
[rich@localhost ~]$
```

The du command displays the disk space used by each directory, and the last line shows the total disk space used by that directory. If you want to see only the total space used by a directory, use the −s option. Type **du -sh /home** to see the space used by the /home directory, for example. The command produces output that looks like this:

```
89M  /home
```

# Viewing System Information with the /proc File System

Your Linux system has a special /proc file system. You can find out many things about your system from this file system. In fact, you can even change kernel parameters through the /proc file system (just by writing to a file in that file system), thereby modifying the system's behavior.

The /proc file system isn't a real directory on the hard drive but a collection of data structures in memory, managed by the Linux kernel, that appears to you as a set of directories and files. The purpose of /proc (also called the *process file system*) is to give you access to information about the Linux kernel, as well as to help you find out about all processes currently running on your system.

You can access the /proc file system just as you access any other directory, but you have to know the meaning of various files to interpret the information. Typically, you use the cat or more command to view the contents of a file in /proc. The file's contents provide information about some aspect of the system.

As with any directory, start by looking at a detailed directory listing of /proc. To do so, log in as root and type **ls -l /proc** in a terminal window. In the output, the first set of directories (indicated by the letter d at the beginning of the line) represents the processes currently running on your system. Each directory that corresponds to a process has the process ID (a number) as its name.

**WARNING**

Notice also a very large file named /proc/kcore; that file represents the *entire* physical memory of your system. Although /proc/kcore appears in the listing as a huge file, no single physical file occupies that much space on your hard drive, so don't try to remove the file to reclaim disk space.

Several files and directories in /proc contain interesting information about your Linux PC. The /proc/cpuinfo file, for example, lists the key characteristics of your system, such as processor type and floating-point processor information. You can view the processor information by typing **cat /proc/cpuinfo**. Here's what appears when cat /proc/cpuinfo is run on a sample system:

```
[rich@localhost ~]$ cat /proc/cpuinfo
Processor      : 0
vendor_id      : GenuineIntel
cpu family     : 6
model          : 126
model name     : Intel(R) Core(TM) i7-1065G7 CPU @ 1.30GHz
stepping       : 5
cpu MHz        : 1497.594
cache size     : 8192 KB
physical id    : 0
siblings       : 1
core id        : 0
cpu cores      : 1
apicid         : 0
initial apicid: 0
fpu            : yes
fpu_exception  : yes
cpuid level    : 22
wp             : yes
flags          : fpu vme de pse tsc msr pae mce cx8 apic sep mtrr pge mca cmov
 pat pse36 clflush mmx fxsr sse sse2 ht syscall nx rdtscp lm constant_tsc
   rep_good
 nopl xtopology nonstop_tsc cpuid tsc_known_freq pni pclmulqdq monitor
   ssse3 cx16
 pcid sse4_1 sse4_2 x2apic movbe popcnt aes xsave avx rdrand hypervisor lahf_lm
abm 3dnowprefetch invpcid_single fsgsbase avx2 invpcid rdseed clflushopt
md_clear flush_l1d arch_capabilities
bugs           : spectre_v1 spectre_v2 spec_store_bypass swapgs itlb_multihit
bogomips       : 2995.18
clflush size   : 64
cache_alignment: 64
address sizes  : 39 bits physical, 48 bits virtual
power management:

[rich@localhost ~]$
```

This output is from an Intel Core i7-1065G7 CPU @ 1.30GHz. The listing shows many interesting characteristics of the processor. The bogomips line in the /proc/ cpuinfo file shows the BogoMIPS for the processor, as computed by the Linux kernel when it boots. (BogoMIPS is something that Linux uses internally to time-delay loops.)

Table 2-6 summarizes some of the files in the /proc file system that provide information about your Linux system. You can view some of these files on your system to see what they contain but note that not all files shown in Table 2-6 are present on your system. The specific contents of the /proc file system depend on the kernel configuration and the driver modules that are loaded (which in turn depend on your PC's hardware configuration).

**TABLE 2-6** **Some Files and Directories in /proc**

| File Name | Content |
|---|---|
| /proc/acpi | Information about Advanced Configuration and Power Interface (ACPI) — an industry-standard interface for configuration and power management on laptops, desktops, and servers. |
| /proc/bus | Directory with bus-specific information for each bus type, such as PCI. |
| /proc/cmdline | The command line used to start the Linux kernel (such as ro root=LABEL=/ rhgb). |
| /proc/cpuinfo | Information about the CPU (the microprocessor). |
| /proc/devices | Available block and character devices in your system. |
| /proc/dma | Information about DMA (direct memory access) channels that are used. |
| /proc/driver/rtc | Information about the PC's real-time clock (RTC). |
| /proc/filesystems | List of supported file systems. |
| /proc/ide | Directory containing information about IDE devices. |
| /proc/interrupts | Information about interrupt request (IRQ) numbers and how they're used. |
| /proc/ioports | Information about input/output (I/O) port addresses and how they're used. |
| /proc/kcore | Image of the physical memory. |
| /proc/kmsg | Kernel messages. |
| /proc/loadavg | Load average (average number of processes waiting to run in the past 1, 5, and 15 minutes). |
| /proc/locks | Current kernel locks (used to ensure that multiple processes don't write to a file at the same time). |
| /proc/meminfo | Information about physical memory and swap-space usage. |
| /proc/misc | Miscellaneous information. |

| File Name | Content |
|---|---|
| /proc/modules | List of loaded driver modules. |
| /proc/mounts | List of mounted file systems. |
| /proc/net | Directory with many subdirectories that contain information about networking. |
| /proc/partitions | List of partitions known to the Linux kernel. |
| /proc/pci | Information about PCI devices found on the system. |
| /proc/scsi | Directory with information about SCSI devices found on the system (present only if you have a SCSI device). |
| /proc/stat | Overall statistics about the system. |
| /proc/swaps | Information about the swap space and how much is used. |
| /proc/sys | Directory with information about the system. You can change kernel parameters by writing to files in this directory. (Using this method to tune system performance requires expertise to do properly.) |
| /proc/uptime | Information about how long the system has been up. |
| /proc/version | Kernel version number. |

**TIP**

You can navigate the /proc file system just as you'd work with any other directories and files in Linux. Use the more or cat command to view the contents of a file.

# Understanding Linux Devices

Linux treats all devices as files and uses a device just as it uses a file — opens it, writes data to it, reads data from it, and closes it when finished. This ability to treat every device as a file is possible because of *device drivers*, which are special programs that control a particular type of hardware. When the kernel writes data to the device, the device driver does whatever is appropriate for that device. When the kernel writes data to the DVD drive, for example, the DVD device driver puts that data on the physical medium of the DVD disk.

Thus, the device driver isolates the device-specific code from the rest of the kernel and makes a device look like a file. Any application can access a device by opening the file specific to that device.

# Device files

Applications can access a device as though it were a file. These files, called *device files*, appear in the /dev directory in the Linux file system.

If you use the ls command to look at the list of files in the /dev directory, you see several thousand files. These files don't mean that your system has several thousand devices. The /dev directory has files for all possible types of devices, which is why the number of device files is so large.

How does the kernel know which device driver to use when an application opens a specific device file? The answer is in two numbers called the *major* and *minor device numbers*. Each device file is mapped to a specific device driver through these numbers.

To see an example of the major and minor device numbers, type the following command in a terminal window:

```
ls -l /dev/sda
```

You see a line of output similar to the following:

```
brw-rw----. 1 root disk 8, 0 Apr 29 18:31 /dev/sda
```

In this line, the major and minor device numbers appear just before the date. In this case, the major device number is 8, and the minor device number is 0. The kernel selects the device driver for this device file by using the major device number.

You don't have to know much about device files and device numbers except to be aware of their existence.

**TECHNICAL STUFF**

In case you're curious, all the major and minor numbers for devices are assigned according to device type. The Linux Assigned Names And Numbers Authority (LANANA) assigns these numbers. You can see the current device list at www.lanana.org.

## Block devices

The first letter in the listing of a device file also provides an important clue. For the /dev/sda device, the first letter is b, which indicates that /dev/hda is a *block device* — one that can accept or provide data in chunks (typically, 512 bytes or 1KB). By the way, /dev/sda refers to the first hard drive on your system (the C: drive in Windows). Hard drives, USB memory sticks, and DVD drives are examples of block devices.

## Character devices

If the first letter in the listing of a device file is c, the device is a *character device* — one that can receive and send data one character (1 byte) at a time. The serial port and parallel ports, for example, are character devices. To see the specific listing of a character device, type the following command in a terminal window:

```
ls -l /dev/ttyS0
```

The listing of this device is similar to the following:

```
$ ls -l /dev/ttyS0
crw-rw----. 1 root dialout 4, 64 Apr 26 23:57 /dev/ttyS0
$
```

Note that the first letter is c because /dev/ttyS0 — the first serial port — is a character device.

## Network devices

Network devices that enable your system to interact with a network — such as Ethernet and dial-up Point-to-Point Protocol (PPP) connections — are special because they need no file to correspond to the device. Instead, the kernel uses a special name for the device. Ethernet devices, for example, are named eth0 for the first Ethernet card, eth1 for the second one, and so on. PPP connections are named ppp0, ppp1, and so on.

Because network devices aren't mapped to device files, no files corresponding to these devices are in the /dev directory.

# Persistent device naming with udev

Starting with the Linux kernel 2.6, a new approach for handling devices was added, based on the following features:

>> **sysfs:** The kernel provides the sysfs file system, which is mounted on the /sys directory of the file system. The sysfs file system displays all the devices in the system as well as lots of information about each device, including the location of the device on the bus, attributes such as name and serial number, and the major and minor numbers of the device.

>> **/sbin/hotplug:** This program is called whenever a device is added or removed and can do whatever is necessary to handle the device.

>> **/sbin/udev:** This program takes care of dynamically named devices based on device characteristics such as serial number, device number on a bus, or a user-assigned name based on a set of rules that are set through the text file /etc/udev/udev.rules.

**REMEMBER**

The udev program's configuration file is /etc/udev/udev.conf. Based on settings in that configuration file, udev creates device nodes automatically in the directory specified by the udev_root parameter. To manage the device nodes in the /dev directory, for example, udev_root should be defined in /etc/udev/udev.conf as follows:

```
udev_root="/dev/"
```

# Managing Loadable Driver Modules

To use any device, the Linux kernel must contain the driver. If the driver code is linked into the kernel as a *monolithic* program (a program in the form of a single large file), adding a new driver means rebuilding the kernel with the new driver code. Rebuilding the kernel means that you have to reboot the PC with the new kernel before you can use the new device driver. Luckily, the Linux kernel uses a modular design that does away with rebooting hassles. Linux device drivers can be created in the form of modules that the kernel can load and unload without having to restart the PC.

**TECHNICAL STUFF**

Driver modules are one type of a broader category of software modules called *loadable kernel modules.* Other types of kernel modules include code that can support new types of file systems, modules for network protocols, and modules that interpret different formats of executable files.

## Loading and unloading modules

You can manage the loadable device driver modules by using a set of commands. You have to log in as root to use some of these commands. Table 2-7 summarizes a few common module commands.

If you have to use any of these commands, log in as root, or type either **su** or **sudo** in a terminal window to become root.

To see what modules are currently loaded, type **lsmod.** You see a long list of modules. The list that you see depends on the types of devices installed on your system.

**TABLE 2-7**     **Commands to Manage Kernel Modules**

| This Command | Does the Following |
|---|---|
| insmod | Inserts a module into the kernel. |
| rmmod | Removes a module from the kernel. |
| depmod | Determines interdependencies among modules. |
| ksyms | Displays a list of symbols along with the name of the module that defines the symbol. |
| lsmod | Lists all currently loaded modules. |
| modinfo | Displays information about a kernel module. |
| modprobe | Inserts or removes a module or a set of modules intelligently. (If module A requires B, for example, modprobe automatically loads B when asked to load A.) |

The list displayed by lsmod includes all types of Linux kernel modules, not just device drivers. For example, if you're using Rocky Linux, which uses the XFS file system by default, you'll find the libcrc32c and xfs modules installed.

**REMEMBER**

Another commonly used module command is modprobe. Use modprobe when you need to manually load or remove one or more modules. The best thing about modprobe is that you don't need to worry if a module requires other modules to work. The modprobe command automatically loads any other module needed by a module. To manually load the sound driver, use the command

```
modprobe snd-card-0
```

This command causes modprobe to load everything needed to make sound work.

**TIP**

You can use modprobe with the –r option to remove modules. To remove the sound modules, use the following command:

```
modprobe –r snd-card-0
```

This command gets rid of all the modules that the modprobe snd-card-0 command loaded.

## Understanding the /etc/modprobe.d files

How does the modprobe command know that it needs to load the snd-intel8x0 driver module? The answer's in the configuration files beneath the /etc/modprobe.d directory. The files there, all ending in the extension .conf, contain instructions that tell modprobe what it should load when it loads a module.

To view the contents of a particular configuration file, type

```
cat /etc/modprobe.d/xxx.conf
```

Where xxx is the name of the configuration file that you want to view.

# Scheduling Jobs in Linux

As a system administrator, you may have to run some programs automatically at regular intervals or execute one or more commands at a specified time in the future. Your Linux system includes the facilities to schedule jobs to run at any future date or time you want. You can also set up the system to perform a task periodically or just once. Here are some typical tasks you can perform by scheduling jobs on your Linux system:

>> Back up the files in the middle of the night.

>> Download large files in the early morning when the system isn't busy.

>> Send yourself messages as reminders of meetings.

>> Analyze system logs periodically and look for any abnormal activities.

You can set up these jobs by using the at command or the crontab facility of Linux. The next few sections introduce these job-scheduling features of Linux.

## Scheduling one-time jobs

If you want to run one or more commands at a later time, you can use the at command. The atd *daemon* — a program designed to process jobs submitted with at — runs your commands at the specified time and mails the output to you.

Some Linux distributions (such as Ubuntu) don't install the at program by default. You can use the standard software installation process for your Linux distribution (see Book 1, Chapter 5) for doing that.

Before you try the at command, you need to know that the following configuration files control which users can schedule tasks by using the at command:

>> /etc/at.allow contains the names of the users who may use the at command to submit jobs.

» /etc/at.deny contains the names of users who are not allowed to use the at command to submit jobs.

If these files aren't present, or if you find an empty /etc/at.deny file, any user can submit jobs by using the at command. The default in Linux is an empty /etc/at.deny file; when this default is in place, anyone can use the at command. If you don't want some users to use at, simply list their usernames in the /etc/at.deny file.

To use at to schedule a one-time job for execution at a later time, follow these steps:

**1.** **Run the at command with the date or time when you want your commands to be executed.**

When you press Enter, the at> prompt appears, as follows:

```
[rich@localhost ~]$ at 21:30
warning: commands will be executed using /bin/sh
at>
```

This method is the simplest way to indicate the time when you want to execute one or more commands; simply specify the time in a 24-hour format. In this case, you want to execute the commands at 9:30 tonight (or tomorrow, if it's already past 9:30 p.m.). You can, however, specify the execution time in many ways. (See Table 2-8 for examples.)

**2.** **At the at> prompt, type the commands you want to execute as though you were typing at the shell prompt.**

After each command, press Enter and continue with the next command.

**3.** **When you finish entering the commands you want to execute, press Ctrl+D to indicate the end.**

Here's an example that shows how to execute the ps command at a future time:

```
at> ps
at> <EOT>
job 2 at Fri Apr 29 21:30:00 2022
[rich@localhost ~]$
```

After you press Ctrl+D, the at command responds with the <EOT> message, a job number, and the date and time when the job will execute.

**TABLE 2-8**

## Formats for the at Command for the Time of Execution

| Command | When the Job Will Run |
|---|---|
| at now | Immediately |
| at now + 15 minutes | 15 minutes from the current time |
| at now + 4 hours | 4 hours from the current time |
| at now + 7 days | 7 days from the current time |
| at noon | At noon today (or tomorrow, if it's already past noon) |
| at now next hour | Exactly 60 minutes from now |
| at now next day | At the same time tomorrow |
| at 17:00 tomorrow | At 5:00 p.m. tomorrow |
| at 4:45pm | At 4:45 p.m. today (or tomorrow, if it's already past 4:45 p.m.) |
| at 3:00 Dec 28, 2018 | At 3:00 a.m. on December 28, 2018 |

After you enter one or more jobs, you can view the current list of scheduled jobs with the atq command. The output of this command looks similar to the following:

```
[rich@localhost ~]$ atq
2 Fri Apr 29 21:30:00 2022 a rich
[rich@localhost ~]$
```

The first field shows the job number — the same number that the at command displays when you submit the job. The next fields show the day, month, time, and year of execution. The last field shows the jobs pending in the a queue and the username.

If you want to cancel a job, use the atrm command to remove that job from the queue. When you're removing a job with the atrm command, refer to the job by its number, as follows:

```
atrm 2
```

This command deletes job 2.

**TIP**

When a job executes, the output is mailed to you. Type **mail** at a terminal window to read your mail and to view the output from your jobs.

# Scheduling recurring jobs

Although at is good for running commands at a specific time, it's not useful for running a program automatically at repeated intervals. You have to use crontab to schedule such recurring jobs, such as if you want to back up your files to tape at midnight every evening.

You schedule recurring jobs by placing job information in a file with a specific format and submitting this file with the crontab command. The cron daemon — crond — checks the job information every minute and executes the recurring jobs at the specified times. Because the cron daemon processes recurring jobs, such jobs are also referred to as *cron jobs.*

Any output from a cron job is mailed to the user who submits the job. (In the submitted job-information file, you can specify a different recipient for the mailed output.)

Two configuration files control who can schedule cron jobs by using crontab:

» /etc/cron.allow contains the names of the users who are allowed to use the crontab command to submit jobs.

» /etc/cron.deny contains the names of users who are not allowed to use the crontab command to submit jobs.

If the /etc/cron.allow file exists, only users listed in this file can schedule cron jobs. If only the /etc/cron.deny file exists, users listed in this file can't schedule cron jobs. If neither file exists, the default Linux setup enables any user to submit cron jobs.

To submit a cron job, follow these steps:

1. **Prepare a shell script (or an executable program in any programming language) that can perform the recurring task you want to perform.**

   You can skip this step if you want to execute an existing program periodically.

2. **Prepare a text file with information about the times when you want the shell script or program (from Step 1) to execute; then submit this file by using crontab.**

   You can submit several recurring jobs with a single file. Each line with timing information about a job has a standard format with six fields. The first five fields specify when the job runs, and the sixth and subsequent fields constitute the command that runs. Here's a line that executes the my job shell script in a user's home directory at 5 minutes past midnight each day:

```
5 0 * * * $HOME/myjob
```

Table 2-9 shows the meaning of the first five fields. **Note:** An asterisk (*) means all possible values for that field. Also, an entry in any of the first five fields can be a single number, a comma-separated list of numbers, a pair of numbers separated by a hyphen (indicating a range of numbers), or an asterisk.

**TABLE 2-9**

## Format for the Time of Execution in crontab Files

| Field Number | Meaning of Field | Acceptable Range of Values* |
|---|---|---|
| 1 | Minute | 0–59 |
| 2 | Hour of the day | 0–23 |
| 3 | Day of the month | 0–31 |
| 4 | Month | 1–12 (1 means January, 2 means February, and so on) or the names of months using the first three letters — Jan, Feb, Mar, Apr, May, Jun, Jul, Aug, Sep, Oct, Nov, Dec |
| 5 | Day of the week | 0–6 (0 means Sunday, 1 means Monday, and so on) or the three-letter abbreviations of weekdays — Sun, Mon, Tue, Wed, Thu, Fri, Sat |

*An asterisk in a field means all possible values for that field. If an asterisk is in the third field, for example, the job is executed every day.*

If the text file jobinfo (in the current directory) contains the job information, submit this information to crontab with the following command:

```
crontab jobinfo
```

That's it! You're set with the cron job. From now on, the cron job runs at regular intervals (as specified in the job-information file), and you receive mail messages with the output from the job.

To verify that the job is indeed scheduled, type the following command:

```
crontab -l
```

The output of the crontab -l command shows the cron jobs currently installed in your name. To remove your cron jobs, type **crontab -r.**

If you log in as root, you can also set up, examine, and remove cron jobs for any user. To set up cron jobs for a user, use this command:

```
crontab -u username filename
```

Here, *username* is the user for whom you install the cron jobs, and *filename* is the file that contains information about the jobs.

Use the following form of the crontab command to view the cron jobs for a user:

```
crontab -u username -l
```

To remove a user's cron jobs, use the following command:

```
crontab -u username -r
```

*Note:* The cron daemon also executes the cron jobs listed in the systemwide cron job file /etc/crontab. Here's a typical /etc/crontab file from a Linux system (type **cat /etc/crontab** to view the file):

```
SHELL=/bin/bash
PATH=/sbin:/bin:/usr/sbin:/usr/bin
MAILTO=root
HOME=/
# run-parts
01 * * * * root run-parts /etc/cron.hourly
02 4 * * * root run-parts /etc/cron.daily
22 4 * * 0 root run-parts /etc/cron.weekly
42 4 1 * * root run-parts /etc/cron.monthly
```

The first four lines set up several environment variables for the jobs listed in this file. The MAILTO environment variable specifies the user who receives the mail message with the output from the cron jobs in this file.

The line that begins with # is a comment line. The four lines following the run-parts comment execute the run-parts shell script (located in the /usr/bin directory) at various times with the name of a specific directory as argument. Each argument to run-parts — /etc/cron.hourly, /etc/cron.daily, /etc/cron.weekly, and /etc/cron.monthly — is a directory. Essentially, run-parts executes all scripts located in the directory that you provide as an argument.

Table 2-10 lists the directories where you can find these scripts and when they execute. You have to look at the scripts in these directories to know what executes at these intervals.

**TABLE 2-10**

## Script Directories for cron Jobs

| Directory Name | Script Executes |
|---|---|
| /etc/cron.hourly | Every hour |
| /etc/cron.daily | Each day |
| /etc/cron.weekly | Weekly |
| /etc/cron.monthly | Once each month |

**TIP**

If your Linux system uses the Systemd startup method, you can also use the systemd timer unit files for scheduling jobs to run. To view the list of currently scheduled jobs, type **systemctl list-timers**.

# Introducing Some GUI System Administration Tools

Each Linux distribution comes with GUI tools for performing system administration tasks. The GUI tools prompt you for input and then run the necessary Linux commands to perform the task. Although slight differences exist among them, the tools have become more uniform as time has passed.

Figure 2-2 shows the System Monitor utility in Rocky Linux with the File Systems tab selected. You can also choose Processes (shown in Figure 2-3) to kill a process, stop it, change priority, and so on.

A graphical look at the current state of the system is available on the Resources tab (shown in Figure 2-4); you can change nothing here other than colors used to represent each item. In this case, a quick look at the resources shows no outbound network activity at all; therefore, connectivity should be the first thing you investigate if you're troubleshooting the client.

As I mention earlier in this chapter, some distributions have more inclusive tools than others. Whereas Ubuntu and Rocky Linux have the Settings graphical utility (shown in Figure 2-5), for example, SUSE has the YaST Control Center. Aside from the fact that YaST has more options, the interfaces are very similar.

As you can see from Figure 2-5, the GUI tool is truly meant to be a one-stop-shopping spot for all your system administration chores.

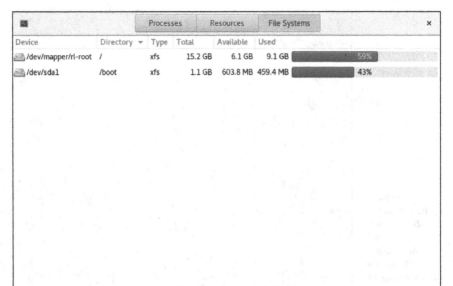

**FIGURE 2-2:**
The File Systems
tab in System
Monitor within
Rocky Linux.

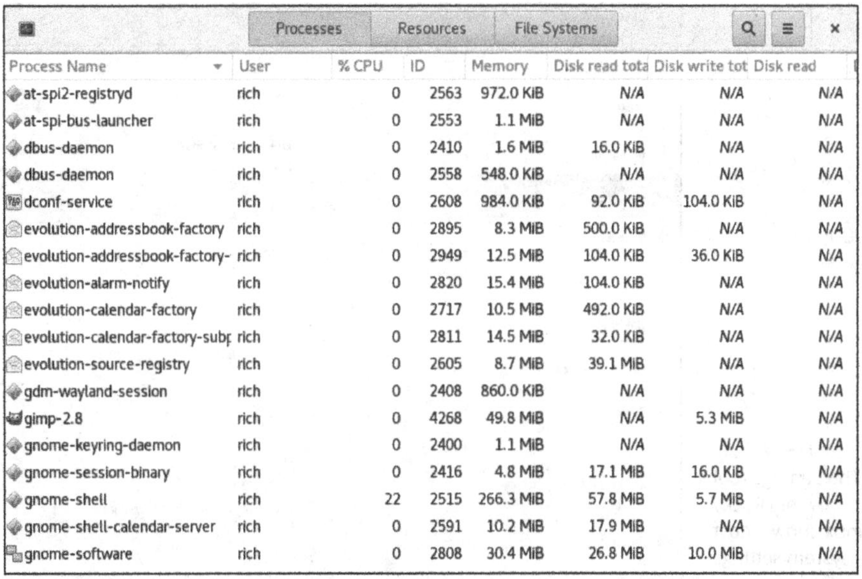

**FIGURE 2-3:**
The options
available on the
Processes tab of
System Monitor
within Rocky
Linux.

Most Linux distributions include GUI utilities that perform system administration chores. If you use any of these GUI utilities to perform a task that requires you to be root, the utility typically pops up a dialog box that prompts you for the root password (except in Ubuntu, in which the GUI tools prompt for your normal user password). Just type the password and press Enter. If you don't want to use the utility, click Cancel.

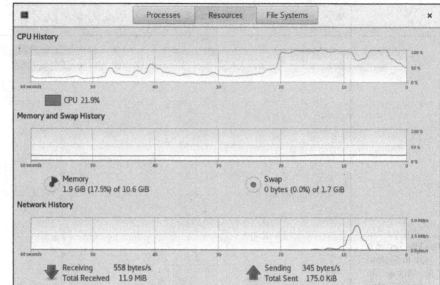

**FIGURE 2-4:**
The Resources
tab of System
Monitor within
Rocky Linux
shows the
current state of
the system.

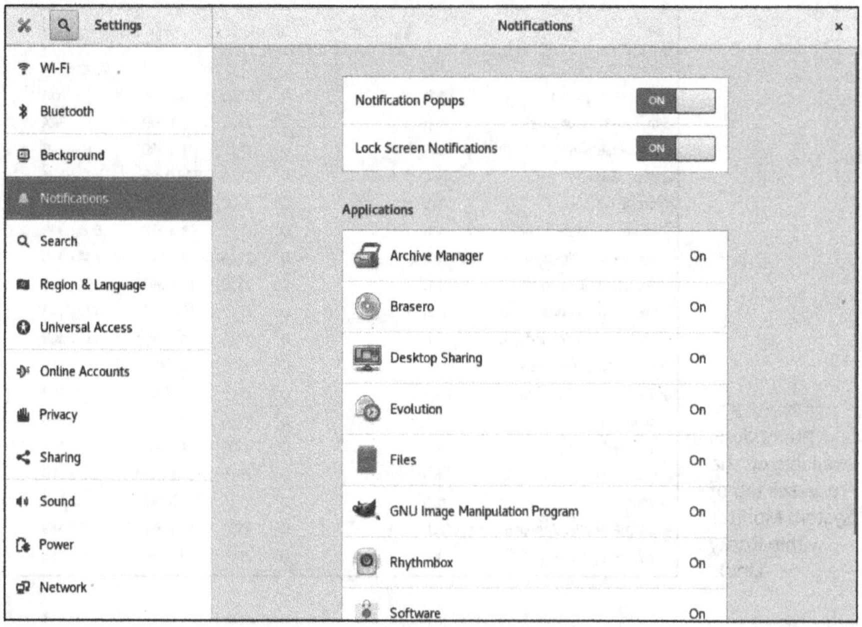

**FIGURE 2-5:**
The Settings tool
within Rocky
Linux shows most
system settings
and lets you
make changes.

## IN THIS CHAPTER

» **Managing user accounts**

» **Managing your groups**

» **Working in the user environment**

» **Changing user and group ownerships of files and directories**

# Chapter 3

# Managing Users and Groups

inux is a multiuser system, so it has many user accounts. Even if you've set up a test machine and you're the only user using that system, you'll have a host of system user accounts. Most of these accounts aren't for people to use; they're for running specific programs, because many servers require a unique username and group name. The Apache web server, for example, often runs under the username apache.

User accounts can belong to one or more groups. Typically, each username has a corresponding private group name. By default, each user belongs to that corresponding private group, but you can define other groups for the purpose of providing access to specific files and directories based on group membership.

User and group ownerships of files ensure that only the right people (or the right processes) can access certain files and directories. Managing the user and group accounts is a typical task in system administration. It's not hard to do this part of the job, given the tools that come with Linux as you discover in this chapter.

# Adding User Accounts

You get the chance to add user accounts when you boot your system for the first time after installing Linux. Typically (depending on your distribution), the root account is the only one that has to be created/configured during installation. If you don't add other user accounts when you start the system for the first time, you can add new users later by using a graphical user interface (GUI) user account manager or the useradd command-line command.

**REMEMBER**

Creating user accounts besides root is always a good idea. Even if you're the only user of the system, logging in as a less privileged user is good practice, because that way you can't damage any important system files inadvertently. If necessary, you can either use the su – command to log in as root and then perform any system administration tasks or use the sudo command to run a single command with root privileges.

## Managing user accounts by using a GUI user manager

Most Linux distributions come with a GUI tool for managing user accounts. You can use that GUI tool to add user accounts. The tool displays a list of current user accounts and has an Add button for adding users. For the purposes of illustration, Figure 3-1 shows the Users interface from Settings in Ubuntu.

The basic steps, regardless of the specific GUI tool, are as follows:

1. **Click the Unlock button to allow editing of user accounts.**

   You must have root privileges to add new user accounts, so most GUI tools require you to click a button to unlock the tool for administrator use.

   A dialog box prompts you for your password to allow you to perform administrator functions.

2. **Click the Add User button.**

   A dialog box prompts you for information about the username and password variables for the new user account.

3. **Enter the requested information.**

   The GUI tool takes care of adding the new user account.

4. **(Optional) In some distributions, you can click one of the other tabs for the user to configure additional information.**

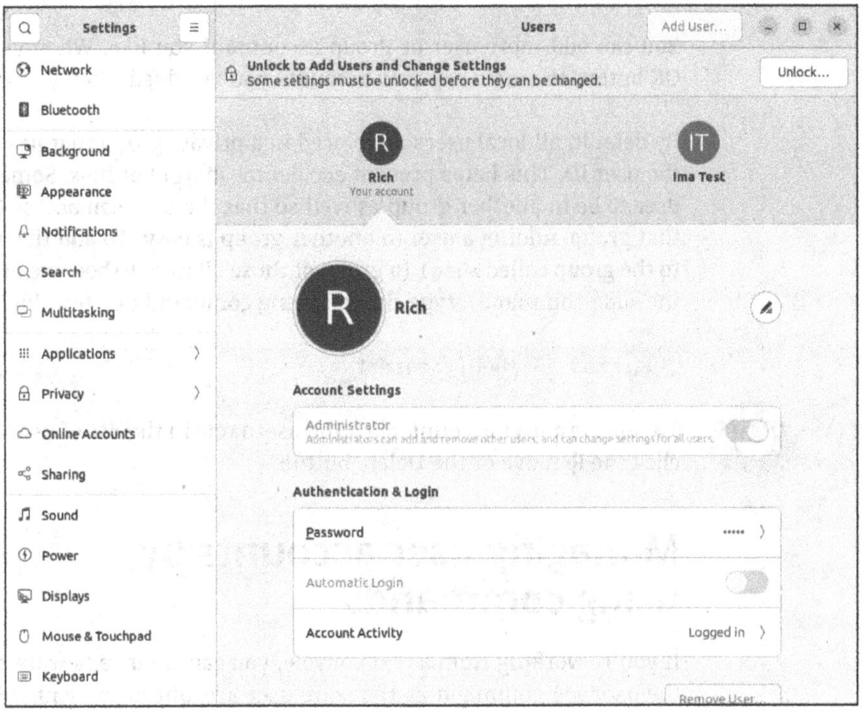

FIGURE 3-1:
The Users
section of the
Ubuntu Settings
dialog box.

Where available, the Details tab allows you to override the defaults for the home directory, shell, and ID information.

The Password Settings tab, when present, allows you to override the defaults for the password configuration. Plug-ins can be used for some parameters but are often used for *quota configuration* (such as size limits on files and the number of inodes that can be created):

- *Soft limits* warn the user.

- *Hard limits* stop the user.

TIP

The tabs other than User Data are used to override the system defaults. If you want to change the system defaults, change the variables in the User and Group Administration interface.

In most distributions, the tool you use to add users is called User and Group Management because it can configure two types of accounts: Users and Groups. Selecting Groups instead of Users allows you to add groups to /etc/group.

To add a new user account, click the Add button and then enter the information requested in the New Local User window. Fill in the requested information (including any add-ins, such as for group quotas) and then click the OK button.

You can add more user or group accounts if you like. When you finish, click the OK button to create any new accounts you've added; then you exit automatically.

By default, all local users are placed in a private group that has the same name as the user ID. This helps prevent accidental sharing of files. Sometimes, you want a user to be in another group as well so that the user can access the files owned by that group. Adding a user to another group is easy. To add the username imatest to the group called wheel (a group of those allowed to become other users by using the sudo command), type the following command in a terminal window:

```
usermod -G wheel imatest
```

**TIP**

To remove a user account, click the username in the list of user accounts and then click the Remove or the Delete button.

## Managing user accounts by using commands

If you're working from a text console, you can create a new user account by using the useradd command as the root user account or by using either su- or sudo. Creating a user account is a two-step process. Follow these steps to add an account for a new user:

1. **Type the following** useradd **command with the** -c **option to create the account and add a comment:**

   ```
   /usr/sbin/useradd -c "Rich Blum" rblum
   ```

2. **Set the password by using the** passwd **command, as follows:**

   ```
   passwd rblum
   ```

   You're prompted for the password twice. If you type a password that someone can easily guess, the passwd program scolds you and suggests that you use a more difficult password.

**TECHNICAL STUFF**

The useradd command consults the following configuration files and directory to obtain default information about various parameters for the new user account:

>> /etc/default/useradd: Specifies the default shell (/bin/bash) and the default home directory location (/home)

>> /etc/login.defs: Provides systemwide defaults for automatic group and user IDs, as well as password-expiration parameters

» `/etc/skel`: A directory that contains the default files that `useradd` creates in the user's home directory

Examine these files with the `cat` or `more` command to see what they contain.

**REMEMBER**

You can delete a user account by using the `userdel` command. Simply type **/usr/sbin/userdel** *username* at the command prompt, where *username* is the name of the user you want to remove. To wipe out that user's home directory as well, type **userdel −r** *username*.

To modify any information in a user account, use the `usermod` command. For user `rblum` to have `root` as the primary group, type the following:

```
usermod −g root rblum
```

**TIP**

To find out more about the `useradd`, `userdel`, and `usermod` commands, type **man useradd**, **man userdel**, or **man usermod**, respectively, in a terminal window.

# Managing Groups

A *group* is something to which users belong. A group has a name and an identification number (ID). After a group is defined, users can belong to one or more of these groups.

You can find all the existing groups listed in `/etc/group`. Here's the line that defines the group named `wheel`:

```
wheel:x:10:root,rblum
```

As this example shows, each line in `/etc/group` has the following format, with four fields separated by colons:

```
groupname:password:GID:membership
```

Table 3-1 explains the meaning of the four fields in a group definition.

If you want to create a new group, you can simply use the `groupadd` command. To add a group called `class` with an automatically selected group ID, type the following command in a terminal window (you have to be logged in as `root`):

```
groupadd class
```

TABLE 3-1

## Meaning of Fields in /etc/group File

| Field Name | Meaning |
| --- | --- |
| groupname | The name of the group (such as wheel). |
| password | The group password. (An x means that the password is stored in the /etc/shadow file.) |
| GID | The numerical group ID (such as 10). |
| membership | A comma-separated list of usernames that belong to this group (such as root,rblum). |

Then you can add users to this group with the usermod command. To add the user rblum to the group named class, type the following commands:

```
usermod -G class rblum
```

If you want to remove a group, use the groupdel command. To remove a group named class, type

```
groupdel class
```

# Exploring the User Environment

When you log in as a user, you get a set of environment variables that controls many aspects of what you see and do on your Linux system. If you want to see your current environment, type the following command in a terminal window:

```
env
```

(By the way, the printenv command also displays the environment, but env is shorter.)

The env command prints a long list of lines. The collection of lines is the current environment; each line defines an environment variable. The env command displays this typical line:

```
HOSTNAME=localhost.localdomain
```

This line defines the environment variable HOSTNAME as localhost.localdomain.

An *environment variable* is nothing more than a name associated with a string. Here is an example of how the environment variable named PATH may be defined for a normal user:

```
PATH=/usr/local/bin:/bin:/usr/bin:/usr/local/sbin:/usr/sbin:/sbin
```

The string to the right of the equal sign (=) is the value of the PATH environment variable. By convention, the PATH environment variable is a sequence of directory names, with names separated by colons ( : ).

Each environment variable has a specific purpose. When the shell has to search for a file, for example, it simply searches the directories listed in the PATH environment variable in the order of their appearance. Therefore, if two programs have the same name, the shell executes the one that it finds first.

In a fashion similar to the shell's use of the PATH environment variable, an editor such as vi uses the value of the TERM environment variable to figure out how to display the file you edit with vi. To see the current setting of TERM, type the following command at the shell prompt:

```
echo $TERM
```

If you type this command in a terminal window, you will see the terminal type assigned to your terminal window, for example:

```
xterm-256color
```

To define an environment variable in bash, use the following syntax:

```
export NAME=Value
```

Here, NAME denotes the name of the environment variable, and Value is the string representing its value. Therefore, you set TERM to the value xterm by using the following command:

```
export TERM=xterm
```

**TIP**

After you define an environment variable, you can change its value simply by specifying the new value with the syntax NAME=new-value. To change the definition of TERM to vt100, for example, type **TERM=vt100** at the shell prompt.

With an environment variable such as PATH, you typically want to append a new directory name to the existing definition rather than define the PATH from scratch. If you download and install the fictional XYZ 5 Development Kit, you have to add the location of the XYZ binaries to PATH. Here's how you accomplish that task:

```
export PATH=$PATH:/usr/xyz/xyz.5.0/bin
```

This command appends the string :/usr/xyz/xyz.5.0/bin to the current definition of the PATH environment variable. The net effect is to add /usr/xyz/xyz.5.0/bin to the list of directories in PATH.

*Note:* You also can write this export command as follows:

```
export PATH=${PATH}:/usr/xyz/xyz.5.0/bin
```

After you type that command, you can access programs in the /usr/xyz/xyz.5.0/bin directory by just typing the program name without the full directory path.

PATH and TERM are only two of several common environment variables. Table 3-2 lists some of the environment variables for a typical Linux user.

**TABLE 3-2**

## Typical Environment Variables in Linux

| Environment Variable | Contents |
|---|---|
| DISPLAY | The name of the display on which the X Window System displays output (typically set to :0.0) |
| HOME | Your home directory |
| HOSTNAME | The host name of your system |
| LOGNAME | Your login name |
| MAIL | The location of your mail directory |
| PATH | The list of directories in which the shell looks for programs |
| SHELL | Your shell (SHELL=/bin/bash for bash) |
| TERM | The type of terminal |

# Changing User and Group Ownership of Files

In Linux, each file or directory has two types of owners: a user and a group. In other words, a user and group own each file and directory. The user and group ownerships can control who can access a file or directory.

To view the owner of a file or directory, use the `ls -l` command to see the detailed listing of a directory. Here's a typical file's information:

```
-rw-rw-r--  1 rblum rblum     1 Apr 23 15:10 test.txt
```

In this example, the first set of characters shows the file's permission setting — who can read, write, or execute the file. The third and fourth fields (in this example, `rblum rblum`) indicate the user and group owner of the file. Each user has a private group that has the same name as the username. Thus, most files appear to show the username twice when you list user and group ownership.

As a system administrator, you may decide to change the group ownership of a file to a common group. Suppose that you want to change the group ownership of the `test.txt` file to the `class` group. To do so, log in as `root` and then type the following command:

```
chgrp class test.txt
```

This `chgrp` command changes the group ownership of `test.txt` to `class`.

You can use the `chown` command to change the user owner. The command has the following format:

```
chown username filename
```

To change the user ownership of a file named `sample.jpg` to `rblum`, type

```
chown rblum sample.jpg
```

The `chown` command can change both the user and group owner at the same time. To change the user owner to `rblum` and the group owner to `class`, type

```
chown rblum.class test.txt
```

In other words, you simply append the group name to the username with a period between the two values.

IN THIS CHAPTER

» Navigating the Linux file system

» Sharing files through NFS

» Mounting the NTFS file system

» Accessing MS-DOS files

# Chapter **4**

# Managing File Systems

A *file system* refers to the organization of files and directories. As a system administrator, you have to perform certain operations to manage file systems on various storage media. You have to know, for example, how to *mount* — add a file system on a storage medium by attaching it to the overall Linux file system. You also have to back up important data and restore files from a backup. Other file-system operations include sharing files with the Network File System (NFS) and accessing Microsoft Windows files. This chapter shows you how to perform all file-system management tasks.

## Exploring the Linux File System

Whether you are studying for the Linux-related certification exams or just trying to understand the working of Linux more, it is important to know that the files and directories in your PC store information in an organized manner, just like paper filing systems. When you store information on paper, you typically put several pages in a folder and then store the folder in a file cabinet. If you have many folders, you probably have some sort of filing system. You might label each folder's tab and then arrange them alphabetically in the file cabinet, for example. You might have several file cabinets, each with lots of drawers, which in turn contain folders full of pages.

Operating systems such as Linux organize information in your computer in a manner similar to your paper filing system. Linux uses a file system to organize all information in your computer. The storage media aren't a metal file cabinet and paper, of course. Instead, Linux stores information on devices such as hard drives, USB drives, and DVD drives.

To draw an analogy between your computer's file system and a paper filing system, think of a disk drive as being the file cabinet. The drawers in the file cabinet correspond to the directories in the file system. The folders in each drawer are also directories — because a directory in a computer file system can contain other directories. You can think of files as being the pages inside the folder — where the actual information is stored. Figure 4-1 illustrates the analogy between a file cabinet and the Linux file system.

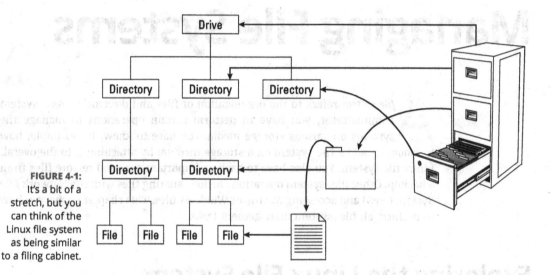

**FIGURE 4-1:** It's a bit of a stretch, but you can think of the Linux file system as being similar to a filing cabinet.

The Linux file system has a hierarchical structure. Directories can contain other directories, which in turn contain individual files.

Everything in your Linux system is organized in files and directories. To access and use documents and programs on your system, you have to be familiar with the file system.

## Understanding the file-system hierarchy

For basic administration and for exam study alike, know that the Linux file system is organized like an upside down tree, with a root directory from which all other directories branch out. When you write a complete pathname, the root directory is represented by a single slash (/). Then there's a hierarchy of files and directories. Parts of the file system can be on different physical drives or in different hard drive partitions.

Linux uses a standard directory hierarchy. Figure 4-2 shows some of the standard parts of the Linux file system. You can create new directories anywhere in this structure.

**FIGURE 4-2:**
The Linux file
system uses
a standard
directory
hierarchy similar
to this one.

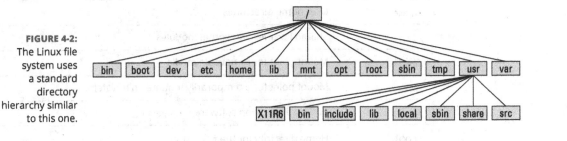

Write the name of any file or directory by concatenating the names of directories that identify where that file or directory is and by using the forward slash (/) as a separator. In Figure 4-2, the usr directory at the top level is written as /usr because the root directory (/) contains usr. On the other hand, the X11R6 directory is inside the usr directory, which is inside the root directory (/). Therefore, the X11R6 directory is uniquely identified by the name /usr/X11R6. This type of full name is a *pathname* because the name identifies the path you take from the root directory to reach a file. Thus, /usr/X11R6 is a pathname.

Each of the standard directories in the Linux file system has a specific purpose. Table 4-1, Table 4-2, and Table 4-3 summarize these directories.

## Mounting a device on the file system

The storage devices that you use in Linux contain Linux file systems and it is good to know this for daily work, but necessary to know this for exam study. Each device has its own local file system, consisting of a hierarchy of directories. Before you can access the files on a device, you have to attach the device's directory hierarchy to the tree that represents the overall Linux file system.

*Mounting* is the operation you perform to cause the file system on a physical storage device (a hard drive partition or a USB memory stick) to appear as part of the Linux file system. Figure 4-3 illustrates the concept of mounting.

TABLE 4-1

## Standard Directories in Linux File System

| Directory | Used to Store |
|-----------|---------------|
| /bin | Executable files for user commands (for use by all users) |
| /boot | Files needed by the bootloader to load the Linux kernel |
| /dev | Device files |
| /etc | Host-specific system configuration files |
| /home | User home directories |
| /lib | Shared libraries and kernel modules |
| /media | Mount point for removable media |
| /mnt | Mount point for a temporarily mounted file system |
| /opt | Add-on application software packages |
| /root | Home directory for the root user |
| /sbin | Utilities for system administration |
| /srv | Data for services (such as web and FTP) offered by this system |
| /tmp | Temporary files |

TABLE 4-2

## The /usr Directory Hierarchy

| Directory | Secondary Directory Hierarchy |
|-----------|-------------------------------|
| /usr/bin | Most user commands |
| /usr/games | Many games install here though they are not technically required to do so other than for historic reasons |
| /usr/include | Directory for *include files* — files that are inserted into source code of applications by using various directives — used in developing Linux applications |
| /usr/lib | Libraries used by software packages and for programming |
| /usr/libexec | Libraries for applications |
| /usr/local | Any local software |
| /usr/sbin | Nonessential system administrator utilities |
| /usr/share | Shared data that doesn't depend on the system architecture (whether the system is an Intel PC or a Sun SPARC workstation) |
| /usr/src | Source code |

TABLE 4-3

## The /var Directory Hierarchy

| Directory | Variable Data |
|-----------|---------------|
| /var/cache | Cached data for applications |
| /var/crash | Dump files from kernel crashes |
| /var/lib | Information relating to the current state of applications |
| /var/lock | Lock files to ensure that a resource is used by one application only |
| /var/log | Log files organized into subdirectories |
| /var/mail | User mailbox files |
| /var/opt | Variable data for packages stored in the /opt directory |
| /var/run | Data describing the system since it was booted |
| /var/spool | Data that's waiting for some kind of processing |
| /var/tmp | Temporary files preserved between system reboots |
| /var/yp | Network Information Service (NIS) database files |

# OVERVIEW OF FHS

The Filesystem Hierarchy Standard (FHS) specifies the organization of files and directories in Unix-like operating systems, such as Linux. FHS defines a standard set of directories and their intended use. The FHS, if faithfully adopted by all Linux distributions, should help improve the interoperability of applications, system administration tools, development tools, and scripts across all Linux distributions. FHS even helps the system documentation (as well as books like this one) because the same description of the file system applies to all Linux distributions. Version 3.0 of FHS is the latest version as of this writing; it was released on June 3, 2015.

FHS is part of the Linux Standard Base (see https://wiki.linuxfoundation.org/lsb/start): a set of binary standards aimed at reducing variations among the Linux distributions and promoting portability of applications. As of this writing, the most current Base is 5.0. To find out more about the Linux Standard Base, check out the home page at https://wiki.linuxfoundation.org/lsb/start.

Figure 4-3 shows two hard drives on the Linux system. Hard drive 1 contains the root file system; hard drive 2 is a separate hard drive that contains user directories. Separate physical devices are mounted at specific mount points on the Linux file system. The system defines a mount point of /home in the file system to mount hard drive 2. After the system mounts the hard drive, users can access files in the file system using the file system path. For example, to access the rich directory on hard drive 2, you would just use the path /home/rich.

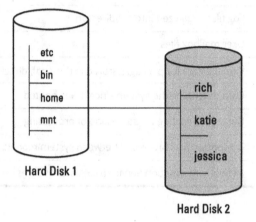

**FIGURE 4-3:**
You have to mount a device on the Linux file system before accessing it.

Hard Disk 1

Hard Disk 2

This is also a common method used for mounting USB memory sticks. Most Linux distributions create a mount point called /media to use for mounting external media devices, such as USB memory sticks. When you insert a USB stick into your computer, the system uses the mount command to relate the physical device file created (such as /dev/sdc) to the mount point in the system. You can also manually use the mount command to mount the device to another location:

```
mount -t vfat /dev/sdc /stick1
```

The -t option tells Linux the file system type used by the device. In this case, the USB memory stick is formatted using the Windows FAT file system, commonly used on memory sticks.

The root user account can use any directory as the mount point, but normal users can only mount devices within their HOME directory structure. If you mount a device on a nonempty directory, however, you can't access the files in that directory until you unmount the device by using the umount command. Therefore, always use an empty directory as the mount point.

REMEMBER

To unmount a device when you no longer need it, use the umount command. You can use either the device name or the mount point name in the umount command:

```
umount /dev/sdc
```

The umount command succeeds as long as no one is using the device. If you get an error when trying to unmount the device, check to see whether the current working directory is on the device. If you're currently working in one of the device's directories, that also qualifies as a use of the device.

## Examining the /etc/fstab file

The mount command has the following general format:

```
mount device-name mount-point
```

You can mount by specifying only the device name or the *mount-point* name, provided that the /etc/fstab file contains an entry for the device mount point. That entry specifies the device name and the file-system type.

In Debian, you can mount a DVD or CD-ROM by typing one of the following commands:

```
mount /dev/cdrom
mount /media/cdrom
```

The /etc/fstab file system table file is a *configuration file* — a text file containing information that the mount and umount commands use. Each line in the /etc/fstab file provides information about a device and its mount point in the Linux file system. Essentially, the /etc/fstab file associates various mount points within the file system with specific devices, which enables the mount command to work from the command line with only the mount point or the device as argument.

Here's a /etc/fstab file from an Ubuntu system. (The file has a similar format in other Linux distributions.)

```
root@Ubuntu22:~$ cat /etc/fstab
# /etc/fstab: static file system information.
#
# Use 'blkid' to print the universally unique identifier for a
# device; this may be used with UUID= as a more robust way to name devices
# that works even if disks are added and removed. See fstab(5).
#
# <file system> <mount point>   <type> <options>       <dump> <pass>
# / was on /dev/sda3 during installation
```

```
UUID=5cfa3b9b-29b5-4f3c-8e15-c77febd8c08d /            ext4
    errors=remount-ro 0        1
# /boot/efi was on /dev/sda2 during installation
UUID=8B9D-4521  /boot/efi      vfat    umask=0077     0      1
/swapfile                                 none          swap   sw
    0       0
root@Ubuntu22:~$
```

The first field on each line shows a device name, such as a hard drive partition, or the unique device ID assigned to the device. The second field is the mount point, and the third field indicates the type of file system on the device. You can ignore the last three fields for now.

This /etc/fstab file shows that the /swapfile device functions as a swap device for virtual memory, which is why the file-system type is set to swap. Linux can use either a file on an existing file system, or a specially formatted file system as swap space for additional memory.

**TECHNICAL STUFF**

The Linux operating system uses the contents of the /etc/fstab file to mount various file systems automatically. During Linux startup, the init process executes a shell script (or the systemd process executes a unit file) that runs the mount -a command. That command reads the /etc/fstab file and mounts all listed file systems (except those with the noauto option). The third field on each line of /etc/fstab specifies the type of file system on that device, and the fourth field shows a comma-separated list of options that the mount command uses when mounting that device on the file system. Typically, you find the defaults option in this field. The defaults option implies (among other things) that the device mounts at boot time, that only the root user can mount the device, and that the device mounts for both reading and writing. If the options include noauto, the device doesn't mount automatically when the system boots.

# Sharing Files with NFS

Sharing files through the NFS is simple and involves two basic steps:

>> On the NFS server, export one or more directories by listing them in the /etc/exports file and by running the /usr/sbin/exportfs command. In addition, you must run the NFS server software package to start the server service.

>> On each client system, use the mount command to mount the directories that the server has exported.

**WARNING**

NFS has security vulnerabilities. Therefore, don't set up NFS on systems that are directly connected to the Internet; be sure to put a firewall between them and the Internet.

The upcoming section walks you through an NFS setup, using an example of two Linux PCs on a LAN. If you're running your Linux systems on a virtual server (such as Oracle's VirtualBox), you'll need to set the guest system's network configuration to use a bridged connection rather than a NAT connection. This allows each guest OS to obtain an IP address on your home LAN.

## Installing NFS

Many Linux systems don't install the NFS software by default, so you'll need to manually install it. For Ubuntu, install the `nfs-kernel-server` package using the apt tool:

```
rich@Ubuntu22:/$ sudo apt install nfs-kernel-server
[sudo] password for rich:
Reading package lists... Done
Building dependency tree... Done
Reading state information... Done
The following additional packages will be installed:
  keyutils libevent-core-2.1-7 libnfsidmap1 nfs-common rpcbind
Suggested packages:
  open-iscsi watchdog
The following NEW packages will be installed:
  keyutils libevent-core-2.1-7 libnfsidmap1 nfs-common nfs-kernel-server
  rpcbind
0 upgraded, 6 newly installed, 0 to remove and 10 not upgraded.
Need to get 616 kB of archives.
After this operation, 2,235 kB of additional disk space will be used.
Do you want to continue? [Y/n]
```

After you install the NFS package, you can check to make sure it's active on the system:

```
rich@Ubuntu22:~$ systemctl status nfs-kernel-server
  nfs-server.service - NFS server and services
     Loaded: loaded (/lib/systemd/system/nfs-server.service; enabled; vendor pr>
     Active: active (exited) since Fri 2022-04-29 18:26:34 EDT; 4min 57s ago
    Process: 922 ExecStartPre=/usr/sbin/exportfs -r (code=exited, status=0/SUCC>
    Process: 925 ExecStart=/usr/sbin/rpc.nfsd (code=exited, status=0/SUCCESS)
   Main PID: 925 (code=exited, status=0/SUCCESS)
        CPU: 4ms

Apr 29 18:26:34 Ubuntu22 systemd[1]: Starting NFS server and services...
```

```
Apr 29 18:26:34 Ubuntu22 systemd[1]: Finished NFS server and services.
rich@Ubuntu22:~$
```

For Rocky Linux, the nfs-utils package is already installed by default, but not active. To activate it you'll need to use the systemctl command:

```
[rich@unknown08002755DFBD ~]$ sudo systemctl enable nfs-server
Created symlink /etc/systemd/system/multi-user.target.wants/nfs-server.service -
    /usr/lib/systemd/system/nfs-server.service.
[rich@unknown08002755DFBD ~]$ sudo systemctl start nfs-server
[rich@unknown08002755DFBD ~]$
```

After you have the NFS server installed and running, the next step is to configure a directory to share.

**WARNING**

If your Linux system uses a firewall program (such as UFW for Ubuntu, or firewalld for Rocky Linux), you'll need to allow NFS traffic through the firewall. For example, on a Rocky Linux system the command would be as follows:

```
[rich@unknown08002755DFBD ~]$ sudo firewall-cmd --add-
    service={nfs,nfs3,mountd,rpc-bind} --permanent
success
[rich@unknown08002755DFBD ~]$ sudo firewall-cmd --reload
success
[rich@unknown08002755DFBD ~]$
```

# Exporting a file system with NFS

To export a file system with NFS, start with the server system that *exports* — makes available to the client systems — the contents of a directory. On the server, you must run the NFS service and also designate one or more file systems to be exported to the client systems.

You have to add an appropriate entry to the /etc/exports file. Suppose that you want to export the /share directory, and you want to enable the hostname testbox to mount this file system for read and write operations. (You can use a host's IP address in place of the host name.) You can do so by adding the following entry to the /etc/exports file:

```
/share testbox(rw)
```

If you use the IP address of a host, the entry might look like this:

```
/share 192.168.1.200(rw)
```

This entry specifies that 192.168.1.200 is the IP address of the host that's allowed full access to the `/share` directory.

After adding the entry in the `/etc/exports` file, manually export the file system by typing the following command in a terminal window:

```
exportfs -a
```

This command exports all file systems defined in the `/etc/exports` file.

After exporting the file system, restart the NFS server using a method appropriate for your Linux distribution. In Rocky Linux, for example, log in as root and type the following command in a terminal window:

```
systemctl restart nfs-server
```

When the NFS service is up, the server side of NFS is ready. Now you can try to mount the exported file system from a client system and access the exported file system.

**TIP**

If you ever make any changes to the exported file systems listed in the `/etc/exports` file, remember to restart the NFS service.

## Mounting an NFS file system

To access an exported NFS file system on a client system, you have to mount that file system on a *mount point* — which is, in practical terms, nothing more than a local directory. Suppose that you want to access the `/share` directory exported from the server named myserver at the local directory `/mnt/myserver` on the client system. To do so, follow these steps:

**1.** Log in as root, and create the directory with the following command:

```
mkdir /mnt/myserver
```

**2.** Type the following command to perform the mount operation:

```
mount myserver:/share /mnt/myserver
```

If you know only the IP address of the server, replace the host name (in this case, myserver) with the IP address.

**3.** Change the directory to /mnt/myserver with the command cd /mnt/myserver.

Now you can view and access exported files from this directory.

To confirm that the NFS file system is indeed mounted, log in as root on the client system, and type **mount** in a terminal window. You see a line similar to the following about the NFS file system:

```
lnbp200:/home/public on /mnt/lnbp200 type nfs (rw,addr=192.168.1.200)
```

# Accessing a DOS or Windows File System

If you're using a legacy machine that you just don't want to throw out and have a really old version of Microsoft Windows installed on your hard drive, you've probably already mounted the DOS or Windows partition under Linux. If not, you can easily mount DOS or Windows partitions in Linux. Mounting makes the DOS or Windows directory hierarchy appear as part of the Linux file system.

## Mounting a DOS or Windows disk partition

To mount a DOS or Windows hard drive partition or storage device in Linux, use the mount command but include the option -t vfat to indicate the file-system type as DOS. If your DOS partition happens to be the first partition on your IDE (Integrated Drive Electronics) drive, and you want to mount it on /dosc, use the following mount command:

```
mount -t vfat /dev/hda1 /dosc
```

The -t vfat part of the mount command specifies that the device you mount — /dev/hda1 — has an MS-DOS file system. Figure 4-4 illustrates the effect of this mount command.

Figure 4-4 shows how directories in your DOS partition map to the Linux file system. What was the C:\DOS directory under DOS becomes /dosc/dos under Linux. Similarly, C:\WINDOWS is now /dosc/windows. You probably can see the pattern. To convert a DOS filename to Linux (when you mount the DOS partition on /dosc), perform the following steps:

1. **Change the DOS names to lowercase.**
2. **Change** C:\ **to** /dosc/.
3. **Change all backslashes (\) to slashes (/).**

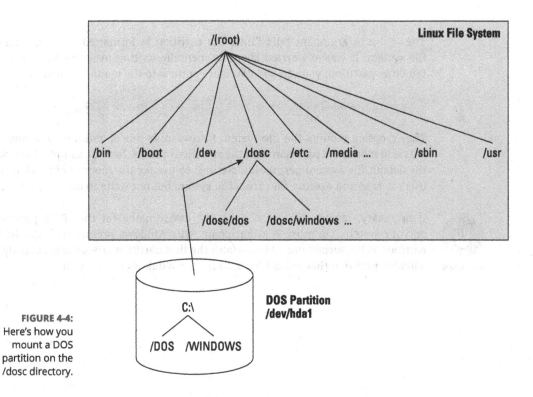

**FIGURE 4-4:**
Here's how you
mount a DOS
partition on the
/dosc directory.

# Mounting an NTFS partition

Nowadays, most PCs come with Windows 10 or Windows 11 preinstalled on the hard drive. Both of these versions of Windows, as well as the older Windows 8, 7, Vista, and XP, typically use the NT File System (NTFS). Linux supports both read and write access to NTFS partitions, and these days all Linux distributions come with the ntfs.ko kernel module, which is needed to access an NTFS partition.

Type the following command to create a mount point for the NTFS partition. (In this case, you're creating a mount point in the /mnt directory.)

```
mkdir /mnt/windir
```

Now you can mount the NTFS partition with the following command:

```
mount /dev/sda2 /mnt/windir -t ntfs
```

The -t ntfs argument tells Linux the partition is formatted using the NTFS file system. If you're worried about accidentally writing over the data on your Windows partition, you can add two more options to the mount command:

```
Mount /dev/sda2 /mnt/windir -t ntfs -r -o umask=0222
```

The -r option mounts the file system in read-only mode, and the -o argument tells it to mount the partition with the specified options. In this example, I provide the default file system permission settings to use for the mount point, allowing users to read and execute files from the system but not write to the file system.

**REMEMBER**

If necessary, replace /dev/sda2 with the device name for the NTFS partition on your system. On most PCs that come with Windows preinstalled, the NTFS partition is the second one (/dev/sda2); the first partition (/dev/sda1) usually is a hidden partition that holds files used for the Windows installation.

# 5
# Managing Linux Servers

# Contents at a Glance

# Chapter **1**

# Hosting Internet Services

L inux has had a rough time breaking into the desktop market, but it has thrived in the server market. These days, just about every company has one or more Linux servers to manage, so it's important to know how Linux servers work and what server software packages are popular these days.

The popularity of Linux servers has a lot to do with their versatility, performance, and cost. This chapter helps get you up to speed on how Linux servers operate and covers the most common server software packages you can install and run in Linux to provide services to your network clients.

## What Is a Linux Server?

Before I dive into Linux server details, let me explain what I mean by a Linux server and show how a Linux server differs from a Linux desktop.

Both Linux desktops and Linux servers use the same Linux kernel, run the same shells, and even have the ability to run the same programs. The difference comes in which programs they primarily run and how those programs run on the system.

Linux desktops primarily focus on personal programs that you run from a graphical user interface (GUI), such as when you browse the Internet or edit a document. The GUI is an easy way for users to interact with the operating system and all files and programs. You start programs by selecting them from a menu system or clicking a desktop icon. In the desktop world, everything is interactive.

Linux servers, however, mostly operate without any human interaction. There's no one sitting at a desktop launching applications (and in fact, many servers don't even have a dedicated monitor and keyboard).

The server runs programs that provide shared resources (called *services*) to multiple users (called *clients*), normally in a network environment. Many services run all the time, even when no clients are actively using them.

Server programs seldom rely on a GUI. Instead, they almost always utilize the Linux shell's command-line interface (CLI) to allow the server administrator to interact with the server, and often, the administrator connects to the server from a remote client to perform any interactive work with the services.

Because there's little interaction with a human operator, servers must know how to launch the programs that provide the services to clients on their own. How the server runs those services can differ from server to server and service to service. The following sections describe how Linux servers start services and how they provide access to those services to clients.

# Launching services

There are two primary ways Linux servers run service programs:

> » As a background process, running at all times, listening for requests
> » As a process spawned by a parent program that listens for the requests

The following sections describe the differences between the two and why they exist.

## Running background processes

When a Linux service program runs continually as a background process, it's called a *daemon*. Linux servers often utilize scripts to launch service daemons as soon as the server boots up (see Book 4, Chapter 2).

Linux daemon programs often end with the letter d to indicate they're daemon processes. Here's an example that shows the MariaDB database server daemon running in the background on a server.

```
rich@Ubuntu22:~$ ps ax | grep mariadb
   883 ?        Ssl    0:00 /usr/sbin/mariadbd
  4234 pts/0    S+     0:00 grep --color=auto mariadb
rich@Ubuntu22:~$
```

The `mariadbd` daemon program listens for network connections from clients. When the daemon receives a request from a client, it processes the request and returns data to the client via the same network channel.

Services that run as daemons must be automatically started by the server. This happens using a startup method (see Book 4, Chapter 2). Two different startup methods are commonly used in Linux:

>> The SysVinit method

>> The Systemd method

The SysVinit method uses scripts to start and stop services, while the Systemd method uses configuration files. Just about all server services have their own startup and shutdown scripts as part of their installation package, so usually you don't need to worry about how that's done. You will, however, want to know how to start, stop, and restart services when necessary.

For Linux systems that use the SysVinit method, you use the `service` program. The format of the `service` program is as follows:

```
service servicename command
```

Where *command* can be `start`, `stop`, `restart`, `reload`, or `status`. So, to stop the MariaDB server service, you issue the following command:

```
service mariadbd stop
```

TIP

You won't see any type of response after issuing the command, so usually it helps to use the `status` command to ensure that the service really did stop.

For Linux systems that use the Systemd method, you use the `systemctl` program:

```
systemctl command servicename
```

Note that in both the `service` and `systemctl` commands, the *servicename* is the name of the service, which may or may not be the same as the daemon program name. For example, with MariaDB, the service name is simply `mariadb`.

**TECHNICAL STUFF**

Note that the name for a background program running in Linux is "daemon" and not "demon," as it is often confused with. Daemons are from Greek mythology and were supernatural beings that provided help to humans when needed.

## Using a super-server

The more services a Linux server supports, the more daemons it must have running in the background, waiting for client requests. Each daemon requires memory resources on the server, even when it's just listening for clients. In the early days of Linux, servers didn't necessarily have lots of resources — thus, the necessity of super-servers.

A *super-server* is a single program that listens for network connections for several different applications. When the super-server receives a request for a service from a client, it spawns the appropriate service program. When the client connection ends, the service program also ends. When a new client connects, the super-server starts a new service program.

The original super-server program created for Linux was the Internet daemon (inetd) application. The inetd program runs as a daemon, listening for specific requests from clients and launching the appropriate service program when needed. The inetd program uses the /etc/inetd.conf configuration file to allow you to define the services for which it handles requests.

The extended Internet daemon (xinetd) application is an advanced version of inetd. It, too, launches service programs as requested by clients, but it contains additional features, such as access control lists (ACLs), more advanced logging features, and the ability to set schedules to turn services on and off at different times of the day or week.

**TIP**

These days, with relatively cheap CPU and memory costs, most Linux servers have plenty of resources available, and system administrators don't have to worry about having too many server services running as daemons in the background just waiting for client connections. This has caused somewhat of a paradigm shift away from using super-servers to using service daemons. In fact, most modern Linux server distributions don't even bother installing the xinetd package by default.

## Listening for clients

A standard Linux server supports lots of services. Usually, a single Linux server will support multiple services at the same time. This means multiple clients will be making requests to the server for multiple services. The trick is getting requests from clients to the correct server service.

Each service, whether it's running as a daemon or running from a super-server, uses a separate network protocol to communicate with its clients. Common service protocols are standardized by the Internet Engineering Task Force (IETF) and published as Request for Comments (RFC) documents. Each server software program communicates with its clients using the protocol specified for its service, such as a web server using Hypertext Transfer Protocol (HTTP) or an email server using Simple Mail Transfer Protocol (SMTP).

The network protocol for a service defines exactly how network clients communicate with the service, using preassigned network ports. Ports are defined within the Transmission Control Protocol (TCP) and User Datagram Protocol (UDP) standards to help separate network traffic going to the same Internet Protocol (IP) address. The IETF assigns different services to different ports for communication. This works similarly to telephone extensions used in a large business: You dial a single phone number to reach the business and then select a separate extension to get to a specific individual within the office. With services, clients use a common IP address to reach a server and then different ports to reach individual services.

The IETF has defined a standard set of ports to common services used on the Internet. These are called well-known ports. Table 1-1 shows just a few of the more common well-known ports assigned.

**TABLE 1-1**  ## Common Internet Well-Known Port Numbers

| Port Number | Protocol | Description |
|---|---|---|
| 20 and 21 | FTP | The File Transfer Protocol is used for sending files to and from a server. |
| 22 | SSH | The Secure Shell protocol is used for sending encrypted data to a server. |
| 23 | Telnet | Telnet is an unsecure protocol for providing an interactive interface to the server shell. |
| 25 | SMTP | The SMTP is used for sending email between servers. |
| 53 | DNS | The Domain Name System (DNS) provides a name service to match IP addresses to computer names on a network. |
| 67 | DHCP | The Dynamic Host Configuration Protocol (DHCP) enables client computers to obtain a valid IP address on a network automatically. |
| 80 | HTTP | The HTTP allows clients to request web pages from servers. |

**TABLE 1-1** *(continued)*

| Port Number | Protocol | Description |
|---|---|---|
| 109 and 110 | POP | The Post Office Protocol (POP) allows clients to communicate with a mail server to read messages in their mailboxes. |
| 137–139 | SMB | Microsoft servers use the Server Message Block (SMB) protocol for file and print sharing with clients. |
| 143 and 220 | IMAP | The Internet Message Access Protocol (IMAP) provides advanced mailbox services for clients. |
| 389 | LDAP | The Lightweight Directory Access Protocol (LDAP) provides access to directory services for authenticating users, workstations, and other network devices. |
| 443 | HTTPS | The secure version of HTTP provides encrypted communication with web servers. |
| 2049 | NFS | The Network File System (NFS) provides file sharing between Unix and Linux systems. |

A host of Linux services are available for serving applications to clients on the network. The /etc/services file contains all the ports defined on a Linux server.

The following sections explore the different types of services you'll find on Linux servers and lists some of the more common Linux applications that provide those services.

# Serving the Basics

There are some basic Internet services that Linux servers are known to do well and that have become standards across the Internet. The three Internet services Linux servers provide are as follows:

>> Web services

>> Database services

>> Email services

The following sections discuss each of these types of Linux services and show you the open-source software packages commonly used to support them.

# Web services

By far the most popular use of Linux servers on the Internet is as a web server. Linux-based web servers host the majority of websites, including many of the most popular websites.

As is true for many Linux applications, there are multiple programs that you can use to build a Linux web server. The following are the most popular ones you'll run into and should know about.

## The Apache server

The Apache web server was at one time the most popular web server on the Internet. It was developed from the first web server software package created by the National Center for Supercomputing Applications (NCSA) at the University of Illinois.

The Apache web server has become popular due to its modularity. Each advanced feature of the Apache server is built as a plug-in module. When features are incorporated as modules, the server administrator can pick and choose just which modules a particular server needs for a particular application. This helps reduce the amount of memory required to run the Apache server daemons on the system.

## The NGINX server

The NGINX web server (pronounced "engine X") is the relatively new guy on the block. Released in 2004, NGINX was designed as an advanced replacement for the Apache web server, improving on performance and providing some additional features, such as working as a web proxy, mail proxy, web page cache, and even load-balancing server.

The core NGINX program has a smaller memory footprint than the larger Apache program, making it ideal for high-volume environments. It's capable of handling more than 10,000 simultaneous network client connections.

One configuration that's becoming popular is to use a combination of the NGINX web server as a load-balancing front end to multiple Apache web servers on the back end. This takes advantage of both the NGINX server's capabilities of handling large traffic volumes and the Apache web server's versatility in handling dynamic web applications.

## The lighthttpd package

On the other end of the spectrum, there may be times you need a lightweight web server to process incoming client requests for a network application. The lighthttpd (pronounced "lighty") package provides such an environment.

The lighthttpd web server is known for low memory usage and low CPU usage, making it ideal for smaller server applications, such as in embedded systems. It also incorporates a built-in database, allowing you to combine basic web and database services in a single package.

# Database services

Storing and retrieving data are important features for most applications. The use of standard text files is often enough for simple data storage applications, but there are times when more advanced data storage techniques are required.

The advent of the relational database allowed applications to quickly store and retrieve data. Relational database servers allowed multiple clients to access the same data from a centralized location. The Structured Query Language (SQL) provides a common method for clients to send requests to the database server and retrieve the data.

Many popular commercial database servers are available for Unix and Windows (and even Linux), but a few high-quality open-source databases have risen to the top in the Linux world. These database server packages offer many (if not most) of the same features as the expensive commercial database packages and can sometimes even outperform the commercial packages.

The following sections discuss the most popular open-source database servers you'll encounter when working in the Linux environment.

## The PostgreSQL server

The PostgreSQL database server started out as a university project and became an open-source package available to the public in 1996. The goal of the PostgreSQL developers was to implement a complete object-relational database management system to rival the popular commercial database servers of the day.

PostgreSQL is known for its advanced database features. It follows the standard atomicity, consistency, isolation, and durability (ACID) guidelines used by commercial databases and supports many of the fancy features you'd expect to find in a commercial relational database server, such as transactions, updatable views, triggers, foreign keys, functions, and stored procedures.

PostgreSQL is very versatile, but with versatility comes complexity. In the past, the PostgreSQL database had a reputation for being somewhat slow, but it has made vast improvements in performance. Unfortunately, old reputations are hard to shake, and PostgreSQL still struggles to gain acceptance in the web world.

## The MySQL server

Unlike the PostgreSQL package, the MySQL database server didn't originally try to compete with commercial databases. Instead, it started out as a project to create a simple but fast database system. No attempt was made to implement fancy database features; it just offered basic features that performed quickly.

Because of its focus on speed, the MySQL database server became the de facto database server used in many high-profile Internet web applications. The combination of a Linux server running the Apache web server and the MySQL database server while utilizing the PHP programming language became known as the LAMP platform; it can be found in Linux servers all over the world.

Since its inception, the MySQL database has added features that can rival those found in PostgreSQL and commercial databases. However, staying true to its roots, MySQL still maintains the option of utilizing the faster storage engine that it became famous for.

## The MariaDB server

In 2008, the MySQL project was acquired by Sun Microsystems. In 2010, when Oracle purchased Sun Microsystems, by default, it also took control of MySQL development. Having a commercial database company in charge of an open-source database project scared many people in the open-source community into thinking MySQL could be discontinued. Shortly after the purchase, a group of MySQL developers left Oracle to start the MariaDB project. MariaDB is an exact replica of MySQL, using the same source code and having the same features. Many Linux distributions now use MariaDB by default instead of MySQL, so don't be alarmed if you see that.

## The MongoDB server

With the rising popularity of object-oriented programming and application design, the use of object-oriented databases has also risen. Currently, one of the most popular object-oriented methods of storing data is called NoSQL.

As its name suggests, a NoSQL database system stores data differently than the traditional relational database systems using SQL. A NoSQL database doesn't create tables but instead stores data as individual documents. Unlike relational tables, each NoSQL document can contain different data elements, with each data element being independent from the other data elements in the database.

One NoSQL database package that is gaining in popularity is the MongoDB package. MongoDB was released in 2009 as a full NoSQL-compliant database management system. It stores data records as individual JavaScript Object Notation (JSON) elements, making each data document independent of the others.

The MongoDB database server supports many relational database features, such as indexes, queries, replication, and even load balancing. It allows you to incorporate JavaScript in queries, making it a very versatile tool for querying data.

**WARNING**

The MongoDB server installs with a default of no security — anyone can connect to the server to add and retrieve data records. This "gotcha" has been a problem for even some high-profile websites where data has been breached. Be careful when using a MongoDB database for your web applications.

## Mail services

At one time, email was the backbone of the Internet. Just about everyone had an email address, and it was crucial to be plugged into an email server to communicate with the world. These days, newer technology (such as texting, tweeting, and messaging) is taking over, but email is still a vital operation for most Internet users. Just about every Linux server installation uses some type of email server package.

Instead of having one monolithic program that handles all the pieces required for sending and receiving mail, Linux uses multiple small programs that work together in the processing of email messages. Figure 1-1 shows you how most open-source email software modularizes email functions in a Linux environment.

As you can see in Figure 1-1, the Linux email server is normally divided into three separate functions:

>> The mail transfer agent (MTA)

>> The mail delivery agent (MDA)

>> The mail user agent (MUA)

MUA is the program that interacts with end users, allowing them to view and manipulate email messages. Therefore, the MUA programs don't usually run on the server side; instead, they run on the client side. Graphical applications such as Evolution and KMail are popular for reading email in Linux desktop environments. The MTA and MDA functions are found on the Linux server. The following sections show the more common MTA and MDA applications you'll see in Linux.

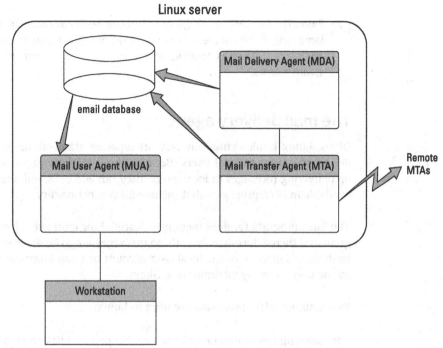

Linux server

email database

Mail Delivery Agent (MDA)

Mail User Agent (MUA)

Mail Transfer Agent (MTA)

Remote MTAs

Workstation

## The mail transfer agent

The MTA is responsible for handling both incoming and outgoing email messages on the server. For each outgoing message, the MTA determines the destination host of the recipient address. If the destination host is a remote mail server, the MTA must establish a communication link with another MTA program on the remote host to transfer the message.

There are quite a few MTA software packages for the Linux environment, but the Linux+ exam focuses on three of them:

>> **sendmail:** The sendmail MTA package gained popularity by being extremely versatile. Many of the features in sendmail have become synonymous with email systems — virtual domains, message forwarding, user aliases, mail lists, and host masquerading. Unfortunately, sendmail is very complex to configure correctly. Its large configuration file is sometimes overwhelming for novice mail administrators to handle.

>> **Postfix**: The Postfix MTA was written as a modular application, using several different programs to implement the MTA functionality. One of Postfix's best features is its simplicity. Instead of one large complex configuration file, Postfix uses just two small configuration files with plaintext parameters and value names to define the functionality.

>> **Exim:** The Exim MTA package sticks with the sendmail model of using one large program to handle all the email functions. It attempts to avoid queuing messages as much as possible, relying instead on immediate delivery in most environments.

### The mail delivery agent

Often, Linux implementations rely on separate stand-alone MDA programs to deliver messages to local users. Because these MDA programs concentrate only on delivering messages to local users, they can add bells and whistles that aren't available in MTA programs that include MDA functionality.

The MDA program receives messages destined for local users from the MTA program and then determines how those messages are to be delivered. Messages can be delivered directly to the local user account or to an alternate location defined by the user, often by incorporating filters.

Two common MDA programs are used in Linux:

>> **binmail:** The binmail program is the most popular MDA program used in Linux. Its name comes from its normal location in the system, /bin/mail. It has become popular thanks to its simplicity. By default, binmail can read email messages stored in the standard /var/spool/mail directory, or you can point it to an alternative mailbox.

>> **procmail:** The procmail program was written by Stephen R. van den Berg and has become so popular that many Linux implementations install it by default. The popularity of procmail comes from its versatility in creating user-configured recipes that allow a user to direct how the server processes received mail. A user can create a personal .procmailrc file in their $HOME directory to direct messages based on regular expressions to separate mailbox files, forward messages to alternative email addresses, or even send messages directly to the /dev/null file to trash unwanted email automatically.

# Serving Local Networks

Besides running large Internet web and database applications, Linux servers are also commonly used in local network environments to provide simple network services. Running a local network requires lots of behind-the-scenes work, and the Linux server is up to the task. This section walks through the most common services you'll find used on all sizes of local networks.

# File servers

These days, the sharing of files has become a necessity in any business environment. Allowing multiple employees to create and edit files in a common folder can greatly improve collaboration efforts in any project.

Sharing files via a web server is common in a wide area network (WAN) environment, but there are easier ways to do that within a local area network (LAN). There are two basic methods for sharing files in a LAN environment:

>> **Peer-to-peer:** In a peer-to-peer network, one workstation enables another workstation to access files stored locally on its hard drive. This method allows collaboration between two employees on a small local network but becomes somewhat difficult if you need to share data between more than two people.

>> **Client–server:** The client–server method of file sharing utilizes a centralized file server for sharing files that multiple clients can access and modify as needed. However, with the centralized file server, an administrator must control who has access to which files and folders, protecting them from unauthorized access.

In the Linux world, two common server software packages are used for sharing files: NFS and Samba.

## NFS

The Network File System is a protocol used to share folders in a network environment. With NFS, a Linux system can share a portion of its virtual directory on the network to allow access by clients and other servers.

In Linux, the software package used to accomplish this is `nfs-utils`. The `nfs-utils` package provides both the drivers to support NFS and the underlying client and server software to share local folders on the network and connect to remote folders shared by other Linux systems on the local network. Using `nfs-utils`, your Linux system can mount remotely shared NFS folders almost as easily as if they were on a local hard drive partition.

## Samba

These days, Microsoft Windows workstations and servers have become the norm in many business environments. Windows workstations and servers can use NFS, but the default file-sharing method used in Windows is the Server Message Block protocol, created by Microsoft. Microsoft servers use proprietary software, but Microsoft has released the SMB protocol as a network standard, so it's possible to create open-source software that can interact with Windows servers and clients using SMB.

The Samba software package (note the clever use of embedding SMB in the name) was created to allow Linux systems to interact with Windows clients and servers. With Samba, your Linux system can act either as a client, connecting to Windows server shared folders, or as a server, allowing Windows workstations to connect to shared folders on the Linux system. Samba does take some work to configure the correct parameters to manage access to your shared folders.

## Print servers

In a business environment, having a printer for every person in the office is somewhat of a wasted expense. The ability to share network printers has become a requirement for most offices and has become popular in many home environments, too.

The standard Linux print-sharing software package is called the Common Unix Printing System (CUPS). The CUPS software allows a Linux system to connect to any printer resource, either locally or via a network, by using a common application interface that operates over dedicated printer drivers. The key to CUPS is the printer drivers. Many printer manufacturers create CUPS drivers for their printers so Linux systems can connect with their printers. For connecting to network printers, CUPS uses the Internet Printing Protocol (IPP).

Besides connecting to a network printer, the CUPS system also allows you to share a locally attached printer with other Linux systems. This allows you to connect a printer to a Linux server and share it among multiple users in a local network.

TIP

The Samba software package can also interact with printers shared on Microsoft networks. You can connect your Linux workstation to printers shared on Windows networks using Samba, or you can even share your own locally attached Linux printer with Windows workstations.

## Network resource servers

Running a local network requires quite a few different resources to keep clients and servers in sync. This is especially true for larger networks where network administrators must manage many different types of clients and servers.

Fortunately, Linux provides a few different service packages that network administrators can use to make their lives easier. The following sections walk through some of the basic network-oriented services that you may see on a Linux server.

## IP addresses

Every device on a local network must have a unique IP address to interact with other devices on the network. For a small home network that may not be too difficult to manage, but for large business networks that task can be overwhelming.

To help simplify that requirement, developers have created the Dynamic Host Configuration Protocol (DHCP). Clients can request a valid IP address for the network from a DHCP server. A central DHCP server keeps track of the IP addresses assigned, ensuring that no two clients receive the same IP address.

These days, you can configure many different types of devices on a network to be a DHCP server. Most home broadband routers provide this service, as do most server-oriented operating systems, such as Windows servers and, of course, Linux servers.

The most popular Linux DHCP server package is maintained by the Internet Systems Consortium (ISC) and is called DHCPd. Just about all Linux server distributions include this in their software repositories.

After you have the DHCPd server running on your network, you'll need to tell your Linux clients to use it to obtain their network addresses. This requires a DHCP client software package. For Linux DHCP clients, there are three popular packages you can use:

» dhclient

» dhcpcd

» pump

Most Debian- and Red Hat–based distributions use the dhclient package, and they even install it by default when a network card is detected during the installation process. The dhcpcd and pump applications are less known, but you may run into them.

## Logging

Linux maintains log files that record various key details about the system as it runs. The log files are normally stored locally in the /var/log directory, but in a network environment it can come in handy to have Linux servers store their system logs on a remote logging server.

The remote logging server provides a safe backup of the original log files, plus a safe place to store logs in case of a system crash or a break-in by an attacker.

Two main logging packages are used in Linux, and which one a system uses depends on the startup software it uses (see Book 4, Chapter 2):

>> rsyslogd: The SysVinit and Upstart systems utilize the rsyslogd service program to accept logging data from remote servers.

>> journald: The Systemd system utilizes the journald service for both local and remote logging of system information.

Both rsyslogd and journald utilize configuration files that allow you to define just how data is logged and which clients the server accepts log messages from.

## Name servers

Using IP addresses to reference servers on a network is fine for computers, but humans usually require some type of text to remember addresses. Enter the Domain Name System. DNS maps IP addresses to a host naming scheme on networks. A DNS server acts as a directory lookup to find the names of servers on the local network.

Linux servers use the Berkeley Internet Name Domain (BIND) software package to provide DNS naming services. The BIND software package was developed in the very early days of the Internet (the early 1980s) at the University of California, Berkeley, and is released as open-source software.

The main program in BIND is the name daemon, named, the server daemon that runs on Linux servers and resolves hostnames to IP addresses for clients on the local network. The beauty of DNS is that one BIND server can communicate with other DNS servers to look up an address on remote networks. This allows clients to point to only one DNS name server and be able to resolve any IP address on the Internet!

TIP

The DNS protocol is text based and is susceptible to attacks, such as hostname spoofing. The DNS Security Extensions (DNSSEC) protocol incorporates a layer of encryption around the standard DNS packets to help provide a layer of security in the hostname lookup process. Make sure your BIND installation supports DNSSEC for the proper security.

## Network management

Being responsible for multiple hosts and network devices for an organization can be overwhelming. Trying to keep up with which devices are active or which servers are running at capacity can be a challenge. Fortunately for administrators, there's a solution.

The Simple Network Management Protocol (SNMP) provides a way for an administrator to query remote network devices and servers to obtain information about their configuration, status, and even performance. SNMP operates in a simple client–server paradigm. Network devices and servers run an SNMP server service that listens for requests from SNMP client packages. The SNMP client sends requests for data from the SNMP server.

The SNMP standards have changed somewhat drastically over the years, mainly to help add security and boost performance. The original SNMP version 1 (SNMPv1) provided for only simple password authentication of clients and passed all data as individual plaintext records. SNMP version 2 (SNMPv2) implemented a basic level of security and provided for the bulk transmission of monitoring data to help reduce the network traffic required to monitor devices. The current version (SNMPv3) utilizes both strong authentication and data encryption capabilities and provides a more streamlined management system.

The most popular SNMP software package in Linux is the open-source net-snmp package. This package has SNMPv3 compatibility, allowing you to securely monitor all aspects of a Linux server remotely.

## Time

For many network applications to work correctly, both servers and clients need to have their internal clocks coordinated with the same time. The Network Time Protocol (NTP) accomplishes this. It allows servers and clients to synchronize on the same time source across multiple networks, adding or subtracting fractions of a second as needed to stay in sync.

For Linux systems, the ntpd program synchronizes a Linux system with remote NTP servers on the Internet. It's common to have a single Linux server use ntpd to synchronize with a remote time standard server and then have all other servers and clients on the local network sync their times to the local Linux server.

# Chapter **2**

# Managing a Web Server

I n the server environment, the most popular use of Linux is as a web server. Linux web servers dominate the Internet. They're also very popular for hosting corporate intranet applications. Everything from serving static web pages to hosting dynamic web applications often runs faster and more efficiently on a Linux server platform.

In this chapter, I cover how to install and configure the two most popular web server software packages used in Linux environments, Apache and NGINX.

## Linux Web Servers

Many different types of web server software packages are available for the Linux platform, but two have risen to the top and are most commonly used in the Linux environment: Apache and NGINX.

This section provides some background on each server and explains how to use them in your network environment.

### Apache

By far the most used web server on the Internet is the Apache web server application, an open-source project maintained by the Apache Software Foundation.

Because it's open source, it's available free of charge for any purpose, commercial or private, and is commonly included in most Linux distribution repositories, making it easy to install.

Over the years, the Apache web server project has pioneered many new features that define just what web servers should support:

>> **Loadable dynamic modules:** The ability to activate and deactivate features on the fly as the web server is running

>> **Scalable multi-session support:** The ability to easily handle multiple client requests at the same time

>> **Limiting concurrent connections:** The ability to limit the number of clients that can connect at the same time to help prevent system overload

>> **Bandwidth throttling:** The ability to regulate the output from the web server to prevent overloading the network, even if the system can handle more connections

>> **Web caching (also called web proxy):** The ability to store web pages requested by multiple clients and read subsequent requests from the cache rather than from the original data source

>> **Load balancing (also called reverse proxy):** The ability to act as a single point of connection for clients and then redirect requests to multiple back-end servers for processing

>> **Common Gateway Interface (CGI):** The ability to forward web page content to internal server programs, commonly used for processing embedded scripting code

>> **Virtual hosting:** The ability to host multiple domains on a single web server

>> **User-based web page hosting:** The ability to allow individual users on the system to host their own web pages

With Apache, all these features (plus a lot more) are easily enabled or disabled using simple text-based configuration files.

TIP

One confusing issue with the Apache web server is that two separate versions are currently supported. The 1.3.x version thread supports older installations of the Apache web server; it's mostly maintained to support bug fixes and security patches for legacy systems. New Apache web server installations should use the 2.x version thread. Most Linux distributions differentiate the two versions by calling the 2.x version Apache2.

# NGINX

Although it can operate as a standard web server, the NGINX (pronounced "engine X") web server is better known as a reverse proxy server. As you can probably guess, a reverse proxy server does the opposite of what a web proxy server does. Instead of processing requests from multiple clients to a single web server, a reverse proxy server processes requests from a single client to multiple web servers. This technique is also known as *load balancing*.

A load-balancing server receives HTTP requests from clients and sends them to a specific server in a pool of common web servers for processing. Each web server in the pool contains the same data and can process the same HTTP requests. The load-balancing process helps distribute the client load on multiple web servers in a high-traffic environment, helping prevent overloading and slow performance.

# The Apache Web Server

With the overall popularity of the Apache web server, most Linux distributions have easy installation packages that make setting up a basic Apache web server easy. The difficult part comes if you need to customize special features. This section walks through the installation of a basic Apache web server setup and how to dig into the Apache configuration files to help customize your web environment.

## Installing an Apache server

You can easily check whether the Apache web server is already installed on your system by opening a web browser and entering the URL **http://localhost**. If the default Apache web page appears, you should be good! If you need to install the Apache software, most Linux server distributions include the Apache web server software as easy-to-install software packages. For example, in the Ubuntu Linux server distribution, the Apache web server package is called apache2. You install the basic Apache server using a single package:

```
$ sudo apt-get install apache2
```

This installs the latest version of the Apache 2.x web server supported by the Ubuntu server version. After you install the Apache server, the installation package automatically configures the server to start at boot time, and serve data files from the /var/www/html directory on the server.

After the Apache server is running you can open a browser and connect to your Linux server. Figure 2-1 shows the default index.html file that is created for Ubuntu servers.

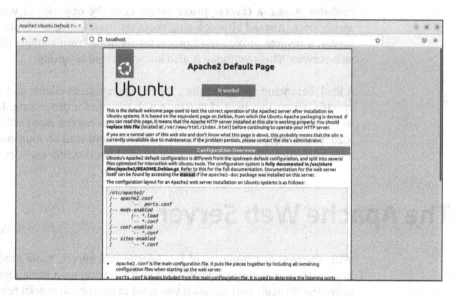

**FIGURE 2-1:**
The default
Apache web page
for Ubuntu.

For Red Hat–based Linux servers, the Apache package is called httpd (this is because the name of the Apache server program is httpd). You can use the standard dnf package installer to install it:

```
$ sudo dnf install httpd
```

Although not specified in the filename, this is the Apache 2.x version of the server. Unlike the Ubuntu Linux distribution, the Red Hat package doesn't automatically start the Apache web server, nor does it start it at boot time. To start the server and ensure that it automatically starts at boot time, you'll need to use these systemctl commands:

```
$ sudo systemctl start httpd
$ sudo systemctl enable httpd
```

Because Red Hat servers have firewall protection enabled by default, you'll also need to allow HTTP connections through the firewall:

```
$ sudo firewall-cmd –zone=public –add-service=http —permanent
```

The Red Hat–based distributions also serve data files from the /var/www/html directory by default. Figure 2-2 shows the default index.html file that is created for Rocky Linux.

**FIGURE 2-2:**
The default
Apache web page
for Rocky Linux.

You can start, stop, restart, and check the status of the Apache program using the apache2ctl utility (some Red Hat–based distributions such as Rocky Linux use apachectl even for the 2.x versions). Table 2-1 shows the commands you can use with apache2ctl.

The status and fullstatus commands are a handy way to check on the Apache web server. However, they display the Apache status as a web page, which requires a text-based command-line browser. Most Linux distributions don't install a command-line browser by default. The Lynx command-line browser is the most popular and is available in most Linux distribution repositories.

TIP

The core Apache software package for both Ubuntu and Red Hat installs a basic web server without many additional features. To customize the web server to support advanced features such as server-side programming, you'll have to install additional software packages. Unfortunately, different Linux distributions bundle different Apache features into different software packages. Consult your specific Linux distribution documentation to determine which packages you need to install to support the Apache features you want to use.

TABLE 2-1

## The apache2ctl Utility Commands

| Command | Description |
| --- | --- |
| start | Starts the Apache server |
| stop | Stops the Apache server, terminating any active connections |
| restart | Restarts the Apache server, closing any existing connections |
| fullstatus | Displays a full status report from the Apache server |
| status | Displays a short status report from the Apache server |
| graceful | Restarts the Apache server, but existing connections are not terminated |
| graceful-stop | Stops the Apache server, but existing connections are not terminated |
| configtest | Parses the configuration files and reports any syntax errors |
| help | Displays the list of commands |

# Configuring an Apache server

A great feature of the Apache web server is that it uses simple text-based configuration files to manage the behavior of the server. The configuration file controls every feature of the server, giving you complete control over just how the Apache web server operates.

Unfortunately though, there isn't a standard location or filename for the Apache configuration file. The main locations and files that you'll need to remember are

» /etc/apache/apache.conf: Apache 1.3.x installation for Ubuntu systems

» /etc/apache2/apache2.conf: Apache2 installation for Ubuntu systems

» /etc/httpd/conf/httpd.conf: Apache 1.3.x and 2.x installation for Red Hat systems

Another confusing issue that you'll most likely run into is that not all the Apache configuration settings are necessarily stored in one configuration file. Often, Linux distributions move configuration settings for separate features into their own configuration files and use the INCLUDE directive in the main configuration file to include them into the configuration. You'll need to consult the documentation for your specific Linux distribution on how the Apache configuration files are arranged.

The following sections walk you through some of the different configuration settings that you'll run into in standard Apache configurations.

## Basic setup

When you look inside an Apache configuration file, the first you'll see are lots of lines that start with a pound sign (#). The pound sign denotes a comment line, allowing you to embed comments within the configuration file.

You define actual configuration settings using a directive keyword and then, optionally, a value for the setting like this:

```
DocumentRoot "/var/www/html"
```

This directive sets the default directory for the Apache server to the /var/www/ html directory on the Linux server. As you peruse the configuration file, you'll see lots of directives setting basic features for the server. Table 2-2 shows the main settings that you'll be interested in.

By default, settings that you define in the main configuration area are called global settings. They apply to the main Apache web server when it starts.

You can also define conditional settings, that only apply when specific conditions are met, such as if an environment variable is defined.

You define conditional settings as a block of directives. The block uses the following format:

```
<IfDefine variable>
    Directive
</IfDefine>
```

The <IfDefine> marker defines the start of the block, and the </IfDefine> marker defines the end of the block. The Apache server processes only the directives listed in the block if the variable is set.

**TABLE 2-2**

## Common Apache Configuration Directives

| Directive | Description |
|-----------|-------------|
| Listen | The TCP port (and optional IP address) to listen for client requests |
| User | The user account used to start the Apache server daemon |
| Group | The group account used to start the Apache server daemon |
| ServerAdmin | Email address of the server administrator |
| ServerName | The domain name of the server |
| ServerRoot | The location of the base configuration files |
| DocumentRoot | The location of the default data directory |
| DirectoryIndex | The default file served when a client requests an index of a directory |
| ErrorDocument | The file to serve when a specific error type occurs |
| ErrorLog | The log file location to use for logging error messages |
| LogFormat | The format of each log file entry |
| AccessFileName | The file that lists restrictions on web page files in a directory |
| Include | Includes configuration settings defined in an external file |
| StartServers | The number of servers to start to handle concurrent requests |
| MaxClients | The maximum number of servers to handle concurrent requests |
| MinSpareServers | The minimum number of extra servers to have running |
| MaxSpareServers | The maximum number of extra servers to have running |
| LoadModule | Load and enable the specified feature module into the server |

Likewise, you can use module settings that apply only when specific modules are loaded. The ‹IfModule› condition specifies directives that are processed only when a specified module is loaded using the LoadModule directive.

Finally, you can use directory settings that apply only to specific directories on the server. The ‹Directory› condition specifies the directives that apply only to the directory path specified in the setting:

```
<Directory /var/www/html/mydata>
   Directive
</Directory>
```

The directives specified in this block apply only when clients attempt to access files stored in that directory.

## Apache logs

The Apache web server creates two types of log files by default:

>> Error logs

>> Access logs

As you can probably guess, the error log keeps track of any errors that occur while the Apache web server is running. The location of the error log is defined using the ErrorDocument directive in the configuration file. Usually the error log is located in the /var/log/apache2/error.log file in Ubuntu servers, and the /var/log/httpd/error_log file in Red Hat servers (note the underscore instead of the period in the filename).

You can customize the format for entries in the error log using the LogFormat directive in the configuration file. By default, error log entries look like this:

```
# cat error_log
[Sat Mar 27 09:55:58.296217 2021] [core:notice] [pid 6142:tid
 140605549128000] SELinux policy enabled; httpd running as context
system_u:system_r:httpd_t:s0
[Sat Mar 27 09:55:58.298306 2021] [suexec:notice] [pid 6142:tid
140605549128000] AH01232: suEXEC mechanism enabled (wrapper: /usr/sbin/suexec)
AH00558: httpd: Could not reliably determine the server's fully qualified
domain name, using 192.168.1.92. Set the 'ServerName' directive globally to
   suppress this message
[Sat Mar 27 09:55:58.336220 2021] [lbmethod_heartbeat:notice] [pid 6142:tid
140605549128000] AH02282: No slotmem from mod_heartmonitor
[Sat Mar 27 09:55:58.336554 2021] [http2:warn] [pid 6142:tid
140605549128000] AH02951: mod_ssl does not seem to be enabled
[Sat Mar 27 09:55:58.337692 2021] [mpm_event:notice] [pid 6142:tid
140605549128000] AH00489: Apache/2.4.37 (centos) configured -- resuming
normal operations
[Sat Mar 27 09:55:58.337702 2021] [core:notice] [pid 6142:tid
140605549128000] AH00094: Command line: '/usr/sbin/httpd -D FOREGROUND'
[Sat Mar 27 09:58:37.678050 2021] [autoindex:error] [pid 6146:tid
```

```
140604646274816] [client 192.168.1.71:60218] AH01276: Cannot serve
directory /var/www/html/: No matching DirectoryIndex (index.html) found,
and server-generated directory index forbidden by Options directive
```

Notice that the entries in the error log aren't necessarily all errors. In this example, the Apache web server is documenting notices that appear when it starts up.

The access log is normally located in the same directory as the error log and
is called either access.log (for Ubuntu servers) or access_log (for Red Hat
servers). It documents all requests made by clients. By default, the access log
entries look like this:

```
192.168.1.71 - - [27/Mar/2021:09:58:37 -0400] "GET / HTTP/1.1" 403 4288 "-"
"Mozilla/5.0 (Windows NT 10.0; Win64; x64) AppleWebKit/537.36 (KHTML, like
Gecko) Chrome/89.0.4389.90 Safari/537.36"
192.168.1.71 - - [27/Mar/2021:09:58:37 -0400] "GET
/noindex/common/css/styles.css HTTP/1.1" 200 71634 "http://192.168.1.92/"
"Mozilla/5.0 (Windows NT 10.0; Win64; x64) AppleWebKit/537.36 (KHTML, like
Gecko) Chrome/89.0.4389.90 Safari/537.36"
192.168.1.71 - - [27/Mar/2021:09:58:37 -0400] "GET
/noindex/common/css/bootstrap.min.css HTTP/1.1" 200 99548
"http://192.168.1.92/" "Mozilla/5.0 (Windows NT 10.0; Win64; x64)
AppleWebKit/537.36 (KHTML, like Gecko) Chrome/89.0.4389.90 Safari/537.36"
192.168.1.71 - - [27/Mar/2021:09:58:37 -0400] "GET
/noindex/common/images/pb-apache.png HTTP/1.1" 200 103267
"http://192.168.1.92/" "Mozilla/5.0 (Windows NT 10.0; Win64; x64)
AppleWebKit/537.36 (KHTML, like Gecko) Chrome/89.0.4389.90 Safari/537.36"
192.168.1.71 - - [27/Mar/2021:09:58:37 -0400] "GET
/noindex/common/images/pb-centos.png HTTP/1.1" 200 13122
"http://192.168.1.92/" "Mozilla/5.0 (Windows NT 10.0; Win64; x64)
AppleWebKit/537.36 (KHTML, like Gecko) Chrome/89.0.4389.90 Safari/537.36"
192.168.1.71 - - [27/Mar/2021:09:58:37 -0400] "GET
/noindex/common/images/centos-header.png HTTP/1.1" 200 28888
"http://192.168.1.92/noindex/common/css/styles.css" "Mozilla/5.0 (Windows
NT 10.0; Win64; x64) AppleWebKit/537.36 (KHTML, like Gecko)
Chrome/89.0.4389.90 Safari/537.36"
192.168.1.71 - - [27/Mar/2021:09:59:29 -0400] "-" 408 - "-" "-"
192.168.1.71 - - [27/Mar/2021:10:06:53 -0400] "GET /badpage.html HTTP/1.1" 404
    196 "-" "Mozilla/5.0 (Windows NT 10.0; Win64; x64) AppleWebKit/537.36 (KHTML,
    like Gecko) Chrome/89.0.4389.90 Safari/537.36"
192.168.1.71 - - [27/Mar/2021:10:06:53 -0400] "GET /favicon.ico HTTP/1.1" 404
    196 "http://192.168.1.92/badpage.html" "Mozilla/5.0 (Windows NT 10.0; Win64;
    x64) AppleWebKit/537.36 (KHTML, like Gecko) Chrome/89.0.4389.90
    Safari/537.36"
192.168.1.71 - - [27/Mar/2021:10:07:45 -0400] "-" 408 - "-" "-"
```

The access log not only documents the file request but also can document the browser type of the client, the OS of the client, and the IP address. You can customize the output using the LogFormat directive as well.

## User web hosting

The default configuration for most Linux distribution Apache servers is to provide one location for hosting files, called the document root. The DocumentRoot directive defines this location; for both Ubuntu and Red Hat servers, by default, it is set to the /var/www/html directory. Any files or directories that you want to make available to web clients are normally placed under that directory structure.

The Apache web server also provides a feature that allows users on the Linux system to host their own files. To enable this feature, add the UserDir directive to the global configuration settings. The UserDir directive specifies the name of the directory in each user's HOME directory where they can host files. The most common setting is

```
UserDir public_html
```

To access files in the user's public_html directory, you must specify the username in the URL. For example, to access the file /home/rich/public_html/test.html, you'd use the URL http://localhost/~rich/test.html.

**WARNING**

To allow access to files in your public_html directory, you must grant read and execute privileges to the user or group account that runs the Apache web server. That user or group will need read and execute privileges to the public_html directory, as well as to the user's HOME directory. This can make things somewhat complicated for protecting other files in the user's HOME directory.

## Virtual web hosting

The basic configuration for an Apache web server assumes that the host is serving files for a single server — namely, the server name or IP address that the Apache software is running on. However, Apache also allows you to host web pages for multiple domain names or IP addresses on a single physical server. This is ideal for businesses that support multiple customers such as Internet service providers (ISPs).

The ability to host multiple web environments on a single physical server is called *virtual web hosting*. There are two ways to implement virtual web hosting in Apache:

>> Name-based virtual hosting

>> IP-based virtual hosting

With name-based virtual hosting, the physical server has multiple host names that point to its IP address in the Domain Name System (DNS). You then must configure the Apache web server to use separate directories based on the host name the client uses in the URL request to connect. You do that using the NameVirtualHost directive, and separate <VirtualHost> blocks, one for each virtual host:

```
NameVirtualHost 192.168.1.77

<VirtualHost 192.168.1.77>
    ServerName www.myhost1.com
    DocumentRoot /var/www/html/host1
</VirtualHost>

<VirtualHost 192.168.1.77>
    ServerName www.myhost2.com
    DocumentRoot /var/www/html/host2
</VirtualHost>
```

The <VirtualHost> directive defines the IP address that the server listens on. Then you must create a separate <VirtualHost> block to define the IP address and use the ServerName directive to define the host name that the client uses in the request. Each separate host name points to a different DocumentRoot area by specifying separate DocumentRoot directives.

With IP-based virtual hosting, the server must listen for incoming requests on multiple IP addresses. Each IP address is assigned a different host name in the DNS.

With IP-based virtual hosting you must define multiple IP addresses on the server either by having separate physical network cards in the server or by defining multiple IP addresses for the same network interface using the ip network command (see Book 3, Chapter 4).

After you configure your Linux server to support multiple IP addresses, you must configure the Apache web server to listen to each IP address using multiple Listen directives. After that, just define separate <VirtualHost> blocks to define the host name and DocumentRoot area for each IP address:

```
Listen 192.168.1.77:80
Listen 192.168.1.78:80
<VirtualHost 192.168.1.77>
    Servername www.myhost1.com
    DocumentRoot /var/www/html/myhost1
```

```
</VirtualHost>
<VirtualHost 192.168.1.78>
    Servername www.myhost2.com
    DocumentRoot /var/www/html/myhost2
</VirtualHost>
```

One advantage to IP-based virtual hosting is that you can have two separate Apache programs running at the same time, each one listening on a different IP address. Each Apache program can have a separate configuration, making it easier to separate out settings for each server.

## Creating a secure web server

Protecting data transmitted across the Internet has become a high priority for most corporations. These days it's recommended to use HTTPS (the secure version of HTTP) for all web transactions.

The Apache web server supports HTTPS sessions, but it requires quite a bit of work. You must have a private/public key pair to use for the encryption, as well as a signed certificate to validate your public key to clients. Creating an HTTPS server with Apache involves six steps:

1. **Install the Apache SSL module.**

2. **Create a public/private key pair.**

3. **Create a Certificate Signing Request (CSR).**

4. **Have the CSR signed by a trusted Certificate Authority (CA) to create a certificate.**

5. **Install the certificate and key files in your Apache setup.**

6. **Configure Apache to use the certificate.**

To use encryption on your Linux system, you'll need to ensure that the mod_ssl Apache module is installed. You'll also need the OpenSSL software package installed so your server can handle certificates.

There are a few additional configuration items you'll need to add or change to support HTTPS connections. For the Listen directive, ensure that you have a separate line to listen on TCP port 443, the default port for HTTPS:

```
Listen 443
```

Also, look for the <VirtualHost> block that defines the area that you want to protect with encrypted communication. In that block, add these new directives:

```
SSLEngine On
SSLCertificateFile    /etc/apache2/certs/mycert.pem
SSLCertificateKeyFile    /etc/apache2/certs/myserver.key
```

These lines enable encryption on the Apache server and add the certificate and private key needed for HTTPS. Now your network clients should be able to connect to your Apache web server using the HTTPS protocol.

# The NGINX Server

The Apache web server had been the most popular web server running on the Internet, but it's getting some serious competition from a new player. The NGINX web server has made some great strides in popularity because it's used for some very high-profile commercial websites.

One of the benefits of NGINX is that it doesn't use separate program threads to handle each client as Apache does. Instead, it uses an asynchronous architecture that allows it to spawn client threads within the main program as needed. This helps reduce the memory footprint required for each client that connects to the web server, so the same server can handle more clients.

Another benefit of NGINX is its ability to work as a reverse proxy server. This allows you to place a main NGINX server at the front end of your network and place your application servers behind a firewall, protected from the Internet. Your website visitors connect to the NGINX server on the front, and it forwards the requests to the back-end servers.

This section walks you through the basics of setting up an NGINX server and how to use it as a basic reverse proxy server.

## Installing NGINX

Because it's relatively new, some Linux distributions don't include the NGINX software in their main software repositories. Fortunately, the Ubuntu and Red Hat Linux server distributions do, so installing it is easy. For an Ubuntu server use the following:

```
$ sudo apt-get install nginx
```

And for a Red Hat server use the following:

```
$ sudo dnf install nginx
```

These commands install the NGINX server program and configuration files. For Ubuntu servers, the NGINX server starts automatically but for Red Hat servers, you'll need to manually start it and set it to start at boot time:

```
$ sudo systemctl start nginx
$ sudo systemctl enable nginx
```

Unlike Apache, the NGINX software doesn't have a command-line application to control the server, so in both Ubuntu and Red Hat environments, you have to use the standard systemctl command to determine the status of the server or to start or stop the server.

**REMEMBER**

Also, if you haven't already done so, you'll need to open the HTTP service on the firewall for Red Hat servers.

Because NGINX works as a normal web server, it will start on TCP port 80, the default HTTP network port. If you already have the Apache web server installed on your system, you'll need to stop it while testing NGINX, and then stop NGINX if you want to restart the Apache web server. Alternatively, you can configure them to listen on different TCP ports so they can both run at the same time.

**TIP**

When you've successfully installed NGINX, you can test out the default web settings by opening your browser and going to the server address, as shown in Figure 2-3.

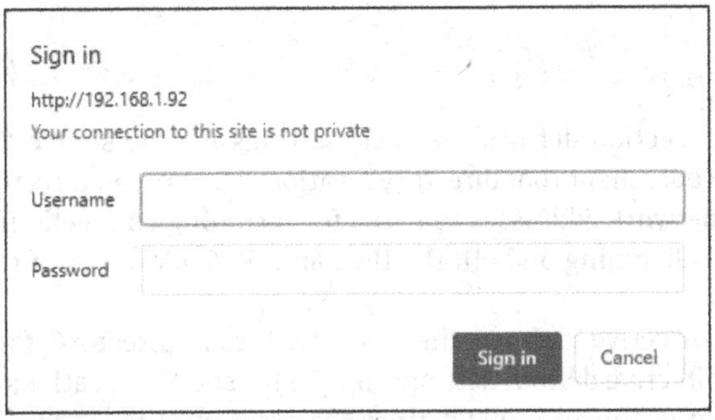

Sign in

http://192.168.1.92
Your connection to this site is not private

Username

Password

Sign in    Cancel

**FIGURE 2-3:**
The NGINX
default web page
in Rocky Linux.

# Configuring NGINX

As you would expect, the configuration files for NGINX are stored in the /etc/ nginx directory. The nginx.conf file is the main configuration file, but as with the Apache web server, NGINX uses the include directive to allow configuration settings to be defined in external files. For Ubuntu servers, the main website directives are defined in the /etc/nginx/sites-enabled/default file.

The NGINX configuration has many of the same features as the Apache web server, so looking at the basic configuration, you'll probably be able to pick out most of the settings:

```
server {
        listen          80 default_server;
        listen          [::]:80 default_server;
        server_name     _;
        root            /usr/share/nginx/html;

        # Load configuration files for the default server block.
        include /etc/nginx/default.d/*.conf;

        location / {
        }

        error_page 404 /404.html;
            location = /40x.html {
        }

        error_page 500 502 503 504 /50x.html;
            location = /50x.html {
        }
    }
```

The server section defines the basic settings for the server. The root directive defines the document root directory location. The listen directives define the TCP ports and network addresses to listen for incoming connections. In this example, the server is listening on both the IPv4 and IPv6 addresses of the Linux server.

The root directive defines the document root directory for the server. The location directive defines settings unique for specific locations on the server. The entry shown in this example defines the error messages that should be returned when a file is not found in the root directory or is temporarily unavailable.

The beauty of NGINX is in the location section. Here, you can define proxy addresses for multiple back-end web servers to implement the reverse proxy feature. Thanks to this feature, the NGINX web server is gaining in popularity and may very soon become the de facto web server in Linux.

These steps demonstrate how to test a web server using the Telnet command-line command. This allows you to submit HTTP requests to the server and see the HTTP response codes that it returns. To do that, follow these steps:

1. **Log in as** root, **or acquire** root **privileges by using** su **or** sudo **with each of the following commands.**

2. **Ensure that you have Apache web server installed.**

   Open a command prompt, and type **sudo apt install apache2** to install the Apache web server package on your Ubuntu server, or **sudo dnf install httpd** to install Apache on your Red Hat server.

3. **For Red Hat servers, start the Apache web server by typing** sudo systemctl start httpd.

4. **Test the Apache web server by typing** telnet localhost 80 **at a command line (you may have to also install the Telnet package on your system).**

   If your system has the Apache web server running, you should be greeted by the Telnet banner, but nothing from the Apache web server — it's waiting for your request.

5. **Request the default web page from the server by typing** GET / **and pressing Enter to submit the request.**

   The Apache web server should return the HTML code contained in the index.html file from the /var/www/html directory.

6. **Test attempting to retrieve an invalid web page.**

   Connect to the Apache web server by typing **telnet localhost 80** at a command line. At the prompt, type **GET /badfile.html** and press Enter.

   You should see some HTML code for a generic error message web page that the browser would display, informing you that it could not find the file on the system.

7. **Remove the Telnet package from your server (it can be a security risk if left enabled).**

REMEMBER

# Chapter 3

# Managing a Database Server

n the old days, if you wanted to store data in or retrieve data from a program or shell script, you had to create a file, read data from the file, parse the data, and then save the data back into the file. Searching for data in the file meant reading every record in the file to look for your data. Nowadays, with databases being all the rage, interfacing your programs and shell scripts with professional-quality open-source databases is a snap. The two most popular open-source databases used in the Linux world are MySQL and PostgreSQL. This chapter shows you how to get these databases running on your Linux system. It also walks you through working with these databases from the command line.

## Using the MySQL/MariaDB Database

By far, the most popular database available in the Linux environment has been the MySQL database. Its popularity has grown as a part of the Linux, Apache, MySQL, PHP (LAMP) server environment, which many Internet web servers use for hosting online stores, blogs, and applications.

In 2008, Sun Microsystems purchased MySQL AB, which was the original developer and supporter of the MySQL open-source project. However, in 2010, Oracle purchased Sun Microsystems, making it the current owner of the MySQL project. Oracle has kept the MySQL project open source (and maintains that it will continue to do so), but many of the original MySQL developers have left Oracle to branch out on their own and start a new database project called MariaDB (named after one of the daughters of the founder of MySQL, Michael Widenius).

The MariaDB open-source project is a clone of MySQL, maintaining nearly 100 percent compatibility with MySQL (this is completely legal in the open-source world). Any code written for MySQL will run just fine on a MariaDB system. Because the MariaDB project is not supported by a large corporation, it has attracted a strong following in the open-source community, and now many Linux distributions have moved to using MariaDB as a replacement for MySQL.

This section explains how to install a MariaDB database in your Linux environment and how to create the necessary database objects to use in your shell scripts.

## Installing MariaDB

Both Ubuntu and Rocky Linux include the MariaDB package in their repositories, so installing a MariaDB server is a snap. For an Ubuntu system, use apt to install the mariadb-server package:

```
rich@Ubuntu22:~$ sudo apt install mariadb-server
Reading package lists... Done
Building dependency tree... Done
Reading state information... Done
The following additional packages will be installed:
  galera-4 gawk libcgi-fast-perl libcgi-pm-perl libconfig-inifiles-perl
  libdaxctl1 libdbd-mysql-perl libdbi-perl libfcgi-bin libfcgi-perl
  libfcgi0ldbl libhtml-template-perl libmariadb3 libmysqlclient21 libndctl6
  libpmem1 libsigsegv2 libterm-readkey-perl liburing2 mariadb-client-10.6
  mariadb-client-core-10.6 mariadb-common mariadb-server-10.6
  mariadb-server-core-10.6 mysql-common socat
Suggested packages:
  gawk-doc libmldbm-perl libnet-daemon-perl libsql-statement-perl
  libipc-sharedcache-perl mailx mariadb-test
The following NEW packages will be installed:
  galera-4 gawk libcgi-fast-perl libcgi-pm-perl libconfig-inifiles-perl
  libdaxctl1 libdbd-mysql-perl libdbi-perl libfcgi-bin libfcgi-perl
  libfcgi0ldbl libhtml-template-perl libmariadb3 libmysqlclient21 libndctl6
  libpmem1 libsigsegv2 libterm-readkey-perl liburing2 mariadb-client-10.6
  mariadb-client-core-10.6 mariadb-common mariadb-server mariadb-server-10.6
  mariadb-server-core-10.6 mysql-common socat
```

```
0 upgraded, 27 newly installed, 0 to remove and 13 not upgraded.
Need to get 16.9 MB of archives.
After this operation, 105 MB of additional disk space will be used.
Do you want to continue? [Y/n]
```

After the installation is complete, you can check whether the MariaDB server is running by using the systemctl command:

```
rich@Ubuntu22:~$ systemctl status mariadb
 mariadb.service - MariaDB 10.6.7 database server
    Loaded: loaded (/lib/systemd/system/mariadb.service; enabled; vendor
  preset: enabled)
     Active: active (running) since Wed 2022-04-27 22:59:45 EDT; 4min 22s ago
       Docs: man:mariadbd(8)
             https://mariadb.com/kb/en/library/systemd/
    Process: 3707 ExecStartPre=/usr/bin/install -m 755 -o mysql -g root -d /var/
  run/mysqld (code=exited, stat>
    Process: 3708 ExecStartPre=/bin/sh -c systemctl unset-environment _WSREP_
  START_POSITION (code=exited, sta>
    Process: 3710 ExecStartPre=/bin/sh -c [ ! -e /usr/bin/galera_recovery ] &&
  VAR= ||  VAR=`cd /usr/bin/..;>
    Process: 3750 ExecStartPost=/bin/sh -c systemctl unset-environment _WSREP_
  START_POSITION (code=exited, st>
    Process: 3752 ExecStartPost=/etc/mysql/debian-start (code=exited, status=0/
  SUCCESS)
   Main PID: 3739 (mariadbd)
     Status: "Taking your SQL requests now..."
      Tasks: 8 (limit: 13180)
     Memory: 57.0M
        CPU: 300ms
     CGroup: /system.slice/mariadb.service
             └─3739 /usr/sbin/mariadbd
```

Ubuntu automatically starts the MariaDB server and enables it to start at boot time.

For Red Hat Linux systems, such as Rocky Linux, you use the dnf command to install the mariadb-server package:

```
[rich@localhost ~]$ sudo dnf install mariadb-server
[sudo] password for rich:
Last metadata expiration check: 22:43:01 ago on Tue 26 Apr 2022 02:27:03 PM EDT.
Dependencies resolved.
================================================================================
 Package          Arch    Version                              Repo      Size
================================================================================
Installing:
```

```
 mariadb-server  x86_64 3:10.3.28-1.module+el8.4.0+427+adf35707 appstream  16 M
Installing dependencies:
 mariadb         x86_64 3:10.3.28-1.module+el8.4.0+427+adf35707 appstream 6.0 M
 mariadb-common  x86_64 3:10.3.28-1.module+el8.4.0+427+adf35707 appstream  62 k
 mariadb-errmsg  x86_64 3:10.3.28-1.module+el8.4.0+427+adf35707 appstream 233 k
 perl-DBD-MySQL  x86_64 4.046-3.module+el8.4.0+577+b8fe2d92     appstream 155 k
 perl-DBI        x86_64 1.641-3.module+el8.4.0+509+59a8d9b3     appstream 739 k
Installing weak dependencies:
 mariadb-backup  x86_64 3:10.3.28-1.module+el8.4.0+427+adf35707 appstream 6.1 M
 mariadb-gssapi-server
                 x86_64 3:10.3.28-1.module+el8.4.0+427+adf35707 appstream  50 k
 mariadb-server-utils
                 x86_64 3:10.3.28-1.module+el8.4.0+427+adf35707 appstream 1.1 M
Enabling module streams:
 mariadb              10.3
 perl-DBD-MySQL       4.046
 perl-DBI             1.641

Transaction Summary
================================================================================
Install  9 Packages

Total download size: 31 M
Installed size: 155 M
Is this ok [y/N]:
```

Unlike Ubuntu, Rocky Linux does not automatically start the MariaDB server after you install it:

```
[rich@localhost ~]$ systemctl status mariadb
 mariadb.service - MariaDB 10.3 database server
   Loaded: loaded (/usr/lib/systemd/system/mariadb.service; disabled; vendor pr>
   Active: inactive (dead)
     Docs: man:mysqld(8)
           https://mariadb.com/kb/en/library/systemd/

[rich@localhost ~]$
```

Use the systemctl command to enable MariaDB to start at boot time and to manually start it now:

```
[rich@localhost ~]$ sudo systemctl enable mariadb
Created symlink /etc/systemd/system/mysql.service → /usr/lib/systemd/system/
    mariadb.service.
```

```
Created symlink /etc/systemd/system/mysqld.service → /usr/lib/systemd/system/
    mariadb.service.
Created symlink /etc/systemd/system/multi-user.target.wants/mariadb.service → /
    usr/lib/systemd/system/mariadb.service.
[rich@localhost ~]$ sudo systemctl start mariadb
[rich@localhost ~]$ systemctl status mariadb
 mariadb.service - MariaDB 10.3 database server
   Loaded: loaded (/usr/lib/systemd/system/mariadb.service; enabled; vendor pre>
   Active: active (running) since Wed 2022-04-27 13:12:09 EDT; 22s ago
     Docs: man:mysqld(8)
           https://mariadb.com/kb/en/library/systemd/
  Process: 36791 ExecStartPost=/usr/libexec/mysql-check-upgrade (code=exited, s>
  Process: 36656 ExecStartPre=/usr/libexec/mysql-prepare-db-dir mariadb.service>
  Process: 36632 ExecStartPre=/usr/libexec/mysql-check-socket (code=exited, sta>
 Main PID: 36759 (mysqld)
   Status: "Taking your SQL requests now..."
    Tasks: 30 (limit: 68892)
   Memory: 78.8M
   CGroup: /system.slice/mariadb.service
           └─36759 /usr/libexec/mysqld --basedir=/usr
```

Now the MariaDB server is running and will start every time the Rocky Linux system boots.

## Looking at the MariaDB command prompt

The portal to the MariaDB database is the mysql command (remember that MariaDB is nearly 100 percent compatible with MySQL). The mysql client program allows you to connect to any MySQL or MariaDB database server anywhere on the network, using any user account and password. By default, if you enter the mysql command on a command line without any parameters, it will attempt to connect to a MariaDB server running on the same Linux system using the Linux login username.

Most likely, this isn't how you want to connect to the database, though. There are lots of command-line parameters that allow you to control not only which MariaDB server you connect to but also the behavior of the mysql interface. Table 3-1 shows the command-line parameters you can use with the mysql program.

As you can see, quite a lot of command-line options are available for modifying how you connect to the MariaDB server.

**TABLE 3-1**     **The mysql Command-Line Parameters**

| Short Parameter | Long Parameter | Description |
|---|---|---|
| -? | --help | Displays help information |
| | --abort-source-on-error | Aborts source operations in case of errors |
| | --auto-rehash | Enables automatic rehashing |
| -A | --no-auto-rehash | Disables automatic rehashing |
| -b | --no-beep | Disables beep on errors |
| -B | --batch | Doesn't use a history file |
| | --binary-as-hex | Prints binary data as hex |
| | --character-sets-dir=*name* | Specifies the directory for character set files |
| | --column-type-info | Displays column type information |
| -c | --comments | Preserves comments |
| -C | --compress | Compresses all information sent between the client and the server |
| -# | --debug | Runs a non-debug version, catches any errors, and exits |
| | --debug-check | Checks memory and opens file usage at exit |
| -T | --debug-info | Displays debug information at exit |
| -D | --database=*name* | Specifies the database to use |
| -e | --execute=*name* | Executes the specified statement and exits |
| -E | --vertical | Displays query output vertically, one data field per line |
| -f | --force | Continues if a SQL error occurs |
| -G | --named-commands | Enables named mysql commands |
| -h | --host=*name* | Specifies the MariaDB server hostname (the default is localhost) |
| -H | --html | Displays query output in HTML code |
| -I | --ignore-spaces | Ignores spaces after function names |
| | --init-command=*name* | SQL command to execute when connecting to the server |
| | --line-numbers | Displays line numbers for errors |

| Short Parameter | Long Parameter | Description |
| --- | --- | --- |
| | --local-infile | Enables/disables the LOAD DATA LOCAL INFILE feature |
| -L | --skip-line-numbers | Doesn't display line numbers for errors |
| -n | --unbuffered | Flushes the buffer after each query |
| -N | --skip-column-names | Doesn't display column names in results |
| -o | --one-database | Ignores statements except those for the default database named on the command line |
| | --pager | Uses pager to display results |
| -p | --password | Prompts for the password for the user account |
| -P | --port=# | Specifies the TCP port number to use for the network connection |
| | --progress-reports | Gets progress reports for long-running commands |
| | --prompt=*name* | Sets the command-line prompt |
| | --protocol=*name* | Sets the protocol to use for the connection (tcp, socket, or pipe) |
| -q | --quick | Doesn't cache each query result |
| -r | --raw | Displays column values without escape conversion |
| | --reconnect | Reconnects if the connection is lost |
| -s | --silent | Uses silent mode |
| -S | --socket=*name* | Specifies a socket for connection to the localhost |
| | --ssl | Enables SSL for the connection |
| -t | --table | Displays output in table form |
| | --tee=*name* | Appends output to the specified file |
| -u | --user=*name* | Specifies the user account to log in as |
| -U | --safe-updates | Allows only UPDATE and DELETE statements that specify key values |
| -v | --verbose | Uses verbose mode |
| -w | --wait | If the connection can't be established, waits and retries |
| -X | --xml | Displays query output in XHTML code |

By default, the `mysql` client program attempts to log in to the MariaDB server using your Linux login name. Just as in Linux, the administrator account in MariaDB is called `root`; to log in as the administrator you run the `mysql` command as the Linux `root` user by using the `sudo` command:

```
rich@Ubuntu22:~$ sudo mysql
Welcome to the MariaDB monitor.  Commands end with ; or \g.
Your MariaDB connection id is 31
Server version: 10.6.7-MariaDB-2ubuntu1 Ubuntu 22.04

Copyright (c) 2000, 2018, Oracle, MariaDB Corporation Ab and others.

Type 'help;' or '\h' for help. Type '\c' to clear the current input statement.

MariaDB [(none)]>
```

When you get to the MariaDB command prompt, you can start entering commands to create, modify, and delete user accounts, databases, and tables.

## Using the mysql commands

The `mysql` program uses two different types of commands:

>> Special `mysql` built-in commands

>> Standard SQL statements

The `mysql` program uses its own set of commands that let you easily control the environment and retrieve information about the MariaDB server. Table 3-2 shows these commands.

**TABLE 3-2**     ## The mysql Commands

| Command | Shortcut | Description |
| --- | --- | --- |
| ? | \? | Accesses help |
| clear | \c | Clears the command |
| connect | \r | Connects to the database and server |
| delimiter | \d | Sets a SQL statement delimiter |
| edit | \e | Edits the command with the command-line editor |
| ego | \G | Sends the command to the MariaDB server and displays the results vertically |

| Command | Shortcut | Description |
|---------|----------|-------------|
| exit | \q | Exits from the mysql program |
| go | \g | Sends the command to the MariaDB server |
| help | \h | Displays help |
| nopager | \n | Disables the output pager and sends the output to STDOUT |
| notee | \t | Doesn't send output to the output file |
| pager | \P | Sets the pager command to the specified program (used more as default) |
| print | \p | Prints the current command |
| prompt | \R | Changes the mysql command prompt |
| quit | \q | Quits from the mysql program (same as exit) |
| rehash | \# | Rebuilds the command completion hash table |
| source | \. | Executes the SQL script in the specified file |
| status | \s | Retrieves status information from the MariaDB server |
| system | \! | Executes a shell command on the system |
| tee | \T | Appends all output to the specified file |
| use | \u | Uses another database |
| charset | \C | Changes to another character set |
| warnings | \W | Shows warnings after every statement |
| nowarning | \w | Doesn't show warnings after every statement |

You can use either the full command or the shortcut command directly from the mysql command prompt:

```
MariaDB [(none)]> \s
--------------
mysql  Ver 15.1 Distrib 10.6.7-MariaDB, for debian-linux-gnu (x86_64) using
   EditLine wrapper

Connection id:      31
Current database:
Current user:       root@localhost
SSL:                Not in use
```

```
Current pager:      stdout
Using outfile:      ''
Using delimiter:    ;
Server:             MariaDB
Server version:     10.6.7-MariaDB-2ubuntu1 Ubuntu 22.04
Protocol version:   10
Connection:         Localhost via UNIX socket
Server characterset:    utf8mb4
Db    characterset:     utf8mb4
Client characterset:    utf8mb3
Conn. characterset:     utf8mb3
UNIX socket:        /run/mysqld/mysqld.sock
Uptime:             22 min 18 sec

Threads: 1  Questions: 61  Slow queries: 0  Opens: 33  Open tables: 26
Queries per second avg: 0.045
--------------

MariaDB [(none)]>
```

Besides its own built-in commands, the mysql program also implements all the standard Structured Query Language (SQL) commands supported by the MariaDB server. (The "Creating database objects" section in this chapter discusses these commands in more detail.)

One uncommon SQL command that the mysql program implements is the SHOW command. Using this command, you can extract information about the MariaDB server, such as the databases and tables created:

```
MariaDB [(none)]> SHOW DATABASES;
+--------------------+
| Database           |
+--------------------+
| information_schema |
| mysql              |
| performance_schema |
| sys                |
+--------------------+
4 rows in set (0.010 sec)

MariaDB [(none)]> USE mysql;
Reading table information for completion of table and column names
You can turn off this feature to get a quicker startup with -A

Database changed
MariaDB [mysql]> SHOW TABLES;
```

```
+---------------------------+
| Tables_in_mysql           |
+---------------------------+
| column_stats              |
| columns_priv              |
| db                        |
| event                     |
| func                      |
| general_log               |
| global_priv               |
| gtid_slave_pos            |
| help_category             |
| help_keyword              |
| help_relation             |
| help_topic                |
| index_stats               |
| innodb_index_stats        |
| innodb_table_stats        |
| plugin                    |
| proc                      |
| procs_priv                |
| proxies_priv              |
| roles_mapping             |
| servers                   |
| slow_log                  |
| table_stats               |
| tables_priv               |
| time_zone                 |
| time_zone_leap_second     |
| time_zone_name            |
| time_zone_transition      |
| time_zone_transition_type |
| transaction_registry      |
| user                      |
+---------------------------+
31 rows in set (0.001 sec)

MariaDB [mysql]>
```

In this example, I use the SHOW SQL command to display the databases currently
configured on the MariaDB server and then the USE SQL command to connect to
a single database. Your mysql session can be connected to only one database at
a time.

You'll notice that after each command I add a semicolon (;). The semicolon indicates the end of a command to the mysql program. If you don't use a semicolon, it prompts you for more data:

```
MariaDB [mysql]> SHOW
    -> DATABASES;
+--------------------+
| Database           |
+--------------------+
| information_schema |
| mysql              |
| performance_schema |
| sys                |
+--------------------+
4 rows in set (0.000 sec)

MariaDB [mysql]>
```

This feature can come in handy when you're working with long commands. You can enter part of the command on a line, press Enter, and then continue on the next line. This can continue for as many lines as you like until you use the semicolon to indicate the end of the command.

**TIP**

Throughout this chapter, I use uppercase letters for SQL commands. This has become a common way to write SQL commands, but the mysql program allows you to specify SQL commands using either uppercase or lowercase.

## Creating database objects

Before you can start storing data in the MariaDB server, you'll need a few database objects to work with. At a minimum, you'll want to have the following:

>> A unique database to store your application data

>> A unique user account to access the database from your programs

>> One or more data tables to organize your data

You build all these objects using the mysql program. The mysql program interfaces directly with the MariaDB server, using SQL commands to create and modify each of the objects.

You can send any type of SQL commands to the MariaDB server using the mysql program. This section walks you through the different SQL statements you'll need to build the basic database objects for your shell scripts.

## Creating a database

The MariaDB server organizes data into databases. A database usually holds the data for a single application, separating it from other applications that use the database server. Creating a separate database for each application helps eliminate confusion and data mix-ups.

The SQL statement required to create a new database is

```
CREATE DATABASE name;
```

That's pretty simple. Of course, you must have the proper privileges to create new databases on the MariaDB server. The easiest way to do that is to run the mysql program as the root user account:

```
rich@Ubuntu22:~$ sudo mysql
Welcome to the MariaDB monitor.  Commands end with ; or \g.
Your MariaDB connection id is 33
Server version: 10.6.7-MariaDB-2ubuntu1 Ubuntu 22.04

Copyright (c) 2000, 2018, Oracle, MariaDB Corporation Ab and others.

Type 'help;' or '\h' for help. Type '\c' to clear the current input statement.

MariaDB [(none)]> CREATE DATABASE test;
Query OK, 1 row affected (0.000 sec)

MariaDB [(none)]>
```

You can see whether the new database was created by using the SHOW DATABASES command:

```
MariaDB [(none)]> SHOW DATABASES;
+--------------------+
| Database           |
+--------------------+
| information_schema |
| mysql              |
| performance_schema |
| sys                |
| test               |
+--------------------+
5 rows in set (0.001 sec)

MariaDB [(none)]>
```

Yes, it was successfully created. You should now be able to connect to the new database:

```
MariaDB [(none)]> USE test;
Database changed
MariaDB [test]> SHOW TABLES;
Empty set (0.000 sec)

MariaDB [test]>
```

The SHOW TABLES command allows you to see if there are any tables created. The Empty set result indicates that there aren't any tables to work with yet. Before you start creating tables, however, there's one other thing you need to do.

## Creating a user account

So far, you've seen how to connect to the MariaDB server using the root administrator account. This account has total control over all the MariaDB server objects (much like how the root Linux account has complete control over the Linux system).

Just like in the Linux world, it's extremely dangerous to use the root MariaDB account for normal applications. If there is a breach of security and someone figures out the password for the root user account, all sorts of bad things could happen to your system (and data).

To prevent that, it's wise to create a separate user account in MariaDB that has privileges only for the database used in the application. You do this with the GRANT SQL statement:

```
MariaDB [test]> GRANT SELECT,INSERT,DELETE,UPDATE ON test.* TO rich IDENTIFIED
    BY 'test';
Query OK, 0 rows affected (0.009 sec)

MariaDB [test]>
```

That's quite a long command. Let's walk through the pieces and see what it's doing.

The first section defines the privileges the user account has on which database(s). The SELECT, INSERT, DELETE, UPDATE statement allows the user account to query the database data (the select privilege), insert new data records, delete existing data records, and update existing data records. The test.* entry defines the database and tables the privileges apply to. This is specified in the following format:

```
database.table
```

As you can see from this example, you're allowed to use wildcard characters when specifying the database and tables. This format applies the specified privileges to all the tables contained in the database named test.

Finally, with the TO statement you specify the user account(s) the privileges apply to. The neat thing about the GRANT command is that if the user account doesn't exist, it creates it. The IDENTIFIED BY portion allows you to set a default password for the new user account.

You can test the new user account directly from the mysql program:

```
rich@Ubuntu22:~$ mysql test -p
Enter password:
Welcome to the MariaDB monitor.  Commands end with ; or \g.
Your MariaDB connection id is 35
Server version: 10.6.7-MariaDB-2ubuntu1 Ubuntu 22.04

Copyright (c) 2000, 2018, Oracle, MariaDB Corporation Ab and others.

Type 'help;' or '\h' for help. Type '\c' to clear the current input statement.

MariaDB [test]>
```

The first parameter specifies the default database to use (test); the –p option tells mysql to prompt for the user's password. After entering the password assigned to the rich user account, you're connected to the server.

Now that you've got a database and a user account, you're ready to create some tables for the data. But first, let's take a look at the other database server you can use.

# Using the PostgreSQL Database

The PostgreSQL database started out as an academic project named Postgres, demonstrating how to incorporate advanced database techniques into a functional database server. Over the years, Postgres evolved into the PostgreSQL open-source project and became one of the most advanced open-source database servers available for the Linux environment.

This section walks you through getting a PostgreSQL database server installed and running, and then setting up a user account and database to work with in your programs.

# Installing PostgreSQL

Similar to MariaDB, most Linux distributions include the PostgreSQL package in their standard software repositories. For Ubuntu, you'll want to install the postgresql package:

```
rich@Ubuntu22:~$ sudo apt install postgresql
[sudo] password for rich:
Reading package lists... Done
Building dependency tree... Done
Reading state information... Done
The following additional packages will be installed:
  libcommon-sense-perl libjson-perl libjson-xs-perl libllvm14 libpq5
  libtypes-serialiser-perl postgresql-14 postgresql-client-14
  postgresql-client-common postgresql-common sysstat
Suggested packages:
  postgresql-doc postgresql-doc-14 isag
The following NEW packages will be installed:
  libcommon-sense-perl libjson-perl libjson-xs-perl libllvm14 libpq5
  libtypes-serialiser-perl postgresql postgresql-14 postgresql-client-14
  postgresql-client-common postgresql-common sysstat
0 upgraded, 12 newly installed, 0 to remove and 8 not upgraded.
Need to get 42.4 MB of archives.
After this operation, 161 MB of additional disk space will be used.
Do you want to continue? [Y/n]
```

As part of the installation process, Ubuntu starts the PostgreSQL server and enables it to start at boot time:

```
rich@Ubuntu22:~$ systemctl status postgresql
  postgresql.service - PostgreSQL RDBMS
     Loaded: loaded (/lib/systemd/system/postgresql.service; enabled; vendor pr>
     Active: active (exited) since Wed 2022-04-27 15:24:25 EDT; 28min ago
    Process: 4889 ExecStart=/bin/true (code=exited, status=0/SUCCESS)
   Main PID: 4889 (code=exited, status=0/SUCCESS)
        CPU: 993us

Apr 27 15:24:25 Ubuntu22 systemd[1]: Starting PostgreSQL RDBMS...
Apr 27 15:24:25 Ubuntu22 systemd[1]: Finished PostgreSQL RDBMS.
rich@Ubuntu22:~$
```

For Red Hat Linux–based distributions, such as Fedora and Rocky Linux, you'll want to install the postgresql-server package:

```
[rich@localhost ~]$ sudo dnf install postgresql-server
[sudo] password for rich:
```

```
Last metadata expiration check: 1 day, 1:34:29 ago on Tue 26 Apr 2022 02:27:03
    PM EDT.
Dependencies resolved.
================================================================================
 Package            Arch   Version                            Repo        Size
================================================================================
Installing:
 postgresql-server x86_64 10.17-2.module+el8.5.0+685+b03fcc47  appstream 5.1 M
Installing dependencies:
 libpq             x86_64 13.3-1.el8_4                         appstream 196 k
 postgresql        x86_64 10.17-2.module+el8.5.0+685+b03fcc47  appstream 1.5 M
Enabling module streams:
 postgresql               10

Transaction Summary
================================================================================
Install  3 Packages

Total download size: 6.8 M
Installed size: 26 M
Is this ok [y/N]:
```

When the installation completes, use the `systemctl` command to enable
PostgreSQL to start at boot time:

```
[rich@localhost ~]$ sudo systemctl enable postgresql
Created symlink /etc/systemd/system/multi-user.target.wants/postgresql.service
    → /usr/lib/systemd/system/postgresql.service.
[rich@localhost ~]$
```

However, before you can start the server, you must first initialize the PostgreSQL
database by running the `postgresql-setup` command as the root user account:

```
[rich@localhost ~]$ su -c '/usr/bin/postgresql-setup' --initdb
Password:
 * Initializing database in '/var/lib/pgsql/data'
 * Initialized, logs are in /var/lib/pgsql/initdb_postgresql.log
[rich@localhost ~]$ sudo systemctl start postgresql
[rich@localhost ~]$ systemctl status postgresql
 postgresql.service - PostgreSQL database server
   Loaded: loaded (/usr/lib/systemd/system/postgresql.service; enabled; vendor
   pres>
   Active: active (running) since Wed 2022-04-27 16:03:50 EDT; 20s ago
  Process: 4718 ExecStartPre=/usr/libexec/postgresql-check-db-dir postgresql
  (code=>
 Main PID: 4721 (postmaster)
    Tasks: 8 (limit: 68892)
```

```
Memory: 16.0M
CGroup: /system.slice/postgresql.service
        —4721 /usr/bin/postmaster -D /var/lib/pgsql/data
        —4722 postgres: logger process
        —4724 postgres: checkpointer process
        —4725 postgres: writer process
        —4726 postgres: wal writer process
        —4727 postgres: autovacuum launcher process
        —4728 postgres: stats collector process
        —4729 postgres: bgworker: logical replication launcher
```

After you've installed the PostgreSQL database server, logging into the PostgreSQL server is slightly different than from the MariaDB server. The MariaDB server maintains its own internal database of users that can be granted access to database objects. PostgreSQL also has this capability, but most PostgreSQL implementations (including Ubuntu and Rocky Linux) utilize the existing Linux system user accounts to authenticate PostgreSQL users.

Using the system user accounts for an application authentication can sometimes be confusing, but it does make for a nice, clean way to control user accounts in PostgreSQL. You simply need to ensure that each PostgreSQL user has a valid account on the Linux system instead of having to worry about a whole separate set of user accounts.

Another major difference for PostgreSQL is that the administrator account in PostgreSQL is called postgres not root. Because of this requirement, when you install PostgreSQL on your Linux system, there must be a Linux user account named postgres. This user account is created during the software package installation process in both Ubuntu and Rocky Linux.

# Looking at the PostgreSQL command interface

The PostgreSQL command-line client program is called psql. This program provides complete access to the database objects configured in the PostgreSQL server. This section describes the psql command and shows you how to use it to interact with your PostgreSQL server.

## Connecting to the server

The psql client program provides the command-line interface to the PostgreSQL server. As you would expect, it uses command-line parameters to control what features are enabled in the client interface. Each option uses either a long or short name format. Table 3-3 shows the command-line parameters available.

TABLE 3-3

# The psql Command-Line Parameters

| Short Name | Long Name | Description |
|---|---|---|
| -a | --echo-all | Displays all SQL lines processed from a script file in the output |
| -A | --no-align | Sets the output format to unaligned mode, with data not displayed as a formatted table |
| -c | --command | Executes the specified SQL statement and exits |
| -d | --dbname | Specifies the database to connect with |
| -e | --echo-queries | Echoes all queries to the screen |
| -E | --echo-hidden | Echoes hidden psql meta-commands to the screen |
| -f | --file | Executes SQL commands from the specified file and exits |
| -F | --field-separator | Specifies the character used to separate column data when in unaligned mode (with the default being a comma) |
| -h | --host | Specifies the IP address or hostname of the remote PostgreSQL server |
| -H | --html | HTML table output mode |
| -l | --list | Displays a list of available databases on the server and exits |
| -L | --log-file | Sends a session log to a file |
| -n | --no-readline | Disables enhanced command-line editing |
| -o | --output | Redirects query output to the specified file |
| -p | --port | Specifies the PostgreSQL server TCP port to connect with |
| -P | --pset | Sets the table printing option specified to a specified value |
| -q | --quiet | Quiet mode; doesn't display output messages |
| -R | --record-separator | Uses the specified character as the record separator (with the default being the newline character) |
| -s | --single-step | Prompts to continue or cancel after every SQL query |
| -S | --single-line | Specifies that the Enter key defines the end of a SQL query instead of a semicolon |
| -t | --tuples-only | Disables column headers and footers in table output |
| -T | --table-attr | Uses the HTML table tag specified when in HTML mode |
| -U | --username | Uses the specified username to connect to the PostgreSQL server |

*(continued)*

**TABLE 3-3** *(continued)*

| Short Name | Long Name | Description |
|---|---|---|
| –v | --variable | Sets the specified variable to a specified value |
| –V | --version | Displays the psql version number and exits |
| –W | --password | Forces a password prompt |
| –x | --expanded | Enables expanded table output to display additional information for records |
| –X | --nopsqlrc | Doesn't process the psql startup file |
| –z | --field-separator-zero | Sets the field separator to zero bytes |
| –? | --help | Displays the psql command line help and exits |

As mentioned in the previous section, the administrative account for PostgreSQL is called postgres. Because PostgreSQL uses Linux user accounts to validate users, you must be logged in as the postgres Linux account to access the PostgreSQL server as the postgres user.

To get around this problem, you can use the sudo command to run the psql command-line program as the postgres user account:

```
[rich@localhost ~]$ sudo --login -u postgres
[postgres@localhost ~]$ psql
psql (10.17)
Type "help" for help.

postgres=#
```

The default psql prompt indicates the database you're connected to (postgres). The pound sign (#) in the prompt indicates that you're logged in with the administrative user account. You're now ready to start entering some commands to interact with the PostgreSQL server.

## The psql commands

Similarly to the mysql program, the psql program uses two different types of commands:

>> Standard SQL statements

>> PostgreSQL meta-commands

PostgreSQL meta-commands allow you to easily extract information about the database environment as well as set features for the psql session. A meta-command is indicated by using a backslash (\). There are lots of PostgreSQL meta-commands for lots of different settings and features, but there's no reason to start worrying about them all right away. The most commonly used ones are as follows:

>> \l to list the available databases

>> \c to connect to a database

>> \dt to list the tables in a database

>> \du to list the PostgreSQL users

>> \z to list table privileges

>> \? to list all the available meta-commands

>> \h to list all the available SQL commands

>> \q to exit the database

If you ever need to find a meta-command, just enter the \? meta-command. You'll see a list of all the available meta-commands and explanations of them.

To test the meta-commands, use the \l meta-command to list the available databases:

```
postgres=# \l
                                List of databases
    Name    |   Owner  | Encoding |   Collate   |    Ctype    |   Access privileges
------------+----------+----------+-------------+-------------+----------------------
 postgres   | postgres | UTF8     | en_US.UTF-8 | en_US.UTF-8 |
 template0  | postgres | UTF8     | en_US.UTF-8 | en_US.UTF-8 | =c/postgres         +
            |          |          |             |             | postgres=CTc/
            |          |          |             |             | postgres
 template1  | postgres | UTF8     | en_US.UTF-8 | en_US.UTF-8 | =c/postgres         +
            |          |          |             |             | postgres=CTc/postgres
(3 rows)

postgres=#
```

The listing shows the available databases on the server along with their features. These databases are the default ones provided by the PostgreSQL server. The postgres database maintains all the system data for the server. The template0 and template1 databases provide default database templates for you to copy when creating a new database.

You're now ready to start working on your own data in PostgreSQL.

# Creating PostgreSQL database objects

This section walks you through the process of creating your database and a user account to access it. You'll see that although some of the work in PostgreSQL is exactly the same as in MariaDB, some of it is completely different.

## Creating a database

Creating a database is one of those actions that's the same in MariaDB. Remember to be logged in as the postgres administrative account to create the new database:

```
[rich@localhost ~]$ sudo --login -u postgres
[sudo] password for rich:
[postgres@localhost ~]$ psql
psql (10.17)
Type "help" for help.

Postgres=# CREATE DATABASE test;
CREATE DATABASE
postgres=#
```

After you create the database, use the \l meta-command to see whether it appears in the listing and then the \c meta-command to connect to it:

```
postgres=# \l
                                  List of databases
    Name    |  Owner   | Encoding |  Collate    |   Ctype     |   Access
  privileges
------------+----------+----------+-------------+-------------+-------------
 postgres   | postgres | UTF8     | en_US.UTF-8 | en_US.UTF-8 |
 template0  | postgres | UTF8     | en_US.UTF-8 | en_US.UTF-8 | =c/
                                                               postgres        +
            |          |          |             |             | postgres=CTc/
                                                               postgres
 template1  | postgres | UTF8     | en_US.UTF-8 | en_US.UTF-8 | =c/
                                                               postgres        +
            |          |          |             |             | postgres=CTc/
                                                               postgres
 test       | postgres | UTF8     | en_US.UTF-8 | en_US.UTF-8 |
(4 rows)

postgres=# \c test
```

```
You are now connected to database "test" as user "postgres".
test=#
```

When you connect to the test database, the psql prompt changes to indicate the new database name. This is a great help when you're ready to create your database objects because you can easily tell where you are in the system.

## Creating user accounts

After creating the new database, the next step is to create a user account that has access to it for your programs. As you've already seen, user accounts in PostgreSQL are significantly different than those in MariaDB.

User accounts in PostgreSQL are called *login roles.* The PostgreSQL server matches login roles to the Linux system user accounts. Because of this, there are two common approaches to creating login roles to run shell scripts that access the PostgreSQL database:

>> Create a special Linux account with a matching PostgreSQL login role to run all your shell scripts.

>> Create PostgreSQL accounts for each Linux user account that needs to run shell scripts to access the database.

For this example, let's choose the second method and create a PostgreSQL account that matches our Linux system account. This way, you can create and run programs that access the PostgreSQL database directly from your Linux user account.

First, you must create the login role:

```
test=# CREATE ROLE rich LOGIN;
CREATE ROLE
test=#
```

That was simple enough. Without the LOGIN parameter, the role is not allowed to log in to the PostgreSQL server, but it can be assigned privileges. This type of role is called a *group role.* Group roles are great if you're working in a large environment with lots of users and tables. Instead of having to keep track of which user has which type of privileges for which tables, you just create group roles for specific types of access to tables and then assign the login roles to the proper group role.

For simple programs and shell scripting, you most likely won't need to worry about creating group roles — just assign privileges directly to the login roles. That's what I do in this example.

However, PostgreSQL handles privileges a bit differently than the way MariaDB does. PostgreSQL doesn't allow you to grant overall privileges to all objects in a database that filter down to the table level. Instead, you need to grant privileges for each individual table you create. Although this is somewhat of a pain, it helps enforce strict security policies. You'll have to hold off on assigning privileges until you've created a table. That's the next step in the process.

# Chapter **4**

# Working with Samba and NFS

f your local-area network (LAN) is like most others, it needs the capability to share files between systems that run Linux and other systems that don't. Though this percentage may be getting smaller as Linux use grows, it's still too large to ignore. Therefore, Linux includes two prominent file-sharing services:

» **Network File System (NFS):** For file sharing with other Unix systems (or PCs with NFS client software)

» **Samba:** For file sharing and print sharing with Windows systems

This chapter describes how to share files by using both NFS and Samba.

## Sharing Files with NFS

Sharing files through NFS is simple and involves two basic steps:

» On the Linux system that runs the NFS server, you export (share) one or more directories by listing them in the /etc/exports file and by running the exportfs command. In addition, you must start the NFS server.

>> On each client system, you use the mount command to mount the directories that your server exported.

The only problem with using NFS is that each client system must support it. Microsoft Windows doesn't ship with NFS, so you have to buy the NFS software separately if you want to share files by using NFS. Using NFS if all systems on your LAN run Linux (or other variants of Unix with built-in NFS support) makes good sense, however.

**WARNING**

NFS has security vulnerabilities, so you shouldn't set up NFS on systems that are directly connected to the Internet without using the RPCSEC_GSS security that comes with NFS version 4 (NFSv4). Version 4.2 was released in November 2016; you should use it for most purposes because it includes all the needed updates.

The next few sections walk you through NFS setup, using an example of two Linux PCs on a LAN.

## Installing NFS

Many Linux systems don't install the NFS software by default, so you'll need to manually install it. For Ubuntu, install the nfs-kernel-server package using the apt tool:

```
rich@Ubuntu22:/$ sudo apt install nfs-kernel-server
[sudo] password for rich:
Reading package lists... Done
Building dependency tree... Done
Reading state information... Done
The following additional packages will be installed:
  keyutils libevent-core-2.1-7 libnfsidmap1 nfs-common rpcbind
Suggested packages:
  open-iscsi watchdog
The following NEW packages will be installed:
  keyutils libevent-core-2.1-7 libnfsidmap1 nfs-common nfs-kernel-server
  rpcbind
0 upgraded, 6 newly installed, 0 to remove and 10 not upgraded.
Need to get 616 kB of archives.
After this operation, 2,235 kB of additional disk space will be used.
Do you want to continue? [Y/n]
```

After you install the NFS package, you can check to make sure it's active on the system:

```
rich@Ubuntu22:~$ systemctl status nfs-kernel-server
 nfs-server.service - NFS server and services
      Loaded: loaded (/lib/systemd/system/nfs-server.service; enabled; vendor pr>
      Active: active (exited) since Fri 2022-04-29 18:26:34 EDT; 4min 57s ago
     Process: 922 ExecStartPre=/usr/sbin/exportfs -r (code=exited, status=0/SUCC>
     Process: 925 ExecStart=/usr/sbin/rpc.nfsd (code=exited, status=0/SUCCESS)
    Main PID: 925 (code=exited, status=0/SUCCESS)
         CPU: 4ms

Apr 29 18:26:34 Ubuntu22 systemd[1]: Starting NFS server and services...
Apr 29 18:26:34 Ubuntu22 systemd[1]: Finished NFS server and services.
rich@Ubuntu22:~$
```

For Rocky Linux, the nfs-utils package is already installed by default but not active. To activate it you'll need to use the systemctl command:

```
[rich@unknown08002755DFBD ~]$ sudo systemctl enable nfs-server
Created symlink /etc/systemd/system/multi-user.target.wants/nfs-server.service -
    /usr/lib/systemd/system/nfs-server.service.
[rich@unknown08002755DFBD ~]$ sudo systemctl start nfs-server
[rich@unknown08002755DFBD ~]$
```

After you have the NFS server installed and running, the next step is to configure a directory to share.

**WARNING**

If your Linux system uses a firewall program (such as UFW for Ubuntu or firewalld for Rocky Linux), you'll need to allow NFS traffic through the firewall. For example, on a Rocky Linux system, the command would be:

```
[rich@unknown08002755DFBD ~]$ sudo firewall-cmd --add-
    service={nfs,nfs3,mountd,rpc-bind} --permanent
success
[rich@unknown08002755DFBD ~]$ sudo firewall-cmd --reload
success
[rich@unknown08002755DFBD ~]$
```

# Exporting a file system with NFS

Start with the server system that *exports* — makes available to the client systems — the contents of a directory. On the server, you must run the NFS service and designate one or more file systems to export.

To export a file system, you have to add an appropriate entry to the /etc/exports file. Suppose that you want to export the /share directory, and you want to enable the host named `testbox` to mount this file system for read and write operations. You can do so by adding the following entry to the /etc/exports file:

```
/share testbox(rw,sync)
```

If you want to give access to all hosts on a LAN, such as 192.168.0.0, you could change this line to

```
/share 192.168.0.0/24(rw,sync)
```

Every line in the /etc/exports file has this general format:

```
Directory host1(options) host2(options) ...
```

The first field is the directory being shared via NFS, followed by one or more fields that specify which hosts can mount that directory remotely and several options in parentheses. You can specify the hosts with names or IP addresses, including ranges of addresses.

The options in parentheses denote the kind of access each host is granted and how user and group IDs from the server are mapped to ID the client. (If a file is owned by root on the server, for example, what owner is that on the client?) Within the parentheses, commas separate the options. If a host is allowed both read and write access, and all IDs are to be mapped to the anonymous user (by default, the anonymous user is named nobody), the options look like this:

```
(rw,all_squash)
```

Table 4-1 shows the options you can use in the /etc/exports file. You find two types of options: general options and user ID mapping options.

After adding the entry in the /etc/exports file, manually export the file system by typing the following command in a terminal window:

```
exportfs -a
```

This command exports all file systems defined in the /etc/exports file.

Now you can start the NFS server processes.

**TIP**

If you ever make any changes in the exported file systems listed in the /etc/exports file, remember to restart the NFS service. To restart a service, invoke the script in the /etc/init.d directory with restart as the argument (instead of the start argument that you use to start the service).

**TABLE 4-1**

# Options in /etc/exports

| Option | Description |
| --- | --- |
| **General Options** | |
| secure | Allows connections only from port 1024 or lower (default) |
| insecure | Allows connections from port 1024 or higher |
| ro | Allows read-only access (default) |
| rw | Allows both read and write access |
| sync | Performs write operations (writing information to the disk) when requested (by default) |
| async | Performs write operations when the server is ready |
| no_wdelay | Performs write operations immediately |
| wdelay | Waits a bit to see whether related write requests arrive and then performs them together (by default) |
| hide | Hides an exported directory that's a subdirectory of another exported directory (by default) |
| no_hide | Causes a directory to not be hidden (opposite of hide) |
| subtree_check | Performs subtree checking, which involves checking parent directories of an exported subdirectory whenever a file is accessed (by default) |
| no_subtree_check | Turns off subtree checking (opposite of subtree_check) |
| insecure_locks | Allows insecure file locking |
| **User ID Mapping Options** | |
| all_squash | Maps all user IDs and group IDs to the anonymous user on the client |
| no_all_squash | Maps remote user and group IDs to similar IDs on the client (by default) |
| root_squash | Maps remote root user to the anonymous user on the client (by default) |
| no_root_squash | Maps remote root user to the local root user |
| anonuid=UID | Sets the user ID of anonymous user to be used for the all_squash and root_squash options |
| anongid=GID | Sets the group ID of anonymous user to be used for the all_squash and root_squash options |

## Mounting an NFS file system

To access an exported NFS file system on a client system, you have to mount that file system on a mount point. The *mount point* is nothing more than a local directory. Suppose that you want to access the /home directory exported from the server named myserver at the local directory /mnt/myserver on the client system. To do so, follow these steps:

1. **Log in as root, and create the directory with this command:**

   ```
   mkdir /mnt/myserver
   ```

2. **Type the following command to mount the directory from the remote system (myserver) on the local directory/mnt/myserver:**

   ```
   mount myserver:/share /mnt/myserver
   ```

After completing these steps, you can view and access exported files from the local directory /mnt/myserver.

To confirm that the NFS file system is indeed mounted, log in as root on the client system, and type **mount** in a terminal window. You see a line similar to the following about the NFS file system:

```
myserver:/share on /mnt/myserver type nfs (rw,addr=192.168.0.4)
```

**TECHNICAL STUFF**

NFS supports two types of mount operations: hard and soft. By default, a mount is hard, which means that if the NFS server doesn't respond, the client keeps trying to access the server indefinitely until the server responds. You can soft-mount an NFS volume by adding the -o soft option to the mount command. For a soft mount, the client returns an error if the NFS server fails to respond and doesn't retry.

# Setting Up a Windows Server Using Samba

If you rely on Windows for file sharing and print sharing, you probably use Windows in your servers and clients. If so, you can still move to a Linux PC as your server without losing the Windows file-sharing and print-sharing capabilities; you can set up Linux as a Windows server. When you install Linux, you also get a chance to install the Samba software package, which performs that setup. All you have to do is select the Windows File Server package group during installation.

**REMEMBER**

After you install and configure Samba on your Linux PC, your client PCs — even if they're running an old Windows operating system or one of the more recent Windows versions — can access shared disks and printers on the Linux PC. To do so, they use the Common Internet File System (CIFS) protocol, the underlying protocol in Windows file and print sharing.

With the Samba package installed, you can make your Linux PC a Windows client, which means that the Linux PC can access the disks and printers that a Windows server manages. At the same time, your Linux PC can be a client to other Windows systems on the network.

The Samba software package has these major components:

» /etc/samba/smb.conf: The Samba configuration file that the Server Message Block (SMB) server uses.

» /etc/samba/smbusers: A Samba configuration file showing the Samba usernames that correspond to usernames on the local Linux PC.

» nmbd: The NetBIOS name server, which clients use to look up servers. (*NetBIOS* stands for *Network Basic Input/Output System* — an interface that applications use to communicate with network transports, such as TCP/IP.)

» nmblookup: A command that returns the IP address of a Windows PC identified by its NetBIOS name.

» smbadduser: A program that adds users to the SMB password file.

» smbcacls: A program that manipulates Windows NT access control lists on shared files.

» smbclient: The Windows client, which runs on Linux and allows Linux to access the files and printer on any Windows server.

» smbcontrol: A program that sends messages to the smbd, nmbd, or winbindd processes.

» smbd: The SMB server, which accepts connections from Windows clients and provides file-sharing and print-sharing services.

» smbmount: A program that mounts a Samba share directory on a Linux PC.

» smbpasswd: A program that changes the password for an SMB user.

» smbprint: A script that enables printing on a printer on an SMB server.

» smbstatus: A command that lists the current SMB connections for the local host.

» smbtar: A program that backs up SMB shares directly to tape drives on the Linux system.

Working with Samba and NFS

» `smbumount`: A program that unmounts a currently mounted Samba share directory.

» `testparm`: A program that ensures that the Samba configuration file is correct.

» `winbindd`: A server that resolves names from Windows NT servers.

The following sections describe how to configure and use Samba.

## Installing Samba

Some Linux distributions install the Samba client by default, but most don't install the Samba server software, which is what you'll need for your Linux system to act as a Windows server. However, most distributions include the Samba server software in their software repositories so installing it is a breeze.

For Debian-based systems, such as Ubuntu, use the apt tool:

```
rich@Ubuntu22:~$ sudo apt install samba
Reading package lists... Done
Building dependency tree... Done
Reading state information... Done
The following additional packages will be installed:
  attr ibverbs-providers libcephfs2 libgfapi0 libgfrpc0 libgfxdr0
  libglusterfs0 libibverbs1 librados2 librdmacm1 python3-dnspython python3-gpg
  python3-markdown python3-pygments python3-requests-toolbelt python3-samba
  python3-tdb samba-common samba-common-bin samba-dsdb-modules
  samba-vfs-modules tdb-tools
Suggested packages:
  python3-sniffio python3-trio python-markdown-doc python-pygments-doc
  ttf-bitstream-vera bind9 bind9utils ctdb ldb-tools ntp | chrony
  smbldap-tools winbind heimdal-clients
The following NEW packages will be installed:
  attr ibverbs-providers libcephfs2 libgfapi0 libgfrpc0 libgfxdr0
  libglusterfs0 libibverbs1 librados2 librdmacm1 python3-dnspython python3-gpg
  python3-markdown python3-pygments python3-requests-toolbelt python3-samba
  python3-tdb samba samba-common samba-common-bin samba-dsdb-modules
  samba-vfs-modules tdb-tools
0 upgraded, 23 newly installed, 0 to remove and 10 not upgraded.
Need to get 12.2 MB of archives.
After this operation, 71.8 MB of additional disk space will be used.
Do you want to continue? [Y/n]
```

For Red Hat–based systems, such as Rocky Linux, use the dnf tool:

```
[rich@unknown08002755DFBD ~]$ sudo dnf install samba
[sudo] password for rich:
Last metadata expiration check: 2:36:05 ago on Fri 29 Apr 2022 10:30:22 AM EDT.
Dependencies resolved.
================================================================================
 Package                Architecture Version              Repository   Size
================================================================================
Installing:
 samba                  x86_64       4.14.5-10.el8_5       baseos       848 k
Installing dependencies:
 samba-common-tools     x86_64       4.14.5-10.el8_5       baseos       500 k
 samba-libs             x86_64       4.14.5-10.el8_5       baseos       169 k

Transaction Summary
================================================================================
Install  3 Packages

Total download size: 1.5 M
Installed size: 4.0 M
Is this ok [y/N]: y
```

In Rocky Linux, as usual, you'll need to enable Samba to start at boot time and manually start it:

```
[rich@unknown08002755DFBD ~]$ sudo systemctl enable smb
Created symlink /etc/systemd/system/multi-user.target.wants/smb.service → /usr/
    lib/systemd/system/smb.service.
[rich@unknown08002755DFBD ~]$ sudo systemctl start smb
[rich@unknown08002755DFBD ~]$
```

And if you have a firewall running on your system, you'll need to open the Samba ports for remote clients to access the Samba server:

```
[rich@unknown08002755DFBD ~]$ sudo firewall-cmd --add-service=samba --permanent
success
[rich@unknown08002755DFBD ~]$ sudo firewall-cmd --reload
success
[rich@unknown08002755DFBD ~]$
```

Now you're ready to set up a directory space to share with the Windows clients on your local network.

# Configuring Samba

To set up the Windows file-sharing and print-sharing services, you can edit the configuration file manually or use a graphical user interface (GUI) tool. Using the GUI tool is much easier than editing a configuration file. Fedora and SUSE come with GUI tools for configuring the Samba server.

If you have to resort to manually configuring Samba, look in the /etc/samba folder for the smb.conf configuration file. To edit it, you'll need root privileges. To add a new directory share, you'll need to start a new section in the file. Each section starts with a label enclosed in brackets, which represents the share name:

```
[sambashare]
    comment = "My Windows share on Rocky"
    path = /share
    read only = no
    browsable = yes
```

After configuring Samba, type the following command in a terminal window to verify that the Samba configuration file is okay:

```
testparm
```

If the command says that it loaded the files, you're all set to go. The testparm command also displays the contents of the Samba configuration file.

**TECHNICAL STUFF**

Samba uses the /etc/samba/smb.conf file as its configuration file. This text file has a syntax similar to that of a legacy Microsoft Windows INI file. You can edit that file in any text editor on your Linux system. Like the old Windows INI files, the /etc/samba/smb.conf file consists of sections with a list of parameters in each section. Each section of the smb.conf file begins with the name of the section in brackets. The section continues until the next section begins or until the file ends. Each line uses the name = value syntax to specify the value of a parameter. As with Windows INI files, comment lines begin with a semicolon (;). In the /etc/samba/smb.conf file, comments may also begin with a hash mark (#).

After setting up a share, you'll need to create a user account to access it. Samba has many advanced authentication features, but for this example, I'll set up a simple user ID and password. To do that, use the smbpasswd utility. This not only lets you create a new user account for a Samba user but also set the password for the account:

```
[rich@unknown08002755DFBD samba]$ sudo smbpasswd -a rich
New SMB password:
```

```
Retype new SMB password:
Added user rich.
[rich@unknown08002755DFBD samba]$
```

Now you're ready to test things out!

## Trying out Samba

You can now connect to your Linux Samba server from any device on your network that supports connecting to Windows shares. That obviously includes Windows workstations, but you can also connect to a Windows share from macOS workstations as well as Linux clients. Depending on which version of Windows you're using, you usually have a Network Neighborhood, Network, or Network icon/option that you can click to see the newly added server. If all else fails, you can specify the name or IP address of your Samba server in the File Manager tool, preceded by two backslashes. When you connect, you'll first be prompted to authenticate — just enter the user ID and password you created with the smbpasswd utility. Figure 4-1 shows the results of connecting to the Samba server.

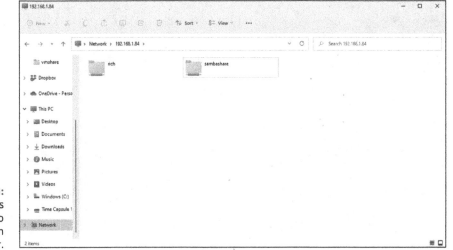

Working with Samba and NFS

**FIGURE 4-1:**
Using Windows File Manager to look at shares on a Samba server.

From here, you can just double-click the share folder to access the files in it.

If you want to experiment with using Samba as a client on your Linux system, use the smbclient program to access shared directories and printers on Windows systems on the LAN and to ensure that your Linux Samba server is working.

## DISCOVERING MORE ABOUT SAMBA

This chapter is only an introduction to Samba. To find out more about Samba, consult the following resources:

- To view Samba documentation online, visit www.samba.org/samba/docs/.
- Read *Using Samba*, 3rd Edition, by Gerald Carter, Jay Ts, and Robert Eckstein (O'Reilly & Associates, 2007)

You should also visit www.samba.org to keep up with the latest news on Samba development. This site also has links to resources for learning Samba.

# Chapter 5

# Managing Mail Servers

E mail is one of the most popular services available on Internet hosts. Email software comes in two parts: a *mail transport agent* (MTA), which physically sends and receives mail messages, and a *mail user agent* (MUA), which reads messages and prepares new messages. While there are several ways of going about implementing this service, the two most popular currently are Postfix, which is growing in popularity, and sendmail, which has been the industry standard for years. This chapter walks you through the basics for getting a Postfix or sendmail email server up and running on your Linux system.

## Working with sendmail

To set up your system as a mail server using the sendmail package, you must configure the sendmail mail transport agent properly. sendmail has the reputation of being a complex but complete mail-delivery system. Just one look at sendmail's configuration file — /etc/mail/sendmail.cf in Fedora or /etc/sendmail.cf in SUSE — can convince you that sendmail is indeed complex. Luckily, you don't have to be an expert on the sendmail configuration file. All you need is one of the predefined configuration files — such as the one installed on your system — to use sendmail.

Your system already has a working sendmail configuration file: /etc/mail/sendmail.cf. The default file assumes that you have an Internet connection and a name server. Provided that you have an Internet connection and that your system has an official domain name, you can send and receive email from your Linux PC.

TIP

The sendmail package has been a staple of mail servers for years, so just about every Linux distribution includes it in the software repository (see Book 1, Chapter 5). However, most Linux distributions don't install it by default. If that's the case with your Linux distribution, just use the appropriate software installation method for your distribution to install the sendmail package.

TECHNICAL
STUFF

To ensure that mail delivery works correctly, your system's name must match the system name that your Internet service provider (ISP) has assigned to you. Although you can give your system any host name you want, other systems can successfully deliver mail to your system only if your system's name is in the ISP's name server.

## The sendmail configuration file

You don't have to understand everything in the sendmail configuration file, send-mail.cf, but you need to know how that file is created. That way, you can make minor changes if necessary and regenerate the sendmail.cf file.

TIP

In SUSE, you can configure sendmail through the YaST Control Center. Choose System⇨Control Center (YaST). Click Network Services on the left side of the window and then click Mail Transfer Agent in the right side of the window. YaST displays a window that you can use to configure sendmail. First, you specify the general settings, followed by the settings for outgoing mail, and finally the settings for incoming mail. After you exit the mail configuration utility, YaST stores the mail settings in the files /etc/sysconfig/sendmail and /etc/sysconfig/mail; then it runs SuSEconfig to update the sendmail configuration file (/etc/sendmail.cf).

You can also generate the sendmail.cf file from m4 macro files — text files in which each line eventually expands to multiple lines that mean something to some program. These macro files are organized into subdirectories in the /usr/share/sendmail-cf directory in Fedora or the /usr/share/sendmail directory in SUSE. You can read the README file in that directory to find out more about the creation of sendmail configuration files.

### The m4 macro processor

The m4 macro processor generates the sendmail.cf configuration file, which comes with the sendmail package in Linux. The main macro file — named sendmail.mc, generic_linux.mc, or linux.mc — is included with the sendmail package.

**TECHNICAL STUFF**

A *macro* is a symbolic name for code that handles some action, usually in a shorthand form that substitutes for a long string of characters. A *macro processor* such as m4 usually reads its input file and copies it to the output, processing the macros along the way. Processing a macro generally involves performing some action and generating some output. Because a macro generates a lot more text in the output than merely the macro's name, the processing of macros is referred to as *macro expansion*.

The m4 macro processor is *stream-based*, which means that it copies the input characters to the output while it's busy expanding any macros. The m4 macro processor doesn't have any concept of lines, so it copies newline characters (which mark the end of a line) to the output. In most m4 macro files, you see dnl, an m4 macro that stands for *delete through newline*. The dnl macro deletes all characters starting at the dnl up to and including the next newline character. The newline characters in the output don't cause any harm; they merely create unnecessary blank lines. The sendmail macro package uses dnl to prevent such blank lines in the output configuration file. Because dnl means to delete everything up to the end of the line, m4 macro files also use dnl as the prefix for comment lines.

To see a simple use of m4, consider the following m4 macro file, which defines two macros (hello and bye) and uses them in a form letter:

```
dnl #################################################
dnl # File: ex.m4
dnl # A simple example of m4 macros
dnl #################################################
define('hello', 'Dear Sir/Madam')dnl
define('bye',
'Sincerely,
Customer Service')dnl
dnl Now type the letter and use the macros
hello,
This is to inform you that we received your recent inquiry.
We will respond to your question soon.
bye
```

Type this text in your favorite text editor and save it in a file named ex.m4. You can name a macro file anything you like, but using the .m4 extension for m4 macro files is customary.

Before you process the macro file by using m4, note the following key points about the example:

>> Use the dnl macro to start all the comment lines, as in the first four lines in the example.

>> End each macro definition with the dnl macro. Otherwise, when m4 processes the macro file, it produces a blank line for each macro definition.

>> Use the built-in m4 command define to define a new macro. The macro name and the value are enclosed between a pair of left and right single quotes (' ... '). Note that you can't use a plain single quote to enclose the macro name and definition.

Now process the macro file ex.m4 by typing the following command:

```
m4 ex.m4
```

m4 processes the macros and displays the following output:

```
Dear Sir/Madam,
This is to inform you that we received your recent inquiry.
We will respond to your question soon.
Sincerely,
Customer Service
```

This output reads like a typical customer-service form letter, doesn't it?

If you compare the output with the ex.m4 file, you see that m4 prints the form letter on standard output, expanding the macros hello and bye into their defined values. If you want to save the form letter in a file called letter, use the shell's output redirection feature, like this:

```
m4 ex.m4 > letter
```

What if you want to use the words *hello* and *bye* in the letter without expanding them? You can do so by enclosing these words in a pair of single quotes (' ... '). You have to do so for other predefined m4 macros, such as define. To use *define* as a plain word, not as a macro to expand, type **'define'**.

## The sendmail macro file

The simple example in the preceding section gives you an idea of how m4 macros are defined and used to create configuration files such as the sendmail.cf file. You find many complex macros stored in files in the /usr/share/sendmail-cf directory in Fedora or the /usr/share/sendmail directory in SUSE. A top-level macro file (called sendmail.mc in Fedora and linux.mc in SUSE), described later in this section, brings in these macro files with the include macro (used to copy a file into the input stream).

**TIP**

To avoid repeatedly mentioning different file and directory names for different distributions such as Fedora and SUSE, I use the file and directory names for Fedora in the following discussions. The general discussions apply to sendmail in all Linux distributions, but you have to replace the file and directory names with those for your specific distribution.

By defining its own set of high-level macros in files located in the /usr/share/ sendmail-cf directory, sendmail essentially creates its own macro language. The sendmail macro files use the .mc extension. The primary sendmail macro file that you configure is sendmail.mc, located in the /etc/mail directory.

Compared with the /etc/mail/sendmail.cf file, the /etc/mail/sendmail.mc file is shorter and easier to work with. Here are some lines from the /etc/mail/ sendmail.mc file that comes with Fedora:

```
divert(-1)dnl
dnl #
dnl # This is the sendmail macro config file for m4. If you make changes to
dnl # /etc/mail/sendmail.mc, you will need to regenerate the
dnl # /etc/mail/sendmail.cf file by confirming that the sendmail-cf package is
dnl # installed and then performing a
dnl #
dnl # /etc/mail/make
dnl #
include('/usr/share/sendmail-cf/m4/cf.m4')dnl
VERSIONID'setup for linux')dnl
OSTYPE('linux')dnl
dnl #
dnl # Do not advertise sendmail version.
dnl #
dnl define('confSMTP_LOGIN_MSG', '$j Sendmail; $b')dnl
dnl #
dnl # default logging level is 9, you might want to set it higher to
dnl # debug the configuration
dnl #
dnl define('confLOG_LEVEL', '9')dnl
dnl #
dnl # Uncomment and edit the following line if your outgoing mail needs to
dnl # be sent out through an external mail server:
dnl #
dnl define('SMART_HOST', 'smtp.your.provider')dn
... lines deleted ...
dnl #
dnl MASQUERADE_AS('mydomain.com')dnl
dnl #
dnl # masquerade not just the headers, but the envelope as well
dnl #
```

```
dnl FEATURE(masquerade_envelope)dnl
dnl #
dnl # masquerade not just @mydomainalias.com, but @*.mydomainalias.com as well
dnl #
dnl FEATURE(masquerade_entire_domain)dnl
dnl #
dnl MASQUERADE_DOMAIN(localhost)dnl
dnl MASQUERADE_DOMAIN(localhost.localdomain)dnl
dnl MASQUERADE_DOMAIN(mydomainalias.com)dnl
dnl MASQUERADE_DOMAIN(mydomain.lan)dnl
MAILER(smtp)dnl
MAILER(procmail)dnl
dnl MAILER(cyrusv2)dnl
```

**TIP**

If you make changes to the /etc/mail/sendmail.mc file, you must generate the /etc/mail/sendmail.cf file by running the sendmail.mc file through the m4 macro processor with the following command (after logging in as root):

```
m4 /etc/mail/sendmail.mc > /etc/mail/sendmail.cf
```

The comments also tell you that you need the sendmail-cf package to process this file.

From the description of m4 macros earlier in this chapter, you see that the sendmail.mc file uses define to create new macros. You also see the liberal use of dnl to prevent too many blank lines in the output.

The other uppercase words (such as OSTYPE, FEATURE, and MAILER) are sendmail macros. These macros are defined in the .m4 files located in the subdirectories of the /usr/share/sendmail-cf directory and are incorporated into the sendmail. mc file with the following include macro:

```
include('usr/share/sendmail-cf/m4/cf.m4')dnl
```

The /usr/share/sendmail-cf/m4/cf.m4 file in turn includes the cfhead.m4 file, which includes other m4 files, and so on. The net effect is as follows: As the m4 macro processor processes the sendmail.mc file, the macro processor incorporates many m4 files from various subdirectories of /usr/share/sendmail-cf.

Here are some key points to note about the /etc/mail/sendmail.mc file:

>> VERSIONID('setup for linux') macro inserts the version information enclosed in quotes into the output.

» OSTYPE('linux') specifies Linux as the operating system. You have to specify this macro early to ensure proper configuration.

Placing this macro right after the VERSIONID macro is customary.

» MAILER(smtp) describes the mailer. According to instructions in the /usr/share/sendmail-cf/README file, MAILER declarations are always placed at the end of the sendmail.mc file, and MAILER(smtp) always precedes MAILER(procmail). The mailer smtp refers to the SMTP mailer.

» FEATURE macros request various special features. FEATURE('blacklist_recipients'), for example, turns on the capability to block incoming mail for certain usernames, hosts, or addresses. The specification of what mail to allow or refuse is placed in the access database (stored in /etc/mail/access.db file). You also need the FEATURE('access_db') macro to turn on the access database.

» MASQUERADE_AS('mydomain.com') causes sendmail to label outgoing mail as having come from the host *mydomain*.com (replace *mydomain* with your domain name). The idea is for a large organization to set up a single sendmail server that handles the mail for many subdomains and makes everything appear to come from a single domain. (Mail from many departments in a university appears to come from the university's main domain name, for example.)

» MASQUERADE_DOMAIN(subdomain.mydomain.com) instructs sendmail to send mail from an address such as user@subdomain.mydomain.com as having originated from the same username at the domain specified by the MASQUERADE_AS macro.

The sendmail macros such as FEATURE and MAILER are described in the /usr/share/sendmail-cf/README file. Consult that file to find out more about the sendmail macros before you make changes to the sendmail.mc file.

## Syntax of the sendmail.cf file

The sendmail.cf file's syntax is designed to be easy for the sendmail program to parse, because sendmail reads this file whenever it starts. Human readability wasn't a primary consideration when the file's syntax was designed. Still, with a little explanation, you can understand the control lines in sendmail.cf.

Each sendmail control line begins with a single-letter operator that defines the meaning of the rest of the line. A line that begins with a space or a tab is considered to be a continuation of the preceding line. Blank lines and lines beginning with a pound sign (#) are comments.

Often, no space appears between the single-letter operator and the arguments that follow the operator, which makes the lines even harder to understand. sendmail. cf uses the concept of a *class* — a collection of phrases. You can define a class named P and add the phrase REDIRECT to that class with the following control line:

```
CPREDIRECT
```

Because everything runs together, the command is hard to decipher. On the other hand, to define a class named Accept and set it to the values OK and RELAY, write the following:

```
C{Accept}OK RELAY
```

This command may be slightly easier to understand because the delimiters (such as the class name, Accept) are enclosed in curly braces.

Other, more recent control lines are even easier to understand. The line

```
O HelpFile=/etc/mail/helpfile
```

defines the option HelpFile as the filename /etc/mail/helpfile. That file contains help information that sendmail uses when it receives a HELP command.

Table 5-1 summarizes the one-letter control operators used in sendmail.cf. Each entry also shows an example of that operator. This table helps you understand some of the lines in sendmail.cf.

**TABLE 5-1** **Control Operators Used in sendmail.cf**

| Operator | Description |
|---|---|
| C | Defines a class, a variable (think of it as a set) that can contain several values. Cwlocalhost adds the name localhost to the class w. |
| D | Defines a macro, a name associated with a single value. DnMAILER-DAEMON defines the macro n as MAILER-DAEMON. |
| F | Defines a class that's been read from a file. Fw/etc/mail/local-host-names reads the names of hosts from the file /etc/mail/local-host-names and adds them to the class w. |
| H | Defines the format of header lines that sendmail inserts into a message. H?P?Return-Path: <$g> defines the Return-Path: field of the header. |
| K | Defines a map (a key-value pair database). Karith arith defines the map named arith as the compiled-in map of the same name. |

| Operator | Description |
|---|---|
| M | Specifies a mailer. The following lines define the `procmail` mailer: `Mprocmail,P=/usr/bin/procmail,F=DFMSPhnu9,S=EnvFromSMTP/HdrFromSMTP,R=EnvToSMTP/HdrFromSMTP,T=DNS/RFC822/X-Unix,A=procmail -Y -m $h $f $u`. |
| O | Assigns a value to an option. `O AliasFile=/etc/aliases` defines the `AliasFile` option to `/etc/aliases`, which is the name of the `sendmail` alias file. |
| P | Defines values for the precedence field. `P junk=-100` sets to -100 the precedence of messages marked with the header field `Precedence: junk`. |
| R | Defines a rule. (A rule has a left side and a right side; if input matches the left side, the right side replaces it. This rule is called *rewriting*.) The rewriting rule `R$* ; $1` strips trailing semicolons. |
| S | Labels a ruleset you can start defining with subsequent R control lines. `Scanonify=3` labels the next ruleset as `canonify` and ruleset 3. |
| T | Adds a username to the trusted class (class `t`). `Troot` adds `root` to the class of trusted users. |
| V | Defines the major version number of the configuration file. |

## Other sendmail files

The `/etc/mail` directory contains other files that `sendmail` uses. These files are referenced in the `sendmail` configuration file, `/etc/mail/sendmail.cf` in Fedora and `/etc/sendmail.cf` in SUSE. Here's how you can search for the `/etc/mail` string in the `/etc/mail/sendmail.cf` file in Fedora:

```
grep "\/etc\/mail" /etc/mail/sendmail.cf
```

Here's what the `grep` command displays as a result of the search on a typical Fedora system:

```
Fw/etc/mail/local-host-names
FR-o /etc/mail/relay-domains
Kmailertable hash -o /etc/mail/mailertable.db
Kvirtuser hash -o /etc/mail/virtusertable.db
Kaccess hash -T<TMPF> -o /etc/mail/access.db
#O ErrorHeader=/etc/mail/error-header
O HelpFile=/etc/mail/helpfile
O UserDatabaseSpec=/etc/mail/userdb.db
#O ServiceSwitchFile=/etc/mail/service.switch
#O DefaultAuthInfo=/etc/mail/default-auth-info
Ft/etc/mail/trusted-users
```

You can ignore the lines that begin with a hash mark or number sign (#) because sendmail treats those lines as comments. The other lines are sendmail control lines that refer to other files in the /etc/mail directory.

Here's what some of these sendmail files are supposed to contain. (Note that not all these files have to be present in your /etc/mail directory, and even when present, some files may be empty.)

>> /etc/mail/access: Names or IP addresses or both of hosts allowed to send mail (useful in stopping *spam* — unwanted email).

>> /etc/mail/access.db: Access database generated from the /etc/mail/access file.

>> /etc/mail/helpfile: Help information for SMTP commands.

>> /etc/mail/local-host-names: Names by which this host is known.

>> /etc/mail/mailertable: Mailer table used to override how mail is routed. (The entry comcast.net smtp:smtp.comcast.net, for example, tells sendmail that mail addressed to comcast.net has to be sent to smtp.comcast.net.)

>> /etc/mail/relay-domains: Hosts that permit relaying.

>> /etc/mail/trusted-users: List of users allowed to send mail using other users' names without a warning.

>> /etc/mail/userdb.db: User database file containing information about each user's login name and real name.

>> /etc/mail/virtusertable: Database of users with virtual-domain addresses hosted on this system.

TECHNICAL
STUFF

The /etc/mail directory sometimes contains other files — /etc/mail/certs and files with the .pem extension — that are meant for supporting Privacy Enhanced Mail (PEM) in sendmail by using the STARTTLS extension to SMTP. The STARTTLS extension uses TLS (more commonly known as Secure Sockets Layer [SSL]) to authenticate the sender and encrypt mail. RFC 2487 describes STARTTLS and is available at http://ietf.org/rfc/rfc2487.txt.

TIP

If you edit the /etc/mail/mailertable file, you have to type the following command before the changes take effect:

```
makemap hash /etc/mail/mailertable < /etc/mail/mailertable
```

Here's an easier way to make sure that you rebuild everything necessary after making any changes. Type the following commands while logged in as root:

```
cd /etc/mail
make
```

The first command changes the current directory to /etc/mail, and the second command runs the make command, which reads a file named Makefile in /etc/mail to perform the steps necessary to rebuild everything.

## The .forward file

Users can redirect their own mail by placing a .forward file in their home directory. The .forward file is a plain-text file with a comma-separated list of mail addresses. Any mail sent to the user is instead forwarded to these addresses. If the .forward file contains a single address, all email for that user is redirected to that single email address. Suppose that a .forward file containing the following line is placed in the home directory of a user named emily:

```
ashley
```

This line causes sendmail to automatically send all email addressed to emily to the username ashley on the same system. User emily doesn't receive mail at all.

You can also forward mail to a username on another system by listing a complete email address. You can add a .forward file with the following line to send messages addressed to username wilbur to the mail address wilbur@somewhereelse.net:

```
wilbur@somewhereelse.net
```

To keep a copy of the message on the original system, in addition to forwarding the message to the preceding specified address, add the following line to the .forward file:

```
wilbur@somewhereelse.net, wilbur\
```

Simply append the username and end the line with a backslash (\). The backslash at the end of the line stops sendmail from repeatedly forwarding the message.

## The sendmail alias file

In addition to the sendmail.cf file, sendmail consults an alias file named /etc/aliases to convert a name to an address. The location of the alias file appears in the sendmail configuration file.

Each alias typically is a shorter name for an email address. The system administrator uses the sendmail alias file to forward mail, to create a mailing list (a single alias that identifies several users), or to refer to a user by several different names. Here are some typical aliases:

```
brown: glbrown
all: jessica, isaac, alex, caleb, glbrown
```

**REMEMBER**

After defining any new aliases in the /etc/aliases file, you must log in as root and make the new alias active by typing the following command:

```
sendmail -bi
```

# Working with Postfix

The Postfix email server was created by Wietse Venema while working at IBM Research as an alternative to the sendmail program, which many administrators find difficult to configure. Many Linux distributions support Postfix as their default email server, including Ubuntu and Rocky Linux.

To install Postfix on a Debian-based Linux distribution such as Ubuntu, use the apt tool:

```
rich@Ubuntu22:~$ sudo apt install postfix
[sudo] password for rich:
Reading package lists... Done
Building dependency tree... Done
Reading state information... Done
Suggested packages:
  procmail postfix-mysql postfix-pgsql postfix-ldap postfix-pcre postfix-lmdb
  postfix-sqlite sasl2-bin | dovecot-common resolvconf postfix-cdb
  postfix-mta-sts-resolver postfix-doc
The following NEW packages will be installed:
  postfix
0 upgraded, 1 newly installed, 0 to remove and 10 not upgraded.
Need to get 1,245 kB of archives.
```

During the installation, three separate dialog boxes appear, prompting you for information about your desired email environment. You have five choices of how to run Postfix:

- **No configuration:** Leaves the default Postfix configuration files
- **Internet site:** Sets Postfix to send and receive email messages directly on the Internet
- **Internet with smarthost:** Sets Postfix to forward all outbound messages to a specific host, but receive incoming mail directly
- **Satellite system:** Sets Postfix to route all mail to a remote smarthost server
- **Local only:** Processes only mail destined for local user accounts on the system

After you select the environment you want, the Postfix installation will automatically change the configuration files to accommodate the selection.

To install Postfix on a Red Hat–based Linux distribution such as Rocky Linux, use the dnf tool:

```
[rich@unknown08002755DFBD ~]$ sudo dnf install postfix
[sudo] password for rich:
Last metadata expiration check: 3:14:04 ago on Fri 29 Apr 2022 10:30:22 AM EDT.
Dependencies resolved.
================================================================================
 Package         Architecture    Version          Repository       Size
================================================================================
Installing:
 postfix         x86_64          2:3.5.8-2.el8    baseos           1.5 M

Transaction Summary
================================================================================
Install  1 Package

Total download size: 1.5 M
Installed size: 4.3 M
Is this ok [y/N]:
```

After Postfix is installed, you'll need to enable it to start up at boot time and start the service. Also, if you plan on your server being able to accept email from outside sources, you'll want to define a firewall rule in firewalld for it:

```
[rich@unknown08002755DFBD ~]$ sudo systemctl enable postfix
Created symlink /etc/systemd/system/multi-user.target.wants/postfix.service → /
   usr/lib/systemd/system/postfix.service.
[rich@unknown08002755DFBD ~]$ sudo systemctl start postfix
[rich@unknown08002755DFBD ~]$ sudo firewall-cmd --add-service=smtp --permanent
success
[rich@unknown08002755DFBD ~]$ sudo firewall-cmd --reload
success
[rich@unknown08002755DFBD ~]$
```

**TIP**

Postfix uses the `/etc/postfix/main.cf` configuration file to store the email server settings. This file is easier to work with than the `sendmail` configuration files, but it does have its own quirks. Check out the Postfix website at www. `postfix.org` for a full discussion and examples on how to configure Postfix.

With either `sendmail` or Postfix installed, you're ready to test things out using a client email package.

# A Mail-Delivery Test

To test out the `sendmail` or Postfix mail transfer agent, you can use the `mail` command to compose and send a mail message to any user account on your Linux system. To install that on a Debian-based Linux distribution, install the `mailutil` package:

```
rich@Ubuntu22:~$ sudo apt install mailutils
Reading package lists... Done
Building dependency tree... Done
Reading state information... Done
The following additional packages will be installed:
  gsasl-common guile-3.0-libs libgsasl7 libmailutils8 libntlm0
  mailutils-common
Suggested packages:
  mailutils-mh mailutils-doc
The following NEW packages will be installed:
  gsasl-common guile-3.0-libs libgsasl7 libmailutils8 libntlm0 mailutils
  mailutils-common
0 upgraded, 7 newly installed, 0 to remove and 10 not upgraded.
Need to get 8,773 kB of archives.
After this operation, 58.9 MB of additional disk space will be used.
Do you want to continue? [Y/n]
```

And for Red Hat–based Linux distributions, it's in the `mailx` package:

```
[rich@unknown08002755DFBD ~]$ sudo dnf install mailx
Last metadata expiration check: 3:15:01 ago on Fri 29 Apr 2022 10:30:22 AM EDT.
Dependencies resolved.
=====================================================================================
 Package         Architecture      Version            Repository        Size
=====================================================================================
Installing:
 mailx           x86_64            12.5-29.el8         baseos            256 k
```

```
Transaction Summary
================================================================================
Install  1 Package

Total download size: 256 k
Installed size: 474 k
Is this ok [y/N]:
```

After you've installed it, you can use the `mail` command to both send and read email messages.

## Using the mail command

As a test, compose a message and send it to yourself. Here's how to send a message with the `mail` command (input in boldface):

```
mail rich
Subject: Test message
This is from my Linux system.

.
```

The `mail` command is a simple mail user agent. In the preceding example, the addressee (`rich`) is specified in the command line. The `mail` program prompts for a subject line. Following the subject, enter the message, and end it with a line that contains only a period. You'll be prompted for a `Cc:`, but leave it blank. After ending the message, the mail user agent passes the message to the mail transport agent for delivery to the specified address. To verify the delivery of mail, type **mail** to run the `mail` command again:

```
rich@Ubuntu22:~$ mail
"/var/mail/rich": 1 message 1 new
>N  1 Rich                Fri Apr 29 18:36  15/452   Test message
?
Return-Path: <rich@Ubuntu22>
X-Original-To: rich
Delivered-To: rich@Ubuntu22.attlocal.net
Received: by Ubuntu22.attlocal.net (Postfix, from userid 1000)
    id 3D482670C9; Fri, 29 Apr 2022 18:36:55 -0400 (EDT)
To: rich@Ubuntu22.attlocal.net
Subject: Test message
User-Agent: mail (GNU Mailutils 3.14)
Date: Fri, 29 Apr 2022 18:36:55 -0400
Message-Id: <20220429173655.3D482670C9@Ubuntu22.attlocal.net>
From: Rich <rich@Ubuntu22>
```

```
This is from my Linux system.

?
```

The question mark prompts you for mail commands such as deleting the message, saving it, or even forwarding it to someone else. Type **man mailx** at the shell prompt to see a list of the commands you can use.

*Note:* If any of your mail server software isn't properly installed, you should be prompted during this test to install any needed components and resolve the problem.

The initial sendmail configuration file is adequate for sending and receiving email, at least within your Linux system. External mail delivery also works, provided that your Linux system has an Internet connection and a registered domain name.

**REMEMBER**

If you have an ISP account that provides your Linux system with a dynamic IP address, you have to use a mail client such as Evolution or Mozilla Mail, which contacts your ISP's mail server to deliver outbound email.

## The mail-delivery mechanism

On an Internet host, the sendmail mail transport agent delivers mail by using Simple Mail Transfer Protocol (SMTP). SMTP-based mail transport agents listen to TCP port 25 and use a small set of text commands to exchange information with other mail transport agents. SMTP commands are simple enough that you can use them manually from a terminal to send a mail message. The telnet command opens a Telnet session to port 25 (the port on which sendmail expects SMTP commands). The sendmail process on the Linux system immediately replies with an announcement.

You can type **HELP** to view a list of SMTP commands. To get help on a specific command, type **HELP***commandname*. Type **HELO localhost** to initiate a session with the host. The sendmail process replies with a greeting. To send the mail message, start with the MAIL FROM: command, which specifies the sender of the message. Next, use the RCPT TO: command to specify the recipient of the message. If you want to send the message to several recipients, provide each recipient's address with the RCPT TO: command.

To enter the mail message, use the DATA command. In response to the DATA command, sendmail displays an instruction that you have to end the message with a period on a line by itself. After you do so and end the message, the sendmail process displays a message indicating that the message is accepted for delivery. Then you can quit the sendmail session with the QUIT command.

# 6

# Security

# Contents at a Glance

IN THIS CHAPTER

» **Establishing basic security**

» **Understanding host-related security issues**

» **Understanding network-related security issues**

» **Interpreting computer security terminology**

» **Keeping up with security news and updates**

# Chapter **1**

# Introducing Linux Security

This chapter explains why you need to worry about security — and offers a high-level view of how to get a handle on security. I explain the idea of an overall security framework and discuss the two key aspects of security: host security and network security. I end the chapter introducing you to the terminology used in discussing computer security.

**TIP**

According to the Objectives listing, 21 percent of the CompTIA Linux+ exam falls under the Security domain. This number should be viewed as being very conservative because so much of administration involves security. You'll find topics related to it appearing in domains such as Administrative Tasks, Essential System Services, and Networking Fundamentals. For that reason, you'll find a lot of security-relevant information in the three chapters of Book 6 and in other chapters as well.

# Why Worry about Security?

In today's networked world, you have no choice but to worry about your Linux system's security. For a stand-alone system or a system used in an isolated local area network (LAN), you have to focus on protecting the system from the users and the users from one another. In other words, you don't want a user to modify or delete system files, whether intentionally or unintentionally, and you don't want a user destroying another user's files (or their own, if you can prevent it).

Because the odds are quite good that your Linux system is connected to the Internet, you have to secure the system from unwanted accesses over the Internet. These intruders — or *crackers*, as they're commonly known — typically impersonate a user, steal or destroy information, and even deny you access to your own system. The latter attack is known as a *denial of service* (DoS) or *distributed denial of service* (DDoS) attack.

By its very nature, an Internet connection makes your system accessible to any other system on the Internet. After all, the Internet connects a huge number of networks across the globe. In fact, the client/server architecture of Internet services, such as Hypertext Transfer Protocol (HTTP) and File Transfer Protocol (FTP), rely on the wide-open network access that the Internet provides. Unfortunately, the easy accessibility to Internet services running on your system also means that anyone on the Internet can easily access your system.

If you operate an Internet host that provides information to others, you certainly want everyone to access your system's Internet services, such as FTP and web servers. These servers often have vulnerabilities, however, that crackers may exploit to harm your system. You need to know about the potential security risks of Internet services and the precautions that you can take to minimize the risk that someone will exploit the weaknesses of your FTP or web server.

You also want to protect your company's internal network from outsiders, even though your goal is to provide information to the outside world through your web or FTP server. You can protect your internal network by setting up an Internet *firewall* — a controlled-access point to the internal network — and placing the web and FTP servers on a host outside the firewall.

# Establishing a Security Framework

The first step in securing your Linux system is setting up a *security policy* — a set of guidelines that states what you enable users (as well as visitors over the Internet) to do on your Linux system. The level of security you establish depends on how you use the Linux system and on how much is at risk if someone gains unauthorized access to your system.

If you're a system administrator for one or more Linux systems in an organization, you probably want to involve company management, as well as users, in setting up the security policy. Obviously, you can't create a draconian policy that blocks all access. (That policy would prevent anyone from effectively working on the system.) On the other hand, if users are creating or using data that's valuable to the organization, you must set up a policy that protects the data from disclosure to outsiders. In other words, the security policy should strike a balance between users' needs and your need to protect the system.

For a stand-alone Linux system or a home system that you occasionally connect to the Internet, the security policy can be just a list of the Internet services that you want to run on the system and the user accounts that you plan to set up on the system. For any larger organization, you probably have one or more Linux systems on a LAN connected to the Internet — preferably through a firewall. (To reiterate, a *firewall* is a device that controls the flow of Internet Protocol [IP] packets between the LAN and the Internet.) In such cases, thinking of computer security systematically (across the entire organization) is best. Figure 1-1 shows the key elements of an organization-wide framework for computer security.

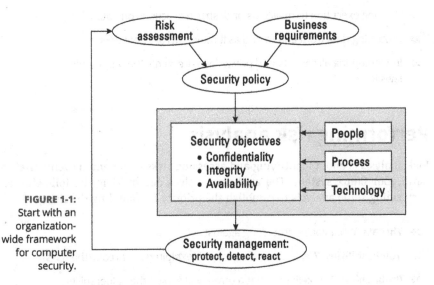

**FIGURE 1-1:**
Start with an organization-wide framework for computer security.

The security framework outlined in Figure 1-1 focuses on

>> Determining the business requirements for security

>> Performing risk assessments

>> Establishing a security policy

>> Implementing a cybersecurity solution that includes people, process, and technology to mitigate identified security risks

>> Continuously monitoring and managing security

The following sections discuss some of the key elements of the security framework.

## Determining business requirements for security

The business requirements for security identify the computer resources and information that you have to protect (including any requirements imposed by applicable laws, such as the requirement to protect the privacy of some types of data). Typical security requirements may include items such as the following:

>> Enabling access to information by authorized users

>> Implementing business rules that specify who has access to what information

>> Employing a strong user-authentication system

>> Denying execution to malicious or destructive actions on data

>> Protecting data from end to end as it moves across networks

>> Implementing all security and privacy requirements that applicable laws impose

## Performing risk analysis

Risk analysis is about identifying and assessing risks — potential events that can harm your Linux system. The analysis involves determining the following and performing some analysis to establish the priority for handling the risks:

>> **Threats:** What you're protecting against

>> **Vulnerabilities:** Weaknesses that may be exploited by threats (the risks)

>> **Probability:** The likelihood that a threat will exploit the vulnerability

>> **Impact:** The effect of exploiting a specific vulnerability

>> **Mitigation:** What to do to reduce vulnerabilities

## Typical threats

Some typical threats to your Linux system include the following:

» **DoS attack:** The computer and network are tied up so that legitimate users can't make use of the systems. For businesses, a DoS attack can mean a loss of revenue. Because bringing a system to its knees with a single computer attack is a bit of a challenge these days, the more common tactic is to point many computers at a single site and let them do the dirty work. Although the purpose and result are the same as ever, this ganging-up is referred to as a distributed (DDoS) attack because more than one computer is attacking the host.

» **Unauthorized access:** The computer and network are used by someone who isn't an authorized user. The unauthorized user can steal information or maliciously corrupt or destroy data. Some businesses may be hurt by the negative publicity resulting from the mere fact that an unauthorized user gained access to the system, even if the data shows no sign of explicit damage.

» **Disclosure of information to the public:** *Disclosure* in this case means the unauthorized release of information. The disclosure of a password file, for example, enables potential attackers to figure out username and password combinations for accessing a system. Exposure of other sensitive information, such as financial and medical data, may be a potential liability for a business.

## Typical vulnerabilities

The threats to your system and network come from exploitation of vulnerabilities in your organization's resources, both computer and people. The following are some common vulnerabilities:

» People's foibles (divulging passwords, losing security cards, and so on)

» Internal network connections (routers, switches)

» Interconnection points (gateways [routers and firewalls] between the Internet and the internal network)

» Third-party network providers (Internet service providers [ISPs], long-distance carriers) with looser security

» Operating-system security holes (potential holes in Internet servers, such as those associated with sendmail, named, and bind)

» Application security holes (known weaknesses in specific applications)

## The 1-2-3 of risk analysis (probability and effect)

To perform risk analysis, assign a numeric value to the probability and effect of each potential vulnerability. To develop a workable risk analysis, do the following for each vulnerability or risk:

1. **Assign subjective ratings of low, medium, and high to the probability.**

   As the ratings suggest, low probability means a lesser chance that the vulnerability will be exploited; high probability means a greater chance.

2. **Assign similar ratings to the effect.**

   What you consider to be the effect is up to you. If the exploitation of a vulnerability would affect your business greatly, assign it a high effect rating.

3. **Assign a numeric value to the three levels — low = 1, medium = 2, and high = 3 — for both probability and effect.**

4. **Multiply the probability by the effect.**

   You can think of this product as being the *risk level*.

5. **Decide to develop protections for vulnerabilities that exceed a specific threshold for the product of probability and effect.**

   You might choose to handle all vulnerabilities that have a probability × effect value greater than 6, for example.

If you want to characterize the probability and effect with finer gradations, use a scale of, say, 1 through 5 instead of 1 through 3, and follow the same steps.

# Establishing a security policy

Using risk analysis and any business requirements that you may have to address (regardless of risk level) as a foundation, you can craft a security policy for the organization. Such a security policy typically addresses high-level objectives such as ensuring the confidentiality, integrity, and availability of data and systems.

The security policy typically addresses the following areas:

>> **Authentication:** Examples include which method is used to ensure that a user is the real user, who gets access to the system, the minimum length and complexity of passwords, how often users change passwords, and how long a user can be idle before that user is logged out automatically.

>> **Authorization:** Examples include what different classes of users can do on the system and who can have the root password.

>> **Data protection:** Examples include what data must be protected, who has access to the data, and whether encryption is necessary for some data.

>> **Internet access:** Examples include restrictions on LAN users from accessing the Internet, what Internet services (such as web and social media) users can access, whether incoming emails and attachments are scanned for viruses, whether the network has a firewall, and whether virtual private networks (VPNs) are used to connect private networks across the Internet.

>> **Internet services:** Examples include what Internet services are allowed on each Linux system; the existence of any file servers, mail servers, or web servers; what services run on each type of server; and what services, if any, run on Linux systems used as desktop workstations.

>> **Security audits:** Examples include who tests whether the security is adequate, how often security is tested, and how problems found during security testing are handled.

>> **Incident handling:** Examples include the procedures for handling any computer security incidents, who must be informed, and what information must be gathered to help with the investigation of incidents.

>> **Responsibilities:** Examples include who is responsible for maintaining security, who monitors log files and audit trails for signs of unauthorized access, and who maintains the security policy.

## Implementing security solutions (mitigation)

After you analyze the risks (vulnerabilities) and develop a security policy, you must select the *mitigation approach:* how to protect against specific vulnerabilities. You develop an overall security solution based on security policy, business requirements, and available technology. This solution makes use of people, process, and technology, and includes the following:

>> Services (authentication, access control, encryption)

>> Mechanisms (username and password, firewalls)

>> Objects (hardware, software)

Because it's impossible to protect computer systems from all attacks, solutions identified through the risk management process must support three integral concepts of a holistic security program:

>> **Protection:** Provide countermeasures such as policies, procedures, and technical solutions to defend against attacks on the assets being protected.

>> **Detection:** Monitor for potential breakdowns in the protective measures that could result in security breaches.

>> **Reaction (response):** Respond to detected breaches to thwart attacks before damage occurs; often requires human involvement.

Because absolute protection from attacks is impossible to achieve, a security program that doesn't incorporate detection and reaction is incomplete.

## Managing security

In addition to implementing security solutions, you also need to implement security management measures to continually monitor, detect, and respond to any security incidents.

The combination of the risk analysis, security policy, security solutions, and security management provides the overall security framework. Such a framework helps establish a common level of understanding of security concerns and a common basis for the design and implementation of security solutions.

# Securing Linux

After you define a security policy, you can proceed to secure the system according to the policy. The exact steps depend on what you want to do with the system, whether the system is a server or workstation, and how many users must access the system.

To secure the Linux system, you have to handle two broad categories of security issues:

>> **Host-security issues:** These issues relate to securing the operating system and the files and directories on the system.

>> **Network-security issues:** These issues refer to the threat of attacks over the network connection.

**TIP**

If your host is connecting to a large network, Directory Services can become a significant issue. Directory Services security is outside the scope of this book, but you can find information about it by searching online.

## Understanding the host-security issues

Here are some high–level guidelines to address host security (some of which I cover in detail in Book 6, Chapter 2):

» When installing Linux, select only the package groups that you need for your system. Don't install unnecessary software. If your system is used as a workstation, for example, don't install most of the servers (web server, news server, and so on).

» Create initial user accounts, and make sure that all passwords are strong enough that password-cracking programs can't guess them. Linux includes tools that enforce strong passwords.

» Set file ownerships and permissions to protect important files and directories.

» If mandatory access-control capabilities are available, enable them. Support for this feature has been incorporated, through Security Enhanced Linux (SELinux) since kernel 2.6. The best way to think of SELinux is as a wrapper that can be placed around standard Linux to provide more security measures. AppArmor is favored over SELinux in some distributions but it serves the same purpose and offers similar features to SELinux.

» Use the GNU Privacy Guard (GnuPG) to encrypt or decrypt files with sensitive information and to authenticate files that you download from the Internet. GnuPG comes with Linux, and you can use the gpg command to perform tasks such as encrypting or decrypting a file and digitally signing a file. (See Book 6, Chapter 2 for an explanation of digital signatures.)

» Use file-integrity checking tools, such as Tripwire, to monitor any changes to crucial system files and directories. Visit www.tripwire.com for the commercial version.

» Periodically check various log files for signs of any break-ins or attempted break-ins. These log files are in the /var/log directory of your system.

» Install distribution security updates as soon as they're available and tested. These security updates fix known vulnerabilities in Linux. Be sure to test each update on non-production machines before rolling it out to your production servers.

**TIP**

You can spend a great deal of time *hardening* your server — locking down the services on it to make it as secure across the network as possible. But don't overlook the fact that someone can pick up the server and walk right out the door with it. When locking down a system, be sure that you also physically secure it with locked doors and cables where necessary.

## Understanding network-security issues

The issue of security comes up as soon as you connect your organization's internal network to the Internet. You need to think of security even if you connect a single computer to the Internet, but security concerns are more pressing when an entire internal network is opened to the world.

If you're an experienced system administrator, you already know that the cost of managing an Internet presence doesn't worry corporate management; management's main concern is security. To get management's backing for the website, you have to lay out a plan to keep the corporate network secure from intruders.

You may think that you can avoid jeopardizing the internal network by connecting only external servers such as web and FTP servers to the Internet, but employing this simplistic approach isn't wise. This approach is like deciding not to drive because you might have an accident. Not having a network connection between your web server and your internal network also has the following drawbacks:

>> You can't use network file transfers, such as SFTP or HTTPS, to copy documents and data from your internal network to the web server.

>> Users on the internal network can't access the corporate web server.

>> Users on the internal network don't have access to web servers on the Internet. Such a restriction makes a valuable resource — the web — inaccessible to the users in your organization.

A practical solution to this problem is to set up an Internet firewall and to put the web server on a highly secured host outside the firewall.

In addition to using a firewall, here are some steps you can take to address network security (explained further in Book 6, Chapter 2):

>> Enable only those Internet services you need on a system. In particular, don't enable services that aren't properly configured.

>> Use Secure Shell (ssh) for remote logins. Don't use the r commands, such as rlogin and rsh.

» Don't use unsecure legacy Internet services, such as FTP or Telnet, that send data in plain text across the Internet. Instead, use encrypted protocols such as SFTP, SSH, and HTTPS.

» Promptly fix any known vulnerabilities of Internet services that you choose to run. Typically, you can download and install the latest security updates from your Linux distribution's online update sites.

# Delving Into Computer Security Terminology and Tools

Computer books, magazine articles, and experts on computer security use some terms that you need to know to understand discussions of computer security (and to communicate effectively with security vendors).

TIP

Table 1-1 describes some commonly used computer security terms. If you're taking the ComptTIA Linux+ exam, port scanning and setuid are important.

**TABLE 1-1**     Common Computer Security Terminology

| Term | Description |
| --- | --- |
| Application gateway | A proxy service that acts as a gateway for application-level protocols, such as FTP, HTTP, NNTP, and SSH. |
| Authentication | The process of confirming that a user is indeed who they claim to be. The typical authentication method is a challenge-response method wherein the user enters a username and secret password to confirm their identity. |
| Backdoor | A security weakness that a cracker places on a host to bypass security features. |
| Bastion host | A highly secured computer that serves as an organization's main point of presence on the Internet. A bastion host typically resides on the perimeter network, but a *dual-homed host* (with one network interface connected to the Internet and the other to the internal network) is also a bastion host. |
| Buffer overflow | A security flaw in a program that enables a cracker to send an excessive amount of data to that program and to overwrite parts of the running program with code in the data being sent. The result is that the cracker can execute arbitrary code on the system and possibly gain access to the system as a privileged user. The exec-shield feature of the Linux kernel protects against buffer overflows. |

*(continued)*

**TABLE 1-1** *(continued)*

| Term | Description |
|---|---|
| Certificate | An electronic document that identifies an entity (such as a person, an organization, or a computer) and associates a public key with that identity. A certificate contains the certificate holder's name, a serial number, an expiration date, a copy of the certificate holder's public key, and the digital signature of the certificate authority so that a recipient can verify that the certificate is real. |
| Certificate authority (CA) | An organization that validates identities and issues certificates. |
| Confidentiality | For data, a state of being accessible to no one but authorized users (usually achieved by encryption). |
| Cracker | A person who breaks into (or attempts to break into) a host, often with malicious intent. |
| DDoS | A variant of the denial-of-service (DoS) attack that uses a coordinated attack from a distributed system of computers rather than a single source. It often uses worms to spread to — and take control of — multiple computers that can then attack the target. |
| Decryption | The process of transforming encrypted information into its original, intelligible form. |
| Digital signature | A one-way MD5 (Message Digest algorithm 5) or SHA-1 (Secure Hash Algorithm-1) hash of a message encrypted with the private key of the message originator, used to verify the integrity of a message and ensure nonrepudiation. |
| DMZ | Another name for the perimeter network. (DMZ originally stood for *demilitarized zone,* the buffer zone separating the warring North and South in Korea and Vietnam.) |
| DoS | An attack that uses so many of the resources on your computer and network that legitimate users can't access and use the system. From a single source, the attack overwhelms the target computer with messages and blocks legitimate traffic. It can prevent one system from being able to exchange data with other systems or prevent the system from using the Internet. |
| Dual-homed host | A computer with two network interfaces. (Think of each network as a home.) |
| Encryption | The process of transforming information so that it's unintelligible to anyone but the intended recipient. The transformation is performed by a mathematical operation between a key and the information. |
| Exploit tools | Publicly available and sophisticated tools that intruders of various skill levels can use to determine vulnerabilities and gain entry into targeted systems. |
| Firewall | A controlled-access gateway between an organization's internal network and the Internet. A dual-homed host can be configured as a firewall. |
| Hash | The result when a mathematical function converts a message to a fixed-size numeric value known as a *message digest* (or *hash*). The MD5 algorithm, for example, produces a 128-bit message digest; SHA-1 generates a 160-bit message digest. The hash of a message is encrypted with the private key of the sender to produce the digital signature. |

| Term | Description |
| --- | --- |
| Host | A computer on a network that's configured to offer services to other computers on the network. |
| Integrity | For received data, a state of being the same as originally sent (that is, unaltered in transit). |
| IP spoofing | An attack in which a cracker figures out the IP address of a trusted host and then sends packets that appear to come from the trusted host. The attacker can send packets but can't see responses. But the attacker can predict the sequence of packets and essentially send commands that set up a backdoor for future break-ins. |
| IPSec (IP Security Protocol) | A security protocol for the network layer of the OSI networking model, designed to provide cryptographic security services for IP packets. IPSec provides encryption-based authentication, integrity, access control, and confidentiality. (For information on IPSec for Linux, visit www.ipsec-howto.org.) |
| Logic bomb | A form of sabotage in which a programmer inserts code that causes the program to perform a destructive action when some triggering event occurs, such as terminating the programmer's employment. |
| Nonrepudiation | A security feature that prevents the sender of data from being able to deny having sent the data. |
| Packet | A collection of bytes, assembled according to a specific protocol, that serves as the basic unit of communication on a network. On TCP/IP networks, for example, the packet may be referred to as an *IP packet* or a *TCP/IP packet.* |
| Packet filtering | Selective blocking of packets according to type of packet (as specified by the source and destination IP address or port). |
| Perimeter network | A network between the Internet and the protected internal network. The perimeter network (also known as DMZ) is where the bastion host resides. |
| Port scanning | A method of discovering which ports are open (in other words, which Internet services are enabled) on a system, performed by sending connection requests to the ports, one by one. This procedure is usually a precursor to further attacks; two port-scanning tools to know are nmap and netstat. |
| Proxy server | A server on the bastion host that enables internal clients to access external servers (and enables external clients to access servers inside the protected network). Proxy servers are available for various Internet services, such as FTP and HTTP. |
| Public key cryptography | An encryption method that uses a pair of keys — a private key and a public key — to encrypt and decrypt the information. Anything encrypted with the public key can be decrypted only with the corresponding private key, and vice versa. |
| Public Key Infrastructure (PKI) | A set of standards and services that enables the use of public key cryptography and certificates in a networked environment. PKI facilitates tasks such as issuing, renewing, and revoking certificates, and generating and distributing public and private key pairs. |
| Screening router | An Internet router that filters packets. |

*(continued)*

**TABLE 1-1** *(continued)*

| Term | Description |
|---|---|
| setuid program | The set user ID program (called either setuid or suid) runs with the permissions of the program owner, regardless of who actually runs it. If root owns a setuid/suid program, that program has root privileges regardless of who started the program. Crackers often exploit vulnerabilities in setuid programs to gain privileged access to a system. Similarly, set group ID (sgid) programs are used to run with the permissions of the group, regardless of who runs the program, and have their own similar vulnerabilities. |
| Sniffer | Synonymous with *packet sniffer* — a program that intercepts routed data and examines each packet in search of specified information such as passwords transmitted in clear text. |
| Spyware | Any software that covertly gathers user information through the user's Internet connection and usually transmits that information in the background to someone else. Spyware can also gather information about email addresses and even passwords and credit card numbers. Spyware is similar to a Trojan horse in that users are tricked into installing spyware when they install something else. |
| Symmetric key encryption | An encryption method wherein the same key is used to encrypt and decrypt the information. |
| Threat | An event or activity, deliberate or unintentional, with the potential for causing harm to a system or network. |
| Trojan horse | A program that masquerades as a benign program but is really a backdoor used for attacking a system. Attackers often install a collection of Trojan horse programs that enable the attacker to freely access the system with root privileges yet hide that fact from the system administrator. Such collections of Trojan horse programs are called *rootkits*. |
| Virus | A self-replicating program that spreads from one computer to another by attaching itself to other programs. |
| Vulnerability | A flaw or weakness that may cause harm to a system or network. |
| War-dialing | Using simple programs that dial consecutive phone numbers looking for modems. |
| War-driving | A method of gaining entry into wireless computer networks that uses a computer, antennas, and a wireless network card and that involves patrolling locations to gain unauthorized access. |
| Worm | A self-replicating program that copies itself from one computer to another over a network. |

Table 1-2 lists some commonly used computer security tools. I discuss some of these tools in other chapters, where they are related to specific topics; others are relevant only to security.

**TABLE 1-2**  **Common Computer Security Tools**

| Tool | Description |
|---|---|
| chage | With this command, you can modify the time between required password changes (both minimum and maximum number of days), the number of days of warning to be given that a change must be made, and expiration date. |
| find | One of the most powerful all-around tools, this command allows you to find almost anything on machine if you can come up with the right syntax. Among the plethora of choices, you can find files created by a user, by a group, or on a certain date, with certain permissions. |
| lsof | An acronym for *list open files*, this utility does just that. Depending on the parameters used, you can choose to see files opened by a specific process or by a specific user. |
| netstat | To see the status of the network, including network connections, routing tables and statistics per interface, this tool does it all. A similar command, ss, is intended to replace much of the functionality here. |
| nmap | This tool is used to scan the network and create a map of what's available on it. This capability makes it an ideal tool for port scanning and security auditing. |
| passwd | A utility (not the file by the same name that holds user account information), with which users can change their passwords at the command line whenever necessary. Many users don't know that this utility exists, so they change their passwords when required through one of the graphical interface tools. |
| su | To temporarily become another user, su can be used within the current user's session. Another shell is created; upon exiting this second shell, the user goes back to the original session. This utility can be used to become the root user or any other user (provided the corresponding password is given). |
| sudo | Instead of creating a new session (as su requires) to perform a job with elevated privileges, sudo enables the user to just run that task with elevated privileges. |
| ulimit | Resource limits on shells can be set or viewed using this command to keep one user from excessively hogging system resources. |
| usermod | This utility can be thought of as an enhanced version of chage. It can it used to set/change password expiration parameters and to specify a default shell, lock or unlock an account, and so on. |

# Keeping Up with Security News and Updates

To keep up with the latest security alerts, you may want to visit one or both of the following sites on a daily basis:

>> CERT Software Engineering Institute of Carnegie Mellon University at `www.sei.cmu.edu/`

>> U.S. Computer Emergency Readiness Team (US-CERT) at `www.us-cert.gov`

If you prefer to receive regular security updates through email, you can also sign up for (subscribe to) various mailing lists:

>> **US-CERT National Cyber Alert System:** Follow the directions at `www.us-cert.gov` to subscribe to this mailing list. The Cyber Alert System features four categories of security information through its mailing lists:

- *Current Activity:* Alerts that provide technical information about vulnerabilities in various common software products.

- *Alerts:* Alerts sent when vulnerabilities affect the general public. Each alert outlines the steps and actions that nontechnical home and corporate computer users can take to protect themselves from attacks.

- *Bulletins:* Weekly summaries of security issues and new vulnerabilities along with patches, workarounds, and other actions that users can take to help reduce risks.

- *Tips:* Advice on common security issues for nontechnical computer users.

>> **Red Hat Security Center:** Although this site (`https://access.redhat.com/security/`) focuses on Red Hat, many of the vulnerabilities listed here apply to Linux as a whole.

Chapter **2**

# Securing Linux

To secure your Linux system, you have to pay attention to both host security and network security. The distinction between the two types of security is somewhat arbitrary, because securing the network involves securing the applications on the host that relate to which Internet services your system offers.

This chapter first examines host security and then explains how you can secure network services (mostly by not offering unnecessary services), how you can use a firewall to stop unwanted network packets from reaching your network, and how to use Secure Shell (SSH) for secure remote logins.

*Host* is the techie term for your Linux system, especially when you use it to provide services on a network. But the term makes sense even when you think of the computer by itself as the host for everything that runs on it: the operating system and all applications. A key aspect of computer security is securing the host.

# Securing Passwords

Historically, Unix passwords are stored in the /etc/passwd file, which any user can read. A typical old-style /etc/passwd file entry for the root user looks like this:

```
root:t6Z7NWDK1K8sU:0:0:root:/root:/bin/bash
```

The fields are separated by colons (:), and the second field contains the password in encrypted form. To check whether a password is valid, the login program encrypts the plain-text password that the user enters and compares the password with the contents of the /etc/passwd file. If the passwords match, the user is allowed to log in.

Password-cracking programs work just like the login program except that these programs choose one word at a time from a dictionary, encrypt the word, and compare the encrypted word with the encrypted passwords in the /etc/passwd file for a match. To crack the passwords, the intruder needs access to the /etc/passwd file or to a copy of it. Often, crackers use weaknesses of various Internet servers (such as mail and FTP) to get a copy of the /etc/passwd file.

**REMEMBER**

Copies of files also exist on backup media, so be sure to store media securely, away from unauthorized eyes.

Over the years, passwords have become more secure in Linux due to several improvements, including shadow passwords and pluggable authentication modules (PAMs, described in the next two sections). You can install shadow passwords or a PAM easily while you install Linux. During Linux installation, you typically get a chance to configure the authentication. If you enable MD5 security and enable shadow passwords, you automatically enable more secure passwords within Linux and make it much more difficult for crackers to ascertain the stored values.

## Shadow passwords

Obviously, leaving passwords lying around where anyone can get at them — even if the passwords are encrypted — is bad security. Instead of storing passwords in the /etc/passwd file (which any user capable of accessing the system can read), Linux now stores them in a shadow password file, /etc/shadow. Only the super-user (root) can read this file. Here's the entry for root in the new-style /etc/passwd file:

```
root:x:0:0:root:/root:/bin/bash
```

In this case, the second field contains x instead of an encrypted password. The x is the *shadow password*. The actual encrypted password is now stored in the /etc/shadow file, where the entry for root is like this:

```
root:$1$AAAni/yN$uESHbzUpy9Cgfoo1Bf0tS0:11077:0:99999:7:-1:-1:134540356
```

The format of the /etc/shadow entries with colon-separated fields resembles the entries in the /etc/passwd file, but the meanings of most of the fields differ. The first field is still the username and the second one is the encrypted password.

The remaining fields in each /etc/shadow entry control when the password expires. You don't have to interpret or change these entries in the /etc/shadow file. Instead, use the chage command to change the password expiration information. For starters, you can check a user's password expiration information by using the chage command with the -1 option, as follows (while logged in as root):

```
chage -l root
```

This command displays expiration information, including how long the password lasts and how often you can change the password.

If you want to ensure that the user is forced to change a password at regular intervals, you can use the -M option to set the maximum number of days that a password stays valid. To make sure that user rich is prompted to change the password in 90 days, for example, log in as root and type the following command:

```
chage -M 90 rich
```

You can use the command for each user account to ensure that all passwords expire when appropriate and that all users choose new passwords.

# Pluggable authentication modules (PAMs)

In addition to improving the password file's security by using shadow passwords, Linux improves the encryption of the passwords stored in the /etc/shadow file by using the MD5 message-digest algorithm described in RFC 1321 (www.ietf.org/rfc/rfc1321.txt). MD5 reduces a message of any length to a 128-bit message digest (or *fingerprint*) of a document so that you can digitally sign it by encrypting it with your private key. MD5 works quite well for password encryption, too.

Another advantage of MD5 over older-style password encryption is that whereas older passwords were limited to a maximum of eight characters, new passwords encrypted with MD5 can be much longer. Longer passwords are harder to guess, even if the /etc/shadow file falls into the wrong hands.

You can tell that MD5 encryption is in effect in the /etc/shadow file. The encrypted passwords are longer and they all sport the $1$ prefix, as in the second field of the following sample entry:

```
root:$1$AAAni/yN$uESHbzUpy9Cgfoo1Bf0tS0:11077:0:99999:7:-1:-1:134540356
```

An add-on program module called a pluggable authentication module (PAM) performs the MD5 encryption. Linux PAMs provide a flexible method for authenticating users. By setting the PAM's configuration files, you can change your authentication method on the fly without modifying vital programs that verify a user's identity (such as login and passwd).

Linux uses PAM capabilities extensively. The PAMs reside in many modules; their configuration files are in the /etc/pam.d directory of your system. Check out the contents of this directory on your system by typing the following command:

```
ls /etc/pam.d
```

Each configuration file in this directory specifies how users are authenticated for a specific utility.

# Protecting Files and Directories

One important aspect of securing the host is protecting important system files — and the directories that contain these files. You can protect the files through file ownership and the permission settings that control who can read, write, or (in the case of executable programs) execute the file.

The default Linux file security is controlled through the following settings for each file or directory:

>> User ownership

>> Group ownership

>> Read, write, execute permissions for the owner

>> Read, write, execute permissions for the group

>> Read, write, execute permissions for others (everyone else)

# Viewing ownerships and permissions

You can see settings related to ownership and permissions for a file when you look at a detailed listing with the `ls -l` command. For example, in Ubuntu, type the following command to see the detailed listing of the `/etc/services` file:

```
ls -l /etc/services
```

The resulting listing looks something like this:

```
-rw-r--r-- 1 root root 12813 Mar 27  2021 /etc/services
```

The first set of characters describes the file permissions for user, group, and others. The third and fourth fields show the user and group that own this file. In this case, user and group names are the same: `root`.

# Changing file ownerships

You can set the user and group ownerships with the `chown` command. If the file `/dev/hda` should be owned by the user `root` and the group `disk`, you type the following command as `root` to set up this ownership:

```
chown root.disk /dev/hda
```

To change the group ownership alone, use the `chgrp` command. Here's how you can change the group ownership of a file from whatever it was earlier to the group named `accounting`:

```
chgrp accounting ledger.out
```

# Changing file permissions

Use the `chmod` command to set the file permissions. To use `chmod` effectively, you have to specify the permission settings. One way is to concatenate one or more letters from each column of Table 2-1 in the order shown: Who/Action/Permission.

To give everyone read and write access to all files in a directory, type **chmod a+rw ***. To permit everyone to execute a specific file, type **chmod a+x** *filename*.

**TABLE 2-1** ## File Permission Codes

| Who | Action | Permission |
|---|---|---|
| u (user) | + (add) | r (read) |
| g (group) | – (remove) | w (write) |
| o (others) | = (assign) | x (execute) |
| a (all) | s (set user ID) | |

Another way to specify a permission setting is to use a three-digit sequence of numbers. In a detailed listing, the read, write, and execute permission settings for the user, group, and others appear as the sequence

```
rwxrwxrwx
```

with dashes in place of letters for disallowed operations. Think of rwxrwxrwx as being three occurrences of the string rwx. Now assign the values r=4, w=2, and x=1. To get the value of the sequence rwx, simply add the values of r, w, and x. Thus, rwx = 7. With this formula, you can assign a three-digit value to any permission setting. If the user can read and write the file but everyone else can only read the file, for example, the permission setting is rw-r--r--, and the value is 644. Thus, if you want all files in a directory to be readable by everyone but writable only by the user, use the following command:

```
chmod 644 *
```

## Setting default permission

What permission setting does a file get when you (or a program) create a new file? The answer is what is known as the *user file-creation mask*, which you can see and set by using the umask command.

Type **umask**, and the command prints a number showing the current file-creation mask. For the root user, the mask is set to 022, whereas the mask for other users is 002. To see the effect of this file-creation mask and to interpret the meaning of the mask, follow these steps:

1. **Log in as** root, **and type the following command:**

   touch junkfile

   This command creates a file named junkfile with nothing in it.

2. **Type** ls -l junkfile **to see that file's permissions.**

You see a line similar to the following:

```
-rw-r--r-- 1 root root 0 Aug 24 10:56 junkfile
```

Interpret the numerical value of the permission setting by converting each three-letter permission in the first field (excluding the first letter) to a number between 0 and 7. For each letter that's present, the first letter gets a value of 4, the second letter is 2, and the third is 1. rw- translates to 4+2+0 (because the third letter is missing), or 6. Similarly, r-- is 4+0+0 = 4. Thus, the permission string -rw-r--r-- becomes 644.

3. **Subtract the numerical permission setting from 666.**

What you get is the umask setting. In this case, 666 – 644 results in a umask of 022. Thus, a umask of 022 results in a default permission setting of 666 – 022 = 644. When you rewrite 644 in terms of a permission string, it becomes rw-r--r--.

To set a new umask, type **umask** followed by the numerical value of the mask. Here's how you go about it:

1. **Figure out what permission settings you want for new files.**

If you want new files that can be read and written only by the owner and no one else, the permission setting looks like this:

```
rw-------
```

2. **Convert the permissions to a numerical value by using the conversion method that assigns 4 to the first field, 2 to the second, and 1 to the third.**

Thus, for files that are readable and writable only by their owner, the permission setting is 600.

3. **Subtract the desired permission setting from 666 to get the value of the mask.**

For a permission setting of 600, the mask becomes 666 – 600 = 066.

4. **Use the** umask **command to set the file-creation mask by typing** umask 066.

REMEMBER

A default umask of 022 is good for system security because it translates to files that have read and write permission for the owner and read permissions for everyone else. The bottom line is that you don't want a default umask that results in files that are writable by the whole world.

# Checking for set user ID permission

Another permission setting can be a security hazard. This permission setting, called the *set user ID* (or setuid and/or suid for short), applies to executable files. When the suid permission is enabled, the file executes under the user ID of the file's owner. In other words, if an executable program is owned by root and the suid permission is set, the program runs as though root is executing it no matter who executed the program. The suid permission means that the program can do a lot more (such as read all files, create new files, and delete files) than a normal user program can do. Another risk is that if a suid program file has a security hole, crackers can do a lot more damage through such programs than through other vulnerabilities.

You can find all suid programs with a simple find command:

```
find / -type f -perm /4000
```

You see a list of files such as the following:

```
/bin/su
/bin/ping
/bin/eject
/bin/mount
/bin/ping6
/bin/umount
/opt/kde4/bin/fileshareset
/opt/kde4/bin/artswrapper
/opt/kde4/bin/kcheckpass
... lines deleted ...
```

Many of the programs have the suid permission because they need it, but you should check the complete list to make sure that it contains no strange suid programs (such as suid programs in a user's home directory).

If you type **ls -l /bin/su**, you see the following permission settings:

```
-rwsr-xr-x 1 root root 25756 Aug 19 17:06 /bin/su
```

The s in the owner's permission setting (–rws) tells you that the suid permission is set for the /bin/su file, which is the executable file for the su command that you can use to become root or another user.

# Encrypting and Signing Files with GnuPG

Linux comes with the GNU Privacy Guard (GnuPG or GPG) encryption and authentication utility. With GnuPG, you can create your public and private key pair, encrypt files with your key, and digitally sign a message to authenticate that it's from you. If you send a digitally signed message to someone who has your public key, the recipient can verify that you signed the message.

## Understanding public key encryption

The basic idea behind public key encryption is to use a pair of keys — one private and the other public — that are related but can't be used to guess one from the other. Anything encrypted with the private key can be decrypted only with the corresponding public key, and vice versa. The public key is for distribution to other people; you keep the private key in a safe place.

You can use public key encryption to communicate securely with others; Figure 2-1 illustrates the basic idea. Suppose that Alice wants to send secure messages to Bob. Each person generates public key and private key pairs, after which they exchange their public keys. When Alice wants to send a message to Bob, she encrypts the message by using Bob's public key and sends the encrypted message to him. Now the message is secure from eavesdropping, because only Bob's private key can decrypt the message and only Bob has that key. When Bob receives the message, he uses his private key to decrypt the message and read it.

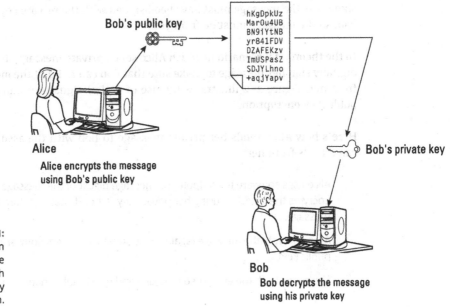

**Bob's public key**

```
hKgDpkUz
MarOu4UB
BN91YtNB
yr841FDV
DZAFEKzv
ImUSPasZ
SDJYLhno
+aqjYapv
```

**Alice**
Alice encrypts the message
using Bob's public key

**Bob's private key**

**Bob**
Bob decrypts the message
using his private key

**FIGURE 2-1:**
Bob and Alice can
communicate
securely with
public key
encryption.

At this point, you might say, "Wait a minute! How does Bob know that the message really came from Alice? What if someone else uses Bob's public key and sends a message as though it came from Alice?" This situation is where digital signatures come in.

## Understanding digital signatures

The purpose of digital (electronic) signatures is the same as that of pen-and-ink signatures but how you sign digitally is different. Unlike a pen-and-ink signature, your digital signature depends on the message you're signing. The first step in creating a digital signature is applying a mathematical function to the message and reducing it to a fixed-size message digest (also called a *hash* or a *fingerprint*). No matter how big your message is, the message digest is usually 128 or 160 bits, depending on the hashing function.

The next step is applying public key encryption. Simply encrypt the message digest with your private key and you get the digital signature for the message. Typically, the digital signature is added to the end of the message, and voilà — you get an electronically signed message.

What good does the digital signature do? Well, anyone who wants to verify that the message is indeed signed by you takes your public key and decrypts the digital signature. What that person gets is the message digest (the encrypted hash) of the message. Then he or she applies the same hash function to the message and compares the computed hash with the decrypted value. If the two match, then no one has tampered with the message. Because your public key was used to verify the signature, the message must have been signed with the private key known only to you, so the message must be from you!

In the theoretical scenario in which Alice sends private messages to Bob, Alice can digitally sign her message to make sure that Bob can tell that the message is really from her. Figure 2-2 illustrates the use of digital signatures along with normal public key encryption.

Here's how Alice sends her private message to Bob with the assurance that Bob can tell it's from her:

1. Alice uses software to compute the message digest of the message and then encrypts the digest by using her private key — her digital signature for the message.

2. Alice encrypts the message (again, using some convenient software *and* Bob's public key).

3. She sends both the encrypted message and the digital signature to Bob.

4. Bob decrypts the message, using his private key.

5. Bob decrypts the digital signature, using Alice's public key, which gives him the message digest.

6. Bob computes the message digest of the message and compares it with what he got by decrypting the digital signature.

7. If the two message digests match, Bob can be sure that the message really came from Alice.

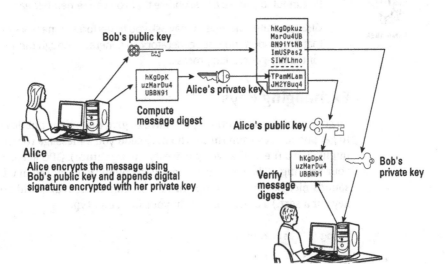

## Using GPG

GPG includes the tools you need to use public key encryption and digital signatures. You can figure out how to use GPG gradually as you begin using encryption. The following sections show some of the typical tasks you can perform with GPG.

### Generating the key pair

The steps for generating the key pairs are as follows:

1. **Type** gpg --gen-key.

   GPG prompts you for your name, your email address, and a comment to make it easier to associate the key pair with your name.

2. **Type each piece of requested information and press Enter.**

3. **When GPG gives you a chance to change the information or confirm it, confirm by typing o and pressing Enter.**

   GPG prompts you for a passphrase that protects your private key.

4. **Type a long phrase that includes lowercase and uppercase letters, numbers, and punctuation marks — the longer the better — and then press Enter.**

   Be careful to choose a passphrase that you can remember easily.

**REMEMBER**

GPG generates the keys. It may ask you to perform some work on the PC so that the random-number generator can generate enough random numbers for the key-generation process.

## Exchanging keys

To communicate with others, you have to give them your public key. You also have to get public keys from those who may send you a message (or from someone who might sign a file so that you can verify the signature). GPG keeps the public keys in your key ring. (The key ring is simply the public keys stored in a file, but the name sounds nice because everyone has a key ring in the real world and these keys are keys of a sort.) To list the keys in your key ring, type

```
gpg --list-keys
```

To send your public key to someone or to place it on a website, you have to export the key to a file. The best way is to put the key in what GPG documentation calls ASCII-armored format, with a command like this:

```
gpg --armor --export rich@test.localhost > richkey.asc
```

This command saves the public key in ASCII-armored format (which looks like garbled text) in the file named richkey.asc. You replace the email address with your email address (the one you used when you created the key), and replace the output filename with something different.

After you export the public key to a file, you can mail that file to others or place it on a website for use by others.

When you import a key from someone, you typically get it in ASCII-armored format as well. If you have a us-cert@us-cert.gov GPG public key in a file named uscertkey.asc (obtained from the link at www.us-cert.gov/pgp/email.html), you import it into the key ring with the following command:

```
gpg --import uscertkey.asc
```

Use the gpg --list-keys command to verify that the key is in your key ring. Here's what you might see when typing **gpg --list-keys** on the system:

```
gpg: checking the trustdb
gpg: marginals needed: 3  completes needed: 1  trust model: pgp
gpg: depth: 0 valid:   1 signed:   0 trust: 0-, 0q, 0n, 0m, 0f, 1u
gpg: next trustdb check due at 2024-03-17
/home/rich/.gnupg/pubring.kbx
--------------------------------
pub   rsa2048 2022-03-18 [SC] [expires: 2024-03-17]
      B264BC4A3C47AFCFA540D5CC8C137F2052C0B54D
uid            [ultimate] Rich Blum <rich@test.localhost>
sub   rsa2048 2022-03-18 [E] [expires: 2024-03-17]
```

The next step is checking the fingerprint of the new key. Type the following command to get the fingerprint of the key you downloaded from US CERT:

```
gpg --fingerprint us-cert@us-cert.gov
```

GPG prints the fingerprint, as follows:

```
pub 2048R/F0E187D0 2018-09-08 [expires: 2019-10-01]
Key fingerprint = 049F E3BA 240B 4CF1 3A76 06DC 1868 49EC F0E1 87D0
uid US-CERT Operations Key &lt;us-cert@us-cert.gov&gt;
```

At this point, you need to verify the key fingerprint with someone at the US-CERT organization.

If you think that the key fingerprint is good, you can sign the key and validate it. Here's the command you use to sign the key:

```
gpg --sign-key us-cert@us-cert.gov
```

GPG asks for confirmation and then prompts you for your passphrase. After that, GPG signs the key.

**WARNING**

Because key verification and signing are potential weak links in GPG, be careful about which keys you sign. By signing a key, you say that you trust the key to be from that person or organization.

## Signing a file

You may find signing files to be useful if you send a file to someone and want to assure the recipient that no one tampered with the file and that you did in fact send the file. GPG makes signing a file easy. You can compress and sign a file named message with the following command:

```
gpg -o message.sig -s message
```

To verify the signature, type

```
gpg --verify message.sig
```

To get back the original document, type

```
gpg -o message --decrypt message.sig
```

Sometimes, you don't care about keeping a message secret but you want to sign it to indicate that the message is from you. In such a case, you can generate and append a clear-text signature with the following command:

```
gpg -o message.asc --clearsign message
```

This command appends a clear-text signature to the text message. Here's a typical clear-text signature block:

```
-----BEGIN PGP SIGNATURE-----
Version: GnuPG v1.4.2 (GNU/Linux)
iD8DBQFDEhAtaHW1HHs4pygRAhiqAJ9Qj0pPMgKVBuokDyUZaEYVsp6RIQCfaoBm
9zCwrSAG9mo2DXJvbKS3ri8=
=2uc/
-----END PGP SIGNATURE-----
```

When a message has a clear-text signature appended, you can use GPG to verify the signature with the following command:

```
gpg --verify message.asc
```

If you did indeed sign the message, the last line of the output says that the signature is good.

## Encrypting and decrypting documents

To encrypt a message meant for a recipient, you can use the --encrypt (or -e) GPG command. Here's how you might encrypt a message for US-CERT by using its GPG key:

```
gpg -o message.gpg -e -r us-cert@us-cert.gov message
```

The message is encrypted with the US-CERT public key (without a signature, but you can add the signature with the –s command).

When US-CERT receives the `message.gpg` file, the recipient must decrypt it by using US-CERT's private key. Here's the command that someone at US-CERT can use:

```
gpg –o message --decrypt message.gpg
```

Then GPG prompts for the passphrase to unlock the US-CERT private key, decrypts the message, and saves the output in the file named `message`.

If you want to encrypt a file that no one else has to decrypt, you can use GPG to perform symmetric encryption. In this case, you provide a passphrase to encrypt the file with the following GPG command:

```
gpg –o secret.gpg –c somefile
```

GPG prompts you for the passphrase and asks you to repeat the passphrase (to make sure that you didn't mistype anything). Then GPG encrypts the file, using a key generated from the passphrase.

To decrypt a file encrypted with a symmetric key, type

```
gpg –o myfile --decrypt secret.gpg
```

GPG prompts you for the passphrase. If you enter the correct passphrase, GPG decrypts the file and saves the output (in this example) in the file named `myfile`.

# Monitoring System Security

Even if you secure your system, you have to monitor the log files periodically for signs of intrusion. You may want to use Tripwire (a good tool for detecting any changes made in the system files) so that you can monitor the integrity of critical system files and directories. Your Linux system probably doesn't come with the Tripwire File Integrity Manager package; you have to buy it from www.tripwire. com. After you purchase and install Tripwire, you can configure it to monitor any changes in specified system files and directories on your system.

Periodically examine the log files in the /var/log directory and its subdirectories. Many Linux applications, including some servers, write log information by using the logging capabilities of syslogd or rsyslogd. On Linux systems, the log files written by `syslogd` and `rsyslogd` reside in the `/var/log` directory. Make sure that only the `root` user can read and write these files.

**REMEMBER**

The `syslogd` configuration file is `/etc/syslog.conf`, and the `rsyslogd` configuration file (existing on many newer systems) is `/etc/rsyslog.conf`. The default configuration of `syslogd` generates the necessary log files, but if you want to examine and understand the configuration file, type **man syslog.conf** or **man rsyslog.conf** for more information.

# Securing Internet Services

For an Internet-connected Linux system, or even one on a TCP/IP local-area network (LAN) that's not connected to the Internet, a significant threat is that someone could use one of many Internet services to gain access to your system. Each service — such as mail, web, and FTP — requires running a server program that responds to client requests arriving over the TCP/IP network. Some of these server programs have weaknesses that an outsider could use to log in to your system — maybe with `root` privileges. Luckily, Linux comes with some facilities that you can use to make the Internet services more secure.

**WARNING**

Potential intruders can employ a *port-scanning tool* — a program that attempts to establish a TCP/IP connection at a port and then looks for a response — to check which Internet servers are running on your system. Then, to gain access to your system, intruders can potentially exploit any known weaknesses of one or more services.

## Turning off stand-alone services

To provide Internet services such as web, email, and SFTP, your Linux system has to run server programs that listen to incoming TCP/IP network requests. Some of these servers start when your system boots and they run all the time. Such servers are *stand-alone servers*. The web server and mail server are examples of stand-alone servers.

Another server, `xinetd`, starts other servers that are configured to work under `xinetd`. Some Linux systems use the `inetd` server instead of `xinetd` to start other servers.

Some servers can be configured to run on a stand-alone basis or under a super server such as `xinetd`. The `vsftpd` SFTP server, for example, can be configured to run as a stand-alone server or to run under the control of `xinetd`.

**TIP**

In Debian and Ubuntu, use the `update-rc.d` command to turn off stand-alone servers, and use the `invoke-rc.d` command to start or stop servers interactively. To get a clue about the available services, type **ls /etc/init.d**, and look at all the script files designed to turn services on or off. You have to use these filenames when you want to turn a service on or off. To turn off Samba service, for example, type **update-rc.d -f samba remove**. If the service was already running, type **invoke-rc.d samba stop** to stop the service. You can use the `invoke-rc.d` command to stop any service in a similar manner.

**TIP**

In Fedora and SUSE, you can turn stand-alone servers on and off by using the `systemctl` command. You can get the names of the service scripts by typing **ls /etc/init.d**. Then you can turn off a service (such as Samba) by typing **sudo systemctl stop smb**. If the service was already running, type **/etc/init.d/smb stop** to stop the service. You can run scripts from the `/etc/init.d` directory with the `stop` argument to stop any service in a similar manner.

## Configuring the Internet super server

In addition to stand-alone servers such as web and mail servers, the `inetd` and `xinetd` servers have to be configured separately. These servers are *Internet super servers* because they can start other servers on demand (see Book 5, Chapter 1).

**TIP**

Type **ps ax | grep inetd** to see if your system runs one of these Internet super servers.

Debian and Ubuntu use `inetd`, and Fedora and SUSE use `xinetd`.

The `inetd` server is configured through the `/etc/inetd.conf` file. You can disable a service by locating the appropriate line in that file and commenting it out by placing a pound sign (#) at the beginning of the line. After saving the configuration file, type **/etc/init.d/inetd restart** to restart the `inetd` server.

Configuring the `xinetd` server is a bit more complicated. The `xinetd` server reads a configuration file named `/etc/xinetd.conf` at startup. This file in turn refers to configuration files stored in the `/etc/xinetd.d` directory. The configuration files in `/etc/xinetd.d` tell `xinetd` which ports to listen to and which server to start for each port. Type **ls /etc/xinetd.d** to see a list of the files in the `/etc/xinetd.d` directory on your system. Each file represents a service that `xinetd` can start. To turn off any of these services, edit the file in a text editor, and add a `disable = yes` line in the file. After you make any changes in the `xinetd` configuration files, you must restart the `xinetd` server; otherwise, the changes don't take effect. To restart the `xinetd` server, type **/etc/init.d/xinetd restart**. This command stops the `xinetd` server and then starts it again. When the server restarts, it reads the configuration files, and the changes take effect.

## Configuring TCP wrapper security

A common security feature of `inetd` and `xinetd` is their use of the TCP wrapper to start various services. The *TCP wrapper* is a block of code that provides an access-control facility for Internet services, acting like a protective package for your message. The TCP wrapper can start other services, such as FTP and Telnet, but before starting a service, it consults the `/etc/hosts.allow` file to see whether the host requesting the service is allowed to use that service. If nothing about that host appears in `/etc/hosts.allow`, the TCP wrapper checks the `/etc/hosts.deny` file to see whether it denies the service. If both files are empty, the TCP wrapper provides access to the requested service.

Here are the steps to follow to tighten access to the services that `inetd` and `xinetd` are configured to start:

1. **Use a text editor to edit the** `/etc/hosts.deny` **file, adding the following line to that file:**

   ALL:ALL

   This setting denies all hosts access to any Internet services on your system.

2. **Edit the** `/etc/hosts.allow` **file and add to it the names of hosts that can access services on your system.**

   To enable only hosts from the 192.168.1.0 network and the `localhost` (IP address 127.0.0.1) to access the services on your system, place the following line in the `/etc/hosts.allow` file:

   ```
   ALL: 192.168.1.0/255.255.255.0 127.0.0.1
   ```

3. **If you want to permit a specific remote host access to a specific Internet service, use the following syntax for a line in** `/etc/hosts.allow`:

   *server_program_name*: *hosts*

   Here, *server_program_name* is the name of the server program, and *hosts* is a comma-separated list of the hosts that can access the service. You may also enter *hosts* as a network address or an entire domain name, such as `.mycompany.com`.

# Using Secure Shell for Remote Logins

Linux comes with Open Secure Shell (OpenSSH) software, a suite of programs that provides a secure replacement for the Berkeley r commands: rlogin (remote login), rsh (remote shell), and rcp (remote copy). OpenSSH uses public key cryptography to authenticate users and to encrypt communications between two hosts so that users can log in from remote systems securely and copy files securely.

This section briefly describes how to use the OpenSSH software in Linux. To find out more about OpenSSH and read the latest news about it, visit www.openssh.com or www.openssh.org.

The OpenSSH software is installed during Linux installation. Table 2-2 lists the main components of the OpenSSH software.

**TABLE 2-2**     **Components of the OpenSSH Software**

| Component | Description |
|---|---|
| /usr/sbin/sshd | This SSH daemon must run on a host if you want users on remote systems to use the ssh client to log in securely. When a connection from the ssh client arrives, sshd performs authentication by using public key cryptography and establishes an encrypted communication link with the ssh client. |
| /usr/bin/ssh | Users can run this SSH client to log in to a host that is running sshd. Users can also use ssh to execute a command on another host. |
| /usr/bin/slogin | This component is a symbolic link to /usr/bin/ssh. |
| /usr/bin/scp | This secure-copy program works like rcp but securely. The scp program uses ssh for data transfer and provides the same authentication and security as ssh. |
| /usr/bin/ ssh–keygen | You use this program to generate the public and private key pairs that you need for the public key cryptography used in OpenSSH. The ssh–keygen program can generate key pairs for both RSA and DSA (Digital Signature Algorithm) authentication. (RSA comes from the first initials of the last names of Ron Rivest, Adi Shamir, and Leonard Adleman — the developers of the RSA algorithm.) |
| /etc/ssh/ sshd_config | This configuration file for the sshd server specifies many parameters for sshd, including the port to listen to, the protocol to use, and the location of other files. (The two versions of SSH protocols are SSH1 and SSH2, both supported by OpenSSH.) |
| /etc/ssh/ ssh_config | This configuration file is for the ssh client. Each user can also have an ssh configuration file named config in the .ssh subdirectory of the user's home directory. |

OpenSSH uses public key encryption in which the sender and receiver both have a pair of keys: a public key and a private key. The public keys are freely distributed, and each party knows the other's public key. The sender encrypts data by using the recipient's public key. Only the recipient's private key can decrypt the data.

To use OpenSSH, start the sshd server and then generate the host keys. Here's how:

>> If you want to support SSH-based remote logins on a host, start the sshd server on your system. Type **ps ax | grep sshd** to see whether the server is already running. If it isn't, log in as root, and turn on the SSH service.

>> Generate the host keys with the following command:

```
ssh-keygen -t dsa -f /etc/ssh/ssh_host_key -N ''
```

The -t dsa flag causes the ssh-keygen program to generate DSA keys which the SSH2 protocol uses. If you see a message saying that the file /etc/ssh/ ssh_host_key already exists, the key pairs were generated during Linux installation. You can use the existing file without having to regenerate the keys.

A user who wants to log in by using SSH can use an ssh command like the following

```
ssh 192.168.0.4 -l rich
```

where 192.168.0.4 is the IP address of the other Linux system. Then SSH displays a message:

```
The authenticity of host '192.168.0.4 (192.168.0.4)' can't be established.
RSA key fingerprint is 7b:79:f2:dd:8c:54:00:a6:94:ec:fa:8e:7f:c9:ad:66.
Are you sure you want to continue connecting (yes/no)?
```

Type **yes**, and press Enter. SSH adds the host to its list of known hosts and prompts you for a password on the other Linux system:

```
rich@192.168.0.4's password:
```

After entering the password, you have a secure login session with that system. You can also log in to this account with the following equivalent command:

```
ssh rich@192.168.0.4
```

If you simply want to copy a file securely from another system on the LAN (identified by its IP address, 192.168.0.4), you can use scp like this:

```
scp 192.168.0.4:/etc/X11/xorg.conf
```

This command prompts for a password and securely copies the /etc/X11/xorg.conf file from the 192.168.0.4 host to the system from which the scp command was typed, as follows:

```
rich@192.168.0.4's password: (type the password.)
xorg.conf 100% 2814 2.8KB/s 00:00
```

# Setting Up Simple Firewalls

A *firewall* is a network device or host with two or more network interfaces — one connected to the protected internal network and the other connected to unprotected networks such as the Internet. The firewall controls access to and from the protected internal network.

If you connect an internal network directly to the Internet, you have to make sure that every system on the internal network is properly secured — which can be nearly impossible, because a single careless user can render the entire internal network vulnerable.

A firewall is a single point of connection to the Internet: You can direct all your efforts toward making that firewall system a daunting barrier to unauthorized external users. Essentially, a firewall is a protective fence that keeps unwanted external data and software out and sensitive internal data and software in (see Figure 2-3).

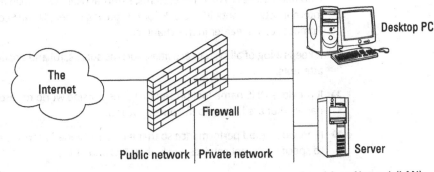

**FIGURE 2-3:**
A firewall protects hosts on a private network from the Internet.

The firewall runs software that examines the network packets arriving at its network interfaces and then takes appropriate action based on a set of rules. The idea is to define these rules so that they allow only authorized network traffic to flow between the two interfaces. Configuring the firewall involves setting up the rules properly. A configuration strategy is to reject all network traffic and then enable only a limited set of network packets to go through the firewall. The authorized network traffic would include the connections necessary to enable internal users to do things such as visit websites and receive email.

To be useful, a firewall must have the following general characteristics:

>> It must control the flow of packets between the Internet and the internal network.

>> It must *not* provide dynamic routing because dynamic routing tables are subject to route *spoofing* — the use of fake routes by intruders. Instead, the firewall uses static routing tables (which you can set up with the route command on Linux systems).

>> It must not allow any external user to log in as root. That way, even if the firewall system is compromised, the intruder is blocked from using root privileges from a remote login.

>> It must be kept in a physically secure location.

>> It must distinguish between packets that come from the Internet and packets that come from the internal protected network. This capability allows the firewall to reject packets that come from the Internet but have the IP address of a trusted system on the internal network.

>> It acts as the SMTP mail gateway for the internal network. Set up the sendmail software so that all outgoing mail appears to come from the firewall system.

>> Its user accounts are limited to a few user accounts for those internal users who need access to external systems. External users who need access to the internal network should use SSH for remote login (see "Using Secure Shell for Remote Logins" earlier in this chapter).

>> It keeps a log of all system activities, such as successful and unsuccessful login attempts.

>> It provides DNS name-lookup service to the outside world to resolve any host names that are known to the outside world.

>> It provides good performance so that it doesn't hinder internal users' access to specific Internet services (such as HTTPS and SFTP).

A firewall can take many forms. Here are three common forms of a firewall:

>> **Packet filter firewall:** This simple firewall uses a router capable of filtering (blocking or allowing) packets according to various characteristics, including the source and destination IP addresses, the network protocol (TCP or UDP), and the source and destination port numbers. Packet filter firewalls are usually placed at the outermost boundary with an untrusted network and

they form the first line of defense. An example of a packet filter firewall is a network router that employs filter rules to screen network traffic.

Packet filter firewalls are fast and flexible, but they can't prevent attacks that exploit application-specific vulnerabilities or functions. They can log only a minimal amount of information, such as source IP address, destination IP address, and traffic type. Also, they're vulnerable to attacks and exploits that take advantage of flaws within the TCP/IP protocol, such as IP address spoofing, which involves altering the address information in network packets to make them appear to come from a trusted IP address.

>> **Stateful inspection firewall:** This type of firewall keeps track of the network connections that network applications are using. When an application on an internal system uses a network connection to create a session with a remote system, a port is also opened on the internal system. This port receives network traffic from the remote system. For successful connections, packet filter firewalls must permit incoming packets from the remote system.

Opening many ports to incoming traffic creates a risk of intrusion by unauthorized users who abuse the expected conventions of network protocols such as TCP. Stateful inspection firewalls solve this problem by creating a table of outbound network connections, along with each session's corresponding internal port. Then this *state table* is used to validate any inbound packets. This stateful inspection is more secure than a packet filter because it tracks internal ports individually rather than opening all internal ports for external access.

>> **Application-proxy gateway firewall:** This firewall acts as an intermediary between internal applications that attempt to communicate with external servers such as a web server. A web proxy receives requests for external web pages from web browser clients running inside the firewall and relays them to the exterior web server as though the firewall was the requesting web client. The external web server responds to the firewall, and the firewall forwards the response to the inside client as though the firewall was the web server. No direct network connection is ever made from the inside client host to the external web server.

Application-proxy gateway firewalls have some advantages over packet filter firewalls and stateful inspection firewalls. First, application-proxy gateway firewalls examine the entire network packet rather than only the network addresses and ports, which enables these firewalls to provide more extensive logging capabilities than packet filters or stateful inspection firewalls.

Another advantage is that application-proxy gateway firewalls can authenticate users directly, whereas packet filter firewalls and stateful inspection firewalls normally authenticate users on the basis of the IP address of the system (that is, source, destination, and protocol type). Given that network addresses can be easily spoofed, the authentication capabilities of application-proxy gateway firewalls are superior to those found in packet filter and stateful inspection firewalls.

The advanced functionality of application-proxy gateway firewalls, however, results in some disadvantages compared with packet filter or stateful inspection firewalls:

- Because of the full packet awareness found in application-proxy gateways, the firewall is forced to spend significant time reading and interpreting each packet. Therefore, application-proxy gateway firewalls generally aren't well suited to high-bandwidth or real-time applications. To reduce the load on the firewall, a dedicated proxy server can be used to secure less time-sensitive services such as email and most web traffic.

- Application-proxy gateway firewalls are often limited in terms of support for new network applications and protocols. An individual application-specific proxy agent is required for each type of network traffic that needs to go through the firewall. Most vendors of application-proxy gateways provide generic proxy agents to support undefined network protocols or applications. Those generic agents, however, tend to negate many of the strengths of the application-proxy gateway architecture; they simply allow traffic to *tunnel* through the firewall.

Most firewalls implement a combination of these firewall functionalities. Many vendors of packet filter firewalls or stateful inspection firewalls have also implemented basic application-proxy functionality to offset some of the weaknesses associated with their firewalls. In most cases, these vendors implement application proxies to provide better logging of network traffic and stronger user authentication. Nearly all major firewall vendors have introduced multiple firewall functions into their products in some manner.

**TIP**

In a large organization, you may also have to isolate smaller internal networks from the corporate network. You can set up such internal firewalls the same way that you set up Internet firewalls.

# Using NAT

Network Address Translation (NAT) is an effective tool that enables you to hide the network addresses of an internal network behind a firewall. In essence, NAT allows an organization to use private network addresses behind a firewall while maintaining the ability to connect to external systems through the firewall.

Here are the three methods of implementing NAT:

>> **Static:** In static NAT, each internal system on the private network has a corresponding external, routable IP address associated with it. This technique is seldom used because unique IP addresses are in short supply.

>> **Hiding:** In hiding NAT, all systems behind a firewall share an external, routable IP address, and the internal systems use private IP addresses. Thus, in a hiding NAT, several systems behind a firewall still appear to be a single system.

>> **Port address translation:** With port address translation, you can place hosts behind a firewall system and still make them selectively accessible to external users.

In terms of strengths and weaknesses, each type of NAT — static, hiding, and port address translation — is applicable in certain situations. The variable is the amount of design flexibility offered by each type. Static NAT offers the most flexibility, but it's not always practical because of the shortage of IP addresses. Hiding NAT technology is seldom used because port address translation offers additional features. Port address translation tends to be the most convenient and secure solution.

# Enabling packet filtering on your Linux system

The Linux kernel has built-in packet filtering software in the form of something called `netfilter`. You use the `iptables` command to set up the rules for what happens to the packets based on the IP addresses in their header and the network connection type.

**TIP**

To find out more about `netfilter` and `iptables`, visit the documentation section of the `netfilter` website at `www.netfilter.org/documentation`.

The built-in packet filtering capability is handy when you don't have a dedicated firewall between your Linux system and the Internet, such as when you connect your Linux system to the Internet through a DSL or cable modem. Essentially, you can have a packet filtering firewall inside your Linux system sitting between the kernel and the applications.

## Using the security level configuration tool

Most Linux distributions, such as Fedora and SUSE, now include GUI tools to turn on a packet filtering firewall and simplify the configuration experience for the user.

In some distributions, you need to install `ufw` (an acronym for Uncomplicated Firewall), which lets you manage a net-filter firewall and simplify configuration. `ufw` serves as a front end to `iptables`, which allows you to enter commands in a terminal window directly through it. The command

```
sudo ufw enable
```

turns the firewall on, and the command

```
sudo ufw status verbose
```

displays such information as the following:

```
Status: active
Logging: on (low)
Default: deny (incoming), allow (outgoing), disabled (routed)
New profiles: skip
```

The default settings are exactly what you're looking for in most cases for a client machine: allowing outgoing traffic and denying incoming traffic.

You can allow incoming packets meant for specific Internet services such as SSH, Telnet, and FTP. If you select a network interface such as eth0 (the first Ethernet card) as trusted, all network traffic over that interface is allowed without any filtering.

**TIP**

In SUSE, to set up a firewall, choose Main Menu⇨ System⇨ YaST. In the YaST Control Center window that appears, click Security and Users on the left side of the window and then click Firewall on the right side. YaST opens a window that you can use to configure the firewall.

You can designate network interfaces (by device name, such as eth0, ppp0, and so on) to one of three zones: internal, external, or demilitarized zone. Then, for that zone, you can specify what services (such as HTTPS, SFTP, and SSH) are allowed. If you have two or more network interfaces and you use the Linux system as a gateway (a router), you can enable forwarding packets between network interfaces (a feature called *masquerading*).

You can also turn on different levels of logging such as logging all dropped packets that attempt connection at specific ports. If you change the firewall settings, choose the Startup category and click Save Settings and Restart Firewall Now.

## Using the iptables command

As I mention earlier in the chapter, the graphical user interface (GUI) firewall configuration tools are just front ends that use the iptables command to implement the firewall. If your Linux system doesn't have a GUI tool, you can use iptables directly to configure firewalling on your Linux system.

Using the iptables command is somewhat complex. The command uses the concept of a *chain*, which is a sequence of rules. Each rule says what to do with a packet if the header contains certain information, such as the source or destination

IP address. If a rule doesn't apply, `iptables` consults the next rule in the chain. By default, there are three chains:

>> INPUT **chain:** Contains the first set of rules against which packets are tested. The packets continue to the next chain only if the INPUT chain doesn't specify DROP or REJECT.

>> FORWARD **chain:** Contains the rules that apply to packets attempting to pass through this system to another system (when you use your Linux system as a router between your LAN and the Internet, for example).

>> OUTPUT **chain:** Includes the rules applied to packets before they're sent out (either to another network or to an application).

When an incoming packet arrives, the kernel uses `iptables` to make a routing decision based on the destination IP address of the packet. If the packet is for this server, the kernel passes the packet to the INPUT chain. If the packet satisfies all the rules in the INPUT chain, the packet is processed by local processes such as an Internet server that's listening for packets of this type.

If the kernel has IP forwarding enabled, and the packet has a destination IP address of a different network, the kernel passes the packet to the FORWARD chain. If the packet satisfies the rules in the FORWARD chain, it's sent out to the other network. If the kernel doesn't have IP forwarding enabled, and the packet's destination address isn't for this server, the packet is dropped.

If the local processing programs that receive the input packets want to send network packets out, those packets pass through the OUTPUT chain. If the OUTPUT chain accepts those packets, they're sent out to the specified destination network.

You can view the current chains, add rules to the existing chains, or create new chains of rules by using the `iptables` command, which normally requires you to be root to interact with. When you view the current chains you can save them to a file. If you've configured nothing else and your system has no firewall configured, typing **iptables -L** should show the following:

```
Chain INPUT (policy ACCEPT)
target prot opt source destination
Chain FORWARD (policy ACCEPT)
target prot opt source destination
Chain OUTPUT (policy ACCEPT)
target prot opt source destination
```

In this case, all three chains — INPUT, FORWARD, and OUTPUT — show the same ACCEPT policy, which means that everything is wide open.

If you're setting up a packet filter, the first thing you do is specify the packets that you want to accept. To accept packets from the 192.168.0.0 network address, add the following rule to the INPUT chain:

```
iptables -A INPUT -s 192.168.0.0/24 -j ACCEPT
```

Now add a rule to drop everything except local loopback (the lo network interface) traffic and stop all forwarding with the following commands:

```
iptables -A INPUT -i ! lo -j REJECT
iptables -A FORWARD -j REJECT
```

The first iptables command, for example, appends to the INPUT chain (-A INPUT) the rule that if the packet doesn't come from the lo interface (-i ! lo), iptables rejects the packet (-j REJECT).

Before rejecting all other packets, you may add more rules to each INPUT chain to allow specific packets in. You can select packets to accept or reject based on many parameters, such as IP addresses, protocol types (TCP, UDP), network interface, and port numbers.

You can do all sorts of specialized packet filtering with iptables. Suppose that you set up a web server and want to accept packets meant for only HTTPS (port 443) and SSH services. The SSH service (port 22) is for you to securely log in and administer the server. Also suppose that the server's IP address is 192.168.0.10. Here's how you might set up the rules for this server:

```
iptables -P INPUT DROP
iptables -A INPUT -s 0/0 -d 192.168.0.10 -p tcp --dport 443 -j ACCEPT
iptables -A INPUT -s 0/0 -d 192.168.0.10 -p tcp --dport 22 -j ACCEPT
```

In this case, the first rule sets up the default policy of the INPUT chain to DROP, which means that if none of the specific rules matches, the packet is dropped. The next two rules say that packets addressed to 192.168.0.10 and meant for ports 443 and 22 are accepted.

**WARNING**

Don't type iptables commands from a remote login session. A rule that begins denying packets from all addresses can also stop what you type from reaching the system; in that case, you may have no way of accessing the system over the network. To avoid unpleasant surprises, always type iptables rules at the console — the keyboard and monitor connected directly to your Linux PC that's running the packet filter. If you want to delete all filtering rules in a hurry, type **iptables -F** to flush them. To change the default policy for the INPUT chain to ACCEPT, type **iptables -t filter -P INPUT ACCEPT**. This command causes iptables to accept all incoming packets by default.

**REMEMBER**

Not every `iptables` command is discussed in this section. You can type **man iptables** to read a summary of the commands. You can also read about `netfilter` and `iptables` at `https://netfilter.org/projects/iptables/index.html`.

After you define the rules by using the `iptables` command, those rules are in memory and are gone when you reboot the system. Use the `iptables-save` command to store the rules in a file. You can save the rules in a file named `iptables.rules` by using the following command:

```
iptables-save > iptables.rules
```

Here's a listing of the `iptables.rules` file generated on a Fedora system:

```
# Generated by iptables-save v1.3.0 on Sun Dec 28 16:10:12 2019
*filter
:FORWARD ACCEPT [0:0]
:INPUT ACCEPT [0:0]
:OUTPUT ACCEPT [6:636]
-A FORWARD -j REJECT --reject-with icmp-port-unreachable
-A INPUT -s 192.168.0.0/255.255.255.0 -j ACCEPT
-A INPUT -i ! lo -j REJECT --reject-with icmp-port-unreachable
COMMIT
# Completed on Sun Dec 28 16:10:12 2019
```

These rules correspond to the following `iptables` commands used to configure the filter:

```
iptables -A INPUT -s 192.168.0.0/24 -j ACCEPT
iptables -A INPUT -i ! lo -j REJECT
iptables -A FORWARD -j REJECT
```

If you want to load these saved rules into `iptables`, use the following command:

```
iptables-restore < iptables.rules
```

# Security Files to Be Aware Of

Table 2-3 lists 11 files, or directories, that security administrators should be aware of and able to explain.

**TABLE 2-3**  **Key Security Files**

| File | Description |
|---|---|
| /etc/nologin | If this file exists, it denies login to all users except root. This file can be handy when maintenance needs to be done and users need to stay off the system for a period of time. Removing the file restores login capability for all users. The file can be created as a text file with any editor, or you can often use the nologin command to create it. |
| /etc/passwd | This file holds much of the user account information and is addressed heavily in this chapter. |
| /etc/shadow | When shadowing is turned on — which it almost always is — password values (hashes) are stored in this file (which is more secure) as opposed to in /etc/passwd. |
| /etc/xinetd.d/* | This directory can be used to store configuration files used by xinetd, the server daemon. |
| /etc/xinetd.conf | This file is the main configuration file used by xinetd, the server daemon. |
| /etc/xinetd.d/* | This directory can be used to store configuration files used by inetd, the Internet daemon. In almost all distributions, inetd has been replaced by xinetd. |
| /etc/inetd.conf | This file is the main configuration file used by inetd, the Internet daemon. |
| /etc/inittab | This file is the initial startup (initialization) table used to identify what starts and stops as the system is booted and changes run states. |
| /etc/init.d/* | This directory can hold configuration files that are used during the change of run states/level and referenced by the inittab file. |
| /etc/hosts.allow | If this file exists, it specifically lists the hosts that are allowed to network with this one. If the file doesn't exist, by default, all hosts are allowed to network with this one. |
| /etc/hosts.deny | If this file exists, it specifically lists the hosts that aren't allowed to network with this one. If the file doesn't exist, by default, all hosts are allowed to network with this one. The three possibilities are having an allow file that identifies only hosts that can network with this one; having a deny file that identifies only hosts that can't connect with this one; and having neither file, which allows all other hosts to network with this one. |

IN THIS CHAPTER

» **Understanding computer security audits**

» **Learning a security test methodology**

» **Reviewing host and network security**

» **Appreciating vulnerability testing**

» **Exploring different security testing tools**

# Chapter **3**

# Vulnerability Testing and Computer Security Audits

When you see the term *audit*, the odds are good that you think of the kind involving taxes. In actuality, many types of audits exist, and one of them is a *computer security audit*. The purpose of a computer security audit, in its simplest form, is to test your system and network security. For larger organizations, an independent auditor can do the security audit (much like auditing of financial statements is done). If you have only a few Linux systems or a small network, you can do the security audit as a self-assessment to figure out whether you're doing everything okay.

This chapter explains how to perform computer security audits and shows you some free tools and resources that can help you test your system's security.

# Understanding Security Audits

An *audit* is an independent assessment of whatever it is you're auditing, so a *computer security audit* is an independent assessment of computer security. If someone conducts a computer security audit of your organization, they focus typically on two areas:

>> **Independent verification** of whether your organization complies with its existing policies and procedures for computer security. This part is the nontechnical aspect of the security audit.

>> **Independent testing** of how effective your security controls (any hardware and software mechanisms that you use to secure the system) are. This part is the technical aspect of the security audit.

You need security audits for the same reason that you need financial audits: to verify that everything's being done the way it's supposed to be done. In public as well as private organizations, management may want to have independent security audits done to assure themselves that their security is A-OK. Regardless of your organization's size, you can always perform security audits on your own, either to prepare for independent security audits or to find whether you're doing everything correctly.

No matter whether you have independent security audits or a self-assessment, here are some of the benefits you get from security audits:

>> Periodic risk assessments that consider internal and external threats to systems and data

>> Periodic testing of the effectiveness of security policies, security controls, and techniques

>> Identification of any significant deficiencies in your system's security (so that you know what to fix)

>> In the case of self-assessments, preparation for any annual independent security testing that your organization may have to face

## Nontechnical aspects of security audits

The nontechnical side of computer security audits focuses on your organization-wide security framework. The audit examines how well the organization has set up and implemented its policies, plans, and procedures for computer security. Here's a list of some items to be verified:

>> Risks are periodically assessed.

>> An entity-wide security program plan is in place.

>> A security program-management structure is in place.

>> Computer security responsibilities are clearly assigned.

>> Effective security-related personnel policies are in place.

>> The security program's effectiveness is monitored and changes are made when needed.

As you might expect, the nontechnical aspects of the security audit involve reviewing documents and interviewing appropriate people to find out how the organization manages computer security. For a small organization or a home PC, expecting plans and procedures in documents is ridiculous. In those cases, simply make sure that you have some technical controls in place to secure your system and your network connection.

# Technical aspects of security audits

The technical side of computer security audits focuses on testing the technical controls that secure your hosts and network. This testing involves determining the following:

>> **How well the host is secured:** Examples include whether all operating system patches are applied, file permissions are set correctly, user accounts are protected, file changes are monitored, and log files are monitored.

>> **How well the network is secured:** Examples include whether unnecessary Internet services are turned off, a firewall is installed, remote logins are secured with tools such as Secure Shell (SSH), and whether Transport Control Protocol (TCP) wrapper access controls are used.

Typically, security experts use automated tools to perform these two security reviews for individual hosts and for the entire network.

# Implementing a Security Test Methodology

A key element of a computer security audit is a security test that checks the technical mechanisms used to secure a host and the network. The security-test methodology follows these high-level steps:

1. **Take stock of the organization's networks, hosts, network devices (routers, switches, firewalls, and so on), and Internet connection.**

2. **If many hosts and network connections exist, determine which important hosts and network devices need to be tested.**

   The importance of a host depends on the kinds of applications it runs. A host that runs the corporate database, for example, is more important than the hosts that serve as desktop systems.

3. **Test the hosts individually.**

   Typically, this step involves logging in as a system administrator and checking various aspects of host security, from passwords to system log files.

4. **Test the network.**

   You usually perform this step by attempting to break through the network defenses from another system on the Internet. If the network has a firewall, the testing checks whether the firewall is configured correctly.

5. **Analyze the test results of both host and network tests to determine vulnerabilities and risks.**

Each type of testing (host and network) focuses on three areas of overall computer security:

» **Prevention:** Includes the mechanisms (nontechnical and technical) that help prevent attacks on the system and the network.

» **Detection:** Refers to techniques such as monitoring log files, checking file integrity, and using intrusion detection systems that detect when someone is about to break into (or has already broken into) your system.

» **Response:** Includes the steps for tasks such as reporting an incident to authorities and restoring important files from backup after a computer security incident occurs.

For host and network security, each area has some overlap. Prevention mechanisms for host security (such as good passwords and file permissions) can also provide network security, for example. Nevertheless, thinking in terms of the three areas — prevention, detection, and response — is helpful.

# Some common computer vulnerabilities

Before you can think about prevention, however, you have to know the types of problems you're trying to prevent — the common security vulnerabilities. The prevention and detection steps typically depend on the specific vulnerabilities. The idea is to check whether a host or a network has the vulnerabilities that crackers exploit.

## Online resources on computer vulnerabilities

Several online resources identify and categorize computer security vulnerabilities:

>> **SANS Institute** publishes a semiweekly high-level executive summary of the most important news articles that have been published on computer security during the past week. You can view past issues and sign up for the new issues at www.sans.org/newsletters/newsbites/?msc=cishp.

>> **CVE** (Common Vulnerabilities and Exposures) is a list of standardized names of vulnerabilities. For more information on CVE, see www.cve.org. Using the CVE name to describe vulnerabilities is common practice.

>> **National Vulnerability Database** is a searchable index of information on computer vulnerabilities, published by the National Institute of Standards and Technology (NIST), a U.S. government agency. You can find the database at https://nvd.nist.gov.

## Typical computer vulnerabilities

Table 3-1 summarizes some common Unix and cross-platform vulnerabilities that apply to Linux.

**TABLE 3-1      Some Vulnerabilities Common to Unix Systems**

| Vulnerability Type | Description |
|---|---|
| BIND DNS | Berkeley Internet Name Domain (BIND) is a package that implements the Domain Name System (DNS), the Internet's name service that translates a name to an IP address. Some versions of BIND have vulnerabilities. |
| Apache Web Server | Some Apache Web Server modules (such as mod_ssl) have known vulnerabilities. Any vulnerability in Common Gateway Interface (CGI) programs used with web servers to process interactive web pages can give attackers a way to gain access to a system. |
| Authentication | User accounts sometimes have no passwords or have weak passwords that are easily cracked by password-cracking programs. |
| CVS, Subversion | Concurrent Versions System (CVS) is a popular source-code control system used in Linux systems. Subversion is another version control system for Linux that is becoming popular. These version control systems have vulnerabilities that can enable an attacker to execute arbitrary code on the system. |
| sendmail | sendmail is a complex program used to transport mail messages from one system to another. Some versions of sendmail have vulnerabilities. |
| SNMP | Simple Network Management Protocol (SNMP) is used to remotely monitor and administer various network-connected systems ranging from routers to computers. SNMP lacks good access control, so an attacker may be able to reconfigure or shut down your system if it's running SNMP. |
| Open Secure Sockets Layer (OpenSSL) | Many applications such as Apache Web Server use OpenSSL to provide cryptographic security for a network connection. Unfortunately, some versions of OpenSSL have known vulnerabilities that could be exploited. |
| Network File System (NFS) and Network Information Service (NIS) | Both NFS and NIS have many security problems (such as buffer overflow, potential for denial-of-service attacks, and weak authentication). Also, NFS and NIS are often misconfigured, which could allow local and remote users to exploit the security holes. |
| Databases | Databases such as MySQL and PostgreSQL are complex applications that can be difficult to configure and secure correctly. These databases have many features that can be misused or exploited to compromise the confidentiality, availability, and integrity of data. |
| Linux kernel | The Linux kernel is susceptible to many vulnerabilities, such as denial of service, execution of arbitrary code, and root-level access to the system. |

# Host-security review

When reviewing host security, focus on assessing the security mechanisms in each of the following areas:

>> **Prevention:** Install operating-system updates, secure passwords, improve file permissions, set up a password for a bootloader, and use encryption.

>> **Detection:** Capture log messages, and check file integrity with Tripwire (a tool that can detect changes in system files).

**TECHNICAL STUFF**

Tripwire started as open-source but no longer is. You can still search for and download the original.

>> **Response:** Make routine backups and develop incident-response procedures.

The following sections review a few of these host-security mechanisms.

## Operating system updates

Linux distributions release updates very quickly. When security vulnerabilities are found, Linux distributions immediately release an update to fix the problem. Many distributions offer online updates that you can enable and use to keep your system up to date. The details of updating the operating system depend on the distribution. (See Book 1, Chapter 5 for information on how to update Linux online.)

## File permissions

Protect important system files with appropriate file ownerships and file permissions. The key procedures in assigning file-system ownerships and permissions are as follows:

>> Figure out which files contain sensitive information and why. Some files may contain sensitive data related to your work or business, whereas many other files are sensitive because they control the Linux system configuration.

>> Maintain a current list of authorized users and what they're authorized to do on the system.

>> Set up passwords, groups, file ownerships, and file permissions to allow only authorized users to access the files.

Table 3-2 lists some important system files in Linux, showing the typical numeric permission setting for each file (which may differ slightly depending on the distribution). See Book 6, Chapter 2 for more information on numeric permission settings.

Another important check is for executable program files that have the setuid permission. If a program has setuid permission and is owned by root, the program runs with root privileges no matter who actually runs the program. You can find all setuid programs with the following find command:

```
find / -perm /4000 -print
```

**TABLE 3-2**    **Important System Files and Their Permissions**

| File Pathname | Permission | Description |
| --- | --- | --- |
| /boot/grub/menu.lst | 600 | GRUB bootloader menu file |
| /etc/cron.allow | 400 | List of users permitted to use cron to submit periodic jobs |
| /etc/cron.deny | 400 | List of users who can't use cron to submit periodic jobs |
| /etc/crontab | 644 | Systemwide periodic jobs |
| /etc/hosts.allow | 644 | List of hosts allowed to use Internet services that are started with TCP wrappers |
| /etc/hosts.deny | 644 | List of hosts denied access to Internet services that are started with TCP wrappers |
| /etc/logrotate.conf | 644 | File that controls how log files rotate |
| /etc/pam.d | 755 | Directory with configuration files for pluggable authentication modules (PAMs) |
| /etc/passwd | 644 | Old-style password file with user account information but not the passwords |
| /etc/rc.d | 755 | Directory with system-startup scripts |
| /etc/securetty | 600 | TTY interfaces (terminals) from which root can log in |
| /etc/security | 755 | Policy files that control system access |
| /etc/shadow | 400 | File with encrypted passwords and password expiration information |
| /etc/shutdown.allow | 400 | Users who can shut down or reboot by pressing Ctrl+Alt+Delete |
| /etc/ssh | 755 | Directory with configuration files for SSH |
| /etc/sysconfig | 755 | System configuration files |
| /etc/sysctl.conf | 644 | Kernel configuration parameters |
| /etc/syslog.conf | 644 | Configuration file for the syslogd server that logs messages |

| File Pathname | Permission | Description |
|---|---|---|
| /etc/udev/udev.conf | 644 | Configuration file for udev — the program that provides the capability to dynamically name hot-pluggable devices and create the device files in the /dev directory |
| /etc/vsftpd | 600 | Configuration file for the Very Secure FTP server |
| /etc/vsftpd.ftpusers | 600 | List of users who aren't allowed to use FTP to transfer files |
| /etc/xinetd.conf | 644 | Configuration file for the xinetd server |
| /etc/xinetd.d | 755 | Directory containing configuration files for specific services that the xinetd server can start |
| /var/log | 755 | Directory with all log files |
| /var/log/lastlog | 644 | Information about all previous logins |
| /var/log/messages | 644 | Main system message log file |
| /var/log/wtmp | 664 | Information about current logins |

You may want to save the output in a file (append *filename* to the command) and then examine the file for any unusual setuid programs. A setuid program in a user's home directory, for example, is unusual.

## Password security

Verify that the password, group, and shadow password files are protected. In particular, the shadow password file has to be write-protected and readable only by root. Table 3-3 shows the password filenames and their recommended permissions.

**TABLE 3-3**    ## Ownership and Permission of Password Files

| File Pathname | Ownership | Permission |
|---|---|---|
| /etc/group | root.root | 644 |
| /etc/passwd | root.root | 644 |
| /etc/shadow | root.root | 400 |

*Incident response* is the policy that tells you what to do if something unusual happens to the system. The policy tells you how to proceed if someone breaks into your system.

Your response to an incident depends on how you use your system and how important the system is to you or your business. For a comprehensive incident response, remember these key points:

>> Figure out how critical and important your computer and network are and identify who or what resources can help you protect your system.

>> Take steps to prevent and minimize potential damage and interruption.

>> Develop and document a comprehensive contingency plan.

>> Periodically test the contingency plan and revise the procedures as appropriate.

# Network-security review

A *network-security review* focuses on assessing the security mechanisms in each of the following areas:

>> **Prevention:** Set up a firewall, enable packet filtering, disable unnecessary inetd or xinetd services, turn off unneeded Internet services, use TCP wrappers for access control, and use SSH for secure remote logins.

>> **Detection:** Use network intrusion detection, and capture system logs.

>> **Response:** Develop incident-response procedures.

Some key steps in assessing the network security are described in the following three subsections.

## Services started by inetd or xinetd

Depending on your distribution, the inetd or xinetd server may be configured to start some legacy Internet services such as Telnet and FTP. It's generally not recommended to use these services, but the decision to turn on some of these services depends on such factors as how the system connects to the Internet and how the system is being used. Usually, you can turn off inetd and xinetd services by commenting out the line; place a pound sign (#) at the beginning of the line.

If you're using `xinetd`, you can see which services are turned off by checking the configuration files in the `/etc/xinetd.d` directory for all the configuration files that have a `disable = yes` line. (The line doesn't count if it's commented out, which is indicated by a # character at the beginning of the line.) You can add a `disable = yes` line to the configuration file of any service that you want to turn off.

Also check the following files for any access controls used with the `inetd` or `xinetd` service:

» `/etc/hosts.allow` lists hosts that are allowed to access specific services.

» `/etc/hosts.deny` lists hosts that are denied access to services.

## Stand-alone services

Many services, such as `apache` and `httpd` (web server) and `sendmail` (mail server), start automatically at boot time, assuming that they're configured to start that way.

In some distributions, you can use the `systemctl` or `chkconfig` command to check which of these stand-alone servers is set to start at various run levels. (See Book 4, Chapter 2 for more information about run levels.) Typically, most systems start up at run level 3 (for text login) or 5 (for graphical login). Therefore, what matters is the setting for the servers in levels 3 and 5. To view the list of servers, type **chkconfig --list | more**. When you do a self-assessment of your network security and find that some servers shouldn't be running, you can turn them off for run levels 3 and 5 by typing **chkconfig --level 35** *servicename* **off**, where *servicename* is the name of the service you want to turn off. For distributions that use the Systemd startup method, type **systemctl --type=service** to list the running services.

In some distributions, you can use a graphical user interface (GUI) tool to see which services are enabled and running at any run level. With YaST, for example, click System on the left side of the window and then click Runlevel Editor on the right side of the window.

When you audit network security, make a note of all the servers that are turned on and then try to determine whether they should really *be* on, according to what you know about the system. The decision to turn on a particular service depends on how your system is used (as a web server or as a desktop system, for example) and on how it's connected to the Internet (such as through a firewall or directly).

### Penetration test

A penetration test is the best way to tell which services are really running on a Linux system. *Penetration testing* involves trying to get access to your system from an attacker's perspective. Typically, you perform this test from a system on the Internet and try to break in or at least get access to services running on your Linux system.

One aspect of penetration testing is seeing which ports are open on your Linux system. The *port number* is a number that identifies a TCP/IP network connection to the system. The attempt to connect to a port succeeds only if a server is running, or "listening," on that port. A port is considered to be open if a server responds when a connection request for that port arrives.

The first step in penetration testing is performing a *port scan* — the automated process of trying to connect to each port number to see whether a valid response comes back. Many available automated tools can perform port scanning; you can install and use a popular port-scanning tool called nmap (described later in this chapter).

After performing a port scan, you know which ports are open and can be exploited. Not all servers have security problems, but many servers have well-known vulnerabilities. An open port provides a cracker a way to attack your system through one of the servers. In fact, you can use automated tools called *vulnerability scanners* to identify vulnerabilities that exist in your system. (I describe some vulnerability scanners later in this chapter.) Whether your Linux system is connected to the Internet directly (through DSL or cable modem) or through a firewall, use the port-scanning and vulnerability-scanning tools to figure out whether you have any holes in your defenses.

# Vulnerability Testing Types

The number-one purpose of penetration testing is to identify vulnerabilities. When you're viewing such a test from this angle, it's important to understand that you have three ways of approaching it: black, white, and gray. These three approaches differ in the amount of information that you assume you have in the beginning. You can use the color with almost any other word — *black box* versus *white box* if a piece of software is doing the testing, for example, *black hat* versus *white hat* if a person is doing the testing, and so on. The following list focuses on the person and uses *box* as the preferred noun:

>> In *black-box testing,* the tests assume no knowledge of the network and look for vulnerabilities that an outsider might stumble across, such as open ports and weak passwords.

Suppose that a bored miscreant came across your network at random and decided to bring it to its knees.

>> In *white-box testing,* the test assumes that the attacker is a knowledgeable insider who's trying to break the system.

Suppose that you just fired a system administrator who wants to get back at you by crashing your network.

>> Between these two extremes lies the realm of *gray-box testing,* which assumes that an insider is behind the problem.

Suppose that someone from shipping is angry about not getting the raise they thought they deserved and wants to make the company pay. The attacker doesn't have the knowledge an administrator would, but they still know more about the systems than a complete outsider would.

# Exploring Security Testing Tools

Many automated tools perform security testing. Some of these tools find the open ports on every system in a range of IP addresses. Others look for the vulnerabilities associated with open ports. Still other tools capture (or *sniff*) those weaknesses and help you analyze them so that you can glean useful information about what's going on in your network.

You can browse a list of the top 100 security tools (based on an informal poll of nmap users) at https://sectools.org. Table 3-4 lists several of these tools by category.

**TIP**

The John the Ripper password-checking tool is one of the best command-line tools an administrator can use to test the strength of user passwords. In most distributions, you have to install it with apt install john, use the unshadow command to create a file containing entries from etc/passwd and etc/shadow, and then look for weaknesses.

nmap (short for *network mapper*) is a port-scanning tool that can rapidly scan large networks and determine which hosts are available on the network, which services they offer, what operating system (and operating-system version) they run, which type of packet filters or firewalls they use, and dozens of other characteristics. You can read more about nmap at https://nmap.org.

**TABLE 3-4** **Some Popular Computer-Security Testing Tools**

| Type | Names of Tools |
|---|---|
| Port scanners | nmap, Strobe |
| Vulnerability scanners | Nessus Security Scanner, SAINT, SARA, Whisker (CGI scanner), ISS Internet Scanner, CyberCop Scanner, Vetescan, Retina Network Security Scanner |
| Network utilities | Netcat, hping2, Firewalk, Cheops, ntop, ping, ngrep, AirSnort (802.11 WEP encryption-cracking tool) |
| Host-security tools | Tripwire, lsof |
| Packet sniffers | tcpdump, Ethereal, dsniff, sniffit |
| Intrusion detection | aide (Advanced Intrusion Detection Environment), Snort, Abacus portsentry, scanlogd, NFR, LIDSSystems (IDSs) |
| Log analysis and monitoring tools | logcolorise, tcpdstats, nlog, logcheck, LogWatch, Swatch |
| Password-checking tool | John the Ripper |

If nmap isn't already installed, you can easily install it on your distribution by using the command apt-get install nmap or the software search facility of YaST (find nmap) or any distribution-specific interface you may have.

If you have permission from your network administrator, you can try nmap to scan your local-area network by typing a command similar to the following (replacing the IP address range with addresses that are appropriate for your network):

```
nmap -O -sS 10.0.2.10-20
```

Following is typical output from that command:

```
Starting Nmap 7.80 ( https://nmap.org ) at 2022-03-16 19:35 EDT
Nmap scan report for ubuntu22 (10.0.2.15)
Host is up (0.000059s latency).
Not shown: 999 closed ports
PORT   STATE SERVICE
22/tcp open  ssh
Device type: general purpose
Running: Linux 2.6.X
OS CPE: cpe:/o:linux:linux_kernel:2.6.32
OS details: Linux 2.6.32
Network Distance: 0 hops
```

```
OS detection performed. Please report any incorrect results at https://nmap.org/
    submit/ .
Nmap done: 11 IP addresses (1 host up) scanned in 1.93 seconds
```

As you can see, nmap displays the names of the open ports and hazards a guess at the operating-system name and version number.

For a quick scan of your own machine, you can use the IP address of 127.0.0.1:

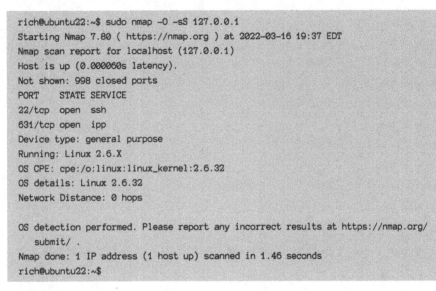

```
rich@ubuntu22:~$ sudo nmap -O -sS 127.0.0.1
Starting Nmap 7.80 ( https://nmap.org ) at 2022-03-16 19:37 EDT
Nmap scan report for localhost (127.0.0.1)
Host is up (0.000060s latency).
Not shown: 998 closed ports
PORT    STATE SERVICE
22/tcp  open  ssh
631/tcp open  ipp
Device type: general purpose
Running: Linux 2.6.X
OS CPE: cpe:/o:linux:linux_kernel:2.6.32
OS details: Linux 2.6.32
Network Distance: 0 hops

OS detection performed. Please report any incorrect results at https://nmap.org/
    submit/ .
Nmap done: 1 IP address (1 host up) scanned in 1.46 seconds
rich@ubuntu22:~$
```

In this example, my Ubuntu system has port 22 open for remote SSH access and port 631 open for access to the CUPS printing service.

# 7
# Scripting

# Contents at a Glance

# Chapter **1**

# Introductory Shell Scripting

As you see throughout many of the preceding chapters, Linux gives you a plethora of small and specialized commands, along with the ability to connect these commands in such a way that one command's output can be used as a second command's input. bash (short for Bourne Again Shell) — the default shell in most Linux systems — provides this capability in the form of I/O redirection and pipes. bash also includes conditionals such as the if statement that you can use to run commands only when a specific condition is true and the for statement that can repeat the set of commands a specified number of times. You can use these features of bash when writing programs called *shell scripts:* task-oriented collections of shell commands stored in a file.

This chapter shows you how to write simple shell scripts that are used to automate various tasks. Many Linux administrators create shell scripts that daily check on the status of the system disk drives, network connections, or any error messages in log files. With shell scripts you don't even need to log into your Linux system to check on things — you can have the shell script email the report directly to you!

# Trying Out Simple Shell Scripts

If you're not a programmer, it's common to feel apprehensive about programming. But you can put that apprehension aside: Shell *scripting* (or programming) can be as simple as storing a few commands in a file that can then be executed. In fact, you can have a useful shell program that has only a single command in it.

Shell scripts are popular among system administrators because they can be used to help automate tasks that you perform often. If a hard drive seems to be getting full, for example, you may want to find all files that exceed some determined size (say, 5MB) and that have not been accessed in the past 30 days. Once the files are found, you may want to send an email message to all the users identified with those large files, requesting that they archive and clean up those files. You can perform all these tasks with a shell script. You might start with the following find command to identify large files:

```
find / –type f –atime +30 –size +5000k –exec ls –l {} \; &gt; /tmp/largefiles
```

This command creates a file named /tmp/largefiles, which contains detailed information about old files taking up too much space. After you get a list of the files, you can use a few other Linux commands — such as sort, cut, and sed — to prepare and send mail messages to users who have large files to clean up. Instead of typing all these commands manually, place them in a file and create a shell script. That, in a nutshell, is the essence of shell scripts — to gather shell commands in a file so that you can easily perform repetitive system administration tasks. Although you can do all this on the command line without a script file, doing so will require you to type the command — complete with parameters and correct syntax — each and every time.

bash scripts, just like most Linux commands, accept command-line options. Inside the script, you can refer to the options as $1, $2, and so on. The special name $0 refers to the name of the script itself.

Here's a typical bash script that accepts arguments:

```
#!/bin/sh
echo "This script's name is: $0"
echo Argument 1: $1
echo Argument 2: $2
```

The first line runs the /bin/sh program, which subsequently processes the rest of the lines in the script. The name /bin/sh traditionally refers to the Bourne shell — the first Unix shell. In most Linux systems, /bin/sh is a symbolic link to /bin/bash, which is the executable program for bash.

Save this simple script in a file named `simple` and make that file executable with the following command:

```
chmod +x simple
```

Now run the script as follows:

```
./simple
```

It displays the following output:

```
This script's name is: ./simple
Argument 1:
Argument 2:
```

The first line shows the script's name. Because you have run the script without arguments, the script displays no values for the arguments.

Now try running the script with a few arguments, like this:

```
./simple "This is one argument" second-argument third
```

This time, the script displays more output:

```
This script's name is: ./simple
Argument 1: This is one argument
Argument 2: second-argument
```

As the output shows, the shell treats the entire string within the double quotation marks as a single argument. Otherwise, the shell uses spaces as separators between arguments on the command line.

This sample script ignores the third argument (and any others that you might give after it in subsequent attempts) because the script is designed to print only the first two arguments, and nothing references $3 or beyond.

# Exploring the Basics of Shell Scripting

Like any programming language, the bash shell supports the following features:

>> Variables that store values, including special built-in variables for accessing command-line arguments passed to a shell script and other special values.

>> The capability to evaluate expressions.

>> Control structures that enable you to loop over several shell commands or execute some commands conditionally.

>> The capability to define functions that can be called in many places within a script. bash also includes many built-in commands that you can use in any script.

The next few sections illustrate some of these programming features through simple examples. It's assumed that you have access to a Bash command-line prompt, either by logging into a console session or by opening a Terminal program from a graphical desktop (see Book 1, Chapter 4).

## Storing stuff

You define variables in bash just as you define environment variables. Thus, you may define a variable as follows:

```
count=12
```

It's important to note that there can't be any spaces embedded in the statement. To use a variable's value, prefix the variable's name with a dollar sign ($). $PATH, for example, is the value of the variable PATH. (This variable is the famous PATH environment variable that lists all the directories that bash searches when trying to locate an executable file.) To display the value of the variable count, use the following command:

```
echo $count
```

bash has some special variables for accessing command-line arguments. As I mention earlier in this chapter, in a shell script, $0 refers to the name of the shell script. The variables $1, $2, and so on refer to the command-line arguments. The variable $* stores all the command-line arguments as a single variable, and $? contains the exit status of the last command the shell executes.

From a bash script, you can prompt the user for input and use the read command to read the input into a variable. Here's an example:

```
echo -n "Enter a value: "
read value
echo "You entered: $value"
```

When this script runs, the read value command causes bash to read whatever is typed in at the keyboard and store that input in the variable called value.

*Note:* The –n option prevents the echo command from automatically adding a new line at the end of the string that it displays. If that's not an option, Enter a value will be displayed, and the value will be read on a line following it. This doesn't change the operation in any way at all — only the aesthetics.

# Calling shell functions

You can group shell commands that you use consistently into a function and assign that function a name. Later, you can execute that group of commands by using the single name assigned to the function. Here's a simple script that illustrates the syntax of shell functions:

```
#!/bin/sh
hello() {
echo -n "Hello, "
echo $1 $2
}
hello Jane Doe
```

When you run this script, it displays the following output:

```
Hello, Jane Doe
```

This script defines a shell function named hello. The function expects two arguments. In the body of the function, these arguments are referenced by $1 and $2. The function definition begins with hello() — the name of the function, followed by parentheses. The body of the function is enclosed in curly braces — { ... }. In this case, the body uses the echo command to display a line of text.

The last line of the example shows how a shell function is called with arguments. In this case, the hello function is called with two arguments: Jane and Doe. The hello function takes these two arguments and prints a line that says Hello, Jane Doe.

# Controlling the flow

In bash scripts, you can control the flow of execution — the order in which the commands are executed — by using special commands such as if, case, for, and while. These control statements use the exit status of a command to decide what to do next. When any command executes, it returns an *exit status:* a numeric value that indicates whether the command has succeeded. By convention, an exit status of zero means that the command has succeeded. (Yes, you read it right: Zero indicates success!) A nonzero exit status indicates that something has gone wrong with the command.

Suppose that you want to make a backup copy of a file before editing it with the vi editor. More important, you want to avoid editing the file if a backup can't be made. Here's a bash script that takes care of this task (the user supplies the path, if necessary, and filename when running the script):

```
#!/bin/sh
if cp "$1" "#$1"
then
vi "$1"
else
echo "Operation failed to create a backup copy"
fi
```

This script illustrates the syntax of the if-then-else structure and shows how the if command uses the exit status of the cp command to determine the next action. If cp returns zero, the script uses vi to edit the file; otherwise, the script displays an error message and exits. By the way, the script saves the backup in a file whose name is the same as that of the original, except for a hash mark (#) added at the beginning of the filename.

TIP

Don't forget the final fi that terminates the if command. Forgetting fi is a common source of errors in bash scripts.

You can use the test command to evaluate any expression and to use the expression's value as the exit status of the command. Suppose that you want a script that edits a file only if it already exists and not create a blank file otherwise, as it normally would. Using test, you can write such a script as follows:

```
#!/bin/sh
if test -f "$1"
then
vi "$1"
else
echo "No such file exists"
fi
```

A shorter form of the test command places the expression in square brackets ([ ... ]). Using this shorthand notation, you can rewrite the preceding script like this:

```
#!/bin/sh
if [ -f "$1" ]
then
vi "$1"
else
echo "No such file exists"
fi
```

*Note:* You must have spaces around the two square brackets for this code to work because the left bracket ([) is an alias to test. If you don't leave the space, it's not seen the same as the name of the alias but rather as a part of the name of what you are trying to run.

Another common control structure is the for loop. The following script adds the numbers 1 through 10:

```
#!/bin/sh
sum=0
for i in 1 2 3 4 5 6 7 8 9 10
do
sum=`expr $sum + $i`
done
echo "Sum = $sum"
```

This example also illustrates the use of the expr command to evaluate an expression. It requires white space on both sides of the operand — the plus sign (+), in this case — and doesn't work properly without it.

The case statement is used to execute a group of commands based on the value of a variable. Consider the following script:

```
#!/bin/sh
echo -n "What should I do -- (Y)es/(N)o/(C)ontinue? [Y] "
read answer
case $answer in
y|Y|"")
echo "YES"
;;
c|C)
echo "CONTINUE"
;;
n|N)
echo "NO"
;;
```

```
*)
echo "UNKNOWN"
;;
esac
```

Save this code in a file named `confirm` and type **chmod +x confirm** to make it executable. Then try it out like this:

```
./confirm
```

When the script prompts you, type one of the characters y, n, or c and then press Enter. The script displays YES, NO, or CONTINUE, respectively. Here's what happens when you type **c** (and then press Enter):

```
What should I do -- (Y)es/(N)o/(C)ontinue? [Y] c
CONTINUE
```

The script displays a prompt and reads the input you type. Your input is stored in a variable named `answer`. Then the `case` statement executes a block of code based on the value of the `answer` variable. When you type **c**, for example, the following block of commands executes:

```
c|C)
echo "CONTINUE"
;;
```

The `echo` command causes the script to display CONTINUE.

From this example, you can see that the general syntax of the `case` command is as follows:

```
case $variable in
value1 | value2)
command1
command2
... other commands ...
;;
value3)
command3
command4
... other commands ...
;;
esac
```

Essentially, the case command begins with the word case and ends with esac. Separate blocks of code are enclosed between the values of the variable, followed by a closing parenthesis and terminated by a pair of semicolons (; ; ).

# Exploring bash's built-in commands

bash has more than 50 built-in commands, including common commands such as cd and pwd, as well as many others that are used infrequently. You can use these built-in commands in any bash script or at the shell prompt. Table 1-1 describes most of the bash built-in commands and their arguments. After looking through this information, type **help** *command* to read more about a specific built-in command. To find out more about the built-in command test, for example, type the following:

```
help test
```

**TABLE 1-1**     ## Summary of Built-in Commands in bash Shell

| This Function | Does the Following |
| --- | --- |
| . *filename* [*arguments*] | Reads and executes commands from the specified *filename* using the optional *arguments*. (Works the same way as the source command.) |
| : [*arguments*] | Expands the *arguments* but doesn't process them. |
| [ *expr* ] | Evaluates the expression *expr* and returns zero status if *expr* is true. |
| alias [*name*[=*value*] ... ] | Allows one *value* to equal another. You could set *xyz* to run *bg*, for example. |
| bg [*job*] | Puts the specified *job* in the background. If no *job* is specified, it puts the currently executing command in the background. |
| break [*n*] | Exits from a for, while, or until loop. If *n* is specified, the *n*th enclosing loop is exited. |
| cd [*dir*] | Changes the current directory to *dir*. |
| command [-pVv] *cmd* [*arg* ... ] | Runs the command *cmd* with the specified arguments (ignoring any shell function named *cmd*). |
| continue [*n*] | Starts the next iteration of the for, while, or until loop. If *n* is specified, the next iteration of the *n*th enclosing loop is started. |

*(continued)*

**TABLE 1-1** *(continued)*

| This Function | Does the Following |
|---|---|
| declare [-frxi] [*name*[=*value*]] | Declares a variable with the specified *name* and optionally, assigns it a *value*. |
| dirs [-l] [+/-*n*] | Displays the list of currently remembered directories. |
| echo [-neE] [*arg* ... ] | Displays the arguments, *arg* ... , on standard output. |
| enable [-n] [-all] | Enables or disables the specified built-in commands. |
| eval [*arg* ... ] | Concatenates the arguments, *arg* ... , and executes them as a command. |
| exec [*command* [*arguments*]] | Replaces the current instance of the shell with a new process that runs the specified *command* with the given *arguments*. |
| exit [*n*] | Exits the shell with the status code *n*. |
| export [-nf] [*name*[=*word*]] ... | Defines a specified environment variable and exports it to future processes. |
| fc -s [*pat*=*rep*] [*cmd*] | Re-executes the command after replacing the pattern *pat* with *rep*. |
| fg [*jobspec*] | Puts the specified job, *jobspec*, in the foreground. If no job is specified, it puts the most recent job in the foreground. |
| hash [-r] [*name*] | Remembers the full pathname of a specified command. |
| help [*cmd* ... ] | Displays help information for specified built-in commands, *cmd*. ... |
| history [*n*] | Displays past commands or past *n* commands, if you specify a number *n*. |
| jobs [-lnp] [ *jobspec* ... ] | Lists currently active jobs. |
| kill [-s *sigspec* \| -*sigspec*] [*pid* \| *jobspec*] ... | Ends the process specified. |
| let *arg* [*arg* ... ] | Evaluates each argument and returns 1 if the last *arg* is 0. |
| local [*name*[=*value*] ... ] | Creates a local variable with the specified *name* and *value* (used in shell functions). |
| logout | Exits a login shell. |
| popd [+/-*n*] | Removes the specified number of entries from the directory stack. |
| pushd [*dir*] | Adds a specified directory, *dir*, to the top of the directory stack. |
| pwd | Prints the full pathname of the current working directory. |

| This Function | Does the Following |
|---|---|
| read [-r] [name ... ] | Reads a line from standard input and parses it. |
| readonly [-f] [name ... ] | Marks the specified variables as read-only so that the variables can't be changed later. |
| return [n] | Exits the shell function with the return value n. |
| set [--abefhkmnptuvxldCHP] [-o option] [arg ... ] | Sets various flags. |
| shift [n] | Makes the n+1 argument $1, the n+2 argument $2, and so on. |
| times | Prints the accumulated user and system times for processes run from the shell. |
| trap [-l] [cmd] [sigspec] | Executes cmd when the signal sigspec is received. |
| type [-all] [-type |-path] name [name ... ] | Indicates how the shell interprets each name. |
| ulimit [-SHacdfmstpnuv [limit]] | Controls resources available to the shell. |
| umask [-S] [mode] | Sets the file creation mask — the default permission to the mode specified for the files. |
| unalias [-a] [name ... ] | Undefines a specified alias. |
| unset [-fv] [name ... ] | Removes the definition of specified variables. |
| wait [n] | Waits for a specified process (n represents its PID) to terminate. |

Doing so displays the following information:

```
test: test [expr]
Exits with a status of 0 (true) or 1 (false) depending on
the evaluation of EXPR. Expressions may be unary or binary. Unary
expressions are often used to examine the status of a file. There
are string operators as well, and numeric comparison operators.
File operators:
-a FILE True if file exists.
-b FILE True if file is block special.
-c FILE True if file is character special.
-d FILE True if file is a directory.
-e FILE True if file exists.
-f FILE True if file exists and is a regular file.
-g FILE True if file is set-group-id.
-h FILE True if file is a symbolic link.
-L FILE True if file is a symbolic link.
-k FILE True if file has its 'sticky' bit set.
```

```
-p FILE True if file is a named pipe.
-r FILE True if file is readable by you.
-s FILE True if file exists and is not empty.
-S FILE True if file is a socket.
-t FD True if FD is opened on a terminal.
-u FILE True if the file is set-user-id.
-w FILE True if the file is writable by you.
-x FILE True if the file is executable by you.
-O FILE True if the file is effectively owned by you.
-G FILE True if the file is effectively owned by your group.
(... Lines deleted ...)
```

Where necessary, the online help from the help command includes a considerable amount of detail.

**WARNING**

Some external programs may have the same name as bash built-in commands. If you want to run any such external program, you must explicitly specify the full pathname of that program. Otherwise, bash executes the built-in command of the same name and never looks for the external program.

Chapter **2**

# Advanced Shell Scripting

The preceding chapter introduced you to some of the power available through shell scripting. All the scripts in that chapter are simple bash routines that allow you to run commands and repeat operations a number of times.

This chapter builds upon that knowledge by showing how to incorporate two powerful tools — sed and awk — into your scripts. These two utilities move your scripts to the place where the only limit to what you can do becomes your ability to figure out how to ask for the output you need. Although sed is the stream editor and awk is a quick programming language, they complement each other so well that it's not uncommon to use one with the other. The best way to show how these tools work is to walk you through some examples.

## Trying Out sed

The following are sample lines of a colon-delimited employee database that has five fields: unique ID number, name, department, phone number, and address.

```
1218:Kris Cottrell:Marketing:219.555.5555:123 Main Street
1219:Nate Eichhorn:Sales:219.555.5555:1219 Locust Avenue
1220:Joe Gunn:Payables:317.555.5555:21974 Unix Way
1221:Anne Heltzel:Finance:219.555.5555:652 Linux Road
1222:John Kuzmic:Human Resources:219.555.5555:984 Bash Lane
```

Imagine that this database has been in existence since the beginning of the company and includes far more than these five entries. Over time, the database has grown to include everyone who now works, or has ever worked, for the company. Several proprietary scripts read from the database, and the company can't afford to be without it. The problem is that the telephone company in one part of the country has changed the 219 prefix to 260, so all entries in the database that use that prefix need to be changed.

This is precisely the task for which sed was created. As opposed to standard (interactive) editors, a *stream editor* works its way through a file line by line and makes changes based on the rules it's given. The rule in this case seems to be to change 219 to 260, but the task isn't quite that simple. To illustrate, if you use the command

```
sed 's/219/260/'
```

the result you get is not completely what you want it to be (all changes are in **bold**):

```
1218:Kris Cottrell:Marketing:260.555.5555:123 Main Street
1260:Nate Eichhorn:Sales:219.555.5555:1219 Locust Avenue
1220:Joe Gunn:Payables:317.555.5555:26074 Unix Way
1221:Anne Heltzel:Finance:260.555.5555:652 Linux Road
1222:John Kuzmic:Human Resources:260.555.5555:984 Bash Lane
```

The changes in the first, fourth, and fifth lines are correct. But in the second line, the first occurrence of 219 appears in the employee ID number rather than in the phone number and was changed to 260. If you wanted to change more than the very first occurrence in a line, you could slap a g (for *global*) into the command:

```
sed 's/219/260/g'
```

That's *not* what you want to do in this case, however, because the employee ID number shouldn't change as a result of this change to the phone prefix. Similarly troublesome, in the third line, a change was made to the address because it contains the value that's being searched for; no change should have been made to this line at all because the employee doesn't have the 219 telephone prefix.

The first rule of using sed is always to identify what makes the location of the string you're looking for unique. If the telephone prefix were encased in parentheses, it would be much easier to isolate. In this database, though, that isn't the case; the task becomes a bit more complicated.

If you said that the telephone prefix must appear at the beginning of the field (denoted by a colon), the result would be much closer to what you want:

```
sed 's/:219/:260/'
```

Again, bolding has been added to show the changes that this command will produce:

```
1218:Kris Cottrell:Marketing:260.555.5555:123 Main Street
1219:Nate Eichhorn:Sales:260.555.5555:1219 Locust Avenue
1220:Joe Gunn:Payables:317.555.5555:26074 Unix Way
1221:Anne Heltzel:Finance:260.555.5555:652 Linux Road
1222:John Kuzmic:Human Resources:260.555.5555:984 Bash Lane
```

Although the accuracy has increased, there's still the problem of the third line in the limited sample (and you don't know how many other lines would be affected in the larger database). Because the colon helped identify the start of the string, it may be tempting to turn to the period to identify the end:

```
sed 's/:219./:260./'
```

But once again, the result still isn't what you hoped for (note the third line):

```
1218:Kris Cottrell:Marketing:260.555.5555:123 Main Street
1219:Nate Eichhorn:Sales:260.555.5555:1219 Locust Avenue
1220:Joe Gunn:Payables:317.555.5555:260.4 Unix Way
1221:Anne Heltzel:Finance:260.555.5555:652 Linux Road
1222:John Kuzmic:Human Resources:260.555.5555:984 Bash Lane
```

The problem, in this instance, is that the period has the special meaning of standing for *any character*, so a match is found whether the 219 is followed by a period, a 7, or any other single character. Whatever the character, it's replaced with a period. The replacement side of things isn't the problem; the search needs to be tweaked. By using the \ character, you can override the special meaning of the period and specify that you're indeed looking for a period and not any single character:

```
sed 's/:219\./:260./'
```

The result becomes

```
1218:Kris Cottrell:Marketing:260.555.5555:123 Main Street
1219:Nate Eichhorn:Sales:260.555.5555:1219 Locust Avenue
1220:Joe Gunn:Payables:317.555.5555:21974 Unix Way
1221:Anne Heltzel:Finance:260.555.5555:652 Linux Road
1222:John Kuzmic:Human Resources:260.555.5555:984 Bash Lane
```

And with that, the mission is accomplished.

# Working with awk and sed

The second example to look at involves a legacy database of books that includes the International Standard Book Number (ISBN) of each title. In the old days, ISBN numbers were ten digits and included an identifier for the publisher and a unique number for each book. ISBN numbers are now 13 digits for new books and have been so for several years. Old books (those published before the first of 2007) have both the old 10-digit number and a new 13-digit number that can be used to identify them because the longer number is a variation on the shorter. For this example, to bring the database up to current standards, the existing 10-digit number will stay in the database, and a new field — holding the ISBN-13 number — will be added to the end of each entry.

To come up with the ISBN-13 number for the existing entries in the database, you start with 978 and then use the first 9 digits of the old ISBN number. The 13th digit is a mathematical calculation (a *check digit*) obtained by doing the following:

1. Add all odd-placed digits (the first, the third, the fifth, and so on).

2. Multiply all even-placed digits by 3 and add them.

3. Add the total of Step 2 to the total of Step 1.

4. Find out what you need to add to round the number up to the nearest 10.

   This value becomes the 13th digit.

Consider the 10-digit ISBN 0743477103. It first becomes 978074347710, and then the steps work out like this:

1. 9+8+7+3+7+1=35.

2. 7*3=21; 0*3=0; 4*3=12; 4*3=12; 7*3=21; 0*3=0; 21+0+12+12+21+0=66.

3. 66+35=101.

4. 110-101=9.

   The ISBN-13 becomes 9780743477109.

The beginning database resembles

```
0743477103:Macbeth:Shakespeare, William
1578518520:The Innovator's Solution:Christensen, Clayton M.
0321349946:(SCTS) Symantec Certified Technical Specialist:Alston, Nik
1587052415:Cisco Network Admission Control, Volume I:Helfrich, Denise
```

And you want the resulting database to change so that each line resembles something like this:

```
0743477103:Macbeth:Shakespeare, William:9780743477109
```

The example that follows accomplishes this goal. It's not the prettiest thing ever written, but it walks you through the process of tackling this problem, illustrating the use of awk and sed. I also include the steps of having the script write to temporary files so that you can examine those files and see their contents at various stages of the operations. Clean programming mitigates the use of temporary files everywhere possible, but that practice also makes it difficult to follow the action at times. That said, here's one solution out of dozens of possibilities. Read on.

## Step 1: Pull out the ISBN

Given the database as it now exists, the first order of business is to pull out the existing ISBN — only the first nine digits, because the tenth digit, which was just a checksum for the first nine, no longer matters — and slap 978 onto the beginning. The nine digits you want are the first nine characters of each line, so you can pull them out by using the cut utility:

```
cut -c1-9 books
```

Because a mathematical operation will be performed on the numbers comprising this value, and because that operation works with each digit, add a space between each number and the next one in the new entry:

```
sed 's/[0-9]/& /g'
```

Now it's time to add the new code to the beginning of each entry (the start of every line):

```
sed 's/^/9 7 8 /'
```

Finally, do an extra step: removing the white space at the end of the line just to make the entry a bit cleaner:

```
sed 's/ $//'
```

Then write the results to a temporary file that you can examine to make sure that all is working as it should. Then the full first step becomes

```
cut -c1-9 books | sed 's/[0-9]/& /g' | sed 's/^/9 7 8 /' | sed 's/ $//' > isbn2
```

*Note:* The `sed` operations could be combined in a script file to increase speed and decrease cycles. I'm walking you through each operation step by step to show what's going on, however, and am not worried about creating script files for this one-time-only operation.

Examining the temporary file, you see that the contents are as follows:

```
9 7 8 0 7 4 3 4 7 7 1 0
9 7 8 1 5 7 8 5 1 8 5 2
9 7 8 0 3 2 1 3 4 9 9 4
9 7 8 1 5 8 7 0 5 2 4 1
```

## Step 2: Calculate the 13th digit

You've taken care of the first 12 digits of the ISBN number. Now you need to compute those 12 digits to figure out the 13th value. Because the numbers are separated by a space, awk can interpret them as fields. The calculation takes several steps:

1. Add all the odd-placed digits:

   x=$1+$3+$5+$7+$9+$11

2. Add all the even-placed digits and multiply by 3:

   y=($2+$4+$6+$8+$10+$12)*3

3. Add the total of Step 2 to the total of Step 1:

   x=x+y

4. Find out what you need to add to round the number up to the nearest 10 by computing the modulo when divided by 10 and then subtracting it from 10.

   The following awk command gets everything in place except the transformation:

   ```
   awk '{ x=$1+$3+$5+$7+$9+$11 ; y=$2+$4+$6+$8+$10+$12 ; y=y*3
   ; x=x+y ; y=x%10 ; print y }'
   ```

Everything is finished except subtracting the final result from 10, which is the hardest part. If the modulo is 7, for example, the check digit is 3. If the modulo is 0, however, the check digit doesn't become 10 (10 – 0); it stays 0. My solution is to use the transform function of sed:

```
sed 'y/12346789/98764321/'
```

Combining the two operations into one, the second step becomes

```
awk '{ x=$1+$3+$5+$7+$9+$11 ; y=$2+$4+$6+$8+$10+$12 ; y=y*3 ; x=x+y ; y=x%10 ;
    print y }' | sed 'y/12346789/98764321/' > isbn3
```

Examining the temporary file, you see that the contents are

```
9
4
1
5
```

## Step 3: Add the 13th digit to the other 12

The two temporary files (one with 12 digits and the other with 1) can now be combined to get the correct 13-digit ISBN number. Just as you used cut in the earlier step, you can use paste now to combine the files. The default delimiter for paste is a tab, but you can change that delimiter to anything with the –d option. I use a space as the delimiter and then use sed to strip the spaces (remember that the isbn2 file has spaces between the digits so that they can be read as fields):

```
paste –d" " isbn2 isbn3 | sed 's/ //g'
```

Finally, add a colon as the first character of each entry to make it easier to append the newly computed ISBN to the existing file:

```
sed 's/^/:/'
```

The entire command becomes

```
paste –d" " isbn2 isbn3 | sed 's/ //g' | sed 's/^/:/' > isbn4
```

Examining the temporary file, you see that the contents are

```
:9780743477109
:9781578518524
:9780321349941
:9781587052415
```

## Step 4: Finish the process

The only operation remaining is to append the values in the temporary file to the current database. You use the default tab delimiter in the entry and then strip it out. Technically, you could specify a colon as the delimiter and avoid the last part of the final steps. But you'd rather have your value complete there and be confident that you're stripping characters that don't belong (tabs) instead of adding more characters than should be there. The final command is

```
paste books isbn4 | sed 's/\t//g' > newbooks
```

The final file looks like this:

```
0743477103:Macbeth:Shakespeare, William:9780743477109
1578518520:The Innovator's Solution:Christensen, Clayton M.:9781578518524
0321349946:(SCTS) Symantec Certified Technical Specialist:Alston,
    Nik:9780321349941
1587052415:Cisco Network Admission Control, Volume I:Helfrich,
    Denise:9781587052415
```

Again, you can accomplish this result in many ways. This solution isn't the cleanest, but it does illustrate the down-and-dirty use of sed and awk.

# Final Notes on Shell Scripting

As with any other aspect of computing, it takes a while to get used to shell scripting. After you become comfortable writing scripts, however, you'll find that you can automate any number of operations and simplify your task as an administrator. The following tips can be helpful to keep in mind:

>> After you create a script, you can run it automatically on a one-time basis by using at or on a regular basis by using cron.

>> You can use conditional expressions — such as if, while, and until — to look for events to occur (such as certain users accessing a file they shouldn't) or to let you know when something that should be there goes away (a file is removed or a user terminates, for example).

>> You can set permissions on shell scripts in the same way that you set permissions for other files. You can create scripts that are shared by all members of your administrative group, for example. (Use case to create menus based upon LOGNAME.)

IN THIS CHAPTER

» **Understanding programming**

» **Exploring software-development tools in Linux**

» **Compiling and linking programs with GCC**

» **Using make**

» **Debugging programs with gdb**

» **Understanding the implications of GNU, GPL, and LGPL**

Chapter **3**

# Programming in Linux

L inux comes loaded with all the tools you need to develop software; often, all you have to do is install them. In particular, Linux has all the GNU software-development tools, such as GCC (C and C++ compiler), GNU make, and the GNU debugger. Whereas the previous two chapters look at some simple tools and shell scripts, this chapter introduces you to programming, describes the software-development tools, and shows you how to use them. Although I provide examples in the C and C++ programming languages, the focus isn't on showing you how to program in those languages but on showing you how to use various software-development tools (such as compilers, make, and debugger).

The chapter concludes with a brief explanation of how the Free Software Foundation's GNU General Public License (GPL) may affect any plans you might have to develop Linux software. You need to know about the GPL because you use GNU tools and GNU libraries to develop software in Linux.

# An Overview of Programming

If you've ever written a computer program in any language — even one of the shell scripts from the Chapters 1 and 2 — you can start writing programs on your Linux system quickly. If you've never written a computer program, however, you need two basic resources before you begin to write code: a look at the basics of programming and a quick review of computers and their major parts. This section offers an overview of computer programming — just enough to get you going.

At its simplest, a *computer program* is a sequence of instructions for performing a specific task such as adding two numbers or searching for some text in a file. Consequently, computer programming involves *creating* that list of instructions, telling the computer how to complete a specific task. The exact instructions depend on the programming language that you use. For most programming languages, you have to go through the following steps to create a computer program:

1. **Use a text editor to type the sequence of commands from the programming language.**

   This sequence of commands accomplishes your task. This human-readable version of the program is called the *source file* or *source code.* You can create the source file with any application (such as a word processor) that can save a document in plain-text form.

**REMEMBER**

   Always save your source code as plain text. (The filename depends on the type of programming language.) Word processors can sometimes put extra instructions in their documents that tell the computer to display the text in a particular font or other format. Saving the file as plain text deletes any and all such extra instructions. Trust me: Your program is much better off without such stuff.

2. **Use a *compiler* program to convert that text file — the source code — from human-readable form into machine-readable *object code.***

   Typically, this step also combines several object code files into a single machine-readable computer program — something that the computer can run.

3. **Use a special program called a *debugger* to track down any errors and find which lines in the source file might have caused the errors.**

4. **Go back to Step 1, use the text editor to correct the errors, and repeat the rest of the steps.**

These steps are referred to as the *edit–compile–debug cycle* of programming because most programmers have to repeat this sequence several times before a program works correctly.

In addition to knowing the basic programming steps, you need to be familiar with the following terms and concepts:

» *Variables* are used to store different types of data. You can think of each variable as being a placeholder for data — kind of like a mailbox, with a name and room to store data. The content of the variable is its *value*.

» *Expressions* combine variables by using mathematical operators or text manipulation functions. One expression may add several variables; another may extract a part of a *string* (a series of sequential characters).

» *Statements* perform some action, such as assigning a value to a variable or printing a string.

» *Flow-control statements* allow statements to execute in various orders, depending on the value of some expression. Typically, flow-control statements include for, do-while, while, and if-then-else statements.

» *Functions* (also called *subroutines* or *routines*) allow you to group several statements and give the group a name. You can use functions to execute the same set of statements over and over by invoking the function that represents those statements. Typically, a programming language provides many predefined functions to perform tasks, such as opening (and reading from) a file, and you can create your own functions for similar tasks.

# Exploring the Software-Development Tools in Linux

Linux supports all of the following traditional Unix software-development tools:

» **Text editors** such as vi and emacs for editing the source code. (To find out more about vi, see Book 2, Chapter 6.)

» A **C compiler** for compiling and linking programs written in C — the programming language of choice for writing Unix applications (though nowadays, many programmers are turning to C++ and Java). Linux includes the GNU C and C++ compilers. Originally, the GNU C compiler was known as GCC, which now stands for *GNU Compiler Collection*. (See a description at https://gcc.gnu.org.)

» The **GNU make utility** for automating the software *build process* — the process of combining object modules into an executable or a library. (The operating system can load and run an *executable*; a *library* is a collection of binary code that can be used by executables.)

>> A **debugger** for debugging programs. Linux distributions often include the GNU debugger gdb.

>> A **version control system** to keep track of various revisions of a source file. Quite a few legacy version control system packages are available for Linux, such as the Revision Control System (RCS), Concurrent Versions System (CVS), and Subversion (a replacement for CVS). However, the Git version control system is quickly becoming the de facto standard in the Linux world, because it was created by Linus Torvalds to track files in the Linux project itself.

TIP

You can install these software-development tools in any Linux distribution. In some distributions, the tools are installed by default. If they're not in the distribution you're using, you can type apt-get install gcc and then apt-get install libc6-dev as root in a terminal window (Debian) or choose to install the Development Tools package through the graphical interface (Fedora, SuSE, Ubuntu, and so on).

The next few sections briefly describe how to use these software-development tools to write applications for Linux.

## GNU C and C++ compilers

The most important software-development tool in Linux is GCC — the GNU C and C++ compiler. In fact, GCC can compile three languages: C, C++, and Objective-C (a language that adds object-oriented programming capabilities to C). You use the same gcc command to compile and link both C and C++ source files. The GCC compiler supports ANSI-standard C, making it easy to port any ANSI C program to Linux. In addition, if you've ever used a C compiler on other Unix systems, you should feel right at home with GCC.

### Using GCC

Use the gcc command to invoke GCC. By default, when you use the gcc command on a source file, GCC preprocesses, compiles, and links to create an executable file. You can use GCC options to stop this process at an intermediate stage, however. You might invoke gcc by using the –c option to compile a source file and to generate an object file, but not to perform the link step.

Using GCC to compile and link a few C source files is easy. Suppose that you want to compile and link a simple program made up of two source files. To accomplish this task, use the following program source code. The task that's stored in the file `area.c` computes the area of a circle whose radius is specified at the command line:

```
#include <stdio.h>
#include <stdlib.h>
/* Function prototype */
double area_of_circle(double r);
int main(int argc, char **argv)
{
if(argc < 2)
{
printf("Usage: %s radius\n", argv[0]);
exit(1);
}
else
{
double radius = atof(argv[1]);
double area = area_of_circle(radius);
printf("Area of circle with radius %f = %f\n",
radius, area);
}
return 0;
}
```

You need another file that actually computes the area of a circle. Here's the listing for the `circle.c` file, which defines a function that computes the area of a circle:

```
#include <math.h>
#define SQUARE(x) ((x)*(x))
double area_of_circle(double r)
{
return M_PI * SQUARE(r);
}
```

For such a simple program, of course, you could place everything in a single file, but this example is a bit contrived to show you how to handle multiple files.

To compile these two files and create an executable file named `area`, use this command:

```
gcc -o area area.c circle.c
```

This invocation of GCC uses the −o option to specify the name of the executable file. (If you don't specify the name of an output file with the −o option, GCC saves the executable code in a file named a.out.)

If you have too many source files to compile and link, you can compile the files individually and generate *object files* (that have the .o extension). That way, when you change a source file, you need to compile only that file; you just link the compiled file to all the object files. The following commands show how to separate the compile and link steps for the sample program:

```
gcc −c area.c
gcc −c circle.c
gcc −o area area.o circle.o
```

The first two commands run gcc with the −c option compiling the source files. The third gcc command links the object files into an executable named area. After you've compiled the program, you can run the area program from the command line:

```
rich@Ubuntu22:~$ ./area 5
Area of circle with radius 5.000000 = 78.539816
rich@Ubuntu22:~$
```

## Compiling C++ programs

GNU CC is a combined C and C++ compiler, so the gcc command also can compile C++ source files. GCC uses the file extension to determine whether a file is C or C++. C files have a lowercase .c extension, whereas C++ files end with .C or .cpp.

**REMEMBER**

Although the gcc command can compile a C++ file, that command doesn't automatically link with various class libraries that C++ programs typically require. Compiling and linking a C++ program by using the g++ command is easy because it runs gcc with appropriate options. However, for some distributions (such as Ubuntu) you need to install g++ as a separate package.

Suppose that you want to compile the following simple C++ program stored in a file named hello.C. (Using an uppercase C extension for C++ source files is customary.)

```
#include <iostream>
int main()
{
using namespace std;
cout << "Hello! This is Linux!" << endl;
}
```

To compile and link this program into an executable program named `hello`, use this command:

```
g++ -o hello hello.C
```

The command creates the `hello` executable, which you can run as follows:

```
./hello
```

The program displays the following output:

```
Hello! This is Linux!
```

A host of GCC options controls various aspects of compiling C and C++ programs.

## Exploring GCC options

Here's the basic syntax of the `gcc` command:

```
gcc options filenames
```

Each option starts with a hyphen (–) and usually has a long name, such as `-funsigned-char` or `-finline-functions`. Many commonly used options are short, however, such as `-c`, to compile only, and `-g`, to generate debugging information (needed to debug the program by using the GNU debugger, `gdb`).

You can view a summary of all GCC options by typing the following command in a terminal window:

```
man gcc
```

Then you can browse through the commonly used GCC options. Usually, you don't have to provide GCC options explicitly because the default settings are fine for most applications. Table 3-1 lists some of the GCC options you may use.

## The GNU make utility

When an application is made up of more than a few source files, compiling and linking the files by manually typing the `gcc` command can get tiresome. Also, you don't want to compile every file whenever you change something in a single source file. This is where the GNU `make` utility comes to your rescue.

**TABLE 3-1**     **Common GCC Options**

| Option | Meaning |
| --- | --- |
| -ansi | Supports only ANSI-standard C syntax. (This option disables some GNU C-specific features, such as the __asm__ and __typeof__ keywords.) When used with g++, supports only ISO-standard C++. |
| -c | Compiles and generates only the object file. |
| -D*MACRO* | Defines the macro with the string "1" as its value. |
| -D*MACRO=DEFN* | Defines the macro as *DEFN*, where *DEFN* is some text string. |
| -E | Runs only the C preprocessor. |
| -fallow-single-precision | Performs all math operations in single precision. |
| -fpcc-struct-return | Returns all struct and union values in memory, rather than in registers. (Returning values this way is less efficient, but at least it's compatible with other compilers.) |
| -fPIC | Generates position-independent code (PIC) suitable for use in a shared library. |
| -freg-struct-return | When possible, returns struct and union values registers. |
| -g | Generates debugging information. (The GNU debugger can use this information.) |
| -I *DIRECTORY* | Searches the specified directory for files that you include by using the #include preprocessor directive. |
| -L *DIRECTORY* | Searches the specified directory for libraries. |
| -l *LIBRARY* | Searches the specified library when linking. |
| -o *FILE* | Generates the specified output file (used to designate the name of an executable file). |
| -O0 (two zeros) | Doesn't optimize. |
| -O or -O1 (letter O) | Optimizes the generated code. |
| -O2 (letter O) | Optimizes more than those done for -O. |
| -O3 (letter O) | Performs optimizations even beyond those done for -O2. |
| -Os (letter O) | Optimizes for size (to reduce the total amount of code). |
| -pedantic | Generates errors if any non-ANSI-standard extensions are used. |
| -pg | Adds extra code to the program so that, when run, this program generates information that the gprof program can use to display timing details for various parts of the program. |

| Option | Meaning |
|---|---|
| -shared | Generates a shared object file (typically used to create a shared library). |
| -UMACRO | Undefines the specified macros. |
| -v | Displays the GCC version number. |
| -w | Doesn't generate warning messages. |
| -Wl, OPTION | Passes the OPTION string (containing multiple comma-separated options) to the linker. To create a shared library named libXXX.so.1, for example, use the following flag: -Wl,-soname,libXXX.so.1. |

The make utility works by reading and interpreting a *makefile* — a text file that describes which files are required to build a particular program, as well as how to compile and link the files to build the program. Whenever you change one or more files, make determines which files to recompile, and it issues the appropriate commands for compiling those files and rebuilding the program.

## Makefile names

By default, GNU make looks for a makefile that has one of the following names, in the order shown:

>> GNUmakefile

>> makefile

>> Makefile

In Unix systems, using Makefile as the name of the makefile is customary because it appears near the beginning of directory listings where uppercase names appear before lowercase names.

When you download software from the Internet, you usually find a Makefile together with the source files. To build the software, you only have to type **make** at the shell prompt; make takes care of all the steps necessary to build the software. Note that sometimes you may need to run configuration scripts, install additional packages, or add libraries before running make.

If your makefile doesn't have a standard name (such as Makefile), you have to use the -f option with make to specify the makefile name. If your makefile is called `myprogram.mak`, for example, you have to run `make` using the following command line:

```
make -f myprogram.mak
```

## The makefile

For a program made up of several source and header files, the `makefile` specifies the following:

» The items that `make` creates — usually, the object files and the executable. Using the term *target* to refer to any item that `make` has to create is common.

» The files or other actions required to create the target.

» Which commands to execute to create each target.

Suppose that you have a C++ source file named `form.C` that contains the following preprocessor directive:

```
#include "form.h" // Include header file
```

The object file `form.o` clearly depends on the source file `form.C` and the header file `form.h`. In addition to these dependencies, you must specify how `make` converts the `form.C` file to the object file `form.o`. Suppose that you want `make` to invoke `g++` (because the source file is in C++) with these options:

» -c (compile only)

» -g (generate debugging information)

» -02 (optimize more)

In the `makefile`, you can express these options with the following rule:

```
# This a comment in the makefile
# The following lines indicate how form.o depends
# on form.C and form.h and how to create form.o.
form.o: form.C form.h
g++ -c -g -02 form.C
```

In this example, the first noncomment line shows `form.o` as the target and `form.C` and `form.h` as the dependent files.

**WARNING**

The line following the dependency indicates how to build the target from its dependents. This line must start with a tab. Otherwise, the make command exits with an error message, and you're left scratching your head because when you look at the makefile in a text editor, you can't tell the difference between a tab and a space. Now that you know the secret, the fix is to replace the space at the beginning of the offending line with a single tab.

The benefit of using make is that it prevents unnecessary compilations. After all, you can run g++ (or gcc) from a shell script to compile and link all the files that make up your application, but the shell script compiles everything, even if the compilations are unnecessary. GNU make, on the other hand, builds a target only if one or more of its dependents have changed since the last time the target was built. make verifies this change by examining the time of the last modification of the target and the dependents.

make treats the target as the name of a goal to be achieved; the target doesn't have to be a file. You can have a rule such as this one:

```
clean:
rm -f *.o
```

This rule specifies an abstract target named clean that doesn't depend on anything. This dependency statement says that to create the target clean, GNU make invokes the command rm -f *.o, which deletes all files that have the .o extension (namely, the object files). Thus, the effect of creating the target named clean is to delete the object files.

## Variables (or macros)

In addition to the basic capability of building targets from dependents, GNU make includes many features that make it easy for you to express the dependencies and rules for building a target from its dependents. If you need to compile a large number of C++ files by using GCC with the same options, for example, typing the options for each file is tedious. You can avoid this repetitive task by defining a variable or macro in make as follows:

```
# Define macros for name of compiler
CXX= g++
# Define a macro for the GCC flags
CXXFLAGS= -O2 -g -mcpu=i686
# A rule for building an object file
form.o: form.C form.h
$(CXX) -c $(CXXFLAGS) form.C
```

In this example, CXX and CXXFLAGS are make variables. (GNU make prefers to call them *variables*, but most Unix make utilities call them *macros*.)

To use a variable anywhere in the makefile, start with a dollar sign ($) followed by the variable within parentheses. GNU make replaces all occurrences of a variable with its definition; thus, it replaces all occurrences of $(CXXFLAGS) with the string –O2 –g –mcpu=i686.

GNU make has several predefined variables that have special meanings. Table 3-2 lists these variables. In addition to the variables listed in Table 3-2, GNU make considers all environment variables (such as PATH and HOME) to be predefined variables as well.

**TABLE 3-2**      **Some Predefined Variables in GNU make**

| Variable | Meaning |
|----------|---------|
| $% | Member name for targets that are archives. If the target is libDisp.a(image.o), for example, $% is image.o. |
| $* | Name of the target file without the extension. |
| $+ | Names of all dependent files with duplicate dependencies, listed in their order of occurrence. |
| $< | The name of the first dependent file. |
| $? | Names of all dependent files (with spaces between the names) that are newer than the target. |
| $@ | Complete name of the target. If the target is libDisp.a(image.o), for example, $@ is libDisp.a. |
| $^ | Names of all dependent files, with spaces between the names. Duplicates are removed from the dependent filenames. |
| AR | Name of the archive-maintaining program (default value: ar). |
| ARFLAGS | Flags for the archive-maintaining program (default value: rv). |
| AS | Name of the assembler program that converts the assembly language to object code (default value: as). |
| ASFLAGS | Flags for the assembler. |
| CC | Name of the C compiler (default value: cc). |
| CFLAGS | Flags that are passed to the C compiler. |
| CO | Name of the program that extracts a file from RCS (default value: co). |
| COFLAGS | Flags for the RCS co program. |

| Variable | Meaning |
|---|---|
| CPP | Name of the C preprocessor (default value: $(CC) -E). |
| CPPFLAGS | Flags for the C preprocessor. |
| CXX | Name of the C++ compiler (default value: g++). |
| CXXFLAGS | Flags that are passed to the C++ compiler. |
| FC | Name of the FORTRAN compiler (default value: f77). |
| FFLAGS | Flags for the FORTRAN compiler. |
| LDFLAGS | Flags for the compiler when it's supposed to invoke the linker ld. |
| RM | Name of the command to delete a file (default value: rm -f). |

## A sample makefile

You can write a makefile easily if you use the predefined variables of GNU make and its built-in rules. Consider, for example, a makefile that creates the executable xdraw from three C source files (xdraw.c, xviewobj.c, and shapes.c) and two header files (xdraw.h and shapes.h). Assume that each source file includes one of the header files. Given these facts, here's what a sample makefile may look like:

```
##########################################################
# Sample makefile
# Comments start with '#'
#
##########################################################
# Use standard variables to define compile and link flags
CFLAGS= -g -O2
# Define the target "all"
all: xdraw
OBJS=xdraw.o xviewobj.o shapes.o
xdraw: $(OBJS)
# Object files
xdraw.o: Makefile xdraw.c xdraw.h
xviewobj.o: Makefile xviewobj.c xdraw.h
shapes.o: Makefile shapes.c shapes.h
```

This makefile relies on GNU make's implicit rules. The conversion of .c files to .o files uses the built-in rule. Defining the variable CFLAGS passes the flags to the C compiler.

**TECHNICAL STUFF**

The target named `all` is defined as the first target for a reason: If you run GNU `make` without specifying any targets in the command line (see the `make` syntax described in the following section), the command builds the first target it finds in the `makefile`. By defining the first target `all` as `xdraw`, you can ensure that `make` builds this executable file, even if you don't explicitly specify it as a target. Unix programmers traditionally use `all` as the name of the first target, but the target's name is immaterial; what matters is that it's the first target in the `makefile`.

## How to run make

Typically, you run `make` simply by typing the following command at the shell prompt:

```
make
```

When run this way, GNU `make` looks for a file named GNUmakefile, `makefile`, or Makefile, in that order. If `make` finds one of these `makefiles`, it builds the first target specified in that `makefile`. If `make` doesn't find an appropriate `makefile`, however, it displays the following error message and exits:

```
make: *** No targets specified and no makefile found.  Stop.
```

If your `makefile` happens to have a different name from the default names, you have to use the `-f` option to specify the `makefile`. The syntax of the `make` command with this option is

```
make -f filename
```

where *filename* is the name of the `makefile`.

Even when you have a `makefile` with a default name such as Makefile, you may want to build a specific target out of several targets defined in the `makefile`. In that case, you have to use the following syntax when you run `make`:

```
make target
```

If the `makefile` contains the target named `clean`, for example, you can build that target with this command:

```
make clean
```

Another special syntax overrides the value of a `make` variable. GNU `make` uses the CFLAGS variable to hold the flags used when compiling C files, for example. You can override the value of this variable when you invoke make. Here's an example of how you can define CFLAGS as the option -g -O2:

```
make CFLAGS="-g -O2"
```

In addition to these options, GNU make accepts several command-line options. Table 3-3 lists the GNU make options.

**TABLE 3-3** **Options for GNU make**

| Option | Meaning |
|--------|---------|
| -b | Ignores the variable given but accepts that variable for compatibility with other versions of make. |
| -C DIR | Changes to the specified directory before reading the makefile. |
| -d | Prints debugging information. |
| -e | Allows environment variables to override definitions of similarly named variables in the makefile. |
| -f FILE | Reads FILE as the makefile. |
| -h | Displays the list of make options. |
| -i | Ignores all errors in commands executed when building a target. |
| -I DIR | Searches the specified directory for included makefiles. (The capability to include a file in a makefile is unique to GNU make.) |
| -j NUM | Specifies the number of jobs that make can run simultaneously. |
| -k | Continues to build unrelated targets, even if an error occurs when building one of the targets. |
| -l LOAD | Doesn't start a new job if load average is at least LOAD (a floating-point number). |
| -m | Ignores the variable given but accepts that variable for compatibility with other versions of make. |
| -n | Prints the commands to execute but does not execute them. |
| -o FILE | Does not rebuild the file named FILE, even if it is older than its dependents. |
| -p | Displays the make database of variables and implicit rules. |
| -q | Does not run anything but returns 0 (zero) if all targets are up to date, 1 if anything needs updating, or 2 if an error occurs. |
| -r | Gets rid of all built-in rules. |
| -R | Gets rid of all built-in variables and rules. |

*(continued)*

**TABLE 3-3** *(continued)*

| Option | Meaning |
|---|---|
| −s | Works silently (without displaying the commands as they execute). |
| −t | Changes the time stamp of the files. |
| −v | Displays the version number of make, licensing information, and a copyright notice. |
| −w | Displays the name of the working directory before and after processing the makefile. |
| −W *FILE* | Assumes that the specified file has been modified (used with −n to see what happens if you modify that file). |

# The GNU debugger

Although make automates the process of building a program, that part of programming is the least of your worries when a program doesn't work correctly or when a program suddenly quits with an error message. You need a debugger to find the cause of program errors. Linux includes gdb — the versatile GNU debugger with a command-line interface.

Like any debugger, gdb lets you perform typical debugging tasks, such as the following:

>> Set a breakpoint so that the program stops at a specified line.

>> Watch the values of variables in the program.

>> Step through the program one line at a time.

>> Change variables in an attempt to correct errors.

The gdb debugger can debug C and C++ programs.

## Preparing to debug a program

If you want to debug a program by using gdb, you have to ensure that the compiler generates and places debugging information in the executable. The debugging information contains the names of variables in your program and the mapping of addresses in the executable file to lines of code in the source file. gdb needs this information to perform its functions such as stopping after executing a specified line of source code.

**TIP**

To make sure that the executable is properly prepared for debugging, use the −g option with GCC or G++. You can do this task by defining the variable CFLAGS in the makefile as

```
CFLAGS= -g
```

## Running gdb

The most common way to debug a program is to run gdb by using the following command:

```
gdb progname
```

progname is the name of the program's executable file. After progname runs, gdb displays the following message and prompts you for a command:

```
GNU gdb (Ubuntu 9.2-0ubuntu1~20.04.1) 9.2
Copyright (C) 2020 Free Software Foundation, Inc.
License GPLv3+: GNU GPL version 3 or later <http://gnu.org/licenses/gpl.html>
This is free software: you are free to change and redistribute it.
There is NO WARRANTY, to the extent permitted by law.
Type "show copying" and "show warranty" for details.
This GDB was configured as "x86_64-linux-gnu".
Type "show configuration" for configuration details.
For bug reporting instructions, please see:
<http://www.gnu.org/software/gdb/bugs/>.
Find the GDB manual and other documentation resources online at:
    <http://www.gnu.org/software/gdb/documentation/>.

For help, type "help".
Type "apropos word" to search for commands related to "word".
(gdb)
```

You can type gdb commands at the (gdb) prompt. One useful command, help, displays a list of commands, as the next listing shows:

```
(gdb) help
List of classes of commands:
aliases -- Aliases of other commands
breakpoints -- Making program stop at certain points
data -- Examining data
files -- Specifying and examining files
internals -- Maintenance commands
obscure -- Obscure features
running -- Running the program
stack -- Examining the stack
status -- Status inquiries
support -- Support facilities
tracepoints -- Tracing of program execution without stopping the program
user-defined -- User-defined commands
Type "help" followed by a class name for a list of commands in that class.
```

```
Type "help all" for the list of all commands.
Type "help" followed by command name for full documentation.
Command name abbreviations are allowed if unambiguous.
(gdb)
```

To quit gdb, type **q** and then press Enter.

gdb has a large number of commands but you need only a few to find the cause of an error quickly. Table 3-4 lists the commonly used gdb commands.

**TABLE 3-4**     ## Common gdb Commands

| This Command | Does the Following |
|---|---|
| break *NUM* | Sets a breakpoint at the specified line number, *NUM*. (The debugger stops at breakpoints.) |
| bt | Displays a trace of all stack frames. (This command shows you the sequence of function calls so far.) |
| clear *FILENAME*: *NUM* | Deletes the breakpoint at a specific line number, *NUM*, in the source file *FILENAME*. clear xdraw.c:8, for example, clears the breakpoint at line 8 of file xdraw.c. |
| continue | Continues running the program being debugged. (Use this command after the program stops due to a signal or breakpoint.) |
| display *EXPR* | Displays the value of an expression, *EXPR* (consisting of variables defined in the program), each time the program stops. |
| file *FILE* | Loads the specified executable file, *FILE*, for debugging. |
| help *NAME* | Displays help on the command named *NAME*. |
| info break | Displays a list of current breakpoints, including information on how many times each breakpoint is reached. |
| info files | Displays detailed information about the file being debugged. |
| info func | Displays all function names. |
| info local | Displays information about local variables of the current function. |
| info prog | Displays the execution status of the program being debugged. |
| info var | Displays all global and static variable names. |
| kill | Ends the program you're debugging. |
| list | Lists a section of the source code. |

| This Command | Does the Following |
|---|---|
| make | Runs the make utility to rebuild the executable without leaving gdb. |
| next | Advances one line of source code in the current function without stepping into other functions. |
| print *EXPR* | Shows the value of the expression *EXPR*. |
| quit | Quits gdb. |
| run | Starts running the currently loaded executable. |
| set variable *VAR=VALUE* | Sets the value of the variable *VAR* to *VALUE*. |
| shell *CMD* | Executes the shell command *CMD* without leaving gdb. |
| step | Advances one line in the current function, stepping into other functions, if any. |
| watch *VAR* | Shows the value of the variable named *VAR* whenever the value changes. |
| where | Displays the call sequence. Use this command to locate where your program died. |
| x/F ADDR | Examines the contents of the memory location at address ADDR in the format specified by the letter F, which can be o (octal), x (hex), d (decimal), u (unsigned decimal), t (binary), f (float), a (address), i (instruction), c (char), or s (string). You can append a letter indicating the size of data type to the format letter. Size letters are b (byte), h (halfword, 2 bytes), w (word, 4 bytes), and g (giant, 8 bytes). Typically, ADDR is the name of a variable or pointer. |

## Finding bugs by using gdb

To understand how you can find bugs by using gdb, you need to see an example. The procedure is easiest to show with a simple example, so the following, dbgtst.c, is a contrived program that contains a typical bug:

```
#include <stdio.h>
static char buf[256];
void read_input(char *s);
int main(void)
{
char *input = NULL; /* Just a pointer, no storage for string */
read_input(input);
/* Process command. */
printf("You typed: %s\n", input);
/* ...._*/
return 0;
}
void read_input(char *s)
```

```
{
printf("Command: ");
gets(s);
}
```

This program's main function calls the read_input function to get a line of input from the user. The read_input function expects a character array in which it returns what the user types. In this example, however, main calls read_input with an uninitialized pointer — the bug in this simple program.

Build the program by using gcc with the –g option:

```
gcc –g –o dbgtst dbgtst.c
```

Ignore the warning message about the gets function being dangerous; I'm trying to use the shortcoming of that function to show how you can use gdb to track down errors.

To see the problem with this program, run it and type **test** at the Command: prompt:

```
./dbgtst
Command: test
Segmentation fault
```

The program dies after displaying the Segmentation fault message. For such a small program as this one, you can probably find the cause by examining the source code. In a real-world application, however, you may not immediately know what causes the error. That's when you have to use gdb to find the cause of the problem.

To use gdb to locate a bug, follow these steps:

1. **Load the program under** gdb.

   Type **gdb dbgtst**, for example, to load a program named dbgtst in gdb.

2. **Start executing the program under** gdb **by typing the** run **command, and when the program prompts for input, type some input text.**

   The program fails as it did previously. Here's what happens with the dbgtst program:

   ```
   (gdb) run
   Starting program: /home/rich/dbgtst
   Command: test
   ```

```
Program received signal SIGSEGV, Segmentation fault.
_IO_gets (buf=0x0) at iogets.c:53
53    iogets.c: No such file or directory.
(gdb)
```

3. **Use the** where **command to determine where the program died.**

For the dbgtst program, this command yields output similar to the following:

```
(gdb) where
#0  _IO_gets (buf=0x0) at iogets.c:53
#1  0x00005555555551da in read_input (s=0x0) at dbgtst.c:16
#2  0x0000555555555189 in main () at dbgtst.c:7
(gdb)
```

The output shows the sequence of function calls. Function call #0 — the most recent one — is to the gets C library function. The gets call originates in the read_input function (at line 16 of the file dbgtst.c), which in turn is called from the main function at line 7 of the dbgtst.c file.

4. **Use the** list **command to inspect the lines of suspect source code.**

In dbgtst, you may start with line 16 of the dbgtst.c file, as follows:

```
(gdb) list dbgtst.c:16
11 return 0;
12 }
13 void read_input(char *s)
14 {
15 printf("Command: ");
16 gets(s);
17 }
18
(gdb)
```

After looking at this listing, you can tell that the problem may be the way read_input is called. Then you list the lines around line 7 in dbgtst.c (where the read_input call originates):

```
(gdb) list dbgtst.c:7
2 static char buf[256];
3 void read_input(char *s);
4 int main(void)
5 {
6 char *input = NULL; /* Just a pointer, no storage for string */
7 read_input(input);
```

```
8 /* Process command. */
9 printf("You typed: %s\n", input);
10 /* ... */
11 return 0;
(gdb)
```

At this point, you can narrow the problem to the variable named input. That variable is an array not a NULL (which means zero) pointer.

## Fixing bugs in gdb

Sometimes, you can fix a bug directly in gdb. For the example program in the preceding section, you can try this fix immediately after the program dies after displaying an error message. An extra buffer named buf is defined in the dbgtst program, as follows:

```
static char buf[256];
```

You can fix the problem of the uninitialized pointer by setting the variable input to buf. The following session with gdb corrects the problem of the uninitialized pointer. (This example picks up immediately after the program runs and dies due to the segmentation fault.)

```
(gdb) file dbgtst
A program is being debugged already. Kill it? (y or n) y
Load new symbol table from "/home/rich/sw/dbgtst"? (y or n) y
Reading symbols from /home/rich/sw/dbgtst ... done.
(gdb) list
1 #include <stdio.h>
2 static char buf[256];
3 void read_input(char *s);
4 int main(void)
5 {
6 char *input = NULL; /* Just a pointer, no storage for string */
7 read_input(input);
8 /* Process command. */
9 printf("You typed: %s\n", input);
10 /* ... */
(gdb) break 7
Breakpoint 2 at 0x804842b: file dbgtst.c, line 7.
(gdb) run
Starting program: /home/rich/sw/dbgtst
Breakpoint 1, main () at dbgtst.c:7
7 read_input(input);
(gdb) set var input=buf
```

```
(gdb) cont
Continuing.
Command: test
You typed: test
Processm exited normally.
(gdb)q
```

As the preceding listing shows, if the program is stopped just before `read_input` is called and the variable named input is set to `buf` (which is a valid array of characters), the rest of the program runs fine.

After finding a fix that works in `gdb`, you can make the necessary changes to the source files and make the fix permanent.

# Understanding the Implications of GNU Licenses

You have to pay a price for the bounty of Linux. To protect its developers and users, Linux is distributed under the GNU GPL (General Public License), which stipulates the distribution of the source code.

The GPL doesn't mean, however, that you can't write commercial software for Linux that you want to distribute (either for free or for a price) in binary form only. You can follow all the rules and still sell your Linux applications in binary form.

When writing applications for Linux, there are a number of licenses that may apply (MIT and BSD, for example), but you should be aware of two licenses:

>> The **GNU General Public License** (GPL), which governs many Linux programs, including the Linux kernel and GCC.

>> The **GNU Library General Public License** (LGPL), which covers many Linux libraries.

**WARNING**

The following sections provide an overview of these licenses and some suggestions on how to meet their requirements. Don't take anything in this book as legal advice. Instead, you should read the full text for these licenses in the text files on your Linux system and then show these licenses to your legal counsel for a full interpretation and an assessment of their applicability to your business.

# The GNU General Public License

The text of the GNU General Public License (GPL) is in a file named COPYING in various directories in your Linux system. Type the following command to find a copy of that file in your Linux system for various items:

```
find /usr -name "COPYING" -print
```

After you find the file, you can change to that directory and type **more COPYING** to read the GPL. These are examples of the license accompanying code, and you can find other examples at www.gnu.org/licenses/gpl-3.0.html.

The GPL has nothing to do with whether you charge for the software or distribute it for free; its thrust is to keep the software free for all users. GPL requires that the software be distributed in source-code form and stipulates that any user can copy and distribute the software in source-code form to anyone else. In addition, everyone is reminded that the software comes with absolutely no warranty.

The software that the GPL covers isn't in the public domain. Software covered by GPL is always copyrighted, and the GPL spells out the restrictions on the software's copying and distribution. From a user's point of view, of course, GPL's restrictions aren't really restrictions; the restrictions are benefits because the user is guaranteed access to the source code.

**WARNING**

If your application uses parts of any software that the GPL covers, your application is considered a *derived work*, which means that your application is also covered by the GPL and that you must distribute the source code to your application.

Although the GPL covers the Linux kernel, the GPL doesn't cover your applications that use the kernel services through system calls. Those applications are considered to be normal use of the kernel.

If you plan to distribute your application in binary form (as most commercial software is distributed), you must make sure that your application doesn't use any parts of any software the GPL covers. Your application may end up using parts of other software when it calls functions in a library. Most libraries, however, are covered by a different GNU license, which is described in the next section.

You have to watch out for only a few of the library and utility programs that the GPL covers. The GNU dbm (gdbm) database library is one of the prominent libraries that GPL covers. The GNU bison parser-generator tool is another utility that the GPL covers. If you allow bison to generate code, the GPL covers that code.

**TECHNICAL STUFF**

Other alternatives for the GNU dbm and GNU `bison` aren't covered by GPL. For a database library, you can use the Berkeley database library db in place of gdbm. For a parser-generator, you may use yacc instead of `bison`.

## The GNU Library General Public License

The text of the GNU Library General Public License (LGPL) is in a file named COPYING.LIB. If you have the kernel source installed, a copy of COPYING.LIB file is in one of the source directories. To locate a copy of the COPYING.LIB file on your Linux system, type the following command in a terminal window:

```
find /usr -name "COPYING*" -print
```

This command lists all occurrences of COPYING and COPYING.LIB in your system. The COPYING file contains the GPL, whereas COPYING.LIB has the LGPL.

The LGPL is intended to allow use of libraries in your applications, even if you don't distribute source code for your application. The LGPL stipulates, however, that users must have access to the source code of the library you use — and that users can use modified versions of those libraries.

The LGPL covers most Linux libraries, including the C library (libc.a). Thus, when you build your application on Linux by using the GCC compiler, your application links with code from one or more libraries that the LGPL covers. If you want to distribute your application in binary form only, you need to pay attention to LGPL.

One way to meet the intent of the LGPL is to provide the object code for your application and a makefile that relinks your object files with any updated Linux libraries the LGPL covers.

**REMEMBER**

A better way to satisfy the LGPL is to use *dynamic linking*, in which your application and the library are separate entities, even though your application calls functions that reside in the library when it runs. With dynamic linking, users immediately get the benefit of any updates to the libraries without ever having to relink the application.

You can find the newest version of the license, GPLv3, and a Quick Guide to it at www.gnu.org/licenses/quick-guide-gplv3.html.

# 8

# Linux
# Certification

# Contents at a Glance

# Chapter **1**

# Studying for the Linux Professional Institute Exams

**J**ust as you can attain many levels of degrees through an educational institution (associate's, bachelor's, master's, and doctorate degrees), you can achieve multiple levels of Linux certification. The Linux Professional Institute (LPI; www.lpi.org) is a nonprofit organization committed to Linux certification; it provides different certifications of increasing difficulty to help employers gauge the competency level of prospective Linux administrators. This chapter discusses the different LPI certification exams, allowing you to determine which exam path is right for your Linux career goals.

## Overview of LPI Certification Exams

LPI provides three separate categories of certification in common open-source tools:

> » **Linux Essentials:** Demonstrating the essentials of installing and running a Linux system; oriented toward students learning the basics of Linux

>> **Linux Professionals:** A series of exams intended to test increasing competency for professional Linux administrators

>> **Open Technology:** Two exams intended for additional open-source topics, such as DevOps and BSD administrators

The following sections discuss the Linux Essentials exam in detail, and provide a general overview of what to expect if you decide to go on to the more advanced Linux Professional series of exams.

# Overview of the Linux Essentials Exam

The Linux Essentials Certificate of Achievement was created by the Linux Professional Institute (LPI) to appeal to the academic sector. Students taking semester-based classes in Linux may not get through all the topics necessary to pass the two exams that are needed to gain the Linux Professionals certification, but LPI still wanted to recognize and authenticate their knowledge. This program was created through international collaboration with a classroom focus in mind. As of this writing, the current version is 1.6, and the exam code is 010-160.

**REMEMBER**

Linux Essentials is a certificate of achievement intended to be a much lower-level (subset) certification than the Linux Professionals certification (LPIC). Although Linux Essentials is recommended, it's not required for any of the LPIC professional certification or any other certifications.

The exam has five domains, called *topics*. Table 1-1 shows these topics and their weightings. It's important to note that weightings are always subject to change; it's not uncommon for them to be tweaked a bit over time.

**TABLE 1-1** ### Domains on the Linux Essentials Exam

| Topic | Weighting |
| --- | --- |
| The Linux Community and a Career in Open Source | 7 |
| Finding Your Way on a Linux System | 9 |
| The Power of the Command Line | 9 |
| The Linux Operating System | 8 |
| Security and File Permissions | 7 |

The sections that follow look at each of these topics in more detail.

# Getting involved in the Linux community and finding a career in open source

Table 1-2 shows the subtopics, weight, description, and key knowledge areas for this topic.

**TABLE 1-2**    Breakout of Topic 1

| Subtopic | Weight | Description | Key Areas |
|---|---|---|---|
| Linux Evolution and Popular Operating Systems | 2 | Knowledge of Linux development and major distributions | Open-source philosophy, distributions, and embedded systems<br><br>(The distributions to be cognizant of include Android, Debian, Ubuntu, CentOS, openSUSE, and Red Hat.) |
| Major Open Source Applications | 2 | Awareness of major applications and their uses and development | Desktop applications, server applications, development languages, and package management tools and repositories<br><br>(Topics include OpenOffice.org, LibreOffice, Thunderbird, Firefox, GIMP, Apache HTTPD, NGINX, MySQL, NFS, Samba, C, Java, Perl, shell, Python, dpkg, apt-get, rpm, and yum.) |
| Understanding Open Source Software and Licensing | 1 | Open communities and licensing open-source software for business | Licensing, Free Software Foundation (FSF), and Open Source Initiative (OSI)<br><br>(Topics include GPL, BSD, Creative Commons, Free Software, FOSS, FLOSS, and open-source business models.) |
| ICT Skills and Working in Linux | 2 | Basic Information and Communication Technology (ICT) skills and working in Linux | Desktop skills, getting to the command line, industry uses of Linux, and cloud computing and virtualization<br><br>(Topics include using a browser, privacy concerns, configuration options, searching the web, and saving content.) |

Here are the top ten items to know as you study for this domain:

>> Linux is the best-known example of open-source software so far developed (and still in development).

>> The *shell* is the command interpreter that resides between the user and the operating system. Although many shells are available, the most common today is the bash shell.

- » A plethora of applications and tools is available for use with the various Linux distributions. Many of these tools are also open-source.

- » The Apache Software Foundation distributes open-source software under the Apache license Free and Open Source Software (FOSS).

- » The Free Software Foundation (FSF) supports the free (open-source) software movement and copyleft under the GNU General Public License. *Copyleft* makes it possible for modifications to be made to software while preserving the same rights in the produced derivatives.

- » The Open Source Initiative (OSI) also supports the open-source software movement, as do the GNOME Foundation, the Ubuntu Foundation, and many other organizations.

- » OpenOffice.org was a popular suite of open-source office-productivity software. LibreOffice is a fork of OpenOffice that has eclipsed it in popularity.

- » Samba makes it possible for Linux systems to share files with Windows-based systems.

- » Thunderbird is a popular mail and news client created by the Mozilla Foundation.

- » Many web browsers are available for Linux, and one of the most popular is Mozilla Firefox.

## Finding your way on a Linux system

Table 1-3 shows the subtopics, weights, descriptions, and key knowledge areas for this topic.

Here are the top ten items to know as you study for this domain:

- » Regular expressions — often referred to as *globbing* — can be used with the shells available in Linux to match wildcard characters. Among the possible wildcards, the asterisk (*) matches any number of characters; the question mark (?) matches only one character.

- » Linux is a case-sensitive operating system.

- » Files can be hidden by preceding their names with a single period (.). In pathnames, however, a single period (.) specifies the active directory, and two periods (..) signifies the parent directory.

- » Absolute paths give the full path to a resource, whereas relative paths give directions from where you're currently working. An example of an absolute path is /tmp/eadulaney/file, and an example relative link is ../file.

>> Files can be copied by using cp or moved by using mv. Files can be deleted with rm, and directories (which are created with mkdir) can be removed with rmdir. Recursive deletion can be done with rm -r.

>> To change directories, use the cd command. When this command is used without parameters, it moves you to your home directory. To see what directory you're currently working in, use the pwd (present working directory) command.

>> The ls command has a plethora of options allowing you to list files. The –a option lists all files (including hidden files).

>> Help is available through the manual pages (accessed with the man command) and info (which shows help files stored below /user/info).

>> The whatis command shows which manual pages are available for an entry, and whereis shows the location of the file and all related files (including any manual pages).

>> Many standard utilities allow you to enter the name of the executable followed by --help to obtain help only on the syntax.

**TABLE 1-3**　　**Breakout of Topic 2**

| Subtopic | Weight | Description | Key Areas |
|---|---|---|---|
| Command Line Basics | 3 | Using the Linux command line | Basic shell, command-line syntax, variables, globbing, and quoting<br><br>(Topics include bash, echo, history, PATH env variables, export, and type.) |
| Using the Command Line to Get Help | 2 | Running help commands and navigation of the various help systems, man, and info | The topics include: man files, info command, /usr/share/doc, and locate |
| Using Directories and Listing Files | 2 | Navigating home and system directories and listing files in various locations | Files, directories, hidden files and directories, home directory, and absolute and relative paths<br><br>(Topics include common options for ls, recursive listings, cd, . and .., home, and ~.) |
| Creating, Moving, and Deleting Files | 2 | Creating, moving, and deleting files under the home directory | Files and directories, case sensitivity, and simple globbing and quoting<br><br>(Topics include mv, cp, rm, touch, mkdir, and rmdir.) |

# The power of the command line

Table 1-4 shows the subtopics, weights, descriptions, and key knowledge areas for this topic.

**TABLE 1-4**     ## Breakout of Topic 3

| Subtopic | Weight | Description | Key Areas |
|---|---|---|---|
| Archiving Files on the Command Line | 2 | Archiving files in the user home directory | Files, directories, archives, and compression<br><br>(Topics include `tar` as well as common `tar` options, `gzip`, `bzip2`, `zip`, and `unzip`.) |
| Searching and Extracting Data from Files | 3 | Searching and extracting data from files in the home directory | Command-line pipes, I/O redirection, and basic regular expressions<br><br>(Topics include `grep`, `less`, `cat`, `head`, `tail`, `sort`, `cut`, and `wc`.) |
| Turning Commands into a Script | 4 | Turning repetitive commands into simple scripts | Basic shell scripting and awareness of common text editors<br><br>(Topics include `#!`, `/bin/bash`, variables, arguments, `for` loops, `echo`, and `exit` status.) |

Here are the top ten items to know as you study for this domain:

- » Standard input (`stdin`) is traditionally the keyboard, and standard output (`stdout`) is traditionally the monitor. Both can be redirected, as can standard error (`stderr`), by using the symbols `>`, `>>`, `<`, and `|`.

- » Commands can be joined on the command line by the semicolon (`;`), and each command runs independently. You can also use the pipe (`|`) to send the output of one command as the input of another command.

- » The `cut` command can pull fields from a file, and the fields can be combined by using either `paste` or `join`. The latter offers more features than the former and can be used with conditions.

- » The `wc` command can count the number of lines, words, and characters in a file.

- » The `grep` utility (and its counterparts `egrep` and `fgrep`) can be used to find matches for strings within files.

>> The find command can be used to search the system for files/directories that meet any number of criteria. When these entities are found, the xargs command can be used to look deeper within them for other values (such as in conjunction with grep).

>> You can use the tar command (which can combine multiple files into a single archive) to do backups.

>> In addition to archiving, you can compress files with the gzip or pack command. To uncompress files, use uncompress, unzip, or unpack.

>> Variables can be given at the command line and referenced as $1, $2, and so on, or entered into the executing file with the read command.

>> Logic can be added to scripts by testing conditions with test or [. Commands can execute through if-then-fi deviations or looping (while, until, or for). You can use the exit command to leave a script or use break to leave a loop.

# The Linux operating system

Table 1-5 shows the subtopics, weights, descriptions, and key knowledge areas for this topic.

Here are the top ten items to know as you study for this domain:

>> When run, every command spans at least one process; processes can be viewed with ps or top (which updates the display dynamically).

>> Jobs can run in the foreground or background and be moved between the two. Jobs running in the foreground can be suspended by pressing Ctrl+Z.

>> IPv4 uses 32-bit addresses, each divided into four octets. The first octet identifies the class of address (A, B, or C). The address can be public or private.

>> The ifconfig utility can be used to see the current IP configuration of the network cards.

>> The ping utility is an all-purpose tool for testing connectivity. It sends echo messages to a specified host to see whether that host can be reached. You can use ping with the loopback address (127.0.0.1) to test internal configuration.

>> The route utility displays the routing table and allows you to configure it.

>> The netstat utility shows the current status of ports — those that are open, listening, and so on.

>> The system log is `/var/log/messages`, and this log is where the majority of events are written to by the system log daemon (`syslogd`). Messages routed there can be viewed with the `dmesg` command.

>> The `logrotate` command can be used to automatically archive log files and perform maintenance as configured in `/etc/syslog.conf`.

>> You can manually write entries to log files by using the `logger` command.

**TABLE 1-5**     **Breakout of Topic 4**

| Subtopic | Weight | Description | Key Areas |
|---|---|---|---|
| Choosing an Operating System | 1 | Knowledge of major operating systems and Linux distributions | Windows, Mac, and Linux differences; distribution lifecycle management<br><br>(Topics include GUI versus command line, desktop configuration; maintenance cycles, and Beta and Stable.) |
| Understanding Computer Hardware | 2 | Familiarity with the components that go into building desktop and server computers | Hardware<br><br>(Topics include motherboards, processors, power supplies, optical drives, peripherals, hard drives and partitions, /dev/sd*, and drivers.) |
| Where Data Is Stored | 3 | Where various types of information are stored on a Linux system | Programs and configuration, packages and package databases, processes, memory addresses, system messaging, and logging<br><br>(Topics include ps, top, free, syslog, dmesg, /etc/, /var/log, /boot/, /proc/, /dev/, and /sys/.) |
| Your Computer on the Network | 2 | Querying vital networking settings and determining the basic requirements for a computer on a local area network (LAN) | Internet, network, routers, querying DNaS client configuration, and querying network configuration<br><br>(Topics include route, ip route show, ifconfig, ip addr show, netstat, /etc/resolv.conf, /etc/hosts, IPv4, IPv6, ping, and host.) |

# Security and file permissions

Table 1-6 shows the subtopics, weights, descriptions, and key knowledge areas for this topic.

TABLE 1-6

## Breakout of Topic 5

| Subtopic | Weight | Description | Key Areas |
|---|---|---|---|
| Basic Security and Identifying User Types | 2 | Understanding various types of users on a Linux system | Root, standard, and system users<br><br>(Topics include /etc/passwd, /etc/group, id, who, w, sudo, and su.) |
| Creating Users and Groups | 2 | Creating users and groups on a Linux system | User and group commands, and user IDs<br><br>(Topics include /etc/passwd, /etc/shadow, /etc/group, /etc/skel, id, last, useradd, groupadd, and passwd.) |
| Managing File Permissions and Ownership | 2 | Understanding and manipulating file permissions and ownership settings | File/directory permissions and owners<br><br>(Topics include ls -l, ls -a, chmod, and chown.) |
| Special Directories and Files | 1 | Understanding special directories and files on a Linux system, including special permissions | Using temporary files and directories, and symbolic links<br><br>(Topics include /tmp, /var/tmp, Sticky Bit, ls -d, and ln -s.) |

Here are the top ten items to know as you study for this domain:

>> File and directory permissions can be changed with the chmod command (which accepts numeric and symbolic values).

>> Adding 1000 to standard permissions turns on the sticky bit; adding 2000 turns on the SGID permission. Adding 4000 turns on the SUID permission.

>> Links are created with the ln command. A *hard link* is nothing more than an alias to a file (sharing the same inode). The ln -s command creates a symbolic link that's an actual file with its own inode. The symbolic link contains a pointer to the original file and can span file systems; the hard link can't.

>> User accounts can be added by manually editing the configuration files or using the useradd command; they can be removed with userdel.

>> The groupadd utility can be used to create groups, and groupdel can be used to remove groups. Groups can be modified with groupmod, and users can be moved from one group to another with the newgrp command.

>> Passwords are changed with the passwd command. Older systems stored passwords in /etc/passwd; now passwords are stored in /etc/shadow, where they're more secure.

>> To see who logged on most recently and may still be on the network, you can use the last command.

>> The su command allows you to become another user (returning with exit). If no other username is specified, the root user is implied — hence, the su for *superuser*.

>> Use sudo instead of su when you want to run a command as another user (usually, root) without becoming that user.

>> The who command shows who's logged on; the w command shows information combining who with uptime.

# Overview of the Linux Professionals Exams

The LPI Linux Professionals series of exams is oriented toward the professional Linux administrator, working in a real-world production environment. The series has three levels of formal LPI certification to determine the competency level of Linux administrators:

>> **LPIC-1:** Validates a candidate's ability to install and configure a computer running Linux, configure basic networking, and perform system maintenance tasks from the command line.

>> **LPIC-2:** Validates a candidate's ability to administer small to medium-sized mixed networks.

>> **LPIC-3:** A grouping of advanced certifications that validate a candidate's advanced knowledge of specific Linux topics.

The following sections describe the different Linux Professional Exams in more detail.

## The LPIC-1 exams

The LPIC-1 level of certification exams is designed to validate a candidate's proficiency in basic, real-world Linux administration tasks. LPI has performed extensive surveying of Linux employers to determine the skills most often sought after for junior Linux administrators and incorporated those skills into its LPIC-1 certification. Currently, the LPIC-1 certification is at version 5.0 and consists of two exams that you must pass to gain certification:

>> **101-500 exam:** Tests knowledge of system architecture, Linux installation and package management, GNU and Unix commands, devices, Linux file systems, and the Linux Filesystem Hierarchy Standard (FHS)

>> **102-500 exam:** Tests knowledge of shells and shell scripting, Linux user interfaces and graphical desktops, Linux administrative tasks, essential system services, networking fundamentals, and Linux security

The LPIC-1 101-500 exam covers four topics, with each topic covering several subtopics. Here's a general overview of what's contained in each topic and subtopic, along with the individual weighting on the exams:

>> Topic 101: System Architecture (weight: 8)

- 101.1: Determine and configure hardware settings (weight: 2)

- 101.2: Boot the system (weight: 3)

- 101.3: Change runlevels/boot targets and shut down or reboot system (weight: 3)

>> Topic 102: Linux Installation and Package Management (weight: 12)

- 102.1: Design hard disk layout (weight: 2)

- 102.2: Install a boot manager (weight: 2)

- 102.3: Manage shared libraries (weight: 1)

- 102.4: Use Debian package management (weight: 3)

- 102.5: Use RPM and YUM package management (weight: 3)

- 102.6: Linux as a virtualization guest (weight: 1)

>> Topic 103: GNU and Unix Commands (weight: 26)

- 103.1: Work on the command line (weight: 4)

- 103.2: Process text streams using filters (weight: 2)

- 103.3: Perform basic file management (weight: 4)

- 103.4: Use streams, pipes, and redirects (weight: 4)

- 103.5: Create, monitor, and kill processes (weight: 4)

- 103.6: Modify process execution priorities (weight: 2)

- 103.7: Search text files using regular expressions (weight: 3)

- 103.8: Basic file editing (weight: 3)

>> Topic 104: Devices, Linux File Systems, Filesystem Hierarchy Standard (weight: 14)

- 104.1: Create partitions and file systems (weight: 2)

- 104.2: Maintain the integrity of file systems (weight: 2)

- 104.3: Control mounting and unmounting of file systems (weight: 3)

- 104.4: Subtopic removed

- 104.5: Manage file permissions and ownership (weight: 3)

- 104.6: Create and change hard and symbolic links (weight: 2)

- 104.7: Find system files and place files in the correct location (weight: 2)

Whereas the 101–500 exam covers the basics of Linux administration, the 102–500 exam digs a little deeper into the Linux skills required to perform real-world Linux administrative tasks:

» Topic 105: Shells and Shell Scripting (weight: 8)

- 105.1: Customize and use the shell environment (weight: 4)

- 105.2: Customize or write simple scripts (weight: 4)

» Topic 106: User Interfaces and Desktops (weight: 4)

- 106.1: Install and configure X11 (weight: 2)

- 106.2: Graphical desktops (weight: 1)

- 106.3: Accessibility (weight: 1)

» Topic 107: Administrative Tasks (weight: 12)

- 107.1: Manage user and group accounts and related system files (weight: 5)

- 107.2: Automate system administration tasks by scheduling jobs (weight: 4)

- 107.3: Localization and internationalization (weight: 3)

» Topic 108: Essential System Services (weight: 12)

- 108.1: Maintain system time (weight: 3)

- 108.2: System logging (weight: 4)

- 108.3: Mail Transfer Agent (MTA) basics (weight: 3)

- 108.4: Manage printers and printing (weight: 2)

» Topic 109: Networking Fundamentals (weight: 14)

- 109.1: Fundamentals of Internet protocols (weight: 4)

- 109.2: Persistent network configuration (weight: 4)

- 109.3: Basic network troubleshooting (weight: 4)

- 109.4: Configure client-side DNS (weight: 2)

>> Topic 110: Security (weight: 10)

- 110.1: Perform security administration tasks (weight: 3)
- 110.2: Set up host security (weight: 3)
- 110.3: Securing data with encryption (weight: 4)

As you can tell from these lists, the LPIC-1 exams cover a wide range of Linux topics. However, remember that these are still oriented toward the junior Linux administrator, so they don't dig too deeply into the topics. For that, there are the LPIC-2 exams, discussed in the next section.

## The LPIC-2 exams

The LPIC-2 level of certification by LPI is intended for more experienced Linux administrators, covering more detailed topics regarding running a Linux server in a production environment. Currently at version 4.5, the LPIC-2 certification also consists of two exams.

The 201-450 exam covers these topics:

>> Topic 200: Capacity planning (weight: 8)

>> Topic 201: Linux kernel (weight: 9)

>> Topic 202: System startup (weight: 9)

>> Topic 203: File system and devices (weight: 9)

>> Topic 204: Advanced storage device administration (weight: 8)

>> Topic 205: Network configuration (weight: 11)

>> Topic 206: System maintenance (weight: 6)

The 202-450 exam covers these general topics:

>> Topic 207: Domain Name System (weight: 8)

>> Topic 208: Web services (weight: 11)

>> Topic 209: File sharing (weight: 8)

>> Topic 210: Network client management (weight: 11)

>> Topic 211: Email services (weight: 8)

>> Topic 212: System security (weight: 14)

As you can see from the topic listing, the LPIC-2 certification starts to get into more of the details of designing and maintaining Linux servers. Before taking this examination, it's recommended that you have several months of hands-on Linux administration experience besides just studying the topics.

## The LPIC-3 exams

Finally, the highest level of Linux certification provided by LPI is the LPIC-3 certification. The LPIC-3 certification level is a bit different from the LPIC-1 and LPIC-2 levels in that there are multiple tracks you can take. Each track consists of a single exam that specializes in a specific area related to advanced Linux administration:

>> **Exam 300-300 Mixed Environments:** Covers installing and managing the Samba software package in a mixed Linux and Windows environment

>> **Exam 303-300 Security:** Covers common Linux security topics, including cryptography, certificates, host security, intrusion detection, access control, network security, and vulnerability assessment

>> **Exam 305-300 Virtualization and Containerization:** Covers using Linux in full virtualization environments, using and maintaining containers, and virtual machine deployment and provisioning

>> **Exam 306-300 High Availability and Storage Clusters:** Covers using Linux systems enterprise-wide with an emphasis on high-availability systems and storage

As you can tell from this list, the LPIC-3 level of certifications really start to get into the advanced topics facing Linux administrators today. Each of these certification exams covers a single area of Linux administration, so you can take as many as you feel necessary to prove your advanced Linux administration skills!

# Chapter **2**

# Studying for the CompTIA Linux+ Exam

The preceding chapter examines the Linux Professional Institute (LPI) certification tracks. LPI provides four levels of certification:

» **Linux Essentials,** the lower-level certification

» **LPIC-1,** an entry-level professional certification

» **LPIC-2,** a mid-range professional certification

» **LPIC-3,** the highest level professional certification

In contrast, Computing Technology Industry Association (CompTIA; www.comptia. org) provides just a single Linux certification. The CompTIA Linux+ certification is intended to validate the competencies required of an early-career Linux system administrator in a vendor-neutral manner.

In this chapter, I provide an overview of the CompTIA Linux+ exam and then explore the topics in each of the exam domains.

# Overview of the CompTIA Linux+ Exam

In the first iteration of the CompTIA Linux+ certification, CompTIA joined with LPI to create common LPIC-1 and Linux+ exams. The official name of the certification was CompTIA Linux+ Powered by LPI, certainly a mouthful to say, but a meaningful addition to a résumé. The certification was awarded by CompTIA but it consisted of two exams by the LPI: LX0-103 and LX0-104. Accordingly, at the time of taking the exams, a candidate could choose to have the test scores forwarded to LPI and gain the Level 1 certification (LPIC-1) at the same time.

However, in 2019, CompTIA chose to go its own way, creating a separate Linux+ exam. Version XK0-004 of the Linux+ exam was a new exam that was no longer equivalent to the LPIC-1 exams. You could also no longer claim dual certification from both organizations unless you took the separate exams.

The current iteration of the Linux+ exam is version XK0-005. It remains separate from the LPI exams. The new Linux+ certification requires a single exam, consisting of a maximum of 90 questions that must be answered in 90 minutes. The Linux+ exam not only utilizes multiple-choice, multiple-response, and fill-in-the-blank questions but also incorporates performance-based questions, placing you in a virtual Linux environment where you need to enter specific commands to solve a task. To take the Linux+ exam, CompTIA recommends that you have the A+ and Network+ certifications, along with 12 months of practical Linux administrator experience. The exam covers common tasks in major Linux distributions, including the Linux command line, basic maintenance, installing and configuring workstations, and networking. There are four domains on the one exam, as shown in Table 2-1.

**TABLE 2-1**  ## Domains on the Linux+ XK0-005 Exam

| Domain | Weighting |
| --- | --- |
| 1.0 System Management | 32% |
| 2.0 Security | 21% |
| 3.0 Scripting, Containers, and Automation | 19% |
| 4.0 Troubleshooting | 28% |

As you can tell from Table 2-1, the new Linux+ exam covers a wide range of topics. The following sections dive into the subtopics contained in each domain in more detail to give you an idea of what you'll need to study to prepare for the exam.

# System Management

The System Management domain is somewhat of a catchall domain for common Linux administrator skills. Table 2-2 lists the subtopics that this domain contains.

TABLE 2-2

## The System Management Domain

| Subtopic | Name |
|----------|------|
| 1.1 | Summarize Linux fundamentals. |
| 1.2 | Given a scenario, manage files and directories. |
| 1.3 | Given a scenario, configure and manage storage using the appropriate tools. |
| 1.4 | Given a scenario, configure and use the appropriate processes and services. |
| 1.5 | Given a scenario, use the appropriate networking tools or configuration files. |
| 1.6 | Given a scenario, build and install software. |
| 1.7 | Given a scenario, manage software configurations. |

This domain contains questions related to the following specific topics:

» The Linux Filesystem Hierarchy Standard (FHS), the basic boot process, device types, compiling packages from source, storage concepts, and listing hardware information

» File and directory operations; editing files; compressing, archiving, and backing up files; file metadata; soft and hard links; and copying files between systems

» Disk partitioning, mounting devices, file system management, monitoring storage space, working with logical volumes, RAID, and storage area network (SAN) devices

» System services, scheduling services, process management

» Managing network interfaces, name resolution, network monitoring tools, remote networking tools

» Package management, sandbox applications, and system updates

» Updating configuration files, configuring kernel options, and configuring common system services

As you can tell from the list, the System Management domain covers a fairly wide assortment of basic Linux skills.

# Security

The Security domain covers the topics related to running a secure Linux environment that you would expect. Table 2-3 shows the breakout of the Security domain subtopics.

TABLE 2-3

## The Security Domain

| Subtopic | Name |
|----------|------|
| 2.1 | Summarize the purpose and use of security best practices in a Linux environment. |
| 2.2 | Given a scenario, implement identity management. |
| 2.3 | Given a scenario, implement and configure firewalls. |
| 2.4 | Given a scenario, configure and execute remote connectivity for system management. |
| 2.5 | Given a scenario, apply the appropriate access controls. |

This domain contains questions related to the following specific topics:

>> Managing public key infrastructure (PKI) certificates, certificate use cases, authentication, and Linux hardening

>> Account creation and deletion and account management

>> Firewall use cases, common firewall technologies, and key firewall features

>> Secure Shell (SSH), and executing commands as another user

>> File permissions, Security-Enhanded Linux (SELinux), AppArmor, and command-line utilities

The Security domain is somewhat of a catchall for anything related to having a secure Linux environment, often a big topic in Linux exams, and it includes user accounts and file permissions.

# Scripting, Containers, and Automation

The Scripting, Containers, and Automation domain covers more advanced administrative topics. Table 2-4 shows the subtopics contained in this domain.

**TABLE 2-4**

## The Scripting, Containers, and Automation Domain

| Subtopic | Name |
|----------|------|
| 3.1 | Given a scenario, create simple shell scripts to automate common tasks. |
| 3.2 | Given a scenario, perform basic container operations. |
| 3.3 | Given a scenario, perform basic version control using Git. |
| 3.4 | Summarize common infrastructure as code technologies. |
| 3.5 | Summarize container, cloud, and orchestration concepts. |

This domain contains questions related to the following specific topics:

>> Shell script elements, common script utilities, environment variables, and relative and absolute paths

>> Container management and image operations

>> Using the Git software version control package

>> File formats and utilities used in infrastructure as code environments, continuous integration/continuous deployment (CI/CD), and advanced Git topics related to CI/CD environments

>> Kubernetes benefits and application use cases; single-node, multicontainer use cases; container persistent storage; container networks; service mesh; bootstrapping; and container registries

Shell scripting has long been a part of Linux administration but using containers is a relatively new topic, and it's covered in detail in the new Linux+ exam structure.

# Troubleshooting

We all wish we lived in a world where things never went wrong but that's not the case. Having good troubleshooting skills is a must for all Linux administrators, and the Linux+ exam questions tests you on your troubleshooting abilities. Table 2-5 shows the subtopics contained in this domain.

TABLE 2-5

## The Troubleshooting Domain

| Subtopic | Name |
|---|---|
| 4.1 | Given a scenario, analyze and troubleshoot storage issues. |
| 4.2 | Given a scenario, analyze and troubleshoot network resource issues. |
| 4.3 | Given a scenario, analyze and troubleshoot central processing unit (CPU) and memory issues. |
| 4.4 | Given a scenario, analyze and troubleshoot user access and file permissions. |
| 4.5 | Given a scenario, use systemd to diagnose and resolve common problems with a Linux system. |

This domain contains questions related to these topics:

>> Storage latency, low throughput, input/output operations per second, capacity issues, file system issues, device issues, and mount option problems

>> Network configuration issues, firewall issues, network interface issues, bandwidth limitations, name resolution issues, and testing remote systems

>> Runaway processes, zombie processes, high CPU utilization, high load averages, high run queues, CPU times, CPU process priorities, memory exhaustion, out of memory, swapping, and CPU or memory hardware issues

>> User login issues, file access issues, password issues, privilege elevation, and disk quota issues

>> systemd unit files, and common problems associated with systemd services not starting

The Troubleshooting domain doesn't really introduce any new topics per se, but it does take a closer look at what you should do if something goes wrong on your Linux system. Notice all the "given the scenario" type of subtopics contained in this domain. You can expect to see questions that outline a specific problem, and you'll need to come up with the specific solution to solve the problem. Also note that because the new Linux+ exam utilizes performance-based questions, you may be placed in a virtual Linux command-line environment and be expected to enter actual commands (in the correct order) to solve the problem.

# Chapter **3**

# Other Linux Certifications

P revious chapters look at the Linux Professional Institute (LPI) and Computing Technology Industry Association (CompTIA) Linux certification exams. As important as those exams are, they're far from the only Linux certifications available.

In this chapter, I cover other vendor-neutral certifications and some of the most popular vendor-specific Linux certifications.

# Vendor-Neutral Certifications

Two other popular organizations that provide vendor-neutral Linux certifications are the Linux Foundation and GIAC. This section describes the Linux certification offerings from both of these organizations.

## The Linux Foundation

The Linux Foundation (www.linuxfoundation.org) was organized in 2000 as a merger between Open Source Development Labs and the Free Standard Group. Its main goal is to support the growth of Linux and promote its use in commercial enterprises. The Linux Foundation is the official host of the Linux kernel project as well as several popular open-source packages such as Kubernetes and the Xen project.

The Linux Foundation provides training and certification for a host of different open-source topics, including Linux administration. Its current Linux administrator certification offerings include the following:

>> **Certified IT Associate:** A preprofessional certificate geared toward those new to Linux

>> **Certified System Administrator:** Geared toward early-career administrators, testing basic Linux operation skills for managing a Linux system

>> **Certified Engineer:** Oriented toward the Linux professional with three to five years of experience who wants to demonstrate the ability to deploy and configure Linux in an enterprise environment

TIP

Besides its Linux certifications, the Linux Foundation also provides certifications for Cloud and Container, Blockchain, Web and Applications, and DevOps.

## The GIAC Certifications

GIAC Certifications (www.giac.org) develops and administers certifications in the information security sector. In the past, you could often find its GIAC Unix Security Administrator (GCUX) certificate listed as a popular Linux certification, but that specific certification has been discontinued. Instead, GIAC is focusing on providing certifications for more specific areas of security interest:

>> Cloud Security

>> Cyber Defense

>> Cybersecurity and IT Essentials

>> Digital Forensics and Incident Response

>> Incident Response and Threat Hunting

>> Operating System and Device In-depth

>> Penetration Testing and Ethical Hacking

>> Security Awareness

>> Security Management, Legal, and Audit

Each of these topics can be beneficial for Linux administrators working in a corporate environment where security is a must.

# Vendor-Specific Certifications

Several vendors offer certifications that authenticate specialization in their specific distributions of Linux. The following are three of those vendors and their most popular certifications:

>> **Red Hat** (www.redhat.com)**:** Some of the most recognized certifications are from Red Hat. At the entry level, the company offers Red Hat Certified System Administrator (RHCSA) certification. The more recognized Red Hat Certified Engineer (RHCE) certification builds upon RHCSA, and the pinnacle certification is Red Hat Certified Architect (RHCA).

>> **SUSE** (www.suse.com)**:** SUSE certification is available at various levels: SUSE Certified Administrator (SCA), SUSE Certified Engineer (SCE), and SUSE Enterprise Architect (SEA). Both SCA and SCE are available in several tracks: Enterprise Linux, OpenStack Cloud, Enterprise Storage, and Systems Management. To become SEA-certified, you must have two of the SCE certifications, three SCA certifications, and one certification from any other track.

>> **Oracle** (www.oracle.com)**:** Oracle, the company that acquired Sun Microsystems and its rich history of Linux, offers both Oracle Certified Associate (OCA) and Oracle Certified Professional (OCP) certifications.

# Index

## Symbols

- (dash), 134, 142
- (hyphen), 493
. (dots), 134
. (period), 518
/ (forward slash), 134, 163, 299
: (colon), 162, 293
; (semicolon), 230, 382
\ (backslash), 134, 230, 369
| (pipe), 231, 244
+ (plus sign), 474
= (equal sign), 293
# (pound sign; hash mark), 283, 337, 382
$ (dollar sign), 470
$? variable, 498
$% variable, 498
$* variable, 498
$@ variable, 498
$^ variable, 498
$< variable, 498
* (asterisk), 233–235, 282
? (question mark), 233–235, 356
[ ] (bracket), 234
< (less-than sign), 232
> (greater-than sign), 232

## A

absolute navigation, 140
absolute paths, 518
access logs, Apache server, 339–341
access point (AP), 204–205
AccessFileName directive, 338
ACPI Shutdown function (VirtualBox), 50

acpi=off boot option, 72
action field, 256
Activities overview area, GNOME, 91
ad hoc mode, 201
Add/Remove Applications program, 79
address command, 214
addrlabel command, 214
Adjust Window Size, 51
Advanced Encryption Standard (AES), 202
After line, 261–262
alias command, 236, 475
alias file, 395–396
allowcddma boot option, 72
Amarok, 128
answer variable, 474
Apache server
    access logs, 339–341
    basic setup, 337–339
    configuring, 336–343
    creating secure web server, 343–344
    error logs, 339–341
    features, 332
    installing, 333–336
    overview, 319, 331–332
    user web hosting, 341
    virtual web hosting, 341–343
    vulnerabilities, 454
Apache Software Foundation, 518
apic boot option, 72
appearance, customizing, 92
applets
    Cinnamon desktop, 106–107
    MATE desktop, 110

Xfce desktop, 113–114
application gateway, 413
Application Launcher, KDE Plasma, 95
Application layer (TCP/IP), 186
application-proxy gateway firewall, 441–442
apropos command, 236
apt tool, 380, 396
AR variable, 498
ARFLAGS variable, 498
arguments, 58
ARPANET, 187
AS variable, 498
ASCII-armored format, 429
ASFLAGS variable, 498
ash shell, 16
assumptions, in this book, 2–3
asterisk (*), 233–235, 282
asymmetric DSL (ADSL), 177–178. *See also* DSL (Digital Subscriber Line)
at command, 278–280
atd daemon program, 278
atrm command, 280
audio
    GNOME Sound options, 125
    KDE Plasma multimedia settings, 126–127
    listening to, 124–129
    MP3 libraries, 127
    players
        Amarok, 128
        Rhythmbox, 128
    streaming versus downloading, 128
    troubleshooting, 124
authentication, 408, 413, 454

authorization, 409
AVI files, 129
awk language, 482–486

## B

backdoor, 413
background, customizing, 92
background processes, running, 314–315
backing up files, administrator's duties, 250
backslash (\), 134, 230, 369
bandwidth throttling, 332
base station, 202
Bash shell
  built-in commands, 475–478
  commands
    combining, 231
    controlling input and output, 231–233
    for file management, 230
    format, 228–229
    syntax of, 228–230
    wildcards, 233–235
  controlling flow of execution, 471–474
  defined, 228
  defining variables, 469–470
  described, 16
  programming features, 469–470
  starting, 56–57
  using, 228–235
.bash_history file listing, 138
bastion host, 413
Berkeley Internet Name Domain (BIND) software, 328
bg command, 238, 475
/bin directory, 229, 300
binary files, 237
BIND (Berkeley Internet Name Domain) software, 328
BIND DNS, 454

binmail program, 324
bit bucket, 233
black hat, 460
black-box testing, 460–461
BogoMIPS, 271
/boot directory
  defined, 300
  /grub/menu.lst file, 456
boot disk, creating, 28–30
boot messages, 54
boot process
  Systemd method, 259–263
  SysVinit method, 252–259
bootable DVD
  booting from, 31
  creating, 28–29
bootable USB stick, creating, 29–30
booting, 53
Bourne, Stephen, 16
Bourne shell, 16
bracket ([ ]), 233–235
breadcrumbs, 150
break command, 475
break NUM command, 504
bt command, 504
buffer, 165
buffer overflow, 413

## C

C compiler, 489
C programming language, 490
C++ programming language, 490, 492–493
cable modem connections
  compared to DSL, 175
  data transfer speeds, 182
  general discussion, 175
  LAN connections, 197–198
  overview of function, 180–182
  typical setup, 182–184

Cable Modem Termination System (CMTS), 182
cal command, 243
Carrier-Sense Multiple Access/ Collision Detection (CSMA/ CD), 191
case statement, 473
cat command, 155, 230, 237, 245
CC variable, 498
cd command, 236, 475, 519
CD-ROMs, managing, 76–77
CentOS, 67
CERT Software Engineering Institute of Carnegie Mellon University, 418
certificate authorities (CAs), 414
certificates, 414
certification. See Linux certification
certified engineer, 536
certified IT associate, 536
certified system administrator, 536
CFLAGS variable, 498
CGI (Common Gateway Interface), 332
chage command, 417
charset command, 357
check digit, 482
chgrp command, 295
chkconfig command, 258
chmod command, 236, 423
chown command, 143, 295
CIFS (Common Internet File System), 379
Cinnamon desktop
  applets, 106–107
  desklets, 106–107
  features, 104–105
  general discussion, 103–104
  history of, 104–105
  menu, 105
  spices, 106–107
  system settings, 105–106

cut command, 237, 520

CVE (Common Vulnerabilities and Exposures), 453

CVS (Concurrent Version System), 454

CXX variable, 499

CXXFLAGS variable, 499

# D

daemon, 314

dash (-), 134, 142

dash, GNOME 3, 91

Data Over Cable Service Interface Specification (DOCSIS), 182

data protection, 409

database objects, creating, 370–372

database projects, creating, 360–363

database servers

 MariaDB server, 321, 349–363

 MongoDB server, 321–322

 MySQL server, 321

 PostgreSQL server, 320, 363–372

databases

 creating, 361–362

 vulnerabilities, 454

date command, 242

dbgtst program, 507

dd command, 237

Debian. *See also* Linux distributions

 configuring Internet super server, 435

 distributions based on, 18–19

 inetd server, 435

 installing mailutil package, 397

 installing Postfix, 396

 installing Samba, 380

 mounting DVD or CD-ROM, 303

 network configuration files, 208

popularity, 17

root password, 60

run levels, 254

Systemd method in, 259

text mode installation, 64

turning off stand-alone servers, 435

 update-rc.d command, 435

debugger

 defined, 488, 490

 finding bugs, 505–508

 fixing bugs, 508–509

 gdb commands, 504–505

 overview, 502

 preparing to debug, 502

 running gdb, 502–503

declare command, 476

decryption, 414, 432–433

default command, 263, 264

delimiter command, 356

denial of service (DoS) attack, 216, 404, 407, 414

depmod command, 277

derived work, 510

desklets, 106–107

desktop

 Cinnamon, 103–107

 GNOME, 87–92

 KDE Plasma, 93–101

 MATE, 107–110

 Xfce, 111–114

detection, 452, 455, 458

/dev directory, 229, 231, 300

device drivers, 273

device files

 block devices, 274

 character devices, 275

 network devices, 275

 udev program, 275

Devices menu (VirtualBox), 51–52

df command, 268–269

dhclient package, 327

DHCP (Dynamic Host Configuration Protocol), 188, 189, 209, 317, 327

dhcpcd package, 327

DHCPd server, 327

diff command, 237

digital signature, 414, 428–429

Digital Subscriber Line. *See* DSL (Digital Subscriber Line)

directories. *See also* files

 base, 135

 creating, 140, 147

 defined, 133–134

 deleting, 148

 opening directories, 146–147

 protecting, 422–425

 removing, 140

DirectoryIndex directive, 338

dirs command, 476

disable command, 263

disclosure, 407

disk performance and usage, 267–270

display *EXPR* command, 504

display=IP_address:0 boot option, 72

displays, settings for, 92

distributed denial of service (DDoS) attack, 404, 414

DistroWatch.com (website), 19

DivX files, 129

dmesg command, 65

DMZ, 414

dnf tool, 381, 397

DNS (Domain Name System), 317, 342

DNS Security Extensions (DNSSEC) protocol, 328

DOCSIS (Data Over Cable Service Interface Specification), 182

DocumentRoot directive, 338, 341

dollar sign ($), 470

Dolphin file manager, KDE Plasma

iptables command, 444–447

ISBN (International Standard Book Number), 482–485

ISC (Internet Systems Consortium), 327

ISO image, 67

isolate command, 263

ISOLINUX, 54

## J

JavaScript Object Notation (JSON), 322

jobs
  cron, 281–283
  one-time, 278–280
  recurring, 281–283
  scheduling, 278–283

jobs command, 476

join command, 520

journalct command, 67–68

journald program, 67, 328

JSON (JavaScript Object Notation), 322

## K

Kate text editor, 160–161

KDE (K Desktop Environment) Plasma desktop
  Application Launcher, 95
  desktop, 96–98
  desktop settings, 100–101
  Dolphin file manager, 149–151
  general discussion, 13–14, 93–94
  Kate text editor, 160–161
  KFind utility, 152–153
  KMail, 121–123
  Konsole, 226–227
  KWrite text editor, 159–160
  logging out from, 61
  multimedia settings, 126–127
  panel, 96

system settings, 99–100
  terminal window, 57
  widgets, 98–99

KDE Dragon, 130

kernel modules, 11

kernel ring buffer, 65–66

key pairs, generating, 429–430

KFind utility, KDE Plasma, 152–153

kickstart file, 72

kill command, 238, 242, 476, 504

KMail, 121–123

KNOPPIX
  boot commands, 68–70
  partitioning tool, 26–27
  text mode installation, 64

Konsole, opening, 226–227

korn shell, 16

ks boot option, 72

ks=kickstartfile boot option, 72

ksyms command, 277

KVM, 40

KWrite text editor, 159–160

## L

l2tp command, 214

LANs (local area networks)
  connecting to Internet, 196–198
  setting up with cable, 197–198
  setting up with DSL, 197–198
  sharing files in, 325
  wired (Ethernet)
    cables, 192–193
    overview of function, 191–192
    setting up, 190–195
    switch, 192–193
    TCP/IP, 185–190, 185–198
  wireless network
    ad hoc mode, 201
    configuring, 205–206

configuring access points, 204–205
    connection diagram and notes, 203–204
    infrastructure mode, 201
    security specifications, 201–202
    setting up hardware, 203–204
    standards for, 199–201

LDAP (Lightweight Directory Access Protocol), port number, 318

ldd command, 238

LDFLAGS variable, 499

less command, 237

less-than sign (<), 232

let arg command, 476

LGPL (Library General Public License), 511

/lib directory, 300

libcrc32c module, 277

Library General Public License (LGPL), 511

LibreOffice, 115–116, 518

lighthttpd package, 319–320

link command, 214

Linux
  general discussion, 7–8
  installing
    approaches for, 21–22
    creating boot disk, 28–30
    disabling secure boot feature, 27–28
    first boot after, 36–37
    keyboard, selecting, 32
    language, selecting, 31
    minimal installation, 32
    normal installation, 32
    options in, 33–34
    by partitioning an existing drive, 24–26, 34–35
    by replacing an existing operating system, 21–22

Simple Mail Transfer Protocol (SMTP), 186, 189, 317, 400

Simple Network Management Protocol (SNMP), 190, 454

Simultaneous Authentication of Equals (SAE), 202

skipddc boot option, 73

SMB (Server Message Block), port number, 318

smbadduser program, 379

smbcacls program, 379

smbclient Windows client, 379

smbcontrol program, 379

smbd SMB server, 379

smbmount program, 379

smbpasswd program, 379, 382

smbprint script, 379

smbstatus command, 379

smbtar program, 379

smbumount program, 38

SMTP (Simple Mail Transfer Protocol), 186, 189, 317, 400

snapshot, VirtualBox, 50

sniffer, 416, 461–462

SNMP (Simple Network Management Protocol), 328–329

soft limits, 289

soft mount, 378

software, installing, 79–83

software-development tools
GNU C and C++ compilers, 490–493
GNU debugger, 502–509
GNU make utility, 493–501
overview, 489–490

sort command, 237, 245

source code, 488

source command, 357

source file, 488

specialized Linux distributions, 18–19

spices, 106–107

split command, 237, 245

spoofing, 440

spyware, 416

SQL (Structured Query Language), 320

/srv directory, 300

stand-alone servers, 434–435, 459

standard error, 231, 520

standard input, 231, 520

standard output, 231, 520

start command, 263, 336

starting Linux, 53–55

StartServers directive, 338

startup scripts, 256–257

state table, 441

stateful inspection firewall, 441

statements, 488

status bar command, 263

status command, 335, 336, 357

step command, 505

stop command, 263, 336

stream editor, 480

stream-based macro processor, 387

streaming
audio, 128
defined, 174

Structured Query Language (SQL), 320

su command, 240, 417, 524

subroutines, 488

Subversion, 490

sudo command, 55, 240, 252, 417, 524

super-server program, 316

superuser, 55, 143

SUSE. See also Linux distributions
certifications, 537
configuring Samba, 382
enabling packet filtering, 443
run levels, 254
text mode installation, 64
turning on/off stand-alone servers, 435

xinetd server, 435–436

YaST Control Center, 284

swap space, 9

swapping out, 10, 267

symmetric DSL, 178. See also DSL (Digital Subscriber Line)

symmetric key encryption, 416

Synaptic Package Manager (Ubuntu), 81–82

sysfs file system, 275

syslogd configuration file, 434

system administration
administrators, 249
backups, 250
boot process
/etc/inittab file, 254–255
automatically starting servers at system startup, 258–259
init program, 255–256
manually starting and stopping servers, 257–258
run levels, 253–254
setting default target, 262
startup scripts, 256–257
systemctl program, 262–264
units and targets, 259–260
booting process
Systemd method, 259–264
SysVinit method, 253–259
defined, 249
device files
block devices, 274
character devices, 275
network devices, 275
overview, 274
udev program, 275
driver modules
/etc/modprob.d files, 277–278
loading and unloading, 276–277
overview, 276–278
GUI tools, 284–286
hardware management, 250

Trivial File Transfer Protocol (TFTP), 190

Trojan horse, 416

troubleshooting
  audio, 124
  TCP/IP networks, 216–221

troubleshooting installations
  fatal signal 11 error, 68–70
  PC reboot problem, 71
  using kernel ring buffer, 65–66
  using KNOPPIX boot commands, 68–70
  using log files, 66–67
  using the journal, 67–68

Tunnel command, 214

Tuntap command, 214

type command, 236, 477

# U

Ubuntu
  adding applications in, 80
  adding packages in, 81–82
  apt tool, 380
  boot screen, 54
  configuring Internet super server, 435
  defined, 18
  first boot, 36–37
  inetd server, 435
  installing, 30–35
  installing Postfix, 396–397
  installing Samba, 380
  LiveDVD image, 30–31
  LivePatch feature, 36
  login window, 55
  Synaptic Package Manager, 81–82
  terminal window, 57
  turning off stand-alone servers, 435
  update-rc.d command, 435
  updating, 77–78
  /var/log/syslog file, 67

ufw (Uncomplicated Firewall), 306, 443–444

ulimit command, 417, 477

umask command, 424–425, 477

unalias command, 236, 477

uname command, 58, 238

unauthorized access, 407

uncompress command, 238

underscore (_), 134

Unified Extensible Firmware Interface (UEFI) boot method, 27–28

uniq command, 237

units
  configuring, 261–262
  Systemd, 259–260

Unix System V operating system, 252

unmount command, 303

unset command, 477

update-rc.d command, 258, 435

updating, operating system, 455

upstream data, 181

uptime command, 266

U.S. Computer Emergency Readiness Team (US-CERT), 418

USB drives
  bootable, creating, 29–30
  booting from, 31

US-CERT National Cyber Alert System, 418

uscertkey.asc file, 429

use command, 357

user account management
  adding user accounts, 250, 288–291
  logging in as root user, 251–252
  removing user accounts, 250
  su - command, 251–252
  using commands, 288–290
  using GUI tools, 288–290

User and Group Management tool, 289

User Datagram Protocol (UDP), 186, 317

User directive, 338

user file-creation mask, 424

user interfaces
  command-line interface (CLI), 15–16
  GNOME desktop, 14–15
  KDE Plasma desktop, 13–14
  overview, 12–13
  X Window system, 13

user web hosting, 341

useradd command, 290

userdel command, 291

usermod command, 291–292, 417

users
  changing file ownership, 295
  environmental variables, 293–294
  managing user accounts
    adding user accounts, 250, 288–291
    logging in as root user, 251–252
    removing user accounts, 250
    su - command, 251–252
    using commands, 288–290
    using GUI tools, 288–290

*Using Samba* (Carter et al), 384

/usr directory
  /bin, 300
  /bin/scp component, 437
  /bin/slogin component, 437
  /bin/ssh component, 437
  /bin/ssh-keygen component, 437
  /games, 300
  /include, 300
  /lib, 300
  /libexec, 300

web proxy, 332

web servers

Apache, 331–332

NGINX, 333, 344–347

Web services

Apache server, 319

defined, 316

lighthttpd package, 319–320

NGINX server, 316

whatis command, 236, 519

where command, 505, 507

whereis command, 237

which command, 237

Whisker menu, Xfce desktop, 112–113

white hat, 460

white-box testing, 460–461

widgets, KDE Plasma, 98–99

Wi-Fi (Wireless Fidelity), 199

Wi-Fi Alliance, 202

Wi-Fi Protected Access (WPA), 202

wildcards, 233–235

WIMP (windows, icons, mouse, and pointer), 56

winbindd server, 38

Windows Disc Image Burner, 28–29

Windows Disk Management tool, 25–26

Windows disk partition, mounting, 308–309

Windows operating system, installing as a virtual machine, 23

Windows overview area, GNOME, 91

Wired Equivalent Privacy (WEP), 202

wireless access point (WAP), 204–205

WLANs (wireless local area networks)

ad hoc mode, 201

configuring, 205–206

configuring access points, 204–205

connection diagram and notes, 203–204

infrastructure mode, 201

security specifications, 201–202

setting up hardware, 203–204

standards for, 199–201

WMV files, 129

word processor, 488

workspace selector, GNOME, 91

workspace switcher, MATE, 109

worms, 416

write permission, 143

**X**

X Window system

defined, 13

Wayland, 13

X.org, 13

x/F ADDR command, 505

Xfce desktop

applets, 113–114

general discussion, 111

history of, 111–112

settings manager, 113

Thunar file manager, 151–152

Whisker menu, 112–113

xfrm command, 214

xfs module, 277

xinetd server, 316, 434–436, 458–459

X.org, 13

**Y**

YaST Control Center, 284, 386

Yet another Setup Tool (YaST), 82–83

**Z**

zcat command, 238

zless command, 238

zmore command, 238

zsh shell, 16

## About the Author

**Richard Blum** has worked in the IT industry for more than 35 years as a network and systems administrator. During that time, he has had the opportunity to work with lots of different computer products, including Windows, Netware, Cisco, Avaya, different flavors of Unix, and of course Linux. Over the years, he has also volunteered for several nonprofit organizations to help support small networks that had little financial support. Rich is the author of several Linux-based books for total Linux geeks and teaches online courses in Linux and web programming.

When he's not busy being a computer nerd, Rich enjoys playing organ, piano, and bass guitar, and spending time with his wife, Barbara, and their two daughters, Katie Jane and Jessica.

## Dedication

To my wife, Barbara.

"An excellent wife, who can find? She is far more precious than jewels."

—Proverbs 31:10 (ESV)

## Author's Acknowledgments

First, all praise and glory go to God, who through His Son makes all things possible and gives us the gift of eternal life.

A special thanks goes to all the past authors in the *Linux All-in-One For Dummies* series. I jumped onto this project in this 7th Edition, and it's amazing to think of the great authors who've been involved with guiding this series from the start. I'm glad to be able to build off that tradition and all their hard work.

Many thanks go to the great people at Wiley for their help and guidance in writing this. Thanks to Kelsey Baird for offering me the opportunity to pick up this project. Also, many thanks to Elizabeth Kuball for helping keep the project focused and on track! The technical editor for this book, Guy Hart-Davis, has done an excellent job of finding my mistakes and making suggestions to help make this book better. Thanks, Guy! Thanks also goes to Carole Jelen at Waterside Productions for arranging this gig and keeping my book-writing career on track.

Finally, I'd like to thank my parents, Mike and Joyce Blum, for constantly stressing education over goofing off, and my wife, Barbara, and two daughters, Katie Jane and Jessica, for their love and support, especially while I was working on this project.

## Publisher's Acknowledgments

**Associate Acquisitions Editor:** Kelsey Baird

**Project Editor:** Elizabeth Kuball

**Copy Editor:** Elizabeth Kuball

**Technical Editor:** Guy Hart-Davis

**Production Editor:** Tamilmani Varadharaj

**Cover Image:** © Julien Tromeur/Shutterstock